First World War
and Army of Occupation
War Diary
France, Belgium and Germany

2 DIVISION
Headquarters, Branches and Services
General Staff
28 June 1916 - 2 July 1916

WO95/1291

The Naval & Military Press Ltd
www.nmarchive.com
Published in association with The National Archives

Published by

The Naval & Military Press Ltd

Unit 10 Ridgewood Industrial Park,

Uckfield, East Sussex,

TN22 5QE England

Tel: +44 (0) 1825 749494

www.naval-military-press.com

www.nmarchive.com

This diary has been reprinted in facsimile from the original. Any imperfections are inevitably reproduced and the quality may fall short of modern type and cartographic standards.

Contents

Document type	Place/Title	Date From	Date To
Heading	2nd Division General Staff Aug-Sep 1916		
Heading	2nd Division War Diaries General Staff July 1916 Sept		
Heading	War Diary General Staff 2nd Division July 1916		
Miscellaneous	Field Register Of Communications Received or Despatched.		
Miscellaneous	XIII Corps Memos Instns Received		
Miscellaneous	Memos Instns to Received From Division on Left		
Miscellaneous	Memos & c received from Infy Bdes R.A. R.E. & C of 2nd Divn		
Miscellaneous	Memos Instns to Issued by 2nd Divn	21/07/1916	21/07/1916
War Diary	Camblain L'Abbe.	01/07/1916	17/07/1916
War Diary	Chateau O.10 B.	18/07/1916	20/07/1916
War Diary	Rue De College, Corbie.	21/07/1916	21/07/1916
War Diary	Citadel F. 21 b.	22/07/1916	25/07/1916
War Diary	Copse B A.21.a.45	25/07/1916	25/07/1916
War Diary	Copse "B".	26/07/1916	28/07/1916
War Diary	Copse "B". A.21.a.4.5.	29/07/1916	29/07/1916
War Diary	The Citadel (F.21.b.).	30/07/1916	31/07/1916
Heading	2nd Division General Staff (Original) War Diary Appendices July 1-31st 1916		
Miscellaneous	IVth Corps No. H.R.S. 669/J. 2nd Div. No. G.S.992/16/14.	01/07/1916	01/07/1916
Miscellaneous	A Form. Messages And Signals.		
Operation(al) Order(s)	2nd Division Order No. 108	01/07/1916	01/07/1916
Operation(al) Order(s)	2nd Division Order No. 109	02/07/1916	02/07/1916
Miscellaneous	A Form. Messages And Signals.		
Miscellaneous	2nd Division. Appendix 5	21/06/1916	21/06/1916
Miscellaneous	Fighting Strength 2nd Division	01/07/1916	01/07/1916
Miscellaneous	App 6		
Miscellaneous	2nd Division App 7	02/07/1916	02/07/1916
Miscellaneous	A Form. Messages And Signals.		
Operation(al) Order(s)	2nd Division Order No. 110	03/07/1916	03/07/1916
Operation(al) Order(s)	2nd Division Order No. 111	03/07/1916	03/07/1916
Miscellaneous	C Form (Duplicate). Messages And Signals.		
Miscellaneous	2nd Division App 12	05/07/1916	05/07/1916
Operation(al) Order(s)	2nd Division Instructions No. 138	05/07/1916	05/07/1916
Miscellaneous	2nd Division. Appendix 14	06/07/1916	06/07/1916
Miscellaneous	Operation Order for O plus 14 day. by Br. Genl. T.E. Marshall, Commdg. Hy. Arty. IVth Corps. Appendix 5	07/07/1916	07/07/1916
Miscellaneous	2nd Division.	07/07/1916	07/07/1916
Miscellaneous	A Form. Messages And Signals.		
Miscellaneous	2nd Division.	04/07/1916	04/07/1916
Operation(al) Order(s)	Operation Order No. 10 by Br. Genl. T.E. Marshall, Commdg. Hy. Arty. IVth Corps. Appendix 20	08/07/1916	08/07/1916
Miscellaneous	2nd Division. Appendix 21	09/07/1916	09/07/1916
Miscellaneous	A Form. Messages And Signals.		
Operation(al) Order(s)	2nd Division Order No. 112	09/07/1916	09/07/1916
Miscellaneous	Fighting Strength 2nd Division App23	08/07/1916	08/07/1916
Miscellaneous	2nd Division No. G.S. 791/27. IVth Corps.	08/07/1916	08/07/1916

Operation(al) Order(s)	Correction Slip No. 1 to 2nd Division Order No. 112 dated 9-7-16	13/07/1916	13/07/1916
Operation(al) Order(s)	2nd Division Order No. 113	14/07/1916	14/07/1916
Miscellaneous	Issued with 2nd Divn. Order No. 113 dated 14th July, 1916	14/07/1916	14/07/1916
Miscellaneous	Issued with 2nd Divn. Order 11 dated 14-7-15	14/07/1916	14/07/1916
Miscellaneous	2nd Division Casualty Return For Week Ending 8-7-16. App28	08/07/1916	08/07/1916
Operation(al) Order(s)	IVth Corps Order No: 116. App 28	14/07/1916	14/07/1916
Miscellaneous	Table To Accompany IV Corps Order No. 116 dated 14th July, 1916	14/07/1916	14/07/1916
Miscellaneous	2nd Division. Appendix 29	14/07/1916	14/07/1916
Operation(al) Order(s)	IV Corps Order No. 117. App30	15/07/1916	15/07/1916
Miscellaneous	103rd Monchy Breton.		
Operation(al) Order(s)	Correction Slip No. 1 to 2nd Division Order No. 113 dated 14-7-16	15/07/1916	15/07/1916
Operation(al) Order(s)	Addition to 2nd Divn. Order No. 113 d/14-7-16	15/07/1916	15/07/1916
Operation(al) Order(s)	Addition Slip No. 2 to 2nd Division Order No. 113 d/14-7-16	16/07/1916	16/07/1916
Miscellaneous	Fighting Strength. 2nd Division.	15/07/1916	15/07/1916
Miscellaneous	App. 34		
Miscellaneous	2nd Division 2nd Division App35	15/07/1916	15/07/1916
Miscellaneous	A Form. Messages And Signals.		
Operation(al) Order(s)	IV Corps Order No. 118	17/07/1916	17/07/1916
Miscellaneous	A Form. Messages And Signals.		
Operation(al) Order(s)	2nd Division Order No. 114	19/07/1916	19/07/1916
Operation(al) Order(s)	2nd Division Order No. 114	17/07/1916	17/07/1916
Miscellaneous	Entraining Table issued With 2nd Division Order No. 114 dated 19/7/16	19/07/1916	19/07/1916
Miscellaneous	Entraining Table Issued With 2nd Divn. Order No. 144 dated 19-7-16	19/07/1916	19/07/1916
Miscellaneous	Entraining Table Issued With 2nd Divn. Order No. 114 dated 19-7-16	19/07/1916	19/07/1916
Miscellaneous	Entraining Table Issued With 2nd Division Order No. 114 dated 19-7-16	19/07/1916	19/07/1916
Miscellaneous	March Table Issued With 2nd Division Order Noted dated 19-7-16	19/07/1916	19/07/1916
Miscellaneous	First Army. Appx 41	18/07/1916	18/07/1916
Miscellaneous	A Form. Messages And Signals.		
Operation(al) Order(s)	2nd Division Order No. 115. App 43	23/07/1916	23/07/1916
Miscellaneous	A Form. Messages And Signals.		
Miscellaneous	C Form (Duplicate). Messages And Signals.		
Miscellaneous	2nd Division. Casualty Return For Week Ending 22/7/16 App 45	23/07/1916	23/07/1916
Miscellaneous	Fighting Strength. 2nd Division	22/07/1916	22/07/1916
Miscellaneous	App 46		
Heading	2nd Division War Diary General Staff July 1916		
Miscellaneous	A Form. Messages And Signals.		
Operation(al) Order(s)	2nd Division Order No. 117	26/07/1916	26/07/1916
Map	Delville Wood Map		
Miscellaneous	Amendment to 2nd Division Order No. 117	26/07/1916	26/07/1916
Miscellaneous	Amendment No. 2 to 2nd Division Order No. 117 dated 26-7-16	26/07/1916	26/07/1916
Miscellaneous	A Form. Messages And Signals.		
Miscellaneous	Report.		
Miscellaneous	2nd Divn. No. G.S. 935/27.	26/07/1916	26/07/1916

Miscellaneous	A Form. Messages And Signals.		
Miscellaneous	2nd Divn.No. G.S. 1001/1/17	29/07/1916	29/07/1916
Miscellaneous	2nd Divn. No. G.S.1001/1/19	30/07/1916	30/07/1916
Miscellaneous	2nd Divn. No. G.S.1001/1/21	30/07/1916	30/07/1916
Miscellaneous	2nd Divn. No. G.S.1001/1/20	30/07/1916	30/07/1916
Miscellaneous	2nd Divn. No. G.S.1001/1/22	31/07/1916	31/07/1916
Diagram etc	XV Corps. XIII Corps. 2nd Div.		
Miscellaneous	5th Inf. Bde.	31/07/1916	31/07/1916
Miscellaneous	2nd Division	01/08/1916	01/08/1916
Miscellaneous	2nd Divn. No.G.S. 1001/1/51	16/08/1916	16/08/1916
Heading	Cover for Documents. Nature of Enclosures. Operations From 20th July 1916 To Memos Instructions etc Received From Division on Right	20/07/1916	20/07/1916
Operation(al) Order(s)	55th (West Lancashire) Division Order No. 24	06/08/1916	06/08/1916
Operation(al) Order(s)	35th Division Order No. 44	26/07/1916	26/07/1916
Heading	Cover for Documents. Nature of Enclosures. Operations From 20th July 1916 To Memos Instructions etc Received From Division on the Left	20/07/1916	20/07/1916
Operation(al) Order(s)	5th Division Operation Order No. 109	20/07/1916	20/07/1916
Miscellaneous	5th Division. S.485/19	31/07/1916	31/07/1916
Miscellaneous	C Form (Duplicate). Messages And Signals.		
Miscellaneous	C Form (Original). Messages And Signals.		
Heading	Cover for Documents. Nature of Enclosures. Operations From 20th July 1916 To Memos Instructions etc Received From Brigades R. A. R.E. etc of 2nd Division	20/07/1916	20/07/1916
Miscellaneous	Arrangements for Raid by 1st King's on night July 3rd/4th.	03/07/1916	03/07/1916
Miscellaneous	C Form (Original). Messages And Signals.		
Operation(al) Order(s)	5th Inf Bde Order No. 133	03/07/1916	03/07/1916
Miscellaneous		21/07/1916	21/07/1916
Miscellaneous	Notes For Future Operations.	21/07/1916	21/07/1916
Operation(al) Order(s)	5th Infantry Brigade Order No. 142	23/07/1916	23/07/1916
Miscellaneous	Operational File A & B		
Operation(al) Order(s)	99th Inf. Bde Operation Order No. 60	23/07/1916	23/07/1916
Miscellaneous	Summary Of Evacuation.	24/07/1916	24/07/1916
Operation(al) Order(s)	99th Infantry Brigade Operation Notes. No 1	24/07/1916	24/07/1916
Operation(al) Order(s)	2nd Division R.A.M.C. Operation Order No. 47	25/07/1916	25/07/1916
Operation(al) Order(s)	6th Infantry Brigade. Operation Order No. 183	28/07/1916	28/07/1916
Miscellaneous	A Form. Messages And Signals.		
Miscellaneous	2nd Division.		
Miscellaneous	Ref map Montation	30/07/1916	30/07/1916
Miscellaneous	6/Bde	01/08/1916	01/08/1916
Miscellaneous	2nd Div.	01/08/1916	01/08/1916
Operation(al) Order(s)	47th (London) Division Operation Order No. 81	02/07/1916	02/07/1916
Operation(al) Order(s)	47th (London) Division Operation Order No. 82	04/07/1916	04/07/1916
Map	Final Barrage		
Miscellaneous	IVth Corps. No. H.R. S. 669.	04/07/1916	04/07/1916
Miscellaneous	Report on With Cutting From S 30 b Sq to S 24 d. 85	29/07/1916	29/07/1916
Miscellaneous	G. 2188	25/07/1916	25/07/1916
Operation(al) Order(s)	3rd Division Operation Order No: 90	24/07/1916	24/07/1916
Operation(al) Order(s)	55th (West Lancashire) Division Operation Order No. 20	25/07/1916	25/07/1916
Miscellaneous	Notes at Corp Counters Conference	24/07/1916	24/07/1916
Map	Montauban.		
Miscellaneous	Montauban.		
Heading	Tactical Progress Reports. 1st to 16 July 1916		

Miscellaneous	Intelligence Report-2nd Division.	01/07/1916	01/07/1916
Miscellaneous	Report on Operations and Work done-2nd Division.	01/07/1916	01/07/1916
Miscellaneous	Report on Operations and Work done-2nd Division.	02/07/1916	02/07/1916
Miscellaneous	Intelligence Report-2nd Division	02/07/1916	02/07/1916
Miscellaneous	Intelligence Report-2nd Division.	03/07/1916	03/07/1916
Miscellaneous	Report on Operations and Work done-2nd Division.	03/07/1916	03/07/1916
Miscellaneous	Report on Operations and Work done-2nd Division.	04/07/1916	04/07/1916
Miscellaneous	Intelligence Report-2nd Division.	04/07/1916	04/07/1916
Miscellaneous	Report on Operations and Work done-2nd Division.	05/07/1916	05/07/1916
Miscellaneous	Intelligence Report-2nd Division.	05/07/1916	05/07/1916
Miscellaneous	Intelligence Report-2nd Division.	06/07/1916	06/07/1916
Miscellaneous	Report on Operations and Work done-2nd Division.	06/07/1916	06/07/1916
Miscellaneous	Report on Operations and Work done-2nd Division.	07/07/1916	07/07/1916
Miscellaneous	Intelligence Report-2nd Division.	07/07/1916	07/07/1916
Miscellaneous	Report on Operations and Work done-2nd Division.	08/07/1916	08/07/1916
Miscellaneous	Report on Operations and Work done-2nd Division.	09/07/1916	09/07/1916
Miscellaneous	Intelligence Report-2nd Division.	08/07/1916	08/07/1916
Miscellaneous	Intelligence Report-2nd Division.	09/07/1916	09/07/1916
Miscellaneous	Report on Operations and Work done-2nd Division.	10/07/1916	10/07/1916
Miscellaneous	Intelligence Report-2nd Division.	10/07/1916	10/07/1916
Miscellaneous	Intelligence Report-2nd Division.	11/07/1916	11/07/1916
Miscellaneous	Report on Operations and Work done-2nd Division.	11/07/1916	11/07/1916
Miscellaneous	Report on Operations and Work done-2nd Division.	12/07/1916	12/07/1916
Miscellaneous	Intelligence Report-2nd Division.	12/07/1916	12/07/1916
Miscellaneous	Report on Operations and Work done-2nd Division.	13/07/1916	13/07/1916
Miscellaneous	Intelligence Report-2nd Division.	12/07/1916	12/07/1916
Miscellaneous	Report on Operations and Work done-2nd Division	14/07/1916	14/07/1916
Miscellaneous	Intelligence Report-2nd Division.	14/07/1916	14/07/1916
Miscellaneous	Report on Operations and Work done-2nd Division.	15/07/1916	15/07/1916
Miscellaneous	Intelligence Report-2nd Division.	15/07/1916	15/07/1916
Miscellaneous	Report on Operations and Work done-2nd Division.	16/07/1916	16/07/1916
Miscellaneous	Intelligence Report-2nd Division.	16/07/1916	16/07/1916
Miscellaneous			
Heading	2nd Division War Diaries General Staff July 1916		
Heading	Cover for Documents. Nature of Enclosures. Operations From 20th July 1916 To Memos Instructions etc Received From XIIIth Corps.	20/07/1916	20/07/1916
Miscellaneous	3rd Division.	19/07/1916	19/07/1916
Diagram etc	Delville Wood Map		
Miscellaneous	A Form. Messages And Signals.		
Miscellaneous	C Form (Duplicate). Messages And Signals.		
Operation(al) Order(s)	XIII Corps Operation Order No. 31	21/07/1916	21/07/1916
Map	Heavy Artillery will Lift From These Lines At The Times Indicated.		
Miscellaneous	Accompanies XIII Corps Order 31		
Miscellaneous	XIII Corps. 132/81 (G)	21/07/1916	21/07/1916
Miscellaneous	C Form (Original). Messages And Signals.		
Miscellaneous	2nd Division Q.	22/07/1916	22/07/1916
Miscellaneous	Headquarters, XIII Corps.	21/07/1916	21/07/1916
Miscellaneous	A Form. Messages And Signals.		
Miscellaneous	XIII Corps Q.S. No.	22/07/1916	22/07/1916
Miscellaneous	C Form (Duplicate). Messages And Signals.		
Miscellaneous	C Form (Original). Messages And Signals.		
Miscellaneous	C Form (Duplicate). Messages And Signals.		
Miscellaneous	2nd Division. XIII Corps. 85/2 (G)	24/07/1916	24/07/1916
Operation(al) Order(s)	XV Corps Operation Order No. 28	24/07/1916	24/07/1916

Operation(al) Order(s)	XIII Corps Operation Order No. 32	24/07/1916	24/07/1916
Miscellaneous	2nd Division. XIII Corps. 323/5 (G).	24/07/1916	24/07/1916
Miscellaneous	2nd Division.	25/07/1916	25/07/1916
Map	Delville Wood Map		
Miscellaneous	Further Examination Of Prisoner Of 3rd Bn., 52nd I.R. 5th Div:	26/07/1916	26/07/1916
Miscellaneous	2nd Division.	29/07/1916	29/07/1916
Miscellaneous	XIII Corps.	30/07/1916	30/07/1916
Miscellaneous	99th Bde	31/07/1916	31/07/1916
Miscellaneous	99th Inf. Bde.	31/07/1916	31/07/1916
Heading	Cover for Documents. Nature of Enclosures. Operations From 20th July 1916 To Memos Instructions etc Issued By 2nd Division	20/07/1916	20/07/1916
Miscellaneous	5th Inf. Brigade.	02/07/1916	02/07/1916
Miscellaneous	2nd Div.	02/07/1916	02/07/1916
Miscellaneous	A Form. Messages And Signals.		
Miscellaneous	6th Inf. Bde.	03/07/1916	03/07/1916
Miscellaneous	2nd Division	03/07/1916	03/07/1916
Miscellaneous	IVth Corps.	06/07/1916	06/07/1916
Miscellaneous	Appendix "A".		
Miscellaneous	Appendix "B".		
Miscellaneous	A.G.H.Q.	07/07/1916	07/07/1916
Miscellaneous	5th Inf. Bde.	08/07/1916	08/07/1916
Miscellaneous	176th Tunnelling Co. R.E.	08/07/1916	08/07/1916
Miscellaneous	C.R.E., 2nd Divn.	08/07/1916	08/07/1916
Miscellaneous	176 Tunnelling Co. R.E.	10/07/1916	10/07/1916
Miscellaneous	5th Inf. Bde.	08/07/1916	08/07/1916
Miscellaneous	C Form (Duplicate). Messages And Signals.		
Miscellaneous	Headquarters, 6th Inf.Bde. 5th Inf.Bde. 99th Inf.Bde. R.A.	08/07/1916	08/07/1916
Miscellaneous	5th Inf. Bde.	08/07/1916	08/07/1916
Miscellaneous	Redistribution Of Frontage Between Brigades.		
Miscellaneous	5th Inf. Bde.	11/07/1916	11/07/1916
Miscellaneous	Orders For Carrying Parties.	11/07/1916	11/07/1916
Miscellaneous	Instructions For Placing Skins In The Line.	11/07/1916	11/07/1916
Miscellaneous			
Miscellaneous	Instructions For Placing Skins In The Line.	11/07/1916	11/07/1916
Miscellaneous	5th Inf. Bde.	13/07/1916	13/07/1916
Miscellaneous	IVth Corps.	13/07/1916	13/07/1916
Miscellaneous	Notes For Divisional Conference 13-7-1916	13/07/1916	13/07/1916
Miscellaneous	Probable Diary Of Events.		
Miscellaneous	5th Inf. Bde.	21/07/1916	21/07/1916
Operation(al) Order(s)	2nd Division Order No. 115	23/07/1916	23/07/1916
Miscellaneous	5th Infantry Brigade.	23/07/1916	23/07/1916
Miscellaneous	G.O.C. 3rd Division.	25/07/1916	25/07/1916
Miscellaneous	C.R.E., 2nd Divn.	25/07/1916	25/07/1916
Miscellaneous	2nd Divisional Instructions No. 139	25/07/1916	25/07/1916
Map	Water Supply		
Heading	2nd Division War Diary General Staff July 1916		
Map	Delville Wood		
Operation(al) Order(s)	XIII Corps Operation Order No. 32	24/07/1916	24/07/1916
Operation(al) Order(s)	2nd Division Order No. 116	24/07/1916	24/07/1916
Miscellaneous	2nd Divn.	25/07/1916	25/07/1916
Operation(al) Order(s)	XIII Corps Operation Order No. 33	25/07/1916	25/07/1916
Miscellaneous	2nd Division.	25/07/1916	25/07/1916
Operation(al) Order(s)	2nd Division Instructions No. 139	25/07/1916	25/07/1916

Operation(al) Order(s)	2nd Division Order No. 117	26/07/1916	26/07/1916
Miscellaneous	Amendment to 2nd Division Order No. 117	26/07/1916	26/07/1916
Operation(al) Order(s)	XIII Corps Artillery Operation Order No. 6	26/07/1916	26/07/1916
Miscellaneous	Amendment to 2nd Division Order No. 117	26/07/1916	26/07/1916
Miscellaneous	Amendment No. 2 to 2nd Division Order No. 117 dated 26-7-16	26/07/1916	26/07/1916
Miscellaneous	A Form. Messages And Signals.		
Diagram etc	Delville Wood		
Miscellaneous	XIII Corps. Appendix 59	28/07/1916	28/07/1916
Miscellaneous	A Form. Messages And Signals.		
Operation(al) Order(s)	XIII Corps Operation Order No. 34	28/07/1916	28/07/1916
Operation(al) Order(s)	2nd Division Order No. 118	29/07/1916	29/07/1916
Diagram etc	Delville Wood		
Operation(al) Order(s)	Operation Order No. 13 by Brig-General L.W.P. East. C.M.G., D.S.O. Cmdg: Heavy Artillery, XIII Corps. Appendix 64	29/07/1916	29/07/1916
Miscellaneous	Appendix. 65		
Miscellaneous	A Form. Messages And Signals.		
Operation(al) Order(s)	2nd Division Order No. 119	31/07/1916	31/07/1916
Miscellaneous	2nd Division-Casualty Return For Week Ending 29th July, 1916	29/07/1916	29/07/1916
Miscellaneous	Officer Casualties.	29/07/1916	29/07/1916
Miscellaneous	IVth Corps.	02/07/1916	02/07/1916
Miscellaneous	2nd Division	02/07/1916	02/07/1916
Miscellaneous	6th Infantry Brigade	02/07/1916	02/07/1916
Miscellaneous	2nd Division	02/07/1916	02/07/1916
Miscellaneous	6th Infantry Brigade	02/07/1916	02/07/1916
Miscellaneous	Raid by 13th Essex Regt on night of 1/2 July 1916	02/07/1916	02/07/1916
Diagram etc			
Miscellaneous	2nd Division	02/07/1916	02/07/1916
Miscellaneous	2nd Divn	04/07/1916	04/07/1916
Miscellaneous	6th To Bde	04/07/1916	04/07/1916
Miscellaneous	Headquarters 2nd Division.	08/07/1916	08/07/1916
Miscellaneous	5th Bde	08/07/1916	08/07/1916
Miscellaneous	IVth Corps.	08/07/1916	08/07/1916
Miscellaneous	Headquarters 2nd Division	09/07/1916	09/07/1916
Operation(al) Order(s)	5th Infantry Brigade Order No. 135	06/07/1916	06/07/1916
Operation(al) Order(s)	99th Inf.Bde. Operation Order No.54	07/07/1916	07/07/1916
Miscellaneous	IVth Corps.	12/07/1916	12/07/1916
Miscellaneous	Preliminary Report On Hostile Mine Sprung Evening Of 9th Inst In Carency (2)	10/07/1916	10/07/1916
Miscellaneous	2nd Division.	07/07/1916	07/07/1916
Miscellaneous	Headquarters, 2nd Division.	10/07/1916	10/07/1916
Miscellaneous	Hqr 2nd Division	11/07/1916	11/07/1916
Diagram etc	Enlarged 4 Times From Air Photo No. 18A 355		
Miscellaneous	A Form. Messages And Signals.		
Miscellaneous	C Form (Duplicate). Messages And Signals.		
Miscellaneous	A Form. Messages And Signals.		
Miscellaneous	IVth Corps.	04/07/1916	04/07/1916
Miscellaneous	2nd Division.	04/07/1916	04/07/1916
Miscellaneous	C Form (Original). Messages And Signals.		
Miscellaneous	C Form (Duplicate). Messages And Signals.		
Miscellaneous	2nd Division	07/07/1916	07/07/1916
Miscellaneous	A Form. Messages And Signals.		
Miscellaneous	C Form (Original). Messages And Signals.	08/07/1916	08/07/1916
Miscellaneous	IVth Corps No. H.R.S. 669/2	13/07/1916	13/07/1916

Miscellaneous	IV Corps No. H.R.S. 609	13/07/1916	13/07/1916
Miscellaneous	2nd Division.	14/07/1916	14/07/1916
Operation(al) Order(s)	Operation Order For O + 8 Day. By Brigadier General T.E. Marshall, Commanding 4th Corps Heavy Artillery.	01/07/1916	01/07/1916
Miscellaneous	2nd Divn. No. G.S. 92/15/7.	01/07/1916	01/07/1916
Operation(al) Order(s)	Operation Order. By Brigadier-General T.E. Marshall. Commanding. Heavy Artillery. IV Corps.	02/07/1916	02/07/1916
War Diary		28/06/1916	02/07/1916
Miscellaneous	IVth Corps No. H.R.S. 669/K.		
Operation(al) Order(s)	Operation Order For O + 11 Day. By Brigadier-General T.E. Marshall., Commanding. Heavy Artillery. 4th Corps.	04/07/1916	04/07/1916
Miscellaneous	IVth Corps No. R.A. 681/28/64.	04/07/1916	04/07/1916
Operation(al) Order(s)	Operation Order For O + 12 Day. By Brigadier General T.E. Marshall., Commanding Heavy Artillery, IV Corps.	05/07/1916	05/07/1916
Miscellaneous	IVth Corps No. H.R.S. 669/	05/07/1916	05/07/1916
Miscellaneous	IVth Corps No. H.R.S. 669/N.	05/07/1916	05/07/1916
Operation(al) Order(s)	Operation Order For O + 13 Day. By Brigadier General T. E. Marshall., Commanding Heavy Artillery, IV Corps.	06/07/1916	06/07/1916
Miscellaneous	IVth Corps No. H.R.S. 669/0.	06/07/1916	06/07/1916
Operation(al) Order(s)	Operation Order For O + 14 Day. By Brigadier General T. E. Marshall, Commanding Heavy Artillery, IV Corps.	07/07/1916	07/07/1916
Miscellaneous	IV Corps No. H.R.S. 669/P.	07/07/1916	07/07/1916
Miscellaneous	IV Corps No. R.A. 681/31/64	08/07/1916	08/07/1916
Operation(al) Order(s)	Operation Order No. 10 By Brigadier-General T. E. Marshall, Commanding Heavy Artillery, IV Corps.	08/07/1916	08/07/1916
Operation(al) Order(s)	Operation Order For O + 16 Day. By Brigadier General T. E. Marshall. Commanding Heavy Artillery, IV Corps.	09/07/1916	09/07/1916
Miscellaneous	IVth Corps No. H.R.S. 669/Q	09/07/1916	09/07/1916
Miscellaneous	IV Corps No. R.A. 739/4/74	10/07/1916	10/07/1916
Miscellaneous	IVth Corps No. H.R.S. 669/2/A	13/07/1916	13/07/1916
Miscellaneous	IV Corps No. R.A. 681/31/64	13/07/1916	13/07/1916
Miscellaneous	The allotment of Ammunition from noon 12th to noon 20th for all purposes, including Raids is as follows:-	13/07/1916	13/07/1916
Operation(al) Order(s)	Operation Order No. 12. by Brigadier General T. E. Marshall, Commanding. Heavy Artillery, IV Corps.	14/07/1916	14/07/1916
Miscellaneous	IV Corps No. H.R.S. 669/2/B.	14/07/1916	14/07/1916
Miscellaneous		15/07/1916	15/07/1916
Operation(al) Order(s)	Operation Order No. 13. by Brigadier General T. E. Marshall, Commanding Heavy Artillery, IV Corps.	15/07/1916	15/07/1916
Miscellaneous	IVth Corps No. H.R.S. 669/2/C.	15/07/1916	15/07/1916

2ND DIVISION

GENERAL STAFF

AUG - SEP 1916

2nd Division

War Diaries

General Staff

July 1916

—

Sept

Operation Reports in separate files.

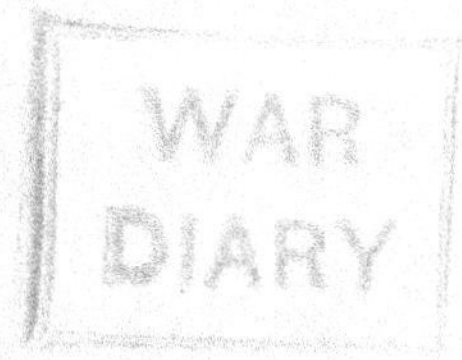

G E N E R A L   S T A F F

2 n d   D I V I S I O N

J U L Y

1 9 1 6

Attached:

Appendices numbered 1 to 70.
(includes casualties).
Reports on Raids.
IV Corps Memos. Orders & Instrns.
XIII -do- -do-
2nd Div. -do- -do-
Right Div. -do- -do-
Left Div. -do- -do-
Units of 2nd Div. -do-
Misc. Divs. -do-
Int. & Progress Reports.

Wt. W 4912/388 50,000 9/14 D. A. & S. Forms/A. 2040/1

Army Form A. 2040.

Index Letter of Register.

Operations from 20th to:

"IN" or "OUT."

GENERAL STAFF 2nd DIVISION

G.S. 1001/

FIELD REGISTER

Of Communications Received or Despatched.

Name of Unit (Regt. [illegible] of SOMME) DATE

Branch of Staff ________ Register opened ________

Section ________ Sub-section ________ " closed ________

INSTRUCTIONS FOR KEEPING REGISTER.

1. Separate registers will be kept for "IN" and "OUT" messages respectively, the necessary alterations being made in the heading to table, etc.

To adapt the register, the following amendments are necessary:—

(*a*) For "IN" messages—Column 2, delete "Despatch"; Column 4, delete "To."

(*b*) For "OUT" messages—Column 2, delete "Receipt"; Column 4, delete "From."

2. Every register will be given an identity number, which is to be inserted for reference in the space provided for that purpose on the cover. In the opposite space will be printed either "IN" or "OUT," according to the purpose for which the register is being used.

3. Column 1.—Messages will be numbered consecutively.

Column 2.—The "time" to be entered is the actual time when the message was received or despatched by the registrar.

Column 3.—"Sender's" number.

(*a*) On incoming messages this will be copied from the message.

(*b*) With outgoing messages this column is only required when the message is transmitted through an intermediary, such as a branch or central registry. When transmitted by the author direct, Column 1 indicates the sender's number, and Column 3 is unnecessary.

Column 4.—"Subject": To be summarized as briefly as possible.

Column 5.—"Action": Intended for a brief note as to the disposal of the message.

XIII Corps Memos Instns &c.

XIIIth Corps. – Memos Instns. received

Date | Branch | Section | Subsection

Sequence No. in Register GS	Time of Receipt / Despatch	Sender's Number	From / To	SUBJECT	Action
1001/2/1	21/7/16	A 694	from [illegible]	Establishment of ammn to be maintained.	P.A. 21/7/16
1001/2/2	21/7/16	G 865	13 Corps	Renewal of general attack by IV Army Reserve army & 6 French army probably on 23rd	P.A. 21/7/16
1001/2/3	21/7/16	132/37 G	13 Corps	Operation Order No 31 of 21/7/16 for operations 22 & 23 July	P.A. 21/7/16
1001/2/3	24/7/16	323/3(G)	[illegible]	Great chances for bold use of snipers & Lewis guns from shell holes [illegible]	Bde RA 25/7
GS 1001/2/4	22/7/16	GS 143/2	[illegible] 13 Corps	Move of 2nd Division less Arty on 23rd into Reserve area	P.A.

Date			Branch	Section	Subsection
Sequence No. in Register	Time of Receipt / Despatch	Sender's Number	From / To	SUBJECT	Action
1001/2/4A	22/7/16	PC/1384	XIII Corps	Orders for move of Field Ambulances	PA
/2/4B	24/7/16	85/26	XIII Corps	13 Corps Operation order 28 of 24 July	PA
/2/4C	24/7/16		[illegible] XIII Corps	XIII Corps O.O. 32 of 24/7/16	PA
/2/4D	24/7/16	132/2/46	[illegible]	General line on which work within XIII Corps area will be carried out	PA, put on file
1001/2/5	25/7/16	132/45	[illegible]	Special Instructions to 2nd Div re bombardment of Delville Wood	Bdes 25/7
1001/2/6	25/7/16	132/46	[illegible]	Boundary between XIII + XV Corps	PA 25/7

Date			Branch	Section	Subsection
Sequence No. in Register	Time of Receipt / Despatch	Sender's Number	From / To	SUBJECT	Action
1001/2/7	25/7	CE 16c/208	CE 13 Corps	asking for list of requirements for dugouts &c	CWE 26/7/16 Reply drawn
1001/2/8	25/7/16		13 Corps	13 Corps O.O. 33 for operations on 27 July & hour of Zero.	PA
" 9.	30.7.16		13th Corps	When Div Commanders have finished with any reports on operations submitted by their CRE the CE 4th Army would like them forwarded to him for his perusal	CRE 2Div 31.7.16
1001/2/10	31/7/16	88/3	RHS	14 Div will relieve 5 Div in right sector XV Corps 1/2 Aug.	G 99 RH 1/8/16

Memos. Instns. &c. received from DIVISION on LEFT.

Date Branch Section Subsection

Sequence No. in Register GS	Time of Receipt / Despatch	Sender's Number	From / To	SUBJECT	Action
1001/3/1	26/7/6	—	5 Divn	O.O. 108 of 26-7-16 for operation 27th July	P.A.

DIVN. on LEFT

Memos &c

Memos &c. received from Infy Bdes. / R.A. R.E. &c. } of 2nd DIVN

Date | Branch | Section | Subsection

Sequence No. in Register	Time of Receipt / Despatch	Sender's Number	From / To	SUBJECT	Action
GS 1001/5/1	22/7/16	-	6 Bde	Notes for future operations	PA
1001/5/2	23/7/16	142	5 Bde	5 Bde order No 142 of 23-7-16 move to Happy Valley.	PA
1001/5/3	23/7/16	60	99 Bde	99 Bde O.O. 60 of 23/7/16 move to Sand Pit Valley.	PA
1001/5/4	23/7/16	4/1121/3	ADMS	Medical Arrts. 2 Divn. Positions of Fd ambs 23/7/16	PA
1001/2/9	24/7/16	4/1140	DDMS	Summary of evacuation	PA
1001/2/10	24/7/16	O No1	99 Bde	99 Bde Operation Notes No 1. of 24-7-16. (Consolidation of positions).	PA

Memos. &c. from INFY BDES. R.A. R.E. &c. 2nd DIVN

Date | Branch | Section | Subsection

Sequence No. in Register	Time of Receipt / Despatch	Sender's Number	From / To	SUBJECT	Action
1001/2/11				Report by Capt. E.B. Denison 1/KRRC.	4 Corps 26/7/16
1001/2/12	26/7/16	RGK 169	99 Bde	Alteration of position of Bde HQ to W Edge of Bernafay Wood Repossession of [illegible]	P.A. 26/7/16
1001/2/13	26/7/16	–	RA 9 Div	Operation Order No 57 of 26 July.	P.A 26/7/16
1001/2/14	31/7/16	–	99th Bde.	Information given by wounded S.A. Soldier found in Delville Wood 27th inst, re inhuman treatment by Germans on retirement of his Brigade from the wood.	13 Corps 2.8.16

Date			Branch	Section	Subsection
Sequence No. in Register	Time of Receipt / Despatch	Sender's Number	From / To	SUBJECT	Action
1001/1/6	25/7/16	P.I. 139	Office.	D.I. 139 Instns re policy to be pursued in new area	Bdes [illegible] 25/7/16
1001/1/7				Water Supply Map 1/40.000	PA
1001/1/8	24/7/16	-	Office	Div. order 116 (relief) 24-7-16	PA
1001/1/9	26/7/16	-	Office	6 Bde will relieve 2 Coys / 99 Bde forming garrison of Montauban	99 Bde [illegible]
1001/1/10	26/7/16	-	2 Div	Shells falling short between 8 + 11 am in S.18.b	XIII Corps 26/7/16
1001/1/11	26/7/16	-	2 Div	Pointing out mistake in 13 Corps orders re Zero hour for 27	4 Corps 26/7/16

2nd DIVN Memos. Instns &c

Memos., Instns &c. issued by

Date | Branch 2nd Divn. Section | Subsection

Sequence No. in Register GS	Time of Receipt / Despatch	Sender's Number	From / To	SUBJECT	Action
1001/1/1	21/1/16	–	2 Div	Bringing to notice certain points re use of TMs. assaults &c &c	Bdes, 10 RCRS, RANS } 21/1/16
1001/1/3	23/1/16	–	2 Divn.	Reconnaissance of line to be carried out by G.O.C. 5 & 99 Bdes	5 & 99 Bdes [illegible]/1/16
1001/1/4	25/1/16	–	2 Divn.	Re establishment of 6 Bde HQ at Picaurin	3 DIV 25/1/16
1001/1/5.	25/1/16	–	2 Div.	Garrison of Montauban will be employed on work on defences under CE of Corps	Bdes CRE 25/1/16

Date			Branch	Section	Subsection
Sequence No. in Register	Time of Receipt / Despatch	Sender's Number	From / To	SUBJECT	Action
1001/1/12	26/7/16		2 Div	Further Examination of Prisoners of 8th Bodn Grenadier Regt	5 & 6 Bde 26/7, 99 Bde only
1001/1/13	27/7/16		2 Div	Short report on operations of 99 Bde on 27-7-16	XIII Corps 27/7
				Further report re above	" 28. 7. 16
14				Relief of 99 Bde by 6 Bde	
1001/1/15	29/7/16		2 Div	Zero hour for operations 30th	
1001/1/16	29/7/16		GS 2 Div	Div Comdr's Chief... to have a ... for consolidation ... attack on Guillemont ...	5 Bde 29/7/16
			N.R.	Cancelled	

Date			Branch	Section	Subsection
Sequence No. in Register	Time of Receipt / Despatch	Sender's Number	From / To	SUBJECT	Action
GS1001/1/17	29/7/16		2 Div	GOC 99 Bde will place one Bn in Div Res. to move at 1 hrs notice from 6 am tomorrow	Bdes + RA 24/7
GS1001/1/18	29/7/16	-	2 Div	GOC considers that much of defensive system concentrated on N + W flank of Delville Wood	6 Bde 29/7
GS1001/1/19	30/7/16	/	2 Div	Re non receipt of reports from 1/OxfLI + 24 RFus	5 Bde 30/7/16
GS1001/1/20	30/7/16	/	2 Div	Div. Comdr wishes ground to be gained by digging. Re comm trench from Waterlot Farm	3 Bdes [illegible] 30/7/16

Date			Branch	Section	Subsection
Sequence No. in Register	Time of Receipt / Despatch	Sender's Number	From / To	SUBJECT	Action
GS 1001/1/21	30/7/16		2 Div	List of trenches to be dug first (afterwards sent on)	Bde CRE [illegible] 31/7/16
GS 1001/1/22	31/7/16		2 Div	Notes — Div. Comdrs Conference 31.7.16	Bdes [illegible] 31/7/16
" 23.	31/7/16		2 Div	Query re 5th Bde Tactical Progress Report up to 4 pm 31st inst.	5th Brigade 31.7.16
GS 1001/1/24	1/8/16		2 Div.	Re maintenance of touch with Divs on right.	13 Corps 1/8/16
GS 1001/1/25	1/8/16		2 Div	Re discontinuance of barrage on E + NE side of Delville Wood	13 Corps 1/8/16

Date | Branch | Section | Subsection

Sequence No. in Register	Time of Receipt / Despatch	Sender's Number	From / To	SUBJECT	Action
1001/1/31	3.8.16		Office	Report on attempt by small party of enemy to enter Delville Wood on night 2/3 August '16	XIII Corps 3.8.16
32	"		"	Forwarding Sketch maps showing Villages of Guillemont and its vicinity	55 Div 3.8.16
				Forwarding 30 copies ea. of following:- Guichy & Guillemont 2 Editions scale 1/5000 " " (clean copies) Notes on information obtained on last attack on Guillemont	6th Bde 3.8.16
				5 copies ditto to 5 Brigade	4.8.16
				10 " " " RA 2 Div	"
33	5.8.16		Office	In Event of this Div carrying out an attack on German Trenches S.18 d. may we use Angle Trench etc for assembly Trenches. Also further asking if any M guns at corner of Delville Wood could assist our attack by firing East along Longueval-Guichy road	17 Div SOR 6 Bde for information 5.8.16
34	5.8.16		Office	2 coys of 10/DCLI will be required to take part in an operation which is to be carried out shortly Select an officer to command the 2 coys and direct him to report to GOC 6th Brigade tomorrow	10/DCLI 6 Bde (for information) 5.8.16
35	6.8.16		Office	With reference to maps forwarded with 13 Corps OO 34 blue line marked "minus 15" runs through our own Trenches S of Waterlot Farm etc	13 Corps 6.8.16

Date			Branch	Section	Subsection
Sequence No. in Register	Time of Receipt / Despatch	Sender's Number	From / To	SUBJECT	Action
GS1001/1/26				Notes for Conference at Div HQ.	
GS1001/1/27	2/8/16	–	GS / 2 Div	Covering party to be provided for new trench being dug S24 b 2.6	5 Bde 2/8
1001/1/28	2/8/16		GS	Zero hour for operations on 3rd Aug	Bde RA, RE Coys, [illegible] 2/8
1001/1/29	2/8/16		GS	Div Comdr's recommendations and decision re capture of Cointing Post (D.O. 120)	Bde RA
1001/1/30	3/8/16		2 Div	Plan of attack on [illegible] 2 Div	XIII Corps

Date			Branch	Section	Subsection
Sequence No. in Register	Time of Receipt / Despatch	Sender's Number	From / To	SUBJECT	Action
1001/1/36	6.8		2 Div	2 Div will probably be relieved by 24 Div on night 8/9	All units 6/8
37.	"		"	Programme of "Chinese Attack" to be made on 7th August	6 Bde 6.8.16
38	6.8.16		2 Division	With ref to map issued with 13 Corps OO No 37, may HQ bombard trench which runs parallel to the Longueval-Guillemont Rd through T.19 a. S.24 b & S.18 d. It shows them left off the Northern portion etc	13 Corps 6.8.16
39				Zero hour for operations	
40	7.8.16		2 Division	Forwarding letter from Genl Kellett (and newspaper cuttings) re wrong statement in press stating that S African and not 99th Bde captured Deville Wood etc	13 Corps 7.8.16
41	7.8.16		2 Division	Forwarding wires received from 17th Division in connection with ~~Delville Wood~~ the situation in Delville Wood not being quite clear, and that the enemy is now occupying a continuous line of trenches inside the wood	13 Corps 7.8.16

Date			Branch	Section	Subsection
Sequence No. in Register	Time of Receipt / Despatch	Sender's Number	From / To	SUBJECT	Action
1001/1/42				Zero hour operations 9th August	
43				Re [illegible]	
44	9.8.16		2 Division	Forwarding map showing positions of some hostile machine guns are marked	13 Corps 9.8.16
45	"		"	Forwarding report on the operations carried out on 8th and 9th August.	13 Corps 9.8.16
46	10.8.16		"	During the move to rest area (the Div) [illegible] Div Arty will be in Bde area as follows	Bdes CRA CRE Q ADMS 10 [illegible]
47	10.8.16		"	Forwarding report re attack by 1/Kings and 1/Middlesex August 8th	XIII Corps 10.8.16
48.	11 8.16		"	Continuation of my G.S/1001/1/45, forward a report from GOC 6th Bde. re attack carried out by the 1/4 Middlesex night 8/9 August	XIII Corps 11.8.16 24th Div

Date Branch Section Subsection

Sequence No. in Register	Time of Receipt / Despatch	Sender's Number	From / To	SUBJECT	Action
1001/1/6	25/7/16	D.I 139	Office.	D.I 139. Instns re policy to be pursued in new area	Bdes 10 R.C.(?) R.A.M.C. Sig. Co. } 25/7/16
1001/1/7				Water Supply Map 1/40.000	P.A.
1001/1/8	24/7/16	–	Office	Divl Order 116 (relief) 24-7-16	P.A.
1001/1/9	26/7/16	–	Office	6 Bde will relieve 2 Coys/99 Bde forming garrison of Montauban	99 Bde 26/7/16
1001/1/10	26/7/16	–	2 Divn	Shells falling short between 8 + 11 am in S.18.b.	XIII Corps 26/7/16
1001/1/11	26/7/16	–	2 Divn	Pointing out mistake in 13 Corps orders re Zero hour for 27"	4 Corps 26/7/16

Date			Branch	Section	Subsection
Sequence No. in Register	Time of Receipt / Despatch	Sender's Number	From / To	SUBJECT	Action
1001/1/49	15.8.16	-	Office	re delay in moving 2 Division from the ANCRE VALLEY area to "D" area	X Corps, V ?, for XIII information 15.8.16
50	16.8.16		Office	Forwarding report called for in GHQ.OB/166 forwarded to 2 Div by 13 Corps re increasing range of Stokes mortars	
51	"		2 Div	Notes on operations	[illegible] 16/8
52	"		"	Forwarding brief statement of the lessons deduced from the fighting in which 2 Div has taken part	13 Corps, 5 Corps for information 16.8.16
53	"	"	2	Forwarding copy of notes on the attack by the French XX and VII Corps on 12th August	[illegible] 16.8.16
54	19.8.16	–	2 Div	Re move of 99 Bde to Bus les Artois on 20.8.16	[illegible] 19/8/16

Date Branch Section Subsection

Sequence No. in Register	Time of Receipt / Despatch	Sender's Number	From / To	SUBJECT	Action

Instructions regarding War Diaries and Intelligence Summaries are contained in F. S. Regs., Part II and the Staff Manual respectively. Title pages will be prepared in manuscript.

WAR DIARY

2nd Division. ~~or~~ General Staff.

~~INTELLIGENCE SUMMARY.~~

(*Erase heading not required.*)

Army Form C. 2118.

Hour, Date, Place	Summary of Events and Information	Remarks and references to Appendices
CAMBLAIN L'ABBE. 1st July, 1916.	Fine and warm.	
5. a.m.	Situation normal. CABARET ROUGE shelled during the night.	
4.25 p.m.	IVth Corps H.R.S. 669/J received..	App. 1.
5.30 p.m.	Situation report. At 11.30 p.m.,3.a.m. and 4 a.m. last night Div. Artillery fired on GIVENCHY for 2 minutes: Enemy's artillery and trench mortars active between 11.a.m. and 1.p.m.: yesterday evening enemy used "box kites" for observation. Hostile aeroplanes active during the morning: marked increase of transport on roads visible from LORETTE RIDGE especially in the case of red cross cars.	
7. p.m.	Operation Order No. 108 issued..	App. 2.
	Railheads unchanged.	
CAMBLAIN L'ABBE. 2nd July, 1916.	Fine and warm.	
5.5 a.m.	Situation normal. Enemy trenches raided successfully. Enemy casualties estimated at 40 killed. One prisoner from 162nd Regt. brought back wounded. Report..	
7. a.m.	2nd Div. Operation Order No. 109 issued..............................	App. 3.
10. a.m.	Further particulars of raid carried out by 13th Essex received.......	App. 4.
11. a.m.	Div. Artillery carried out a bombardment of German trenches between LOVE and IRISH craters.	
4.30 p.m.	IVth Corps Operation Order (H.C.S. 669/K) received..............................	App. 5.
5.30 p.m.	Quiet day. One of our batteries shelled with lachrymatory shells. Some 15 cm shells fired into CARENCY.	
	Fighting strength for week ending 1/7/16 received....................	App. 6.
	Casualty return for week ending 1/7/16 received......................	App. 7.
10.15 p.m.	Div. Artillery co-operated with IVth Corps Heavy Artillery in shelling CITE DE CAUMONT.	
	Railheads unchanged.	

Instructions regarding War Diaries and Intelligence Summaries are contained in F.S. Regs., Part II. and the Staff Manual respectively. Title pages will be prepared in manuscript.

WAR DIARY

2nd Division — General Staff.

~~INTELLIGENCE SUMMARY.~~

(*Erase heading not required.*)

Army Form C. 2118.

Hour, Date, Place	Summary of Events and Information	Remarks and references to Appendices
CAMBLAIN L'ABBE. 3rd July, 1916.	Fine and warm.	
4. a.m.	IVth Corps H.A. and 2nd Div. Artillery bombarded roads and communication trenches near GIVENCHY.	
5. a.m.	Div. Artillery assisted IVth Corps Heavy Artillery in bombardment of CITE DE CAUMONT.	
5. a.m.	Situation report. Situation normal except for slight retaliation for our bombardment.	
9.45 a.m.	IVth Corps H.R.S. 609 received....................................	App. 8.
3. p.m.	IVth Corps H.A. and French Courts bombarded THE PIMPLE.	
5. p.m.	Situation report. Hostile Trench Mortars active in CARENCY Sector from 5. p.m. A battery on LORETTE SPUR shelled with lachrymatory shells.	
7. p.m.	2nd Divn. instructions No. 110 issued..............................	App. 9.
	2nd Divn .instructions No. 111 issued..............................	App. 10.
CAMBLAIN L'ABBE. 4th July, 1916.	Fine up to 2 p.m. Thunderstorms during the afternoon.	
5. a.m.	Situation report. Two mines were exploded close together at 10.45p.m. The near lips were occupied and position consolidated. Enemy barraged ZOUAVE VALLEY for about 15 minutes. Small raiding party 1st Kings, 6th Inf. Bde. entered German trenches about S.15.b.3. and killed two Germans.	
11.20 a.m.	Telegram from G.O.C. 1st Army congratulating those who took part on night of 1st/2nd July received....................................	App. 11
4.20 p.m.	IV Corps H.R.S. 669/N received....................................	App. 12
5.30 p.m.	Situation report. CARENCY shelled yesterday at 5.30 p.m. and at 7 p.m. with 4.2 inch. Our front line in ZOUAVE VALLEY shelled by 77 mm and 4.2 inch when mine was exploded and during the raid: Enemy blew "camouflet" at 3 p.m. at S.8.b.9.2½. No damage was done.	
	Railheads unchanged.	

(73989) W4141—463. 400,000. 9/14. H.&J.Ltd. Forms/C. 2118/10.

Instructions regarding War Diaries and Intelligence Summaries are contained in F. S. Regs., Part II. and the Staff Manual respectively. Title pages will be prepared in manuscript.

WAR DIARY

2nd Division or General Staff.

~~INTELLIGENCE SUMMARY.~~

(*Erase heading not required.*)

Army Form C. 2118.

Hour, Date, Place	Summary of Events and Information	Remarks and references to Appendices
CAMBLAIN L'ABBE.		
5th July, 1916.	Thunderstorms during the day. Fine after 4. p.m.	
5. a.m.	Situation normal.	
5.45 p.m.	Situation report. Very quiet day. Some heavy trench mortaring of left brigade front, otherwise hostile artillery inaction.	
	Railheads unchanged.	
	2nd Division instructions No. 138 issued..............................	App. 13.
CANBLAIN L'ABBE.		
6th July, 1916.	Dull.	
5. a.m.	Situation normal.	
6.15 p.m.	Situation report. Enemy shelled ZOUAVE VALLEY with H.E. and heavy trench mortars between 12 and 2 p.m.: our howitzers retaliated. Our 18 pdrs. shelled hostile trenches at 6.5 p.m. and 7. p.m. last evening when rifle fire was opened on our aeroplanes.	
9.10 p.m.	IVth Corps H.R.S. 669/O received..................................	App. 14.
	Railheads unchanged.	
CAMBLAIN L'ABBE.		
7th July, 1916.	Wet.	
4.55 a.m.	Situation normal.	
1.15 p.m.	IVth Corps heavy artillery O.O.....received..........................	App. 15.
5. p.m.	Situation report. Some trench mortar activity in the CARENCY Sector. Otherwise quiet.	
6.15 p.m.	IVth Corps H.R.S. 669 received......................................	App. 17
	Railheads unchanged.	
	His Majesty the Kings message to all ranks received — — — —	app 18

(73989) W4141—463. 400,000. 9/14. H.&J.Ltd. Forms/C. 2118/10.

Instructions regarding War Diaries and Intelligence Summaries are contained in F. S. Regs., Part II. and the Staff Manual respectively. Title pages will be prepared in manuscript.

Army Form C. 2118.

WAR DIARY

2nd Division. ~~or~~ General Staff.

~~INTELLIGENCE SUMMARY.~~

(*Erase heading not required.*)

Hour, Date, Place	Summary of Events and Information	Remarks and references to Appendices
CAMBLAIN L'ABBE. 8th July, 1916.	Warm and fine.	
5. a.m.	Raid opposite S.3.5. at 1.5 a.m. was successful. Hostile Artillery fire was distributed along the Divisional front and lasted 30 minutes. Otherwise all quiet.	
11.30 a.m.	IVth Corps H.R.S. 629 received........	App. 19.
5.25 p.m.	Situation report. All quiet.	
6.20 p.m.	IVth Corps heavy artillery O.O./10 received........	App. 20.
	Railheads unchanged.	
CAMBLAIN L'ABBE. 9th July, 1916.	Fine and warm.	
5. a.m.	Situation all quiet. ZOUAVE VALLEY shelled between 9. p.m. and 10. p.m.	
	Fighting strength for week ending 8/7/16 received........	App. 23.
2.15 p.m.	IVth Corps H.R.S. 669/Q received........	App. 21.
	2nd Division OperationOrder No. 112 issued........	App. 22.
5.30 p.m.	Enemy reported to have been registering with 4.2 Howitzers on the SOUCHEZ VALLEY. Intermittent shelling with 77.mm in CARENCY Sector.	
	Railheads unchanged.	
	Casualty return for week ending 8.7.16. received	App 28

(73989) W4141—463. 400,000. 9/14. H.&J.Ltd. Forms/C. 2118/10.

Instructions regarding War Diaries and Intelligence Summaries are contained in F. S. Regs., Part II. and the Staff Manual respectively. Title pages will be prepared in manuscript.

WAR DIARY
or
INTELLIGENCE SUMMARY.
(Erase heading not required.)

Army Form C. 2118.

Hour, Date, Place	Summary of Events and Information	Remarks and references to Appendices
CAMBLAIN L'ABBE. 10th July, 1916.	Fine.	
5. a.m.	Last night enemy blew a mine between FOOTBALL and BROADSIDE craters at 8.20 p.m. We consolidated our lip of the crater. Some damage was done to our front line . Otherwise al quiet.	
3. p.m.	G.O.C. First Army inspected officers and men of the 1st Royal Berks, 13th Essex, and 17th R. Fusiliers who had taken part in raids recently.	
5.25 p.m.	Situation normal.	
	Report on raid carried out on night 7th/8th received.................	App. 24.
	Railheads unchanged.	
CAMBLAIN L'ABBE. 11th July, 1916.	Fine.	
5. a.m.	Very quiet night.	
9.30 a.m.	IV Corps H.R.S. 604 received..	App. 25.
5.20 p.m.	Hostile Trench Mortars active 6.30 a.m.and 8. a.m. on the right of the Northern Section. Enemy artillery active against CABARET ROUGE between 1. p.m. and 3. p.m.	
	Railheads unchanged.	
CAMBLAIN L'ABBE. 12th July, 1916.	Dull and some rain in the evening.	
5. a.m.	Enemy snipers active during the night otherwise situation normal.	
5.30 p.m.	Hostile trench mortars active opposite CARENCY sector during the morning until silenced by our artillery. Otherwise situation normal.	
	Railheads unchanged.	

(73989) W4141—463. 400,000. 9/14. H.&J.Ltd. Forms/C. 2118/10.

Army Form C. 2118.

Instructions regarding War Diaries and Intelligence Summaries are contained in F. S. Regs., Part II. and the Staff Manual respectively. Title pages will be prepared in manuscript.

WAR DIARY

2nd Division. or General Staff.

~~INTELLIGENCE SUMMARY.~~

(Erase heading not required.)

Hour, Date, Place	Summary of Events and Information	Remarks and references to Appendices
CAMBLAIN L'ABBE. 13th July, 1916.	Fine.	
5. a.m.	ZOUAVE VALLEY and 130th VALLEY was slightly shelled about 9.30 p.m. otherwise nothing to report.	
	Correction slip No. 1 to 2nd Divn. O.O./112 issued	App. 26.
5.15 p.m.	In the Northern sector enemy trench mortars were very active between 11 a.m. and 12.30 p.m. and succeeded in doing some damage to our trenches. We retaliated with artillery and trench mortars.	
10 p.m.	IV Corps telephoned that 2nd Divn. is to be relieved and to go South. Railheads unchanged.	
CAMBLAIN L'ABBE. 14th July, 1916.	Fine.	
5. a.m.	Situation normal.	
3. a.m.	Relief of 5th Inf. Bde. by 6th Inf. Bde. completed.	
	2nd Divn. Operation Order No. 113 issued..............................	App. 27.
4.45 p.m.	Operation Order IV Corps No. 116 received............................	App. 28.
5. 15 p.m.	Situation normal. Enemy fired shrapnel over the ZOUAVE VALLEY between 10 a.m. and 11 a.m.	
9. p.m.	IV Corps H.R.S. 669/2/B received....................................	App. 29

(73989) W4141—463. 400,000. 9/14. H.&J.Ltd. Forms/C. 2118/10.

Army Form C. 2118.

Instructions regarding War Diaries and Intelligence Summaries are contained in F. S. Regs., Part II. and the Staff Manual respectively. Title pages will be prepared in manuscript.

WAR DIARY
2nd Division or General Staff.
INTELLIGENCE SUMMARY.
(*Erase heading not required.*)

Hour, Date, Place	Summary of Events and Information	Remarks and references to Appendices
CAMBLAIN L'ABBE. 15th July, 1916.	Fine.	
5. a.m.	ZOUAVE VALLEY shelled between 1.30 a.m. and 2.10 a.m.. Otherwise situation normal .	
11.45 a.m.	5th Inf. Bde. marched to DIEVAL area marching past G.O.C. IV Corps on the way.	
5.20 p.m.	Northern end of ZOUAVE VALLEY shelled also SOUCHEZ. Trench mortars active in CARENCY Section.	
5.25 p.m.	IV Corps Operation Order No. 117 received..........................	App. 30.
7. p.m.	Correction Slip No. 1 to O.O./113 issued............................	App. 31.
8.15 p.m.	Addition to 2nd Divn. O.O./113 issued..............................	App. 32.
	Railheads unchanged.	

Instructions regarding War Diaries and Intelligence Summaries are contained in F. S. Regs., Part II. and the Staff Manual respectively. Title pages will be prepared in manuscript.

WAR DIARY
or
INTELLIGENCE SUMMARY.
(Erase heading not required.)

Army Form C. 2118.

Hour, Date, Place	Summary of Events and Information	Remarks and references to Appendices
CAMBLAIN L'ABBE. 16th July, 1916.	Wet.	
5. a.m.	All quiet.	
1.25 a.m.	G.O.C. 140th Infantry Brigade has assumed command of BERTHONVAL Sector.	
7. a.m.	Addition slip No. 2 to 2nd Division O.O./113 issued................	App. 33.
	Fighting strength for week ending 15/7/16 received................	App. 34.
	Casualty Return for week ending 15/7/16 received..................	App. 35.
5.20 p.m.	Yesterday evening trenches W. of KENNEDY CRATER received some minenwerfer and about 50 rounds of 77 mm were fired into the ZOUAVE VALLEY. We retaliated with 18 pdrs and 4.5 howitzers. SOUCHEZ was shelled intermittently with 77 mm this morning.	
	Railheads unchanged.	
CAMBLAIN L'ABBE. 17th July, 1916.	Wet.	
3. a.m.	6th Bde. relieved by 142nd Bde.	
5. a.m.	Situation normal.	
10. a.m.	2nd Division report centre opens at O.10.B.	
3. p.m.	Telegram issued with reference to 2nd Division Order No. 113........	App. 36.
	Railheads unchanged.	

(73989) W4141—463. 400,000. 9/14. H.&J.Ltd. Forms/C. 2118/10.

Army Form C. 2118.

Instructions regarding War Diaries and Intelligence Summaries are contained in F. S. Regs., Part II. and the Staff Manual respectively. Title pages will be prepared in manuscript.

WAR DIARY

2nd Division or General Staff.

~~INTELLIGENCE SUMMARY.~~

(*Erase heading not required.*)

Hour, Date, Place	Summary of Events and Information	Remarks and references to Appendices
CHATEAU O.10.B.		
18th July, 1016.	Wet.	
12.30 a.m.	IV Corps O.O./118 received........	App. 37.
1. a.m.	2nd Division G.528 issued........	App. 38.
	Division resting and training.	
	Railheads unchanged.	
CHATEAU O.10.B.		
19th July, 1916.	Fine.	
2. a.m.	First Army C. 840 received........	App. [illegible].
7. a.m.	2nd Division Order No. 114 issued........	App. 40.
9.40 a.m.	G.H.Q. Q/3072/A received........	App. 41.
	Division resting and training.	
	Railheads unchanged.	
CHATEAU O.10.B.		
20th July, 1916.	Fine.	
4. a.m.	2nd Division H.Q. entrained at DIEVAL.	
8. a.m.	2nd Division H.Q. opened at RUE DE COLLEGE,CORBIE.	
	Division moving by rail from IV Corps Area to join XIII Corps IV Army. Division entrained in accordance with 2nd Division Order No. 114. First train arrived LONGUEAU about 9. a.m. First train at SALEUX about 11 a.m.	

(73989) W4141—463. 400,000. 9/14. H.&J.Ltd. Forms/C. 2118/10.

Instructions regarding War Diaries and Intelligence Summaries are contained in F. S. Regs., Part II. and the Staff Manual respectively. Title Pages will be prepared in manuscript.

WAR DIARY

General Staff ~~or~~ 2nd Division.
~~INTELLIGENCE SUMMARY~~
(Erase heading not required.)

Army Form C. 2118

Place	Date	Hour	Summary of Events and Information	Remarks and references to Appendices
RUE DE COLLEGE, CORBIE. 21-7-16.	21-7-16.		Fine.	
			Infantry Brigades complete, reach their new billetting areas by 7 a.m.	
		1 pm.	13th Corps G.865 received.......... Supply Railhead, HEILLY.	App. 41
CITADEL F.21.b. 22-7-16.			Fine.	
		9-30am	The Division complete, has arrived in billets and bivouacs in area CORBIE - SAILLY LE SEC - MORLANCOURT.	
		3 p.m.	2nd Division Advanced H.Q. opened at CITADEL.	
			13th Corps Order received (G.904)..........	Appx. 29
			Railheads unchanged.	

1875 Wt. W593/826 1,000,000 4/15 J.B.C. & A. A.D.S.S./Forms/C. 2118.

Instructions regarding War Diaries and Intelligence Summaries are contained in F. S. Regs., Part II. and the Staff Manual respectively. Title pages will be prepared in manuscript.

WAR DIARY

Genral Staff or 2nd Division.

~~INTELLIGENCE~~ SUMMARY.

(*Erase heading not required.*)

Army Form C. 2118.

Hour, Date, Place	Summary of Events and Information	Remarks and references to Appendices
CITADEL (F.21.b.) 23-7-1916.	Fine.	
7 p.m.	Arrival of the Division in Reserve area(HAPPY VALLEY, SAND PIT VALLEY, BOIS DES TAILLES, MORLANCOURT) reported to XIII Corps.	
2 a.m.	Operation Order No. 115 issued....................................	Appendix 43.
4-15 p.m.	Message No. G.937 received....................................	,, 44
	Casualty Return for week ending 22-7-16 received....................	,, 45
	Fighting Strength for week ending 22-7-16 received..................	,, 46
CITADEL (F.21.b.). 24-7-16.	Fine.	
11-50 a.m	XIII Corps report enemy massing behind GINCHY....	
6-25 p.m.	XIII Corps Operation Order 38 received.............................	Appendix 47
6-35 p.m.	XIII Corps 133/2/49 received..	Appendix 48
	99th Inf. Bde. relieved left sub-section of 3rd Division, LONGUEVAL - DELVILLE WOOD and came under ordersof 3rd Divn.	
11-15 p.m.	2nd Divn. Operation Order 116 issued................................	Appendix 49
CITADEL (F.21.b.). 25-7-16.	Fine.	
5-35 a.m.	99th Inf.Bde. report situation quiet.	
3-0 p.m.	Relief of 76th Bde. by 6th Bde. in Divl. Reserve Bde area completed. 6th Bde. cam under orders of G.O.C., 3rd Divn.	
COPSE B A.21.a.45. 7-50 p.m.	2nd Division Advanced H.Q. opens at COPSE "B", A.21.a.45. and G.O.C. assumed command of Left Section, XIII Corps.	
9-10 p.m.	XIII Corps 133/84(G) received.......................................	Appendix 50
5-50 p.m.	99th Bde. report MONTAUBAN, CATERPILLAR VALLEY and BERNAFAY WOOD heavily shelled.	
10-30 pm.	XIII Corps O.O. 33 received...	Appendix 51
10-40 p.m.	XIII Corps 132/85(G) received.......................................	Appendix 52
	2nd Divn. Instructions 130 issued...................................	Appendix 53

(73989) W4141—463. 400,000. 9/14. H.&J.Ltd. Forms/C. 2118/10.

Instructions regarding War Diaries and Intelligence Summaries are contained in F. S. Regs., Part II. and the Staff Manual respectively. Title Pages will be prepared in manuscript.

WAR DIARY

Army Form C. 2118

General Staff ~~xxx~~ 2nd Division.

INTELLIGENCE SUMMARY

(Erase heading not required.)

Place	Date	Hour	Summary of Events and Information	Remarks and references to Appendices
CØPSE "B"	26-7-1916		Dull.	
		4-15am	Relief of 9th Bde. by 5th Bde. completed.	
		6-0 am	Situation normal. Series of gas shells put over by enemy at 11 p.m. and 2 a.m.	
		7-0 am	2nd Division Operation Order No. 117 issued....................................	Appx.54
		9-10am	XIII Corps R.A. Operation Order No.6 received - - - - - - - - - - - - - - - - -	Appx.55
			Amendment No.1 to 2nd Division Order No.117 issued - - - - - - - - - - - - - -	Appx.56
		6-0 pm	Situation report. There was continuous shelling with H.E. in the vicinity of TRONES WOOD and LONGUEVAL. Enemy artillery have been less active to-day.than yesterday.	
		11-10pm	Amendment No.2 to 2nd Divn. Order No.117 issued - - - - - - - - - - - - - - - -	Appx.57

1875 Wt. W593/826 1,000,000 4/15 J.B.C. & A. A.D.S.S./Forms/C. 2118.

Instructions regarding War Diaries and Intelligence Summaries are contained in F. S. Regs., Part II. and the Staff Manual respectively. Title pages will be prepared in manuscript.

Army Form C. 2118.

WAR DIARY

General Staff ~~xx~~ 2nd Division.
~~INTELLIGENCE SUMMARY~~.
(*Erase heading not required.*)

Hour, Date, Place	Summary of Events and Information	Remarks and references to Appendices
COPSE "B". 27-7-16.	Fine.	
5-50 a.m.	Situation report. Gas shells were fired in the vicinity of BERNAFAY WOOD and MONTAUBAN, also tear shells, in consequence communications and working parties were considerably hampered. One prisoner was captured South of DELVILLE WOOD.	
8-35 a.m.	Report by telephone from 99th Inf.Bde.that left Coy. Right Battn. reached 1st objective 7-26 a.m. Left Battalion reached PRINCES ST line 7-23 a.m.	
10-15 am.	99th Bde. report that 1/K.R.R.C. had reached their final objective, 23/R. Fus. not quite up on their left.	
10-40 am.	99th Bde. telephone that 70 prisoners had arrived at Bde. H.Q.	
10-50 am.	5th Divn. on our left telephoned their right battalion had reached its final objective. Left held up at X roads Duke St.	
12 noon.	3 officers and 70 prisoners arrive at Bde. H.Q.	
12-25 pm.	22nd Royal Fusiliers report that enemy are counter attacking, that K.R.R. are hard pressed and that losses are severe.	
	One Bn. from 6th Brigade put at the disposal of 99th Brigade.	
12-50 pm.	Message from 60th carrier pigeon- Short of ammunition and bombs, reinforcements urgently needed.	
1-15 pm.	Another Bn. and 1 Sec. M.G. Company from 6th Bde. put at disposal of 99th Bde. A third Bn. to take the place of Bn. first moved up near MONTAUBAN.	
1-25 pm.	Pigeon message through Corps that 23rd Royal Fusiliers had reached their final objective.	
3-15 pm.	Enemy reported to be still attacking heavily especially South of PRINCES STREET.	
3-50 pm.	Situation report. We hold our objectives. Heavy counter attacks are being made in vicinity of PRINCES STREET. Three German officers and 160 other ranks have been passed through to Corps Cage.	
7-35 pm.	Report received from General KELLETT commanding 99th Inf. Bde.........	App. 58
8-10 pm.	106th Bde. 35th Division placed at the disposal of G.O.C.,2nd Divn.	
11-45 pm.	Short report on todays operations sent to XIII Corps..................	App. 59

(73989) W4141—463. 400,000. 9/14. H.&J.Ltd. Forms/C. 2118/10.

Instructions regarding War Diaries and Intelligence Summaries are contained in F.S. Regs., Part II. and the Staff Manual respectively. Title pages will be prepared in manuscript.

WAR DIARY

2nd Division. or General Staff.

INTELLIGENCE SUMMARY.

(Erase heading not required.)

Army Form C. 2118.

Hour, Date, Place	Summary of Events and Information	Remarks and references to Appendices
COPSE "B". A.21.a.4.5. 28th July, 1916.	Fine.	
6.45 a.m.	5th Bde. report that there was heavy shelling until 3.30 am . Casualties of 2nd H.L.I. and 17th R.Fus. believed severe.	
7.15 a.m.	Report from 99th Bde.sent off at 6.55 am on position in DELVILLE WOOD. S.Staffs and 17th Middlesex practically relieved. One Bn. of 99th Bde. in support. Shelling is continuous.	
8.35 a.m.	G.O.C. 4th Army congratulates 2nd Divn. on capture of DELVILLE WOOD...	App. 60
7.40 a.m.	17th Middlesex report Germans massing at East End of Wood. Div.Art. ordered to barrage eastern face of wood.	
9.45 a.m.	6th Bde. report that Germans entered DELVILLE WOOD and had manned strong points in E end of PRINCES STREET.	
10.15 a.m.	Report from O.C. S. Staffs received through 6th Inf. Bde. stating his Bn. was being incessantly shelled in DELVILLE WOOD from South East.	
10.25 a.m.	XIII Corps asked to do counter battery work on S.E. of DELVILLE WOOD.	
10.40 a.m.	XIII Corps state that French artillery are doing counter battery work S.E. of DELVILLE WOOD.	
12 noon	G.O.C. 6th Bde.assumes command of left Bde. Section.	
1. p.m.	Gen. Kellett Commanding 99th Inf. Bde.reports that there are no Germans alive in DELVILLE WOOD.	
2.15 p.m.	Message from 17th Middlesex timed 12.20 pm stating that no frontal attack by enemy had taken place, terrific bombardment on DELVILLE WOOD.	
4.6 p.m.	G.O.C. XIII Corps congratulates 2nd Division.	
5.15 p.m.	5th Divn. report that prisoner states that counter attack is to take place on DELVILLE WOOD tonight.	
6.10 p.m.	R.F.C. report that at 2.30 pm that trench between T.19.a.3.0. to S.18.d.2.8. was clear of Germans.	
6.10 p.m.	S. Staffs reported all well in DELVILLE WOOD.	
6.35 p.m.	G.O.C. sends report on operations in continuation of last nights to XIII Corps.	

(73989) W4141—463. 400,000. 9/14. H.&J.Ltd. Forms/C. 2118/10.

Army Form C. 2118.

Instructions regarding War Diaries and Intelligence Summaries are contained in F. S. Regs., Part II. and the Staff Manual respectively. Title pages will be prepared in manuscript.

WAR DIARY
or
2nd Division General Staff. INTELLIGENCE SUMMARY.

(*Erase heading not required.*)

Hour, Date, Place		Summary of Events and Information	Remarks and references to Appendices
COPSE "B". 28/7/16 continued.			
	7. p.m.	Commander in Chief expresses his gratitude to the Div. through Corps Commander.	
	9.50 p.m.	Message sent to 6th Bde. to send out patrols tonight as Corps Commander considers that enemy outside DELVILLE WOOD are willing to surrender in small numbers.	
	10.10 p.m.	XIII Corps O.O./34 received..	App. 61
	10. p.m.	Telephone wires at D.H.Q. cut by shells.	
	10.15 p.m.	S.O.S. signal sent up in front of 6th Bde.	
	10.45 p.m.	6th Bde. report that rifle andshell fire died down considerably.	"
COPSE "B". 29th July, 1916. A.21.a.4.5.		Fine andhot.	
	12.15 a.m.	Report from 5th Bde.timed 10.45 pm stating that enemy were attacking positions in DELVILLE WOOD and LONGUEVAL.	
	4.45 a.m.	6th Bde. report that enemy attacked about 10. pm and were driven back. At 2.30 am enemy were again bombarding heavily.	
	6.10 a.m.	Information received from O.C. 6th Bde.M.G. Coy. that enemy shelling had caused many casualties especially in the S. Staffs.	
	8.40 a.m.	XIII Corps Artillery O.O./7 received......................................	App. [illegible]
	9.5 a.m.	6th Bde. report that shelling inDELVILLE WOOD is considerably less intense.	
	9.15 a.m.	Message (timed 8.55 pm) by pigeon from S.Staffs stating all quiet .	
	11.45 a.m.	Gen. Daly report that DELVILLE WOOD is being held by Lewis Guns, Machine guns and snipers only: also that concentrated hostile artillery fire is reducing the Bde. to insignificant numbers .	
	12 noon	2nd Divn. O.O./118 issued..	App. 63
	1. p.m.	Advanced H.Q. closed at COPSE "B" and open at the CITADEL F.21.b.	
	5.55 p.m.	Situation report. Intermittent shelling by enemy artillery in both sub-sections with occasional short bombardments.	
	c11. 30 p.m.	XIII Corps Heavy Artillery Operation order No.13 received.............	App. 64
		Casualty return for week ending 29.8.16. received —	app 70.

(73989) W4141—463. 400,000. 9/14. H.&J.Ltd. Forms/C. 2118/10.

Instructions regarding War Diaries and Intelligence Summaries are contained in F.S. Regs., Part II. and the Staff Manual respectively. Title pages will be prepared in manuscript.

WAR DIARY

General Staff or 2nd Division.

~~INTELLIGENCE SUMMARY~~.

(Erase heading not required.)

Army Form C. 2118.

Hour, Date, Place	Summary of Events and Information	Remarks and references to Appendices
THE CITADEL(F.21.b.).	Fine and hot.	
30-7-16. 6-10 a.m.	F.O.O. 41st Bde. R.F.A. reports that there is very little rifle or machine gun fire and that German prisoners are being passed to our second line.	
8-28 a.m.	5th Inf.Bde. telephoned that 24/R. Fus. had reached their objective.	
9-30 a.m.	Wounded officer states we are in possession of GUILLEMONT Station.	
10-35 a.m.	5th Inf.Bde. telephoned that attack on GUILLEMONT Station had failed. Col. WALSH, Commdg. 24/R.Fus. was wounded. Report of Oxf. & Bucks L.I. attack..	Appx.. 65
11-30 a.m.	Situation report..	Appx.. 66
12 noon.	XIII Corps telephone that 30th Divn. were out of GUILLEMONT and therefore our second attack was not to take place.	
12-40 p.m.	Engineer officer reports that 24/R. Fus. were in trench they took this morning.	
1-50 p.m.	Situation report from 5th Inf. Bde..................................	Appx.. 67
3-35 p.m.	Pigeon message from 13/Essex to 6th Bde. Casualties in wood very slight. Battn.H.Q. buried by a 9.2" shell, no one killed. Few Germans seen in wood wearing British helmets. O.C. 1/King's R. sends out party to round them up.	
3-45 p.m.	F.O.O. reports that enemy coming through LEUSE Wood in large numbers and that they are holding trenches in front of GUILLEMONT thickly.	
3-57 p.m.	99th Inf.Bde. warned to keep R. Berks at half hour's notice and remainder at a hour's notice.	
5-0 p.m.	F.O.O. reports that 200 men of R.Scots Fus were surrounded by enemy in front of GUILLEMONT.	
6-15 p.m.	6th Bde. report that patrol sent out this morning report no enemy in S.E. of DELVILLE WOOD.	
6-45 p.m.	XIII Corps O.O. No. G121	Appx.. 68
9-0 p.m.	S.O.S. from LONGUEVAL reported.	
9-50 p.m.	F.O.O. reports heavy shelling WATERLOT FARM and TRONES WOOD. Enemy attacking 9 p.m.	
11-40 p.m.	Orders from XIII Corps for 2nd Divn. to move to MINDEN POST to-morrow.	

Instructions regarding War Diaries and Intelligence Summaries are contained in F. S. Regs., Part II. and the Staff Manual respectively. Title pages will be prepared in manuscript.

WAR DIARY
or
INTELLIGENCE SUMMARY.
(Erase heading not required.)

Army Form C. 2118.

Hour, Date. Place	Summary of Events and Information	Remarks and references to Appendices
THE CITADEL. (F.21.b.)		
31-7-16.	Fine and hot.	
12-4 a.m.	Message from 5th Bde. stating that 24/R. Fus. are not holding trench at S.18.d.	
12-33 am.	6th Bde. report that S.O.S. had been sent from DELVILLE WOOD and heavy rifle and machine gun fire could be heard.	
12-45 am.	6th Bde. state that rifle and machine gun fire was less. Hostile artillery active. Our artillery just commencing barrage.	
1-0 a.m.	5th Bde. report all quiet in DELVILLE WOOD.	
7-30 am.	Reported to XIII Corps that we do not hold trench S.18.d.	
5-45 pm	Situation report. Quiet day on the whole. There was some slight shelling of DELVILLE WOOD and LONGUEVAL ALLEY all day. The vicinity of 5th Bde. H.Q. shelled with 5.9".	
7-30 p.m.	2nd Divn. O.O. No. 119 issued......................	Appx. 68

(73989) W4141—463. 400,000. 9/14. H.&J.Ltd. Forms/C. 2118/10.

2nd DIVISION
GENERAL STAFF
No. ________
Date ________

(original)

War Diary
appendices

~~1st to 20-7-16~~

JULY 1-31st 1916

App. 1

IVth Corps No. H.R.S. 669/J.
2nd Div. No. G.S.992/16/14.

2nd Division.

With reference to IVth Corps letter No. H.R.S. 669 of 21st June, 1916

1. The following operations will be carried out tomorrow July 2nd:-

(a) At 11 a.m. the 2nd Division will carry out a bombardment of the enemy's trenches between LOVE ~~and~~ (S.15.a.) and IRISH (S.8.d.) craters. The bombardment will last about 20 minutes.

(b) The Army and IVth Corps Artillery will bombard the enemy's billets at N.19 CITE DE MOULIN at 10.15 p.m. July 2nd and 5.0 a.m. July 3rd, and M.33 CITE DE CAUMONT at 10 p.m. and 10.45 p.m. on July 2nd.

(c) The IVth Corps 6" Howitzers will bombard the enemy's machine gun emplacements opposite the 47th Division front under arrangements to be made between B.G., C.H.A., IVth Corps and G.O.C. 47th Division.

2. At about 4.0 a.m. on July 3rd the IVth Corps Heavy Artillery and 2nd Divisional Artillery will bombard the enemy's roads and communication trenches near GIVENCHY under arrangements to be made between B.G., C.H.A., IVth Corps and G.O.C. 2nd Division.

3. Copies of all orders and instructions with reference to these operations will be forwarded to Corps Headquarters.

4. Please acknowledge by wire.

(Sd) W.A.T.Bowly, Major G.S.
for Brig. General,
General Staff, IVth Corps.

1st July, 1916.

"A" Form.

Army Form C. 2121.

MESSAGES AND SIGNALS.

No. of Message..........

Prefix........ Code..........m. Office of Origin and Service Instructions.	Words	Charge	This message is on a/c of: ....Service. (Signature of "Franking Officer.")	Recd. at..........m Date.......... From.......... By..........
	Sent At..........m. To.......... By..........			

TO 5 & 6 Bdes RA 2nd Div 47th Div IV Corps HA

* Sender's Number	Day of Month	In reply to Number	AAA

Ref 2nd Div Order No 108

para 3a treat 3 for

From			
Place			
Time			

The above may be forwarded as now corrected. (Z) Censor. Signature of Addressor or person authorised to telegraph in his name.

* This line should be erased if not required.

(A1) G. Ltd., London — W.14342/M.41. 150,000 Pads. 12/15. Forms C.2121.

Refer and

1 afe").

.9.b.,

ed to , from inication

German d

will 5th to be d to

Lieut. Colonel,

General Staff, 2nd Division.

Issued at 4 pm

Copy No. 1 to 5th Inf. Bde.
2 6th Inf. Bde.
3 99th Inf. Bde.
4 C.R.A., 2nd Divn.
5 C.R.E., 2nd Divn.
6 A.D.M.S., 2nd Divn.
7 "Q", 2nd Divn.
8 & 9 IVth Corps.) For information.
10 47th Divn.)
11 51st Divn.)
12 IVth Corps Hy.Arty.)
13 - 17 G.S. Records.

Army Form C. 2121.

No. of Message ....

Recd. at ....m.
Date ....
From ....
By ....

..........Service.

..........m.
To ....
By ....

(Signature of "Franking Officer.")

2

3..

TO	FUR	47 DIVN
	FOWL	4 Corps HA
	RA 347	4 Corps

Sender's Number.	Day of Month.	In reply to Number.	AAA
* G 249	27		

Reference GNU order No 108 para 3a time 3 pm

From GNU
Place
Time 11 am

The above may be forwarded as now corrected. (Z)

Censor. Signature of Addressor or person authorised to telegraph in his name.

* This line should be erased if not required.

225,000. W 14642—M 44. H. W & V., Ld. 12/15.

Refer and ... 16.

... will ... trafe").

... S.9.b., ...

...red to ...ne, from ...munication

...e German ...ed

... will ... 5th ... to be ...ed to

Lieut. Colonel,

General Staff, 2nd Division.

Issued at 4 pm

Copy No. 1 to 5th Inf. Bde.
2 6th Inf. Bde.
3 99th Inf. Bde.
4 C.R.A., 2nd Divn.
5 C.R.E., 2nd Divn.
6 A.D.M.S., 2nd Divn.
7 "Q", 2nd Divn.
8 & 9 IVth Corps.) For information.
10 47th Divn.)
11 51st Divn.)
12 IVth Corps Hy.Arty.)
13 - 17 G.S. Records.

SECRET.

Appendix 2

Copy No. 13

2nd DIVISION ORDER No. 108.

Reference Map, 36.B.,1/40,000, and Secret Trench Map, 36.C.S.W.3.

1st July, 1916.

(1). On the 3rd July, the following operations will take place -

(2). Divisional Artillery and Trench Mortars will shoot at 11 a.m. on the PIMPLE ("One round strafe").

(3). (a). French Artillery will shoot at targets in squares S.7.a., S.3.a. and between S.9.a. and S.9.b., beginning at an hour to be communicated later.

S7a

Front line trenches and saps must be cleared to a depth of 250 yards from the German front line, from FOOTBALL Crater on the South to PELLETIER communication trench on the North (both inclusive).

(b). 2nd Divisional Artillery will shrapnel the German trenches after the French Artillery have ceased firing.

(c). At the conclusion of (b), 36th Bde. R.F.A. will telephone the code word " REGINALD " to G.O.C. 5th Inf. Brigade who will then order the trenches to be re-occupied immediately: this will be repeated to Div. H.Q.

[signature] Lieut. Colonel,
General Staff, 2nd Division.

Issued at 4 pm

Copy No.		
1	to 5th Inf. Bde.	
2	6th Inf. Bde.	
3	99th Inf. Bde.	
4	C.R.A., 2nd Divn.	
5	C.R.E., 2nd Divn.	
6	A.D.M.S., 2nd Divn.	
7	"Q", 2nd Divn.	
8 & 9	IVth Corps.	)
10	47th Divn.	) For information.
11	51st Divn.	)
12	IVth Corps Hy.Arty.	)
13 - 17	G.S. Records.	

Appx 3

S E C R E T.
****

Copy No.......

2nd DIVISION ORDER No. 109.
****

Reference Map, 36.B., 1/40,000,
and Secret Trench Map, 36.C.S.W.3.

2nd July, 1918.

(1). 99th Inf. Brigade will relieve 6th Inf. Brigade in BERTHONVAL Section on night 5th/6th July under arrangements made by Brigade Commanders concerned.

(2). On relief, 6th Inf. Brigade will take over billets in the Reserve Brigade area vacated by 99th Inf. Brigade.

(3). Machine gun positions, BAJOLLE, BAJOLLE SWITCH and MAISTRE Lines now occupied by 99th Inf. Bde. will be taken over by 6th Inf. Bde.

(4). While in Divl. Reserve, the Sapping Platoons and Dug-out Platoons 6th Inf. Brigade will be at the disposal of the C.R.E. for work on the rear lines, each Battalion furnishing its Sapping Platoons and Dug-out Platoons in turn for 48 hours.

Geddes.
Lieut. Colonel,
General Staff, 2nd Division.

Issued at 9/.A.M.

Copy No. 1 to 5th Inf.Bde.
2 6th Inf. Bde.
3 99th Inf.Bde.
4 10/D.C.L.I.(Pioneers).
5 R.A., 2nd Divn.
6 R.E., 2nd Divn.
7 2/Signal Co.
8 A.D.M.S., 2nd Divn.
9 A.D.V.S., ,,
10 "Q", 2nd Divn.
11 2nd Div. Train.
12 & 13 IVth Corps.
14 47th Divn.
15 51st Divn.
16 176th Tunnelling Co.R.E.
17 182nd ,, ,,
18 Pioneer Bn., 47th Divn.
19 O.C. Det., R.N. Divn.
20 - 24 G.S. & Records.

"A" Form. Army Form C. 2121.

MESSAGES AND SIGNALS. No. of Message..........

Prefix........ Code............m. | Words | Charge | This message is on a/c of: | Recd. at ....m

Office of Origin and Service Instructions. | Sent | At ....m. | To | By | ....Service. (Signature of "Franking Officer.") | Date | From | By

TO 4 Corps

Sender's Number	Day of Month	In reply to Number	AAA
G 252	2		

Following particulars of raid received by telephone aaa Covering fire of Stokes mortars was effective and party reached enemys trenches without much difficulty aaa Germans inclined to run aaa more than forty germans were killed and in addition dugouts were bombed aaa Our casualties 5 men killed 2 missing 2 Officers 3 men wounded aaa O.C. raiding party was hit in shoulder by shrapnel at commencement but continued in command until the end aaa Prisoner belongs to 162 Regt

From 2nd Div

Place

Time .0 am

The above may be forwarded as now corrected. (Z)

Censor. Signature of Addressor or person authorised to telegraph in his name.

J. B. Belgrave
Major
Gen Staff

* This line should be erased if not required.

(A1) O. Ltd., London — W.14542/M.41. 150,000 Pads. 12/15. Form C.2121.

Appendix 2.

IVth Corps No. H.R.S.669/K.
2nd Div. No. G.S. 992/16/15.

2nd Division.

With reference to IVth Corps letter No. H.R.S. 669 of 21st June, 1916.

1. The following operations will be carried out tomorrow July 3rd, 1916:-

(a) 'One round' bombardment by the Divisional Artillery and Trench Mortars of the 2nd and 47th Divisions at targets and times to be selected by G.Os.C. 2nd and 47th Divisions.

(b) The IVth Corps Heavy Artillery will bombard the PIMPLE and observation posts N and N.E. of it, at a time to be selected by the B.G., C.H.A., IVth Corps, in conjunction with G.O.C. 47th Division.

(c) At 10.15 p.m. and 11 p.m. on July 3rd and at 5.30 am on July 4th the Army and IVth Corps Artillery will bombard the enemy's bille s in LIEVIN.

(d) The French 120 mm 'Courts' will bombard the enemy's trenches in S.3 and S.9 at an hour to be arranged by B.G., C.H.A., IVth Corps in conjunction with G.Os.C. 2nd and 47th Divisions. The artillery of the 2nd and 47th Divisions will shrapnel these trenches when the French guns have ceased firing.

2. During the night July 3rd/4th :-

(a) The IVth Corps Heavy Artillery will bombard the following roads:-

i. N.19.b.5.8 to M.18.d.0.8 to M.23 Central to M.17.b.83
ii. N.20.a.1.9 to crossroads M.22.d.5.0 and north to M.22.b.2.2.
iii. N.20.a.1½.0. to N.31 central, to M.35.b.0.4.
iv. N.25.d.4.5 to M.36.b.6.5.

(b) The 47th Division will carry out a raid at a time and place to be selected by the G.O.C. 47th Division.

3. Copies of all orders and instructions with reference to these operations will be forwarded to Corps Headquarters.

4. Please acknowledge by wire.

(Sd) W.A.T.Bowly, Major GS
for Brig. General,
General Staff, IVth Corps.

2nd July, 1916.

'G' Diary

F I G H T I N G   S T R E N G T H

2nd DIVISION — WEEK ENDING 1st July, 1916.

	"A" Fighting Strength in accordance with 1st Army No.902.A of 3 - 4 - 1916.		"B" Included in Col.A but not actually with unit.		"C" Drafts received since last Return.		Explanation of any discrepancy exceeding one officer and 30 other ranks, other than "C", between Fighting Strength shewn on this Return, and that shewn on last.
	OFFICERS	O.RANKS	OFFICERS	O.RANKS	OFFICERS	O.RANKS	
Headquarters 2nd Div.	19	206	-	-	-	-	
R.Artillery 2/Divn.	90	2887	3	76	-	90	
Y/2 T. M. Battery.	2	23	-	5	-	-	
X/2 T. M. Battery.	2	27	-	-	-	-	
Z/2 T. M. Battery.	2	27	-	-	-	-	
V/2 T. M. Battery.	2	36	-	2	-	-	
R. Engineers.	26	798	1	21	2	9	
H. Q. 5th Inf.Bde.	4	69	-	-	-	-	*(2/Lt. Roberts to General List.
2nd Ox. & Bucks.	42	1033	9	159	-	64	(2/Lt. Johnstone to Engl.(sick)
2nd Highl. Lt. Inf.	42	943	4	182	5	10	(2/Lt. Cannell to Engl. (sick)
17th Roy. Fusiliers.	38*	1041	8	189	1	48	
24th Roy. Fusiliers.	32ø	1030	11	151	-	6	ø(Major Cradock to Engl.(sick)
5th Bde. M. G. Coy.	10	148	-	-	-	-	(Lieut. Nelson to Engl.(sick)
5th Bde. L. M. Batty.(a)	5	68	-	-	-	-	
TOTAL 5th INF.BDE.	168	4329	32	701	6	128	
H. Q. 6th Inf.Bde.	7	124	-	-	-	-	*(2/Lt.R.T.Wilks to Engl.(sick)
1st King's (L'pool)	28	1005	4	210	-	45	(2/Lt.L.Skempton to Engl.(sick)
2nd South Staffs.	34*	1036	8	160	2	64	
13th Essex.	38ø	1015	12	184	1	80	ø(2/Lt.F.A.Webb transf.to 12th Bttn.
17th Middlesex.	38	929	6	202	1	9	(2/Lt.E.C.Johnson,reported as arrived (last week in error.
6th Bde. M. G. Coy.	9	180	1	4	-	2	
6th Bde. L. M. Batty. (a)	4	60	-	-	-	-	
TOTAL 6th INF.BDE.	154	4289	31	760	4	200	
H. Q. 99th Inf.Bde.	5	60	-	-	-	-	*(2 officers wounded.
1st K. R. R. C.	23*	1050	8	202	1	120	(2 officers admitted to hospital and evacuated
1st Roy. Berks.	32ø	750≠	10	172	-	30	(1 officer evacuated out of Div.Area.
22nd Roy. Fusiliers.	43	1083	18	214	1	20	(1 officer transferred to England.
23rd Roy. Fusiliers.	34	1072	8	236	2	65	ø (Lt. Thorne missing.
99th Bde. M. G. Coy.	11	145	2	11	1	1	(2/Lt. Jackson wounded.
99th Bde. L. M. Batty.(a)	3	96	-	-	-	-	≠ 70 other ranks casualties.
TOTAL 99th INF.BDE.	148	4230	41	814	5	236	
10th D.C.L.I.(Pioneers)	26	963	2	14	-	-	
2nd Div. Train.	23	408	3	3	-	-	
R. A. M. C.	31	713	3	10	-	2	
No.3 Mob.Vet.Section.	1	26	-	-	-	-	
TOTAL 2ND DIVISION.	698	18990	116	2408	17	625	

(a) Included in strength of Battalions.

Attached						
1/Sussex (A.T.)Coy.R.E.	4	154	-	-	-	-

(Sd) D. R. Dickinson Capt.
for Major General
Commanding 2nd Division.

1 - 7 - 16.

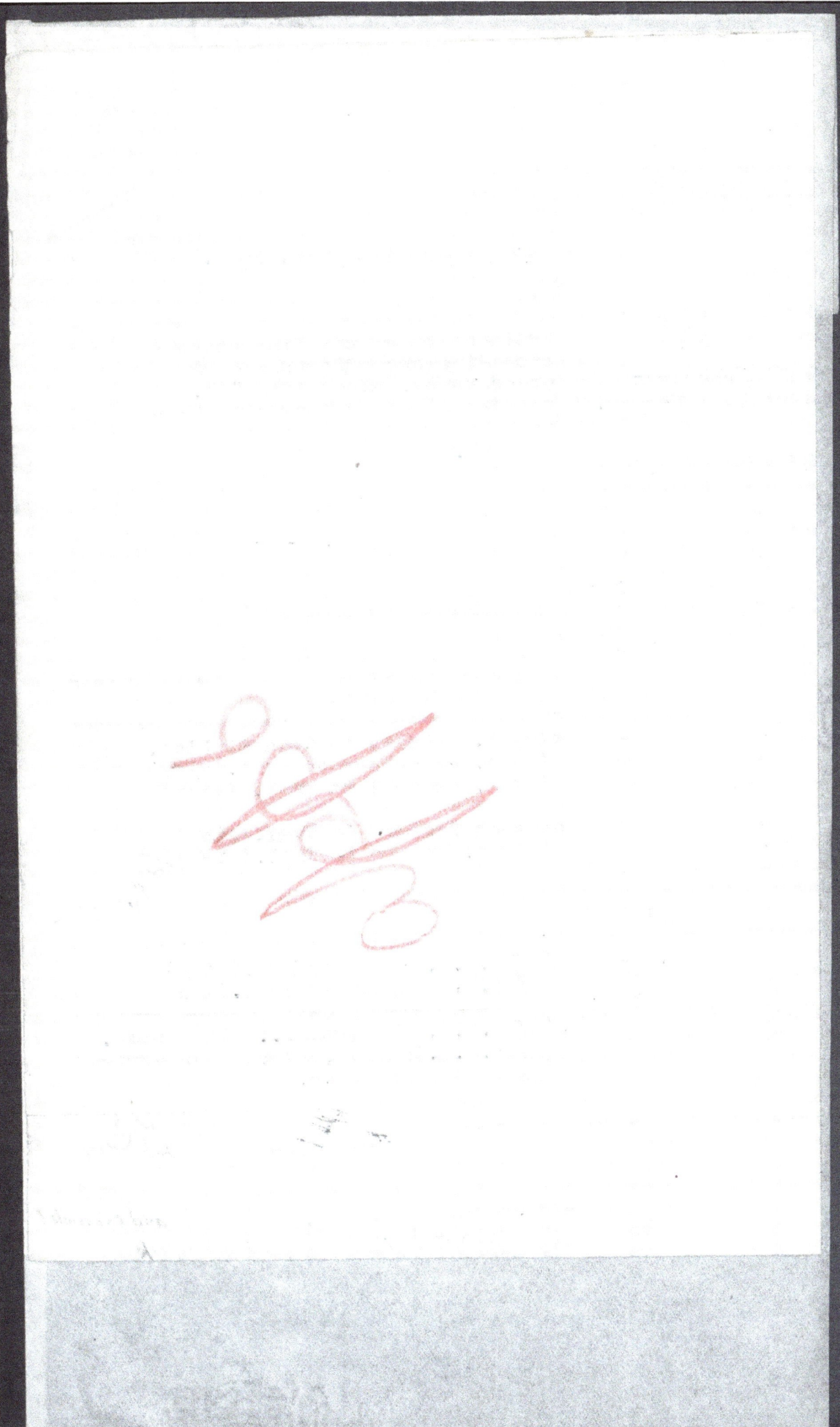

G Branch

appx 7

2nd DIVISION - CASUALTY RETURN FOR ~~WEEK~~ ENDING 1st July, 1916.

UNIT.	KILLED.		WOUNDED.		MISSING.		Names of Officers, and remarks,
	O.	O.R.	O.	O.R.	O.	O.R.	
H.Q., 2nd Divn.							
H.Q., 5th Infy.Bde.							
2/Oxf & Bucks L.I.			1 *	12			*2/Lt. B.C.C.WARDE, 3rd Batt. att.2nd.
2/High. L.I.		5	1 x	16			xLt. H.D.C.CRAIG. 4th Bn.attd. 2nd.
17/Royal Fusiliers.		1	2 %	16			%Lt.A.C.SOMERSET. 2/Lt.L.C.SAYER.
24/Royal Fusiliers,				2			
5th Bde M.G.Coy.							
H.Q., 6th Inf.Bde.							
1/King's Regt.		4		8			
2/S. Staff. R.		2		3			
13/Essex Regt.		3		9			
17/Middlesex Regt.				7			
6th Bde. M.G.Coy.							
H.Q., 99th Inf.Bde.							
1/R. Berks. Regt.		14	1 ø	33	1 #	1	ø2/Lt.E.P.JACKSON, #Lt. H.C.THORNE,
1/K.R.R.C.		1	1 +	9			+2/Lt. W.DUNKELS, 6th Batt. attched 1st.
22/Royal Fusiliers.		2	1 ⊕	6			⊕Lt. T.H.EVANS.
23/Royal Fusiliers.							
99th Bde. M.G.Coy.			1 @				@Capt. C.GRANT, at duty.
No.1 Batty. M.M.G.S.							
H.Q., R.A., 2/Divn.							
34th Bde. R.F.A.							
36th Bde. R.F.A.							
41st Bde. R.F.A.				1			
44th Bde. R.F.A.							
H.Q., R.E., 2/Divn.							
5thField Coy. R.E.							
226th Fd. Coy. R.E.							
1/E.A.Fd. Coy. R.E.							
2/Signal Co. R.E.							
~~173rd T. Coy. R.E.~~		1					
~~252nd T. Coy. R.E.~~				5			
South Irish Horse.							
2/Divl.Cyclist Coy.							
TOTAL.	-	33	8	127	1	1	

H.Q., 2nd Divn.
2/7/1916.

Captain,
for D.A.A. & Q.M.G., 2nd Division.

"A" Form.

MESSAGES AND SIGNALS.

Army Form C. 2121.

No. of Message

Prefix ... Code ... m. | Words | Charge

Office of Origin and Service Instructions.

Sent
At ... m.
To
By

This message is on a/c of:
APPENDIX 8. Service.

(Signature of "Franking Officer.")

Recd. at ... m.
Date
From
By

TO BACHE BEAKE BIBAC C.R.A.
C.R.E. "Q".

Sender's Number.	Day of Month	In reply to Number	
* G.350	7		AAA

Following from Advanced First Army begins AAA The Commander-in-Chief wishes the following wire from His Majesty the King circulated to all ranks begins AAA Please convey to the Army under your command my sincere congratulations on the results achieved in the recent fighting AAA I am proud of my troops none could have fought more bravely AAA GEORGE R.I. ends

From BACCA
Place
Time 9-10am.

(sd) L.Hassell, Capt.
G.S.

The above may be forwarded as now corrected. (Z)

Censor.

Signature of Addressor or person authorised to telegraph in his name.

* This line should be erased if not required.

(1138) Wt. W14042—M44. 300000 Pads. 12/15. Sir J. C. & S.

"A" Form.

MESSAGES AND SIGNALS.

Army Form C. 2121.

No. of Message

Prefix Code m. Words Charge

Office of Origin and Service Instructions.

SECRET

D R

This message is on a/c of: Service.

(Signature of "Franking Officer.")

Recd. at m.

Date

From

By

TO			
5 Bde	RA	9 2 Dvn	47th DIVN
6 Bde	RE	4 Corps	4 Corps HA
99 Bde	ADMS	51 DIVN	

Sender's Number	Day of Month	In reply to Number	AAA
* G 296	3rd		

Ref. 2nd DIVN order No 110 para (1) line 3 for "6/7" read "7/8"

From 2 DIVN

Place

Time 10.45 pm

The above may be forwarded as now corrected.

(Z)

Censor.

Signature of Addressor or person authorised to telegraph in his name. Major General Staff

* This line should be erased if not required.

(4198) Wt. W14042—M44. 300000 Pads. 12/15. Sir J. C. & S.

C R

Reference and Secret

(1). the

(2). r)

(3). :

oming

(4). t.

(5).

other information is to be given.

(6). Acknowledge.

Lieut. Colonel,
General Staff, 2nd Division.

Issued at 7 pm.

Copy No.		Copy No.		
1	to 5th Inf. Bde.	8) 9)	to IVth Corps.	
2	6th Inf. Bde.	10	47th Divn.	For information.
3	99th Inf. Bde.	11	51st Divn.	
4	C.R.A., 2nd Divn.	12	IVth Corps Hy.Arty.	
5	C.R.E., 2nd Divn.	13 - 17	G.S. Records.	
6	A.D.M.S., 2nd Divn.			
7	"Q", 2nd Divn.			

Copy No. 15...

2nd DIVISION ORDER No. 110.

****

Reference Map, 1/40,000,
and Secret Trench Map, 36.B.S.W.3.

3rd July, 1916.

(1). The 5th Inf. Brigade will carry out a raid on the enemy's trenches East of PELLETIER ALLEY on the night 6th/7th July.

Details will be worked out by the G.O.C., 5th Inf. Brigade.

(2). At ZERO hour (which will be communicated later) the Divisional Artillery will barrage the following points :-

S.3.c.8.2. to S.3.c.1.4.) to a depth of
and)
S.9.a.1.6. to S.9.a.½.4.) 100 yds.
also
S.3.c.5½.3. to S.9.a.5.4.

Total - five 18 pdr. Batteries and two 4.5" Howitzer Batteries.

Exact targets will be pointed out to Group Commanders on the ground.

(3). On the return of the raiding party, G.O.C., 5th Inf. Brigade will telephone the code word " CHARLIE" to O.C. 36th Bde. R.F.A. when the barrage will be stopped. It is important that this information should be forthcoming as early as possible.

(4). All identification marks will be removed from officers and men of the raiding party before they start.

(5). All ranks taking part in the raid are to be warned that in the event of capture they are not bound to disclose anything beyond their rank and name. No other information is to be given.

(6). Acknowledge.

[signature]

Lieut. Colonel,

General Staff, 2nd Division.

Issued at 7 p.m.

Copy No. 1 to 5th Inf. Bde.
2 6th Inf. Bde.
3 99th Inf. Bde.
4 C.R.A., 2nd Divn.
5 C.R.E., 2nd Divn.
6 A.D.M.S., 2nd Divn.
7 "Q", 2nd Divn.

Copy No. 8) to IVth Corps.
9)
10 47th Divn.) For
11 51st Divn.) infor-
12 IVth Corps Hy.Arty.) mation.
13 - 17 G.S. Records.

S E C R E T.
****

Appx 10

Copy No. 16

2nd DIVISION ORDER No. 111.

Reference Map, 36.B., 1/40,000, and Secret Trench Map, 36.C.S.W.3.

3rd July, 1916.

Appx 10

(1). The 6th Inf. Brigade will carry out a raid on the enemy's trenches about S.15.c.4½.2. on the night 3rd/4th July.

Details will be worked out by the G.O.C., 6th Inf. Brigade.

A party detailed by the O.C., 182nd Tunnelling Co.R.E. will accompany the Infantry under arrangements to be made between the O.C., and the G.O.C., 6th Inf. Brigade.

(2). The objects of the raid are :-

(a). To ascertain whether the enemy has any mine shafts in the vicinity of this point.
(b). To inflict as much loss as possible on the enemy.
(c). To obtain identifications.

(3). At ZERO hour (which will be notified later) the R.A., Stokes mortars and machine guns will open fire simultaneously.

The R.A. will barrage the following points -

Five 18 pdr. Batteries and one 4.5" Howr. Battery, on crest line from about S.15.a.4.1. to about S.21.b.7.6.

Three 18 pdr. Batteries and 1½ Howr. Batteries on area between German front line S.21.b.3½.5. to S.21.d.5.9. and crest line S.21.b.7.6. to S.21.d.9.9.

One Section 4.5" Howr. on German front line S.15.c.9.1. to S.21.b.0.9.

2" Trench Mortars on front line from ANGEL AVENUE Northwards.

This barrage will be maintained until the raiding party has returned, when the code word " GOFF" will be sent by 6th Inf. Brigade H.Q. to O.C., 41st Bde. R.F.A. The barrage will then stop.

(4). If further artillery support is required, the code word " HUGO" will be telephoned by 6th Inf. Brigade H.Q. to O.C., 41st Bde. R.F.A., when the barrage will be continued. The code word will be repeated to Div.H.Q.

To stop the barrage again, the code word " GOFF" will be repeated.

(5). All identification marks and papers are to be removed from personnel of the raiding party.

(6). Every officer and man is to be cautioned that, if taken prisoner, he is not to disclose anything except his rank and name.

(7). Acknowledge.

[signature]

Lieut. Colonel,
General Staff, 2nd Division.

Issued at 4 pm.

Copy No. 1 to 5th Inf. Bde.
2 6th Inf. Bde.
3 99th Inf. Bde.
4 C.R.A., 2nd Divn.
5 C.R.E., 2nd Divn.
6 182nd Tng. Co.R.E.
7 A.D.M.S., 2nd Divn.

Copy No.8 to "Q" 2/Div.
9 & 10 IVth Corps.) For
11 51st Divn.)informa-
12 47th Divn.)tion.
13 IVth Corps H.A.)
14 - 18 G.S. Records.

"C" Form (Duplicate).
MESSAGES AND SIGNALS.

Army Form C. 2123.

No. of Message

Prefix: SM KI 39 DCO 475

Service Instructions.

Charges to Pay. £ s. d.

Office Stamp.

Handed in at DCO Office 10.43 m. Received 10.54 a.m.

TO 2nd Divn

Sender's Number	Day of Month	In reply to Number	AAA
G926	4-7-16		

G06 First Army wishes to congratulate all who took part in raids carried out on night of 27th/28th June opposite ANGRES and on night of 1st/2nd July at about S.15.b.4½.2.

FROM PLACE & TIME: 4 Corps 10.45 am

W 15660—M 151 75,000 Pads. H & S 4/16 Forms/C.2123. (5668)

App. 12

IVth Corps No. H.R.S. 669/N
2nd Div. No. G.S. 992/16/21.

2nd Division.

During the nights of July 5th/6th and 6th/7th the IVth Corps Heavy Artillery and the Artillery of the 47th Division will bombard the following roads at times to be selected by the B.G., C.R.A., IVth Corps in conjunction with the G.O.C. 47th Divn

(i) N.19.b.5.8 to M.18.d.0.8 to M.23 central: and M.17.b.6.3 to M.22 central to M.21.d.9.2.

(ii) N.20.a.1.9 to cross roads M.22.d.5.0 and thence North to M.22.b.2.2.

(iii) N.20.a.1½.0 to N.31 central to M.35.b.0.6 to M.33.d.8.3.

(iv) N.25.d.5.7½ to M.36.b.8.5 to M.35.a.6.1.

No fire will be brought to bear on the road N.20.a.0.½ to M.28.d.6.6.

2. The maximum amount of ammunition to be expended will be as under:-

500	rounds of	18-pounder,	per night.
30	"	4.5" howr.	" "
40	"	60 pounder	" "

3. Please acknowledge by wire.

(Sd) W.A.T.Bowly, Major, G.S.
for Brigadier General,
General Staff, IVth Corps.

5th July, 1916.

Diary

App 13

S E C R E T .

2nd DIVISION INSTRUCTIONS No. 138.

5th July, 1916.

Laying and Maintenance of telephone lines.

The following instructions are to be observed in connection with the laying and maintenance of telephone lines in the Divisional Area :-

(A). In back area.

(1). No permanent lines are to be touched without reference to O.C. Signals, Division.

(2). No cables of any description are to be laid along poles of permanent lines, or on poles already supporting any airline or cable.

(3). No cables of any description are to be laid along hedges or on trees on which already a cable exists, without reference to O.C. Signals, Division.

(4). All overhead road crossings must give at least 17 feet clearance.

(B). In the forward area.

(1). Cables in the trenches must be stapled not lower than 8" and not higher than 2'6" from floor of trench. There is sufficient space for any number of lines likely to be laid in one trench on a surface of 1'10" .

(2). When a new cable is laid up a communication trench in which a number of cables already exist, it should be laid on the side of the trench on which there are the fewest cables unless the nature of the side renders this unsatisfactory or unless the cable is much more exposed by so doing.

(3). The greatest care must be taken to avoid crossing other cables already stapled to the wall of the trench. Every cable should as far as is possible be kept the same height from the bottom of the trench throughout its whole length. With care this is possible and it is very noticeable how, in many cases, no effort has hitherto been made to do this, in consequence, cables along the wall of a trench become inextricably mixed up.

(4). Cables must not be stretched too tight round corners and must lie flat along the wall of the trench. They must follow the exact contour of the trench- i.e. be stapled back in all recesses etc. A coil of slack must be pinned to the wall of the trench every 300 yards so that the cable can be loosened if required after it has been laid in the first case.

(5). Where cables cross side trenches- roads etc., they must always be buried and NEVER taken overhead.

(6).........

(6). Cables must be labelled whilst being laid every 100 yards. No regular supply of labels can be assured and consequently units must make efforts to provide their own labels.

(7). Every cable in a trench requires patrolling daily and every inch of cable examining. Men on patrol duty must always take a supply of staples and labels with which to improve their cables.

(8). If for any reason it is decided to lay a cable across country where trenches exist the cable must be laid well away from the trench and not be allowed to cross any trench without being buried under the floorboards.

(C). ECONOMY of CABLE.

(1). There exists at present shortage of every sort of cable. Every unit is responsible for clearing away disused cables in their area and for salving any serviceable cable for relaying.

(2). When brigades are in reserve, if a battalion Hd. Qtrs. is near an existing Signal Office which accepts telegrams from brigade for the battalion a separate direct line must not be laid by the brigade but orderlies sent from the battalion to the existing Signal Office.

(3). When battalions are not in the trenches telephone lines to companies are NOT to be laid except in special cases when permission must be obtained from O.C. Signals, Division.

[signature]

Lieut. Colonel,

General Staff, 2nd Division.

Issued to :-

5th Inf. Bde.
6th Inf. Bde.
99th Inf. Bde.
10th D.C.L.I. (Pioneers).
C.R.A., 2nd Divn.
C.R.E., 2nd Divn.
2/Signal Company.
"Q", 2nd Divn.

S E C R E T.
****

Appendix 14.

IVth Corps No.H.R.S. 669/9

2nd Division.

----

1. During the night July 7th/8th

(a). The 2nd Division will carry out a raid on the enemy's trenches about S.9.a.0.8½. at a time to be selected by G.O.C., 2nd Division.

(b). ~~The IVth Corp~~

2. At 12 noon and 10 p.m. July 7th the IVth Corps Heavy Artillery will co-operate with the 1st Corps Heavy Artillery in the bombardment of the enemy's billets N.21.a.6.7. andc N.15.d.1.1.

3. Please acknowledge by wire.

6th July, 1916.

(sd) W.A.T. Bowly, Major,
for Br.General,
General Staff, IVth Corps.

S E C R E T. Appendix 15.

Copy No.5.

Operation Order for 0 plus 14 day.
by Br. Genl. T.E. Marshall, Commdg. Hy.Arty.
IVth Corps.

Headquarters,
7th July, 1916.

Reference Map, 1/20,000 Sheet 36.c. Edition 7a.

1. During the night of 7th/8th July, 1916, 15th H.A. Group will fire on roads as follows :-

(a) Same roads as during nights 5/6th, and 6/7th .-

Times :- 9.30 p.m.
10. 0 p.m.
12.25 p.m.

Ammunition allowed - 15 rounds of 60-pounder.

(b) Roads - N.19.b.9½.1. to M.29.c.1.4 to M.28.b.8.6 to M.28.c.0.4 to M.27.d.5½.9½., paying particular attention to portion of road lying in N.19.

Times :- 10.30 p.m.
10.50 p.m.
11.55 p.m.
12.35 a.m.
1. 15. a.m.

Ammunition allowed - 45 rounds of 60-pounder.

(Sd) B.E. BANTING. Captain. R.A.
for Brigade-Major,
Heavy Artillery, IV Corps.

Appendix 17.

S E C R E T. IV Corps H.R.S. 669.

2nd Division.

---

1. The present ammunition situation allows of the following allotment of ammunition to your Division which cancels previous orders :-

	18 pdrs.	4.5".
For to-nights operation.	3,000	300
For your second operation including barrage.	20,000	2,000
For your daily allowance till noon on July 14th including billet and road shoots in accordance with programme.	2,800	350
	25,800	2,650

2. Your defensive dump round the guns should be reduced to 300 rounds 18 pdr per gun, and kept at that figure, and your echelons should be kept full.

H.Q., IVth Corps. (sd) H. DE PREE, Br. General,

7th July, 1916. General Staff, IVth Corps.

"A" Form. Army Form C. 2121.

MESSAGES AND SIGNALS. No. of Message..........

Prefix ...... Code ...... m.	Words	Charge	This message is on a/c of:	Recd. at ...... m.
Office of Origin and Service Instructions.	Sent		Service.	Date 8
	At ...... m.			From
	To			
	By		(Signature of "Franking Officer.")	By

TO BACHE. C.R.A.
BEAKE. C.R.E.
BIBAC. "Q"

Sender's Number.	Day of Month.	In reply to Number.	AAA
* 350	7		

Following from Advanced First Army begins AAA The Commander in Chief wishes the following wire from His Majesty the King circulated to all ranks begins AAA Please convey to the Army under your command my sincere congratulations on the results achieved in the recent fighting AAA I am proud of my troops none could have fought more bravely AAA GEORGE R I ends

From BACCA
Place
Time 9.10 a.m.

The above may be forwarded as now corrected. (Z)
Censor.

[signature] Capt.
General Staff.
Signature of Addressor or person authorised to telegraph in his name.

* This line should be erased if not required.

225,000. W 14042—M 44. H. W & V., Ld. 12/15.

SECRET. Appx 19 IV Corps No. H.R.S.629.

2nd Division.

I forward herewith for your information and necessary action a copy of a minute from G.H.Q. dated 4th July, 1916.

H.Q. IVth Corps.
8th July, 1916.

(Sd) W.A.T.Bowly, Major G.S.
for Brig. General,
General Staff, IVth Corps.

- 2 -

2nd Div. No.
G.S. 261/86.

5th Inf. Bde. 2nd Div. Train.
6th Inf. Bde. A.D.M.S. 2nd Divn.
99th Inf. Bde. A.D.V.S. 2nd Divn.
R.A. 2nd Divn. A.P.M. 2nd Divn.
R.E. 2nd Divn. "Q" 2nd Divn.
2nd Signal Coy.
10th D.C.L.I. (Pioneers).

For information and guidance.
The importance of this matter cannot be too strongly impressed on all ranks.

H.Q. 2nd Divn.
9th July, 1916.

(Sd) J.D.Belgrave, Major,
General Staff, 2nd Divn.

Captured documents and the examination of prisoners have shown beyond all possibility of doubt that information regarding our attack was obtained by the Germans through overhearing telephone ~~conversations~~ messages. We have not yet got full details of the German system of overhearing but there is clear evidence that it is both accurate and extends over large areas.

It should be impressed on all ranks and particularly on officers that leakage of information of this nature, not only prior to an attack but also before raids or in connection with reliefs, inevitably means sacrificing lives. The only sound rule with regard to telephones must be never to mention anything on the telephone that you would not mention in the presence of a hostile agent.

Codes must be freely used where confidential information has to be transmitted. Officers should make it their personal duty to examine frequently the messages which are passing down the telephone wires, and severe desciplinary action must be taken in connection with any infringement of the existing regulations.

This applies equally to the Signal Services, Regimental Signals and Artillery Forward Observing Officers.

Adv.G.H.Q.

4th July, 1916.

(sd) R. Butler, M.Genl. for
Lt. Genl.
C.G.S.

Appendix 20.

SECRET. Copy No. 5.

OPERATION ORDER No. 10
by Br. Genl. T.E. Marshall, Commdg.
Hy. Arty. IVth Corps.

Reference Map, 1/20,000, Sheet 36.C. Edition 7a/8th July, 1916

1. From 11-58 p.m. 8-7-16 to 12-30 a.m. 9-7-16, 15th H.A. group will bombard trenches in M.32.d. paying special attention to the following points -
M.32.d.4.4½. - M.32.d.3½.1½. - M.32.d.7½.3½.(Trench Mortar).
Ammunition allowed 40 rounds of 4.5" Howr.

2. From 12-1 a.m. to 12-25 a.m. 9-7-16, 15th H.A. group will bombard trenches in M.26, paying special attention to the following points :-
M.26.c.8.7. - M.26.c.8½.6. - M.26.c.9.3.
Ammunition Allowed 80 rounds of 4.5" Howr.

3. From 1-20 a.m. to 1-55 a.m. 9-7-16, 15th H.A.Group will bombard trenches in M.26, as in (2), but will, in addition, pay attention to following points -
M.26.d.7.1½. - M.26.d.6.3. - M.26.d.6.4. - M.26.d.8.5. - M.26.b.7.4½.
Ammunition allowed - 80 rounds of 4.5" Howr.

4. From 12-1 a.m. to 12-25 a.m. 9-7-16, French Artillery will bombard following points -
M.26.d.7.1¼. - M.26.d.6.3. - M.26.d.6.4. - M.26.d.8.5. - M.26.b.7.4½.
Ammunition allowed 20 rds of 120mm Court.

5. From 11-58 p.m. 8-7-16 to 12-30 a.m. 9-7-16 and again from 1-58 a.m. to 2-35 a.m., 9-7-16, French Artillery and 15th H.A. Group will bombard the "PIMPLE" with a view to prevent observation from that point.
Ammunition allowed 30 rounds of 120mm Court.
,, ,, 25 ,, 60 pdr. shrapnel.

6. Watches will be synchronised between 9-15 p.m. and 9-30 p.m. 8-7-16.

7. Acknowledge.

(sd) E. Blackburn, Capt. R.A.
Bde. Major, IVth Corps.

Appendix 21.

IVth Corps No. H.R.S.669/Q.

S E C R E T.
****

2nd Division.

----

1. During to-night July 9th/10th the IVth Corps Heavy Artillery and the artillery of the 47th Division will bombard the following roads at times to be selected by the B.G., C.H.A., IV Corps in conjunction with G.O.C. 47th Division. -

(a). Same roads as during nights 5th/6th and 6th/7th July.

(b). Road N.19.b.9½.1. to M.29.c.1.4. to M.28.b.8.6. to M.28.c.0.4. to M.27.d.5½.9½.

Road (b) will not be shelled until the bombardment of roads (a) is completed.

2. Total ammunition allotted :-

600 rounds 18 pdr.
40 ,, 60 pdr.
30 ,, 4.5" Howr.

3. Please acknowledge by wire.

9th July, 1916.

(sd) W.A.T. Bowly, Major for Br Genl.
General Staff, IVth Corps.

"A" Form.

Army Form C. 2121.

MESSAGES AND SIGNALS.

No. of Message...........

Prefix........... Code...........m. Office of Origin and Service Instructions.	Words	Charge	This message is on a/c of: ....Service. (Signature of "Franking Officer.")	Recd. at ....m. Date.......... From.......... By..........
PRIORITY 516 B[illegible]	Sent At..........m. To.......... By..........			

TO: BACHE – RA – RE [illegible] – [illegible] PLE
BEAKE – HDRS ARM [illegible] – [illegible]
[illegible] – 47 Div – 51 Div – 17[illegible] – 182 [illegible]

* Sender's Number	Day of Month	*In reply to Number	AAA
G425	11	[illegible]	

R [illegible] BACCA Order 112 [illegible] 1 [illegible] 12/13 [illegible]

J.B. 12.7

From	BACCA
Place	
Time	[illegible]

The above may be forwarded as now corrected.

Censor.

(Z)

Signature of Addressor or person authorised to telegraph in his name.

* This line should be erased if not required.

(A1) O. Ltd., London.– W.14042/M.44. 150,000 Pads. 12/15. Form C.2121.

SECRET.
****

Copy No. 20......

appx 22

2nd DIVISION ORDER No. 112.
****

Reference Map, 36.C., 1/40,000, and Secret Trench Map, 36.C.S.W.3.

9th July, 1916.

(1). The 6th Inf. Brigade will relieve the 5th Infy. Bde. in the CARENCY Section on the night 12th/13th July under arrangements to be made between Brigade Commanders concerned.

(2). On relief, 5th Inf. Brigade will take over billets vacated by 6th Inf. Brigade in the Reserve Brigade area.

(3). Machine gun positions in the BAJOLLE, BAJOLLE SWITCH and MAISTRE Lines now occupied by the 6th Inf. Brigade, will be taken over by the 5th Inf. Brigade.

(4). The Sapping Platoons and Dug-out Platoons 5th Inf. Brigade will rejoin their units.

(5). Completion of relief will be reported to Div.H.Q.

[signature]

Lieut. Colonel,

General Staff, 2nd Division.

Issued at 7 p.m.

Copy No. 1 to 5th Inf. Bde.
2 6th Inf. Bde.
3 99th Inf. Bde.
4 R.A., 2nd Divn.
5 R.E., 2nd Divn.
6 2/Signal Co.
7 10/D.C.L.I.(Pioneers).
8 A.D.M.S., 2nd Divn.
9 A.P.M., 2nd Divn.
10 2/Div. Train.
11 "Q", 2nd Divn.
12 & 13 IVth Corps.
14 47th Divn.)
15 51st Divn.)
16 176th Tunnelling Co.RE.) For information.
17 182nd ,, ,,)
18 O.C., Det. R. Naval Divn.)
19 - 23 G.S. Records.

FIGHTING STRENGTH

2ND DIVISION — WEEK ENDING 8-7-16.

	"A" FIGHTING STRENGTH IN ACCORDANCE WITH 1ST ARMY No.908.A. OF 3 - 4 - 1915.		"B" INCLUDED IN COL.A BUT NOT ACTUALLY WITH UNIT.		"C" DRAFTS RECEIVED SINCE LAST RETURN		EXPLANATION OF ANY DISCREPANCY EXCEEDING ONE OFFICER AND 30 OTHER RANKS, OTHER THAN "C" BETWEEN FIGHTING STRENGTH SHEWN ON THIS RETURN, AND THAT SHEWN ON LAST.
	Officers	O.Ranks	Officers	O.Ranks	Officers	O.Ranks	
Headquarters 2/Div.	20	192	-	-	-	-	
R.Artillery 2/Div.	66	2880	-	91	-	15	
Y/2 T. M. BATTY.	2	25	-	1	-	-	
X/2 T. M. Batty.	2	27	-	-	-	-	
Z/2 T. M. Batty.	2	27	-	-	-	-	
V/2 T. M. Batty.	2	66	1	5	-	-	
R.Engineers 2/Div.	26	802	1	21	-	4	
H.Q. 5th Inf. Bde.	4	69	-	-	-	-	
2nd Ox.and Bucks.	42	998*	9	121	-	-	*(18 o.ranks wounded, 2 killed and 15 (to hospital and Base.
2nd Highl. L. I.	43	909ø	4	182	2	37	
17th Royal Fusiliers.	38	1032	5	195	1	-	
24th Royal Fusiliers.	32	1015	7	201	-	-	ø(66 o.ranks (Bantams) to No.35 Inf. (Base Depot & 5 o.ranks casualties.
5th Bde. M. G. Coy.	10	144	-	2	-	1	
5th Bde. L. M. Batty.(a)	4	68	-	-	-	-	
TOTAL 5TH INF. BDE.	169	4167	25	701	3	38	
H.Q. 6th Inf. Bde.	6	124	-	-	-	-	#{Capt. W.D.WILKINSON transferred to 27th Middlesex {Lieut. M.OXENBOULD to Engl. for training in Res. Bttn.
1st King's (L'pool)	28	1051	7	195	-	69	*(2/Lt.W.R.G.Benson killed. (2/Lt. S.Caldwell to Engl., sick.
2nd South Staffs.	33*	1035	10	148	1	-	
13th Essex.	35ø	957 ✧	9	182	1	-	✧ 62 o.ranks casualties to receipt mid
17th Middlesex.	36#	920	5	188	-	-	ø(Capt.A.G.Hayward and Lt.F.R.Keeble (wounded. Capt.F.J.Trumble and 2/Lt. (G.Conquest to Engl., sick.
6th Bde. M. G. Coy.	10	177	2	7	1	3	
6th Bde. L. M. Batty.(a)	4	60	-	-	-	-	
TOTAL 6th INF. BDE.	148	4284	35	720	3	72	
H.Q. 99th Inf. Bde.	5	89	-	-	-	-	
1st K. R. R. Corps.	25	1052	2	193	-	15	
1st Royal Berks.	30*	802	7	118	-	38	*(2/Lt.Lane died of wounds. (2/Lt.Hanney to Engl., wounded.
22nd Royal Fusiliers.	45	1057	15	186	1	-	
23rd Royal Fusiliers.	34	1056	6	207	1	-	
99th Bde. M. G. Coy.	11	144	2	9	-	-	
99th Bde. L. M. Batty.(a)	4	74	-	-	-	-	
TOTAL 99th INF. BDE.	146	4200	32	715	1	53	
10th D.C.L.I.(Pioneers)	27	951	4	26	-	-	
2/Divnl. Train.	23	409	3	3	-	-	
R. A. M. C.	31	710	2	14	-	3	
No.3 Mob.Vet.Sec.	1	26	-	1	-	-	
TOTAL 2nd DIVISION	667	18744	100	2295	7	185	

(a) Included in strength of battalions.

[signature] for Major General
Commanding 2nd Division.

8th July, 1916.

Appx 24

SECRET.

2nd Divn No. G.S. 791/27.

IVth Corps.

With reference to the raid carried out last night by the 5th Inf. Bde. against the German sap and front line about S.9.a.9.9., it appears that owing to the heavy and sodden nature of the ground consequent on the recent rain, more time was taken to reach the German trench than had been experienced in practice.

The leading party got into the German trench and a machine gun was seized, but the two men bringing it back were wounded when returning through the German wire, and it was dropped. The 3 officers of the party were all casualties and it appears that when they were put out of action, the party were thrown into confusion.

The casualties were :-

1 officer missing.
2 officers wounded.
8 other ranks missing.
12 other ranks wounded.

The artillery and trench mortars co-operated successfully, and a diversion created by Stokes mortars and machine gun fire which was arranged by the G.O.C. 99th Inf. Brigade, was successful in drawing attention and hostile fire away from the point of attack.

I regret the failure of the operation, the party had been well trained and I am satisfied it was gallantly led.

There is no doubt the Germans are very much on the alert along this Divisional front and I do not propose to carry out any more minor raids for the present.

H.Q., 2nd Divn
8th July, 1916.

(Sd) W.G. WALKER. Major-Genera
Commanding 2nd Division.

S E C R E T.
****

Copy No....19...

App 26

CORRECTION SLIP No. 1
to
2nd DIVISION ORDER No.
112 dated 9-7-16.

13th July, 1916.

Para. 1.

For "night 12th/13th July "

read "night 13th/14th July ".

Para. 4. Delete

and Substitute -

" While in Divisional Reserve, the Sapping and Dug-out Platoons, 5th Inf. Brigade, will be at the disposal of the C.R.E. for work on rear lines, each Battalion furnishing its Sapping Platoons and Dug-out Platoons in turn for 48 hours. "

[signature]

Lieut. Colonel,

General Staff, 2nd Division.

Issued to all recipients
of 2/Divn. Order No. 112.

S E C R E T.
****

Copy No. 21......

app 27

2nd DIVISION ORDER No.113.
****

Reference Map, 36.B., 1/40,000.

14th July, 1916.

(1). The 2nd Division will be relieved by the 47th Division on the 15th July and succeeding days. The detailed moves are given in the attached March Table.

(2). On the 15th July, the 5th Inf. Brigade will move into the DIEVAL area vide attached Table. It will be accompanied by its Machine Gun Company and its Light Trench Mortar Battery.

(3). On the night 15th/16th the 99th Inf. Brigade will be relieved by the 140th Inf. Brigade in the BERTHONVAL Section and will move into the area now occupied by the Reserve Brigade of the Division. It will be accompanied by its Stokes Mortar Battery but not by its Machine Gun Company - see para. 8. On the 16th July it will move into the FRESNICOURT area, vide attached Table.

(4). On the night 16th/17th the 6th Inf. Brigade will be relieved by the 142nd Inf. Brigade in the CARENCY Section and will move into the area now occupied by the Reserve Brigade of the Division. It will be accompanied by its Stokes Mortar Battery, but not by its Machine Gun Company (see para. 8).

(5). 2nd Divisional Artillery will remain in the line for the present and will be relieved by the 37th Divisional Artillery at a date to be notified later.

Guns and telephone wire will be left in the line, and guns of the 37th Division will be taken over.

The 2nd Divisional Artillery will probably move into an area round TANGRY.

Medium Trench Mortar Batteries complete will be withdrawn from the line on the 18th/19th inst. under orders to be issued by the C.R.A.

(6). Field Companies R.E. of the 2nd Division, in the line, will be relieved by Field Companies R.E. of the 47th Division on the same dates as the Infantry Brigades are relieved, and will move as in the attached Table. -

Reliefs will be carried out under arrangements to be made between C.R.E's concerned.

(7). The Pioneer detachments now working in forward areas will be withdrawn on the same nights as the respective Infantry Brigades, and will rejoin their Battalion at VILLERS AU BOIS.

Pioneer detachments working in back area will be withdrawn as soon as possible under orders to be issued through the C.R.E., and will rejoin their Battalion at VILLERS AU BOIS.

The Pioneer Battalion will move to LA COMTE on the morning of the 17th July under the orders of its own Commanding Officer.

(8).........

P.T.O.

(8). The Brigade Machine Gun Companies of the 6th and 99th Inf. Brigades will remain in the line until the night 17th/18th July, when they will be relieved by the Brigade Machine Gun Companies of the 47th Division.

They will then move to CAMBLAIN L'ABBE: the 6th Bde. M.G. Co. will rejoin its Brigade, and the 99th Bde. M.G.Co. will remain at CAMBLAIN L'ABBE until the afternoon of the 18th when it will move to HERMIN.

(9). Field Ambulances will move on the 17th under orders to be issued by the A.D.M.S., to OURTON, FRESNICOURT and LA THIEULOYE. A.D.M.S. will arrange details with A.D.M.S., 47th Division.

(10). All Dug-out and Sapping Platoons will rejoin their units at once under orders to be issued by Brigadiers.

(11). (a). The following Schools will be closed and the personnel will rejoin their units:-

2nd Divn. Officers School on the 15th July.
2nd Divn. Bomb School on the 15th July.
2nd Divn. Gas School on the 15th July.
2nd Divn. Signal School. on the 15th July.

Divisional Intelligence Officers and personnel will rejoin their units.

(b). The Divisional Train, etc., will move under orders to be issued by the A.A. & Q.M.G.

(12). G.O.C. 47th Division will take over command of the Sector from the G.O.C., 2nd Divn. at 10 a.m. on the 17th July when 2nd Division Head Qrs. will close at CAMBLAIN L'ABBE and open at CHATEAU in O.10.b. about 1½ miles North of BAJUS.

(13). Acknowledge.

C. Geddes

Lieut. Colonel,
General Staff, 2nd Division.

Issued at 7 p.m.

Copy No. 1 to 5th Inf. Bde.
2 6th Inf.Bde.
3 99th Inf.Bde.
4 R.A., 2nd Divn.
5 R.E., 2nd Divn.
6 2/Signal Co.
7 10/D.C.L.I. (Pioneers).
8 A.D.M.S., 2nd Divn.

Copy No. 9 to A.D.V.S.2/Div.
10 A.P.M., 2nd Divn.
11 2/Div.Train.
12 "Q", 2/Div.
13 & 14 IVth Corps.)
15 47th Divn.) For
16 60th Divn.) infor-
17 R.N.DIVN.) mation.
18 176 Tng.Co.RE.)
19 182nd ,, ,,)
20 - 24 G.S.Records.

MARCH TABLE. (Issued with 2nd Divn.Order No. 113 dated 14th July, 1918.

Date.	Unit.	Hour of passing Starting Point.	Starting Point.	Route.	Destination.	Remarks.
15th July.	5th Inf.Bde.	Not before 9 a.m.	As arranged by G.O.C. Inf.Bde.	GAUCHIN LEGAL - X rds P.9.d.8.3. - thence by units to billets.	Bde.H.Q., DIEVAL. 2 Bns. DIEVAL. 1 Bn. MAREST. 1 Bn. CAMBLAIN-CHATELAIN. Bde.M.G.Co.) DIEVAL Lt.T.M.Bty.) AREA.	
	E.Ang.Fd.Co.	Not before noon.	As arranged by C.R.E.	GAUCHIN LEGAL - X rds P.9.d.8.3. - LA COMTE.	)BAJUS.)	
Night 15/16th July.	99th Inf.Bde.	On relief.	As arranged by G.O.C. Inf.Bde.	-	Present Reserve Bde. Area, 2nd Divn.	Bde.M.G.Co., remains in the line till night 17/18th JULY.
-	226th Fd.Co.RE	,,	-	-	VILLERS AU BOIS.	
16th July.	99th Inf.Bde.	Not before mid-day.	As arranged by G.O.C. Inf.Bde.	By units to billets.	Bde.H.Q. FRESNICOURT. 1 Bn. FREVILLERS. 1 Bn. HERMIN. 1 Bn. ESTREE CAUCHIE. 1 Bn. FRESNICOURT. Lt.T.M.Bty. FRESNICOURT AREA.	
	226 Co.R.E.	To be arranged with G.O.C. 99th I.Bde.	As arranged by CRE.	As arranged with G.O.C., 99th Inf.Bde.	HOUVELIN.	
Night 16/17th July.	6th Inf.Bde.	On relief.	As arranged by G.O.C. Inf.Bde.	-	Present Reserve Bde. area, 2nd Division.	Bde.M.G.Co. remains in the line till night 17th/18th July.
Night 16/17 July.	5th Fd.Co.RE.	On relief.	-	-	VILLERS AU BOIS.	
17th JULY.	10/D.L.I.	9 a.m.	As arranged by C.O.	CAMBLAIN L'ABBE - ESTREE CAUCHIE - X rds at P.9.d.8.3.	LA COMTE.	

(Continued).

MARCH TABLE. Issued with 2nd Divn. Order 1[illegible] dated 14-7-16 (Continued).

Date.	Unit.	Hour of passing Starting Pt.	Starting Point.	Route.	Destination.	Remarks.
17th JULY.	Div.H.Q. No.11 San.Sec. Div.Co. Mob.Vety.Sec.	10 a.m. 10-10 a.m. 10-15 a.m. 10-25 a.m.	Road Junc. W.6.c.2.9. ,, ,, ,,	ESTREE CAUCHIE - X rds P.9.d. - LA COMTE.	CHATEAU, O.10.b.) Will be notified) later.	
,,	Field Ambulances.	Not before 11 a.m.	As arranged by A.D.M.S.	As arranged by A.D.M.S.	1 Fd.Amb. OURTON. 1 ,, FRESNICOURT. 1 ,, LA THIEULOYE.	
Night 17/18th July.	6th Bde.M.G. Co.	On relief.	-	-	CAMBLAIN L'ABBE.	To rejoin 6th I.Bde.
	99th Bde. M.G. Co.	,,	-	-	,,	
18th JULY.	99th Bde.M.G. Co.	Not before Mid-day.	As arranged by O.C. Coy.	ESTREE CAUCHIE.	HERMIN.	To rejoin 99th Inf. Bde.

NOTE :- The Divisional Train will move under the orders of the A.A. & Q.M.G., 2nd Divn.

"G" Diary.

APP 28

2nd DIVISION - CASUALTY RETURN FOR WEEK ENDING 8-7-16.

UNIT.	KILLED. O.	KILLED. O.R.	WOUNDED. O.	WOUNDED. O.R.	MISSING. O.	MISSING. O.R.	Names of Officers, and Remarks,
H.Q., 2nd Divn.							* 2/Lt. A. ALLEN, at duty.
H.Q., 5th Infy.Bde.							
2/Oxf & Bucks L.I.		2		13			* 2/Captain H. McCULLOCH. at duty.
2/High. L.I.		1	2 *	3			
17/Royal Fusiliers.			2 x	12	1 %	7	xCapt. C.F.S. STEWART. Munster Fus. attac. xLt. S. WOOTTON. %Lt. O.D. POLLAK,
24/Royal Fusiliers,		3	1 #	20			#Lt. E.E. CARRALL-WELCOCKS.
5th Bde M.G.Coy.				2			
5th Bde T.M.Battery.-				4			
H.Q., 6th Inf.Bde.							
1/King's Regt.		1		10			
2/S. Staff. R.	1 ≠			5			≠2/Lt. W.R.G. BENSON, 4th Batt. att. 2nd.
13/Essex Regt.		7	2 ‡	39		3	‡Capt. A.G. HAYWARD, Lt. F.R. KEEBLE,
17/Middlesex Regt.		2		10			
6th Bde. M.G.Coy.							
H.Q., 99th Inf.Bde.							
1/R. Berks. Regt.				1			
1/K.R.R.C.				2			
22/Royal Fusiliers.			1 §	9			§ 2/Lt. F.S. MEEKS, 30th Batt. attch. 22nd.
23/Royal Fusiliers.	1 @			1			@ Capt. R.D. JOHNSON, 16th Bn. att. 23rd.
99th Bde. M.G.Coy.							
No.1 Batty. M.M.G.S.							
H.Q., R.A., 2/Divn.							
34th Bde. R.F.A.							
36th Bde. R.F.A.							
41st Bde. R.F.A.				1			
44th Bde. R.F.A.							
H.Q., R.E., 2/Divn.							
5th Field Coy. R.E.				2			
226th Fd. Coy. R.E.							
1/E.A.Fd. Coy. R.E.							
2/Signal Co. R.E.							
232nd T.Coy. R.E.				1			
South Irish Horse.							
2/Divl. Cyclist Coy.							
TOTAL.	2	16	8	135	1	10	

H.Q., 2nd Divn.
13 / 7 /1916.

W J Liberdale Lieut
for
Captain,
D.A.A. & Q.M.G., 2nd Division.

SECRET.

Copy No. 8 1

app 28 (a)

IV CORPS ORDER No: 116.

14th July, 1916.

1. (a) The 47th Division will relieve the 2nd Division in the Right Sector; the infantry relief to be completed by 10.0 a.m. on 17th July.

(b) At this hour the G.O.C., 47th Division will take over command of the Right Sector and the G.O.C., Royal Naval Division will take over command of the Left Sector.

(c) The G.O.C., Royal Naval Division will then have under his command the 47th Divisional Artillery, the 141st Infantry Brigade holding the SOUCHEZ Section, the 1st Brigade, Royal Naval Division holding the ANGRES Section, and the 2nd Brigade, Royal Naval Division in Divisional Reserve.

2. The details of moves are given on attached Table.

3. (a) The 2nd Divisional Artillery will continue to cover the Right Divisional front until relieved by the artillery of the 37th Division.

(b) The 47th Divisional Artillery will continue to cover the Left Divisional front until relieved by the artillery of the Royal Naval Division.

(c) These reliefs will take place without moving guns or telephone wires.

(d) The Medium Trench Mortar Batteries of the 2nd and 47th Divisions will remain in the line.

4. All R.E. and Medical duties in the Right Sector will be taken over by the 47th Division and those in the Left Sector by the Royal Naval Division by the evening of the 17th July.

5. The Pioneer Battalions will join their respective divisions on the 17th July.

6. (a) The 6th and 99th Brigade Machine Gun Companies will remain in the Right Sector until the night 17th/18th July.

(b) The Corps Motor Machine Gun Battery will come under the orders of the 47th Division to-morrow, but when the G.O.C., 47th Division hands over command of the Left Sector, it will remain in that Sector.

7. Orders regarding the relief of working parties and infantry attached to Tunnelling Companies will be issued later.

8. Acknowledge.

H. De Pree

Brigadier General,
General Staff, IV Corps.

Copy No.		Copy No.	
1	to 2nd Division.	9	to C.E., IV Corps.
2	47th Division.	10	D.A.D.M.S.
3	R.N.Division.	11	D.A.D.A.S.
4	37th Division.	12	18 Sqdn. R.F.C.
5	XVII Corps.	13	B.G., H.A., IV Corps.
6	I Corps.	14	Corps Cavalry
7	Adv: First Army.	15	A.P.M.
8	G.O.C., R.A.	16	File
17	War Diary.		
18.	D.A & Q.M.G.		

Acknowledged

TABLE TO ACCOMPANY IV CORPS ORDER No: 116 dated 14th July, 1916.

Night.	5th Bde.	6th Bde	99th Bde	1st Bde R.N.D.	2nd Bde R.N.D.	140th Bde	141st Bde	142nd Bde.
July 14/15	2nd Div'l Reserve Area.	CARENCY Section	BERTHONVAL Section	ANGRES Section	DIEVAL Area	FRESNICOURT COUPIGNY BOUVIGNY Area	SOUCHEZ Section	HERSIN FOSSE 10 Area.
July 15/16	DIEVAL Area	CARENCY Section	2nd Div'l Reserve Area	ANGRES Section	FRESNI-COURT COUPIGNY Area	BERTHONVAL Section	SOUCHEZ Section	BOUVIGNY huts area.
July 16/17	DIEVAL Area	2nd Div'l Reserve Area	FREVILLERS FRESNI-COURT Area	ANGRES Section	HERSIN Area	BERTHONVAL Section	SOUCHEZ Section	CARENCY Section.

Appendix 29.

S E C R E T.
****

IVth Corps No.H.R.S.669/2/B

2nd Division.

1. The IVth Corps Heavy Artillery will bombard LA CULOTTE to-morrow July 15th at times to be selected by B.G., C.H.A., IVth Corps, in consultation with G.O'sC. 2nd and 47th Divisions.

2. The 2nd Division will carry out a trench mortar bombardment in the CARENCY Section at the discretion of the G.O.C., 2nd Division.

3. Please acknowledge by wire.

(sd) W.A.T. Bowly, Major
G.S. for
Br. General,
General Staff, IVth Corps.

14th July, 1916.

SECRET

COPY No. 1

app 30

IV CORPS ORDER No: 117.
****

15th July, 1918.

1. The 37th Division will carry out the following moves on July 16th :-

(a) 102nd Infantry Brigade, with attached troops, from the area VILLERS BRULIN - CHELERS - BAILLEUL AUX CORNAILLES to DIVION.

(b) 63rd Infantry Brigade and attached troops, from area SARS LEZ BOIS - MAGNICOURT SUR CANCHE - HOUVIN HOUVIGNEUL to area vacated by 102nd Infantry Brigade.

(c) The Divisional Artillery from area REBREUVIETTE - BOURET SUR CANCHE to bivouacs in the area GAUCHIN LEGAL - HERMIN - OLHAIN.

(d) Divisional Headquarters to BRYAS.

An Officer to take over billets for the 102nd Infantry Brigade will report at IV Corps Headquarters, RANCHICOURT, and an officer to take over bivouacs for the Artillery will report to Headquarters 2nd Division at CAMBLAIN L'ABBE, both at 9.30 a. m. July 16th.

2. The Artillery of the 37th Division will take over from the Artillery of the 2nd Division on the nights of the 17th/18th and 18th/19th.

3. The 37th Division will come under the orders of IV Corps from the completion of the moves on the 16th.

4. RAILHEAD for supplies will be BRUAY from 17th instant.

5. Acknowledge.

H. De Pree
Brigadier General,
General Staff, IV Corps.

Issued at 4.30 p.m.

Copy No.		Copy No.	
1 to	2nd Division	8 to	A.D.A.S., IV Corps.
2	37th Division	9	A.D.M.S. ,,
3	47th Division	10	A.P.M. ,,
4	R.N.Division	11	First Army for informn:
5	G.O.C., R.A.	12	Third " " "
6	C.E., IV Corps.	13	I Corps " "
7	D.A. & Q.M.G.	14	XVII Corps. " "

Copy No. 15 File - No. 16 War Diary.

Q. to see

Acknowledged
15.7.

103[d]
MONCHY BRETON.

S E C R E T.
****

Copy No. 25.

App 31

CORRECTION SLIP No.1
to
2nd DIVISION ORDER No.113 dated 14-7-16.

15th July, 1916.

Reference March Table -

16th July - 226th Fd.Co.R.E.

Destination - For "HOUVELIN"
Read "BEUGIN".

17th July - 10/D.C.L.I.

Destination - For "LA COMTE"
Read "OURTON".

17th July.

Delete "2/Div. Co." and "Mob.Vety.Sec."

Further orders will be issued for the move of these units.

Div.H.Q., etc. - Starting Point - For "W.6.c.2.9."
Read "W.16.c.2.9."

N O T E.

2/Div.H.Q. 2nd Echelon,
2/Signal Co. and
No. 11 Sanitary Section
will be billetted in LA COMTE.

C.R.E. will also be billetted in LA COMTE.

G. Belgrave Major
for Lieut. Colonel,
General Staff, 2nd Division.

Issued at 4 pm.

Copy No. 1 to 5th Inf. Bde.
2 6th Inf.Bde.
3 99th Inf.Bde.
4 R.A., 2nd Divn.
5 R.E., 2nd Divn.
6 10/D.C.L.I.
7 A.D.M.S., 2nd Divn.
8 A.P.M. 2nd Divn.
9 2/Div. Train.
10 "Q", 2nd Divn.
11 Camp Commdt.
12 A.D.V.S., 2nd Divn.
13 & 14 IVth Corps,)
15 47th Divn.)
16 60th Divn.) For information.
17 R.N. Divn.)
18 176th Tng.Co RE.)
19 182nd ,, ,,)

Copy No.20 to 2/Sig.Co.
21 - 25 G.S. Records.

S E C R E T.
****

app 32

Copy No. 23

ADDITION
to
2nd Divn. Order No.113 d/14-7-16

15th July, 1916.

With reference to para. 5 -

(1). 37th Divisional Artillery arrive in the area GAUCHIN LEGAL - HERMIN - OLHAIN on the 16th., and will relieve 2nd Div. Artillery on nights 17th/18th and 18th/19th under arrangements made by G.O's C., R.A. 2nd and 37th Divisions.

(2). On relief, 2nd Div. Artillery will move into the GAUCHIN LEGAL area, and will march next day to an area to be notified later.

J B Belgrave Major
for Lieut. Colonel,
General Staff, 2nd Division.

Issued at 8·15 pm

Copies sent to all recipients of 2nd Divn. Order No.113.

S E C R E T.
****

app 33

Copy No. 24...

ADDITION SLIP No. 2.
to
2nd Division Order No. 113 d/14-7-16.

16th July, 1916.

Reference para. (6) -

On 18th July, 5th Field Co. R.E., will move to BEUGIN under arrangements to be made by C.R.E.

[signature] Major for Lieut. Colonel,
General Staff, 2nd Division.

Issued at 7 a.m.

Copies sent to all recipients
of 2nd Divn. Order No.113.

FIGHTING STRENGTH.

2nd DIVISION. WEEK ENDED 15/7/16.

	"A" FIGHTING STRENGTH IN ACCORDANCE WITH 1ST ARMY No.908.A. OF 6 - 4 - 1915.		"B" INCLUDED IN COL.A BUT NOT ACTUALLY WITH UNIT.		"C" DRAFTS RECEIVED SINCE LAST RETURN.		EXPLANATION OF ANY DISCREPANCY EXCEEDING ONE OFFICER AND 30 OTHER RANKS, OTHER THAN "C" BETWEEN FIGHTING STRENGTH SHEWN ON THIS RETURN, AND THAT SHEWN ON LAST.
	Officers	O.Ranks.	Officers	O.Ranks.	Officers	O.Ranks.	
Headquarters 2/Div.	20	192	-	-	-	-	
R.Artillery 2/Div.	93	2910	4	228	7	36	
Y/2 T.M.Batty.	2	23	-	2	-	-	
X/2 T.M.Batty.	2	27	-	-	-	-	
Z/2 T.M.Batty.	2	27	-	-	-	-	
V/2 T.M.Batty.	2	65	1	4	-	-	
R.Engineers 2/Div.	27	786	1	24	-	10	
H.Q.5th Inf.Bde.	4	69	-	-	-	-	
2nd Oxf.& Bucks L.I.	42	971	11	127	-	-	*(1 officer missing, 36 O.R.killed, (wounded & missing. 1 O.R. to base (4 to hospital.
2nd High.L.I.	42	886	8	177	-	-	
17th R.Fusiliers.	37 *	996 *	14	201	-	-	
24th R.Fusiliers.	34 ∅	972 ∅	9	165	4	-	∅ 2 officers transferred to England. 44 O.R. to hospital, wounded and sick.
5th Bde.M.G.Coy.	10	143	2	4	-	2	
5th Bde.L.M.Batty (a)	5	68	-	-	-	-	
TOTAL 5TH INF.BDE.	174	4105	44	674	4	2	
H.Q. 6th Inf.Bde.	5	125	-	-	-	-	
1st King's (L'pool)	28	1047	7	200	-	-	
2nd S.Staffs. Regt.	32	1019	10	147	-	-	* 1 officer transferred to 2nd R. Welsh Regt. O.R. to hospital
13th Essex Regt.	35	936	9	184	-	-	
17th Middlesex Regt.	34	~~887~~ 916	6 *	179 *	-	-	
6th Bde. M.G.Coy.	9	173	2	5	-	-	
6th Bde. T.M.Batty. (a)	4	71	-	-	-	-	
TOTAL 6TH INF.BDE.	147	~~4258~~ 4287	34	715	-	-	
H.Q.99th Inf.Bde.	5	89	-	-	-	-	
22nd R.Fusiliers.	36	1037	10 *	[illegible]			[illegible] England. 1 transferred to England for training duties.
23rd R.Fusiliers.	33	1040	7	212	-	-	
1/R.Berks.	29	812	9	116	-	-	
1/K.R.R.C.	25	1040	8	190	-	2	
99th Bde.M.G.Coy.	11	144	-	10	-	-	
99th Bde.L.M.Batty.(a)	5	71	-	-	-	-	
TOTAL 99th INF.BDE.	136	4162	28	752	-	2	
10th D.C.L.I.(Pioneers)	28	951	5	61	-	-	
2/Divnl.Train.	25	404	3	3	-	-	
R. A. M. C.	31	707	2	15	-	2	
No.3 Mob.Vet.Sec.	1	26	-	-	-	-	
TOTAL 2ND DIVISION.	688	~~18643~~ 18672	122	1784	11	52	

(a) Included in strength of battalions.

15th July, 1916.

[signature] for Major General,
Commanding 2nd Division.

"G" Diary.

2nd Division - CASUALTY RETURN FOR WEEK ENDING 15th July, 1916.

UNIT.	KILLED. O.	KILLED. O.R.	WOUNDED. O.	WOUNDED. O.R.	MISSING. O.	MISSING. O.R.	Names of Officers and remarks.
H.Q., 2nd Division.							
H.Q., 5th Infy. Bde.							
2/Oxf. & Bucks L.I.		2		14		1	
2/High. L.I.	1x			3			xT/Capt. A. HUTTON.
17th R. Fusiliers.		5	3%	12			%(2/Lt.H.R.K.PECHELL, (28th Bn.att.17th.
24th R. Fusiliers.		3	1@	14			(Capt S.J.M.HOLE, (2/Lt.S.H.HEWETT,
5th Bde M.G. Coy.							@ 2/Lt. F.S.MOTT.
5th Bde. T.M. Batty.				1 *			* of 2/H.L.I. attachd.
H.Q., 6th Infy. Bde.							
1/Kings Regt.				1			
2/S. Staff. Regt.							
13th Essex Regt.		2		3			
17th Middlesex Regt.							
6th Bde. M.G. Coy.			1#	2			#2/Lt. R.ELCOCK,) 3rd Kings. att.)
6th Bde. T.M. Batty.							
H.Q., 99th Inf. Bde.							
1/R. Berks Regt.				5			
1/K.R.R.C.		1		6			
22nd R. Fusiliers.		3		2			
23rd R. Fusiliers.		1		5			
99th Bde. M.G. Coy.							
99th T.M. Batty.							
10th D.C.L.I.				11			
H.Q., R.A., 2/Divn.							
34th Bde. R.F.A.							
36th Bde. R.F.A.							
41st Bde. R.F.A.							
V.2.T.M.Battery.							
X.2.T.M.Battery.							
Y.2.T.M.Battery.							
Z.2.T.M.Battery.							
X/R.N.D./T.M.Batty.		1*					* accidentally.
H.Q., R.E., 2/Divn.							
5th Field Coy.R.E.		2		6			
226th Field Coy.				1			
E.A.Fd.Coy. R.E.							
2/Signal Coy.R.E.							
6th Field Ambce.				1			
TOTAL.	1	20	5	87	-	1	

18 / 7 /1916.

Major,
D.A.A. & Q.M.G.,2nd Division.

"A" Form. Army Form C. 2121

MESSAGES AND SIGNALS. No. of Message

Prefix Code m. Words Charge

Office of Origin and Service Instructions.

Sent At m. To By

This message is on a/c of: Appx Service.

(Signature of "Franking Officer.")

Recd. at 96 m. Date From By

TO R.A. 2nd Div.
37th Div.

Sender's Number.	Day of Month	In reply to Number	
* G521	17		AAA

Ref 2nd Div Order 113 para 5 AAA Equipment of 2nd Div Medium Trench Mortar Batteries will remain in the line and will handed over to the 37 Div personnel AAA Personnel of Medium T. M. Batteries 37 Div will relieve personnel of medium T. M. Batteries 2nd Div by the morning of 19th July AAA Equipment of 37 Div medium T. M. Batteries will be taken over by morning of 19th July AAA Details will be arranged by G.O's.C. R. A. concerned AAA Addressed R. A. repeated 37th Div.

From 2nd Div
Place
Time 3p.m.

The above may be forwarded as now corrected (Z)

(Sgd.) J.D.BELGRAVE
Major
Gen.Staff.

Censor. Signature of Addressor or person authorised to telegraph in his name.

* This line should be erased if not required.

(4198) Wt. W14742—M44. 300,000 Pads 12/15. S r J. C. & S.

app 37

SECRET

IV CORPS ORDER NO 118.

Copy No. 1.

17th July, 1916.

---

1. The 2nd Division will move to unoccupied billets in the area S.W. of the Roman Road and S.E. of the PERNES - ST.POL Road (exclusive of VALHUON) with a view to entraining at PERNES, DIEVAL and BRIAS Stations. The entrainment will begin on the night of the 19th July.

2. The moves will be carried out on the 18th, 19th and 20th July, the details of which will be arranged by the 2nd Division.

3. The 6th Infantry Brigade will be clear of ESTREE CAUCHIE by 1 p.m. 18th July at which hour the 63rd Infantry Brigade will arrive to take its place in Corps Reserve, and will be billetted in CAMBLAIN L'ABBE, MAISNIL BOUCHE, GOUY SERVINS and ESTREE CAUCHIE.

4. The 103rd Infantry Brigade will march to the area FRESNICOURT, HERMIN, FREVILLERS, ESTREE CAUCHIE on the 19th July, but will not arrive before 3 p.m. It will move by MAGNICOURT and FREVILLERS, roads North of which places are allotted to the 2nd Division.

5. The Divisional H.Q. 37th Division will open at the Chateau in O.10.b. at noon on the 20th July.

6. Acknowledge.

H. DePreé

H.Q., IV Corps,
17th July, 1916.

Brigadier-General,
General Staff, IV Corps.

Issued at midnight 17th/18th July 1916.

Copy No.	1 2nd Division.	Copy No.	9 A.P.M., IV Corps.
" "	2 37th Division.	" "	10 Adv. First Army (for informn)
" "	3 47th Division.	" "	11 Third Army. "
" "	4 R.N. Division.	" "	12 XVII Corps.
" "	5 G.O.C., R.A.	" "	13 I Corps.
" "	6 D.A. & Q.M.G.	" "	14 18 Sqn. R.F.C.
" "	7 A.D.A.S.	" "	15 File.
" "	8 A.D.M.S.	" "	16 War Diary.

Action taken
CB.

Acknowledged
[illegible]

"A" Form.
MESSAGES AND SIGNALS.

Army Form C. 2121.
No. of Message

Prefix Code m. | Words | Charge | This message is on a/c of: Service. | Recd. at m.
Office of Origin and Service Instructions.
Sent At m. To By
(Signature of "Franking Officer.")
Date From By

To { 5th Brigade | CO | Signals | ADMS
6th Brigade | CRE | Train |
99th Brigade | ADMS | IV Corps |

Sender's Number G. 528 | Day of Month 18 | In reply to Number | AAA

Following moves will take place 18th July aaa 6th Inf Bde to area HOUDAIN BEUGIN part of LA COMTE part of MAGNICOURT BAJUS aaa Troops to be clear of ESTREE CAUCHIE by 12.30 pm aaa Bde HQ HOUDAIN aaa 5th Field Coy RE to LA THIEULOYE aaa To be clear of ESTREE CAUCHIE by 12.45 pm aaa 226th Field Coy RE to ANTIN to be clear of BAJUS by 12 noon aaa East Anglian Field Coy RE to BRYAS to be clear of BAJUS by 11.45 am aaa 5th Inf Bde aaa Bde HQ Trench Mortar Bty and one battalion from DIEVAL to PERNES aaa One battalion from DIEVAL to GRICOURT and BOURS aaa To be clear of DIEVAL by 2 pm aaa Remainder stand fast and Bde HQ to PERNES aaa 99th Inf Bde Bde HQ Trench Mortar Battery and two battalions from

From
Place
Time

The above may be forwarded as now corrected. (Z)
Censor. Signature of Addressor or person authorised to telegraph in his name.
* This line should be erased if not required.

(4'98) Wt. W14 42—M44. 300000 Pads 12/15. Sir J. C. & S.

"A" Form.

MESSAGES AND SIGNALS.

Army Form C. 2121.

No. of Message..........

Prefix .... Code .... m.	Words	Charge	This message is on a/c of:	Recd. at .... m
Office of Origin and Service Instructions.	Sent		..........Service.	Date
	At..........m.			From
	To			
	By		(Signature of "Franking Officer.")	By

TO (2)

Sender's Number.	Day of Month. 18	In reply to Number.	AAA

ESTREE CAUCHIE and FRESNICOURT to DIEVAL to be clear of GAUCHIN LEGAL by 11-30 am aaa Bde Machine Gun Coy as ordered aaa Remainder 81 and [illegible] aaa Bde HQ to DIEVAL aaa Mobile Veterinary Section to DIEVAL to be clear of GAUCHIN LEGAL by 11-45 am aaa 6th Field Ambulance to FERME D'ESTRAYELLE ? 29 C to move in rear of 99th Brigade as far as GAUCHIN LEGAL and thence by Roman road aaa Orders for move on 19th will be issued later aaa Acknowledge

Priority

From 2 Dn

Place

Time 1 am

The above may be forwarded as now corrected.

(Z) C. Deedes Lt Col

Censor. Signature of Addressor or person authorised to telegraph in his name.

* This line should be erased if not required.

225,000. W 14042—M 44. H. W & V., Ld. 12.15.

6

S E C R E T.   Copy No.....

Appx 40

2nd DIVISION ORDER No. 114.
****

Reference Map, 36 B
1/40,000.

19th July, 1916.

1. 2nd Division will move to entraining stations PERNES, DIEVAL and BRIAS, and will entrain in accordance with Tables attached.

2. All troops except the personnel of Infantry Battalions will be at the entraining stations 3 hours before the time at which their train is due to depart. Transport of infantry Battalions with a loading party of 100 men will be at the entraining station 3 hours before the time at which their train is due to depart, and the remainder of the Battalion 1¼ hours before that time.

3. (a) The composition of strategical trains is as follows :-

TYPE COMBATTANT - 33 Covered Trucks.
14 Open Flats.
1 Officers' Coach.

TYPE PATC - 24 Covered Trucks.
23 Open Flats.
1 Officers' Coach.

All trains are "Type Combattant" unless specifically marked as "Parc".

Covered trucks take 40 men or 8 horses; 2 or 3 men can travel in each truck with the horses.

Open Flats vary in size, but 4 pairs of wheels can be taken with limbered ~~wagons~~ vehicles (5 for guns and ammunition wagons); 3 pairs when one 4 wheeled vehicle is not limbered, and only one vehicle in the case of pontoons and ambulances.

Officers' Coach cannot be taken as having more than 4 compartments.

(b) Breast and head ropes for ~~typig~~ tying up horses must be provided by Units, but railway provides lashings for vehicles.

(c) In mixed trains, loading parties will be told off to load all horses and vehicles, and not only those belonging to their own Unit.

(d) R.F.A. will unship traversing handspike.

(e) The R.T.O. is responsible for loading the train.

(4). Officers for duty at entraining stations will be detailed as follows:-

Infantry Brigade Hd. Qrs. at PERNES ....PERNES.
,, ,, ,, at DIEVAL ....DIEVAL.
,, ,, ,, at HOUDAIN .... BRYAS.

These officers will act in co-operation with the R.T.O. and railway entraining staff as may be required. They will proceed by the last train leaving their respective stations. These officers will be handed a copy of the March Table affecting their station by their respective Brigades.

(5).......
P.T.O.

(5). G.O.C., R.A., will detail one subaltern officer, 2 N.C.Os. and 25 men at each of the following stations :-

PERNES
DIEVAL and
BRYAS.

to assist in entraining D.A.C., commencing with trains No. 25, 23 and 24 respectively. These parties will proceed in the last train leaving their respective stations. G.O.C., R.A. will make all arrangements for rationing these parties.

(6) O.C., Divisional Signal Coy. will furnish one motor cyclist for permanent duty at each of the entraining stations PERNES, DIEVAL and BRYAS. The cyclist will be at the disposal of the officer detailed by Infantry Brigades mentioned in para. 4 above, for communication with billetting areas. He will proceed by the last train from the entraining station concerned.

(7) Every unit will entrain its supplies and baggage wagons (from 2nd Div. Train) with its first line transport.

(9) Every unit will entrain with the current day's and the next day's rations and forage. To ensure this, O.C. Divnl. Supply Column will arrange to have one day's supplies for each train load of troops entraining after midday, at the station 2 hours before the time of departure of the train. He will bring sufficient loaders to load up the supplies on the train. These supplies will be handed over to the senior officer on each train, who will be responsible for them being issued to the troops in the train on arrival at the destination.

Lorries used thus will be loaded up again at Supply Railhead before proceeding to the new area.

S.S.O. will submit a statement of the feeding strength of each train load to the O.C. Divnl. Supply Column as soon as possible

(8) Entraining States, shewing men, horses, vehicles, (G.S., 4 wheeled limbered, 2 wheeled) will be handed to R.T.O. 3 hours before departure of train.

(10) Orders regarding the movement of units provided with motor transport will be issued by A.A. & Q.M.G.

Motor Ambulances will proceed by road under orders issued by A.A. & Q.M.G.

(11) Acknowledge.

(Sd) C.Deedes.
Lieut. Colonel,
General Staff, 2nd Division.

Issued at 7 a.m.

Copy No.			Copy No.		
1	to	5th Inf. Bde.	13	to	Camp Commdt.
2	to	6th Inf. Bde.	14		2/Div. Train.
3		99th Inf. Bde.	15		S.S.O. 2nd Divn.
4		10/D.C.L.I.	16		2/Div. Supply Column.
5		R.A. 2nd Divn.	17 & 18		IVth Corps)for
6		R.E. 2nd Divn.	19		Southern Railheads.)information.
7		2/Div. Signal Coy.	20 - 24		G.S.Records.
8		A.D.M.S. 2nd Divn.			
9		A.P.M. 2nd Divn.			
10		A.D.V.S. 2nd Divn.			
11		D.A.D.O.S. 2nd Divn.			
12		"Q" 2nd Divn.			

SECRET.

Copy.No.......

2nd DIVISION ORDER No.114.

Reference Map, 36.B.
1/40,000.

18th July, 1916.

(1). 2nd Division will move to entraining stations PERNES, DIEVAL and BRYAS, and will entrain in accordance with Tables attached.

(2). All troops except the personnel of Infantry Battalions will be at the entraining station 3 hours before the time at which their train is due to depart. Transport of Infantry Battalions with a loading party of 100 men will be at the entraining station 3 hours before the time at which their train is due to depart, and the remainder of the Battalion 1½ hours before that time.

(3).(a). The composition of strategical trains is as follows :-

TYPE COMBATTANT. - 33 Covered Trucks.
14 Open Flats.
1 Officers' Coach.

TYPE PARC - - 24 Covered Trucks.
23 Open Flats.
1 Officers' Coach.

All trains are " Type Combattant" unless specifically marked as " Parc ".

Covered trucks take 40 men or 8 horses; 2 or 3 men can travel in each truck with the horses.

Open Flats vary in size, but 4 pairs of wheels can be taken with limbered vehicles (5 for guns and ammunition wagons); 3 pairs when one 4 wheeled vehicle is not limbered, and only one vehicle in the case of pontoons and ambulances.

Officers' Coach cannot be taken as having more than 4 compartments.

(b). Breast and head ropes for tying up horses must be provided by Units, but railway provides lashings for vehicles.

(c). In mixed trains, loading parties will be told off to load all horses and vehicles, and not only those belonging to their own Unit.

(d). R.F.A. will unship traversing handspike.

(e). The R.T.O. is responsible for loading the train.

(4). Officers for duty at entraining stations will be detailed as follows :-

Infantry Brigade Hd.Qrs. at PERNES................PERNES.
,, ,, ,, at DIEVAL................DIEVAL.
,, ,, ,, at HOUDAIN..............BRYAS.

These officers will act in co-operation with the R.T.O. and railway entraining staff as may be required. They will proceed by the last train leaving their respective stations. These officers will be handed a copy of the March Table affecting their Station by their respective Brigades.

(5).......
P.T.O.

(5). G.O.C., R.A. will detail one subaltern officer, 2 N.C.Os. and 25 men at each of the following stations :-

PERNES,
DIEVAL and
BRYAS,

to assist in entraining D.A.C., commencing with trains No. 25, 23 and 24 respectively. These parties will proceed in the last train leaving their respective stations. G.O.C., R.A. will make all arrangements for rationing these parties.

(6). O.C., Divisional Signal Co. will furnish one motor cyclist for permanent duty at each of the entraining stations PERNES, DIEVAL and BRYAS. The cyclist will be at the disposal of the officer detailed by Infantry Brigades mentioned in para. 4 above, for communication with billotting areas. He will proceed by the last train from the entraining station concerned.

(7). Every unit will entrain its supplies and baggage wagons (from 2nd Divl. Train) with its 1st line transport.

(8). Entraining States, shewing men, horses, vehicles, (G.S., 4 wheeled limbered, 2 wheeled) will be handed to R.T.O. 3 hours before departure of train.

(9). Every unit will entrain with the current day's and the next day's rations and forage. To ensure this, O.C., Divl. Supply Column will arrange to have one day's supplies for each train load of troops entraining after midday, at the station 2 hours before the time of departure of the train. He will bring sufficient loaders to load up the supplies on the train. These supplies will be handed over to the senior officer on each train, who will be responsible for them being issued to the troops on the train on arrival at the destination.

Lorries used thus will be loaded up again at Supply Railhead before proceeding to the new area.

S.S.O. will submit a statement of the feeding strength of each train load to the O.C., Divl. Supply Column as soon as possible.

(10). Orders regarding the movement of units provided with motor transport will be issued by A.A. & Q.M.G.

Motor ambulances will proceed by road under orders issued by A.A. & Q.M.G.

(11). Acknowledge.

[signature]

Lieut. Colonel,
General Staff, 2nd Division.

Issued at 4 am

Copy No.	To	Copy No.	To
1	5th Inf.Bde.	13	Camp Commdt.
2	6th Inf. Bde.	14	2/Div. Train.
3	99th Inf. Bde.	15	S.S.O., 2nd Div.
4	10/D.C.L.I.	16	2/Div.Supply Col.
5	R.A., 2nd Divn.	17 & 18	IVth Corps.) For
6	R.E., 2nd Divn.	19	Southern Railheads.) information.
7	2/Div. Signal Co.	20 - 21	G.S. Records.
8	A.D.M.S., 2nd Divn.		
9	A.P.M., 2nd Divn.		
10	A.D.V.S., 2nd Divn.		
11	D.A.D.O.S. 2nd Divn.		
12	"Q", 2nd Divn.		

0/4/40

Entraining Table issued with 2nd Division Order No. 114 dated 19/7/16.

Date.	Unit.	Serial No.	Billetted at	Entrain-ing Stn.	Route to Ent. Station.	To arrive at Ent. Stn. at: Trnspt & Loading Party.	To arrive at Ent. Stn. at: Unit.	No. of train.	Train leaves.	Remarks.
20th	5th I.Bde. H.Q.	10	PERNES	PERNES (I.13.a)		2 a.m. 20th July		No. 1	4.52 am	
	Bde. M.G. Coy.	16	"	"		"		"	"	
	Sec.Div.Sig.Coy.	15	"	"		"		"	"	by lorry.
	5th L.T.M.Bty.	17	"	"		"		"	"	
	Medium T.M.Bty.	96	GAUCHIN LEGAL Area		via HOUDAIN & CAMBLAIN CHATELAIN	5 a.m.	6.45AM	No. 4	7.52 am	
20th	1 Bn.5th I.Ido.	11	PERNES	"		8 a.m.	9.45am	No. 7	10.52 am	
20th	1 Bn. -do-	12	CAMBLAIN CHATELAIN	"		11 a.m.	12.45pm	No.10	1.52 pm	
20th	1 Bn. -do-	13	MAREST	"		2 p.m.	3.45pm	No. 13	4.52 pm	
20th	1 Bn. -do-	14	BOURS	"	via I.20.c.	5 p.m.	6.45pm	No. 16	7.52 pm	
20th	10th D.C.L.I. (less 1 Coy.)	Part 04	OURTON	"	via BOURS & MAREST	8 p.m.		No. 19	10.52pm.	
20th	226 Field Coy.	84	ANTIN	"	via I.20.c.			"		
	1 Coy.D.C.L.I.	Part 04	OURTON		via OURTON	11 p.m.		No. 22	1.52 am	
20th/21st	6th Field Amb.	91 A	FERME D'ESTRAYELLE (I.23.c)	"	via BOURS & MAREST			"		
	Mob. Vet.Sec.		DIEVAL	"						
21st	1 Bty. R.F.A. ½ No.1 Sec DAC (less G.S. wagons for S.A.A.)	41 ½ 79	GAUCHIN LEGAL Area.	"	via HOUDAIN and CAMBLAIN CHATELAIN	2 a.m.		No. 25 "	4.52 am	Under detailed orders of C.R.A.
21st	1 Bty. R.F.A. ½ No.1 Sec DAC (less G.S. wagons for S.A.A.)	42 ½ 79	"	"	"	5 a.m.		No. 28	7.52 am	

Entraining Table issued with 2nd Division Order No. 114 dated 10/7/16 (continued)

Date	Unit.	Serial No.	Billetted at	Entraining Stn.	Route to Entrng. Stn.	To arrive at Ent. Stn. at Trnspt & Loading Party.	Unit.	No. of train.	Train leaves.	Remarks.
21st	1 Bty. R.F.A.	43	GAUCHIN LEGAL Area.	PERNES (I.13.a)	via HOUDAIN and CAMBLAIN CHATELAIN	8.0 a.m.		No. 31	10.52 am	Under detailed orders of C.R.A.
	¼ No.1 Sec.DAC (less G.S. wagons for SAA)	¼ 79	,,	,,	,,					
21st	H.Q. Bde. R.F.A. (4 battery Bde)	40	,,	,,	,,	11 a.m.		No. 34	1.52 pm	
	1 Bty. R.F.A. (4 guns)	44	,,	,,	,,					
	¼ No.1 Sec DAC (less G.S. wagons for S.A.A.)	¼ 79	,,	,,	,,					
21st	H.Q. D.A.C.	78	,,	,,	,,	2 p.m.		No. 37 parc	4.52 pm	
	No. 1 Sec. DAC 6 G.S. wagons for S.A.A. with drivers and horses.	79	,,	,,	,,					
	No. 2 Sec. DAC 6 G.S. wagons for S.A.A. with drivers and horses.	80	,,	,,	,,			,,		
	H.Q. Div.Train.	part 87	LA COMTE	,,	via OURTON & CAMBLAIN CHATELAIN					Under orders issued by A.A. & Q.M.G.

NOTE. Units must leave billets in sufficient time to reach the station at the time ordered but not before.

1

ENTRAINING TABLE ISSUED WITH [illegible] DIVN. ORDER No.144 dated 1[illegible]-7-1916.

Date.	Unit.	Serial No.	Billettod at	Entraining Sta.	Route to Entraining Sta.	Arriving at Entraining Sta. Transport & Loading party	Arriving at Entraining Sta. Unit.	No. of train.	Train leaves at	Remarks.
20th.	99th I.Bde.HQ.	20	DIEVAL.	DIEVAL. (0.13.c)			1 A.M	2	4.A.M.	
	Sec.Div.Sig.Co	25	,,				,,	2	4 a.,m.	
	H.Q.99 Bde.M.G.Co.	26		,,			,,	2	4 a.m....	To arrive at DIEVAL village by 10-30 pm 19th July & clear the main road. Billets for M.G.Co. as required to be arranged by 99th Bde.
	Div.Hd.Qrs.	01	LA COMTE.	,,	BAJUS.		,,	2	,,	
	H.Q. & No.1 Sec.Div.Sig.Co	05	LA COMTE.	,,	BAJUS.		,,	2	,,	
20th.	1 Bn. 99/Bde.	21	DIEVAL.	,,		4 a.m.	5-45am	5	7 a.m.	
	1 Sec.99th Bde. M.G.Co.	26a.		,,			4 a.m.	5	,, ...	To arrive at DIEVAL village by 10-30 pm 19th, clear of main rd.
20th.	1 Bn. 99th Bde.	22	DIEVAL.	,,		7 a.m.	8-45am	8	10 a.m.	
	1 Sec.99th Bde. M.G.Co.	26b.		,,			7 a.m.	8	,, ...	To arrive at DIEVAL village by 10-30pm 19th & clear the main road.
20th.	1 Bn.99th I.Bde	23	FREVILLERS.	,,	BAJUS.	10 a.m.	11-45am	11	1 p.m.	
	1 Sec.99th Bde. M.G.Co.	26c		,,			10 a.m.	11	,, ...	To arrive at DIEVAL village by 10-30pm 19th and clear the main road.
20th	1 Bn.99th I.Bde	24	HERMIN.	,,	FREVILLERS - BAJUS	1 p.m.	2-45 pm	14	4 p.m.	
	1 Sec.99th Bde M.G.Co.	26d		,,			1 p.m.	14	,,....	To arrive at DIEVAL village by 10-30pm 19th & clear the main road.
20th.	99/L.T.M.Bty.	27	DIEVAL	DIEVAL			4 p.m.	17	7 p.m.	
	5/Fd.Co.R.E.	85	LA THIEULOYE	,,	Rd.Junc.C.19.d.		,,	17	,,......	Not to form up or halt on the BAJUS - LA THIEULOYE - BRYAS road.
	H.Q.R.E.	83	LA COMTE	,,	BAJUS.		,,	17	,,	
	1 Medium T.M. Bty.	97		,,			,,	17	,,......	By lorry.
20th	100th Fd.Amb. (less Motor vehicles).	92	OURTON.	,,	Main road.		7 p.m.	20	10 p.m.	

(Continued)........

ENTRAINING TABLE ISSUED WITH 2nd DIVN. ORDER No. 114 dated 19-7-16. (CONTINUED).

Date.	Unit.	Serial No.	Billetted at	Entraining Sta.	Route to Entraining Sta.	Arriving at Entraining Sta. Loading Party. / Unit.	No. of train.	Train leaves at	Remarks.
20/21st	1 Bty.R.F.A.. ¼ No.2 Sec.DAC (less G.S.wgns for S.A.A.)	51 ¼ 80	GAUCHIN LEGAL Area.	DIEVAL 0.13.c.		10 p.m.	23	1 a.m.	
21st.	1 Bty.RFA. ¼ No.2 Sec.DAC (less G.S. wagons for SAA)	52 ¼ 80	,,	,,		1 a.m.	26	4 a.m.	
21st.	1 Bty.R.F.A. ¼ No.2 Sec.DAC. (less GS wagons for S.A.A.	53 ¼ 80	,,	,,		4 a.m.	29	7 a.m.	
21st.	H.Q. Bde.RFA (4 Bty.Bde,. 1 Bty.RFA(4 guns) ¼ No.2 Sec.DAC (less GS wagons for S.A.A.).	50 54 ¼ 80	,,	,,		7 a.m.	32	10 a.m.	
21st	½ No.4 Sec. D.A.C.	½ 82	,,	,,		10 a.m.	35 parc.	1 p.m.	
21st.	½ No.4 Sect. D.A.C.	½ 82	,,	,,		1 p.m.	38 parc	4 p.m.	

NOTE... Units must leave billets in sufficient time to reach the Station at the time ordered BUT NOT BEFORE.

…INING TABLE ISSUED WITH 2nd DIVISION ORDER No. 114 dated 19-7-1916.

Date.	Unit.	Serial No.	Billetted at	Entraining Sta.	Route to Entraining Sta	To arrive at Entraining Sta: Transport & loading party	To arrive at Entraining Sta: Unit	No. of Train.	Train leaves at	Remarks.
20th JULY	6th I.Bde.HQ.	30	HOUDAIN.	BRYAS. (N.22.c)	Via LA COMTE & LA THIEULOYE	12-30am		No.3	3-29 a.m.	
	Bde.M.G.Co.	36	,,	,,	,,	,,		,,	,,	
	Sec.Div.Sig.Co.	35	,,	,,	,,	,,		,,	,,	
	e/L.T.M.Bty.	37	,,	,,	Via FREVILLERS & LA THIEULOYE	,,		,,	,,......	By Lorry.
	1 Medium T.M. Bty.	98	GAUCHIN LEGAL - area.	,,						
,,	1 Bn. 6th I.Bde	31	HOUDAIN	,,	Via LA COMTE & LA THIEULOYE	3-30am	5-15am	No. 6	6-29 am	
,,	1 Bn. 6th I.Bde	32	HOUVELIN	,,	Via MONCHY BRETON and LA THIEULOYE	6-30am	8-15am	No.9	9-29 a.m	
,,	1 Bn.6th I.Bde	33	BEUGIN	,,	LA COMTE and LA THIEULOYE	9-[illegible]am	[illegible] 10-45am	No.12	11-59 a.m	
,,	1 Bn. 6 I.Bde.	34	BAJUS	,,	Via LA THIEULOYE	12-30am	2-15pm	No. 15	3-29 pm	
,,	E.A.Fd.Co.R.E.	86	BRYAS	,,	Via LA THIEULOYE	3-30 pm		No.18	6-29pm.	
	Salvage Sec. Sany.Sec. Div.Co. Mil.Police.	94	LA COMTE	,,		,,		,,	,,	
,,	5th Fd.Amb.	93	LA THIEULOYE	,,		6-30 pm		No.21	9-29 p.m.	
20/21st JULY	1 Bty.R.F.A. ¼ No.3 Sec.D.A.C (less GS wagons ¼ S.A.A.)	61 81	GAUCHIN LEGAL area.	,,	Via HOUDAIN and CAMBLAIN CHATELAIN.	9-30 pm		No.24	12-29am	Under detailed orders of C.R.A.
,,	1 Bty.R.F.A. ¼ No.3 Sec.DAC (less GS wagons ¼ S.A.A.)	62 81	,, ,,	,, ,,	,, ,,	12-30 a.m. ,,		No.27 ,,	3-29am 21st July	,,
21st JULY	1 Bty.RFA ¼ No.3 Sec.DAC (less GS wagons ¼ S.A.A.)	63 81	,,	BRYAS (N.22.c.)	,,	3-30 a.m.		No.30	6-29 am	,,

(Continued).....

MARCH TABLE ISSUED WITH 2nd DIVISION ORDER No.[illegible] dated [illegible]-7-1918.(Continued).

Date.	Unit.	Serial No.	Billetted at	Entrain-ing Sta.	Route to Entraining Sta.	To arrive at Entraining Sta. at Trnspt & Loading parties.	Unit.	No. of train.	Train leaves at	Remarks.
21st JULY.	¼ No.3 Sec.DAC & 6 GS wagons for SAA with drivers & horses.	½ 81	GAUCHIN LEGAL area.	BRYAS (N.22.c)	Via HOUDAIN & CAMBLAIN CHATELAIN	8-30 a.m.		No.33.	9-29 a.m.	
	HQ.Bde.RFA. (3 Bty.Bde.)	80	,,	,,	,,		,,	,,	,,	
	½ men of Div. Train.	87 to 90	(DIEVAL.) (GRICOURT.) (MAGNICOURT.)	,,			,,	,,	,,	Under detailed order by A.A. & Q.M.G.
	H.Q. Div R.A.	92	,,	,,	,,		,,	,,	,,	
,,	½ men of Div. Train. All horses & Trnspt of Div.Train (less Train H.Q.)	87 to 90	DIEVAL. GRICOURT. MAGNICOURT.	,,		9 a.m.		No. 33 parc	11-59 am	Under detailed order by A.A. & Q.M.G.

NOTE. Units must leave billets in sufficient time to reach the Station at the time ordered but not before.

S E C R E T.   Q/3072 A.

Appx 41

First Army.
Fourth Army.

---

1. The 2nd Division (less all motor vehicles) will be moved by rail from First Army to Fourth Army under arrangements to be made by the Director of Railways. Entrainment will commence on the night July 19/20th. The Infantry of the Division will entrain first.

2. Advanced parties proceeding on July 19th, will report to H.Q. IX Corps at TALMAS.

3. Motor vehicles, except motor cars with Staff Officers, will be despatched in convoys on July 19th and 20th, via:- BRIAS - ST. POL - DOULLENS - TALMAS - PICQUIGNY.

4. First Army will arrange, if necessary, for billets required on the march for motor vehicles and personnel, with Armies concerned.

5. The D.D.S.&.T., First Army will arrange with the D.D.S.&.T., Fourth Army for the despatch of the Divl. Supply Column in such detachments as may be necessary.

6. Arrangements for the entrainment will be made by the Divl. Commander in conjunction with the A.D.R.T.I (BETHUNE), and in accordance with a railway programme to be prepared by the latter officer.

7. Entraining stations will be BRIAS, PERNES and DIEVAL. Detraining stations will be LONGEAU and SALEUX.

8. One Staff Officer of the Division will be located at Headquarters A.D.R.T.I., and another Staff Officer for detrainment purposes at Headquarters A.D.R.T.IV, during the whole period of the move.

9. The detrainment and all subsequent moves will be carried out under the orders of the G.O.C., Fourth Army.

10. The Staff Officer for detrainment will arrange for a statement of billets allotted to each unit to be delivered to O/C Units on or before arrival at detrainment stations.

11. Units will entrain with rations for the day following the day of detrainment.

C.T. Dawkins Major-General,

G.H.Q.

18/7/16.

for Quartermaster General.

Copies: Third Army.
Reserve Army.
2nd Division.
D.T.
D.S.
I.G.C.
D.D.O.S.
D.O.S.
D. Rys.
Adv. Q.
G.S.
A.G.(2).

2

H.Q., 2nd Division.

For information.

RT Lee Major
D.A.Q.M.G.
for Quartermaster General

G.H.Q.
18.7.16.

acknowledged
BB. 19.7

"A" Form. Army Form C. 2121.

MESSAGES AND SIGNALS. No. of Message

Prefix Code m. Words Charge

Office of Origin and Service Instructions.

Sent At m. To By

This message is on a/c of: Service.

(Signature of "Franking Officer.")

Recd. at m. Date From By

TO 2nd Divn

App 29

Sender's Number	Day of Month	In reply to Number	AAA
G 904	22		

Ref. Operation Order No 31 para 1 (c) 13th Corps will attack GUILLEMONT only on 23rd inst aaa French attack on MAUREPAS will not take place aaa GOC. 30th Divn will modify his plan accordingly reporting action proposed to Corps HQ as soon as possible especially what alterations are required in (?) of Corps Arty. aaa Acknowledge

From 13th Corps

Place

Time 3.10 pm

The above may be forwarded as now corrected. (Z)

Censor. Signature of Addressor or person authorised to telegraph in his name.

* This line should be erased if not required.

233146—W. & S. Ltd., London.—W 1753/1402—100,000—7/15. Forms C 2121/10.

"A" Form. Army Form C. 2121.

MESSAGES AND SIGNALS. No. of Message

Prefix Code m. Words Charge
Office of Origin and Service Instructions.
Sent At m. To By
This message is on a/c of: Service.
(Signature of "Franking Officer.")
Recd. at m. Date From By

TO 2nd Divn (App 41)

Sender's Number	Day of Month	In reply to Number	AAA
G 865	31st		

It is probable that the general attack will be renewed by Fourth Army Reserve Army and 6th French Army on 23rd aaa The task of 13th Corps will be a combined attack on the line FALFEMONT FARM GUILLEMONT 1 & 30th Divn. and a detachment of 35th Divn. aaa 3rd Divn. will have as objective the clearance of DELVILLE WOOD and LONGUEVAL VILLAGE and connection of GUILLEMONT with DELVILLE WOOD aaa Meanwhile 3rd Divn will endeavour to gain ground towards GUILLEMONT as far S. as the railway aaa 35th Divn the same South of the railway aaa Consolidation of our own work and

From
Place
Time

The above may be forwarded as now corrected. (Z)
Censor. Signature or Addressor or person authorised to telegraph in his name.

* This line should be erased if not required.

393146—W. & S. Ltd., London.—W 1759/1402—100,000—7/15. Forms C 2121/10.

"A" Form. Army Form C. 2121.

MESSAGES AND SIGNALS. No. of Message

Prefix Code m. | Words | Charge | This message is on a/c of: Service. | Recd. at m. Date From By

Office of Origin and Service Instructions. Sent At m. To By (Signature of "Franking Officer.")

TO (2)

Sender's Number | Day of Month | In reply to Number | AAA

prevention of enemy work to continue with all energy aaa Addsd 2nd 3rd 9th 30th 35th Divns 1st Cavalry Divn and GOC RA repts 15 Corps and p.c. 20 French Corps

From 13 Corps

Place

Time 9.30am

The above may be forwarded as now corrected. (Z)

Censor. Signature of Addressor or person authorised to telegraph in his name.

* This line should be erased if not required.

203146—W. & S. Ltd., London.—W 1789/1402—100,000—7/15. Forms C 2121/10.

S E C R E T.
****

Copy No. 20

2nd DIVISION ORDER No. 115.

Appx 13

Reference Maps, 1/40,000 and 1/20,000.

23rd July, 1916.

(1). The following moves will take place on the 23rd July -

(a). 99th Inf.Bde. to SAND PIT Valley, squares F.13 and 19.

5th Fd.Co.R.E.)
Bearer Div. 100th Fd.Amb.) will remain at MORLANCOURT and will come under orders of G.O.C., 6th Inf. Bde.

99th Inf. Bde. will march to its new area via squares K.9,10,11, to Northern end of BOIS DES TAILLES, thence by road through L.7, L.1, F.25, ARBRE FILIFORME.

99th Inf. Bde. will be clear of MORLANCOURT by 11 a.m. but will not pass road junction K.6.d.8.7. before 10 a.m.

(b). 6th Inf. Bde. will march to an area about the BOIS DES TAILLES, squares K.12 and 18, North of the BRAY - CORBIE road.

6th Inf. Bde. will move via MORLANCOURT, thence by track through squares K.9,10,11, but troops from SAILLY LE SEC can move by road junction J.18.c., thence by main CORBIE - BRAY road; head of column not to reach MORLANCOURT before 11 a.m.; column (including 10/D.C.L.I.) to be clear of SAILLY LE SEC by 10 a.m.

East Anglian Fd.Co.R.E.)
Bearer Div. 5th Fd.Amb.) will march under the orders of G.O.C., 6th Inf. Bde. as far as the N. end of BOIS DES TAILLES, and will proceed thence by the same route as the 99th Inf. Bde. to SAND PIT Valley where they will come under the orders of G.O.C., 99th Inf. Bde.

(c). 5th Inf. Bde.)
226th Fd.Co.R.E.)
Bearer Div. 6th Fd.Amb.) will march to the HAPPY VALLEY, squares F.26 and 27, moving by the SOMME VALLEY road as far as SAILLY LE SEC, thence to BRAY - CORBIE road at J.18.c., thence along the BRAY - CORBIE road. The column will not leave VAUX SUR SOMME before 9-30 a.m.

(d). 10/D.C.L.I. (Pioneers) will move immediately in rear of 6th Inf. Bde. to MORLANCOURT, under orders of G.O.C. 6th Inf. Bde.

(2). (a). Div. Artillery (less Medium Trench Mortar Batteries and S.A.A. Sections and Grenade Wagons D.A.C.) will remain in its present area.

(b). Medium Trench Mortar Batteries, and S.A.A. Sections and Grenade Wagons D.A.C. will move to MORLANCOURT under arrangements to be made by G.O.C., R.A. They will not arrive at MORLANCOURT before 2 p.m. They will march via CORBIE, SOMME VALLEY road as far as SAILLY LE SEC, thence by road junction J.18.c. and road junction K.20.b.

(3)..........

(3). Div. Train will move from its present areas under orders to be issued by the A.A. & Q.M.G.

(4). Advance parties will move to their new areas in sufficient time to ascertain bivouacs, water supply, etc., and to guide the troops to their destinations.

(5). All units will move with watercarts full.

(6). Arrival of troops which is not to be later than 5 p.m., in their new areas will be reported at once to Div. Hd. Qrs.

(7). Advanced Divisional Head Quarters will be at the CITADEL, F.21.b.

(8). Acknowledge.

Lieut. Colonel,

General Staff, 2nd Division.

Issued at 7 a.m.

Copy No.	To	
1	5th Inf. Bde.	
2	6th Inf. Bde.	
3	99th Inf. Bde.	
4	R.A., 2nd Divn.	
5	R.E., 2nd Divn.	
6	2/Signal Co.	
7	10/D.C.L.I.(Pioneers).	
8	A.D.M.S., 2nd Divn.	
9	A.P.M., 2nd Divn.	
10	2/Div. Train.	
11	"Q", 2nd Divn.	
12 & 13	XIIIth Corps.	For information.
14	3rd Divn.	For information.
15	9th Divn.	For information.
16	18th Divn.	For information.
17	30th Divn.	For information.
18	35th Divn.	For information.
19	1st Cavy.Divn.	For information.
20 - 24	G.S. Records.	

"A" Form. Army Form C. 2121.

MESSAGES AND SIGNALS. No. of Message

Prefix Code m. | Words | Charge | This message is on a/c of: | Recd. at m.
Office of Origin and Service Instructions. | Sent At m. To By | Service. (Signature of "Franking Officer.") | Date From By

TO 2nd Divn app 44

Sender's Number	Day of Month	In reply to Number	AAA
G937	23		

30th Division will be prepared to tack GUILLEMONT only or GUILLEMONT and FALFEMONT FARM together on morning of 25th aaa French will attack MAUREPAS when 30th attack FALFEMONT aaa If FALFEMONT not attacked 25th It will be attacked 26th aaa 30th Divn working parties will tonight construct such assembly trenches as are necessary for these attacks under arrangements to be made with 3rd and 35th Divns aaa 30th Divn will arrange to patrol tonight and tomorrow night the whole of the enemy defences to be attacked in order to discover wire cut and damage done aaa Tomorrow night the 30th Divn will take over from 3rd and

From
Place
Time

The above may be forwarded as now corrected. (Z)
Censor. Signature of Addressor or person authorised to telegraph in his name.

* This line should be erased if not required.

35146—W. & S. Ltd., London.—W 1789/1462—100,000—7/15. Forms C 2121/10.

"A" Form. Army Form C. 2121.

MESSAGES AND SIGNALS. No. of Message

Prefix ... Code ... m. | Words | Charge

Office of Origin and Service Instructions.

This message is on a/c of: ... Service.

Sent At ... m. To ... By ...

(Signature of "Franking Officer.") By

Recd. at ... m. Date ... From ... By ...

TO (2)

Sender's Number | Day of Month | In reply to Number | AAA

35th Divns such portions of their respective fronts as are necessary to form up for the attack aaa 3rd and 35th will remain responsible for defence of the front now held aaa Hour of both attacks will be notified later aaa 3rd Divn will continue to consolidate line now held and to gain ground in DELVILLE WOOD and towards GUILLEMONT as far as the railway aaa It will attack the trench parallel to and N.E. of the GUILLEMONT LONGUEVAL Road when 30th Divn attacks GUILLEMONT aaa Addrsd 3rd 30th and 35th Divns. repeated 2nd Divn GOC RA No 9 Squadron RFC. 15 Corps

From 13 Corps

Place

Time 3.35 pm

The above may be forwarded as now corrected. (Z)

Censor. Signature of Addressor or person authorised to telegraph in his name.

* This line should be erased if not required.

93146—W. & S. Ltd., London.—W 1739/1462—100,000—7/15. Forms C 2121,10.

"C" Form (Duplicate). Army Form C. 2123

MESSAGES AND SIGNALS. No. of Message........

	Charges to Pay. £ s. d.	Office Stamp.
Service Instructions. Priority RRC		

Handed in at RRC Office 12.35 a m. Received 2.45 a m.

TO 2nd Div.

Sender's Number	Day of Month	In reply to Number	AAA
G957	24		

GHQ wire that Germans are believed to be massing large forces on line GINCHY-FLERS possibly with a view to counterattack in direction of Montauban aaa Following moves will be carried out immediately aaa two Battalions 106th Brigade now at BAFTET Wood will be placed at disposal of GOC 3rd Division aaa GOC 3rd Division will at once move these two Battalions into the valleys in S22B & S23A where they will dig themselves cover immediately aaa Remainder of 106th Bde to move at once to Montauban & come under orders of GOC 3rd Division aaa 90th Infy Bde near Glatz Redoubt will be placed at disposal of GOC 35th Div aaa Acknowledge aaa Addsd 2nd 3rd 30th

FROM Divs 35th Div Reptd GOC RA 15th Corps
PLACE & TIME & 20th French Corps No. 9 Squadron

W 15680—M 151 75,000 Pads. H & S 4/16 Forms/C.2123. (5688)

R.F.C. 13 Corps 12.25 am

"G" Diary

APP. 45

app 45

2nd Division - CASUALTY RETURN FOR W/E Ending 22/7/16

UNIT.	KILLED. O.	KILLED. O.R.	WOUNDED. O.	WOUNDED. O.R.	MISSING. O.	MISSING. O.R.	Names of Officers and remarks.
H.Q., 2nd Division.							
H.Q., 5th Infy. Bde.							
2/Oxf. & Bucks L.I.							
/High. L.I.							
17th R. Fusiliers.							
24th R. Fusiliers.							
5th Bde M.G. Coy.							
5th Bde. T.M. Batty.							
H.Q., 6th Infy. Bde.							
1/Kings Regt.				2			
2/S. Staff. Regt.							
13th Essex Regt.				1			
17th Middlesex Regt.							
6th Bde. M.G. Coy.							
6th Bde. T.M. Batty.							
H.Q., 99th Inf. Bde.							
1/R. Berks Regt.							
1/K.R.R.C.							
22nd R. Fusiliers.				2			
23rd R. Fusiliers.							
99th Bde. M.G. Coy.							
99th T.M. Batty.							
10th D.C.L.I.							
H.Q., R.A., 2/Divn.							
34th Bde. R.F.A.							
36th Bde. R.F.A.							
41st Bde. R.F.A.							
V.2.T.M.Battery.							
X.2.T.M.Battery.							
Y.2.T.M.Battery.							
Z.2.T.M.Battery.							
H.Q., R.E., 2/Divn.							
5th Field Coy.R.E.							
226th Field Coy.							
E.A.Fd.Coy. R.E.							
2/Signal Coy.R.E.							
TOTAL.	-	-	-	5	-	-	

23/7/1916.

Feilding Major,
D.A.A. & Q.M.G., 2nd Division.

F I G H T I N G   S T R E N G T H.

2nd DIVISION. WEEK ENDED 22/7/16.

	"A" FIGHTING STRENGTH		"B" INCLUDED IN COL. "A" BUT NOT ACTUALLY WITH UNIT.		"C" DRAFTS RECEIVED SINCE LAST RETURN.		EXPLANATION OF ANY DISCREPANCY EXCEEDING ONE OFFICER AND 30 OTHER RANKS, OTHER THAN "C" BETWEEN FIGHTING STRENGTH SHEWN ON THIS RETURN, AND THAT SHEWN ON LAST.
	Officers	O.Ranks.	Officers	O.Ranks.	Officers	O.Ranks.	
Headquarters 2/Divn.	19	182	-	-	-	-	-
R.Artillery 2/Div.	97	2922	4	[illegible]	4	12	
Y/2 T.M.Batty.	2	23	-	[illegible]	-	-	
X/2 T.M.Batty.	2	27	-	-	-	-	
Z/2 T.M.Batty.	2	27	-	-	-	-	
V/2 T.M.Batty.	2	65	1	4	-	-	
R.Engineers 2/Divn.	27	779	-	10	-	3	
H.Q. 5th Inf.Bde.	4	69	-	-	-	-	
2nd Oxf.& Bucks L.I.	41	986	6	60	-	1	# Lt.Col.apptd.Brig.Gen.1st Naval Bde. 2 officers to England wounded.
2nd High.L.I.	30 #	870	5	112	11	-	∅ 1 officer sick & 1 transferred to R.E.
17th R.Fusiliers.	48	989	12	122	3	-	
24th R.Fusiliers.	31 ∅	963	6	107	-	-	
5th Bde.M.G.Coy.	10	142	2	-	-	-	
5th Bde.T.M.Batty.(a)	5	65	-	-	-	-	
TOTAL 5TH INF.BDE.	178	4084	31	401	14	1	
H.Q.6th Inf.Bde.	5	120	-	-	-	-	# 1 officer posted to Signal School BLETCHLEY.
1st King's (L'pool)	33 #	1043	4	160	6	-	∅ 1 officer to England, sick.
2nd S.Staffs.Regt.	38	1025	7	119	6	1	
13th Essex Regt.	36 ∅	952	7	122	2	-	
17th Middlesex Regt.	28	690	4	139	4	1	
6th Bde. M.G.Coy.	9	170	-	4	-	-	
6th Bde.T.M.Batty. (a)	4	71	-	-	-	-	
[illegible]	[illegible]	[illegible]	22	[illegible]	18	2	
H.Q.99th Inf.Bde.	5	92	-	-	-	-	
1st K.R.R.C.	29	1049	1	158	6	-	
1st R.Berks.	[illegible]	[illegible]	6	[illegible]	-	-	
22nd R.Fusiliers.	30	1027	6	93	4	-	
23rd R.Fusiliers.	37	1027	5	135	4	-	
99th Bde.M.G.Coy.	11	144	3	4	-	6	
99th Bde.T.M.Batty. (a)	5	65	-	-	-	-	
TOTAL 99TH INF.BDE.	154	4211	21	472	14	6	
10th D.C.L.I. (Pioneers)	28	960	-	26	-	-	
2/Divnl.Train.	23	404	3	8	-	-	
R.A.M.C.	30	698	2	18	2	7	
No.3 Mob.Vet.Sec.	1	27	2				
TOTAL 2ND DIVISION.	728	16658	84	1706	52	31	

(a) Included in strength of battalions.

22nd July, 1916.

Major General,
Commanding 2nd Division.

app46

2nd Division

War Diaries

General Staff

July 1916

"A" Form.

Army Form C. 2121.

MESSAGES AND SIGNALS.

No. of Message

Prefix ... Code ... m.	Words	Charge	This message is on a/c of:	Recd. at ... m.
Office of Origin and Service Instructions.	Sent		Service.	Date
	At ... m.			From
	To			
5th Bde RE 2 Div	By APM		(Signature of "Franking Officer.")	By

TO 6th Bde, Canadian, Det N... 3 Div, 1 Cav Div, 99th Bde, Q 2 Div, 2 Div G... Officer, 30 Div, 1/ DCLI, Q ... APM, XIII Corps, 36 Div, RA 2 Div, APM, 6 Div — 710

Sender's Number.	Day of Month	In reply to Number	
* G.621	25		AAA

Reference Para 8 of 2nd Div Order No.116

line 2 for S 12 c read F 12 c

From	Heart.
Place	
Time	~~EXRT~~ 9-45am.

The above may be forwarded as now corrected. (Z)

Censor.

J. Belgrave

Major,

General Staff.

Signature of Addressor or person authorised to telegraph in his name.

* This line should be erased if not required.

(1133) Wt. W14042–3.44 300,000 Pads 12/15. Sir J. C. & S.

"A" Form. Army Form C. 2121.

MESSAGES AND SIGNALS. No. of Message...........

Prefix............ Code............m.	Words	Charge	This message is on a/c of :	Recd. at..............m.
Office of Origin and Service Instructions. *	Sent		.... Service.	Date..............
	At..............m.			From..............
	To..............			
	By..............		(Signature of "Franking Officer.")	By..............

TO: OAK, FRUIT, STAR — FUZE, NARWAY — 125

Sender's Number	Day of Month	In reply to Number	AAA
* G 626			

[illegible]

From	
Place	
Time	

The above may be forwarded as now corrected. (Z)

Censor. Signature of Addressor or person authorised to telegraph in his name.

* This line should be erased if not required.

(A1) O. Ltd., London.— W.14012/M.44. 150,000 Pads. 12/15. Form C.2121.

"A" Form. Army Form C. 2121.

MESSAGES AND SIGNALS.

No. of Message...........

Prefix........... Code...........m.	Words	Charge	This message is on a/c of :	Recd. at ....m.
Office of Origin and Service Instructions.	Sent		.... Service.	Date
	At...........m.			From
	To			
	By		(Signature of "Franking Officer.")	By

TO 725

* Sender's Number	Day of Month	In reply to Number	AAA

[illegible] TANK [illegible]

[illegible]

[illegible]

[illegible] FRUIT

STAR [illegible] and NORWAY

From HEART

Place

Time 9.5 pm

The above may be forwarded as now corrected. (Z)

Censor. Signature of Addressor or person authorised to telegraph in his name.

[illegible] Major

* This line should be erased if not required.

(A1) O. Ltd., London— W.14042/M.44. 150,000 Pads. 12/15. Form C.2121.

"A" Form. Army Form C. 2121.

MESSAGES AND SIGNALS. No. of Message...........

Prefix.......... Code..........m. | Words | Charge | This message is on a/c of: ....Service. | Recd. at..........m.
Office of Origin and Service Instructions.

Sent At..........m. To.......... By..........

(Signature of "Franking Officer.")

Date.......... From.......... By..........

TO "Q"
SAUCE
ENGINE

525

Sender's Number	Day of Month	In reply to Number	AAA
* 9636	25		

New boundary between NERVE and Corps on the left is as follows ref map issued with NERVE summary dated 23/7/16 along western side of PELL MELL AAA Along northern side of DOVER STREET AAA Along Eastern side of CHEAPSIDE from junction with DOWN STREET Northwards AAA Between church and Chateau then through DELVILLE WOOD to SE corner of quadrangular copse S11d74 AAA Thence along SE side of LONGUEVAL-FLERS Road AAA A Bde. of the Divn. on our left will take over tonight from OAK the line up to this new boundary between Corps AAA

From ADV HEART
Place
Time 10 pm

The above may be forwarded as now corrected. (Z) [signature]

Censor. Signature of Addressor or person authorised to telegraph in his name.

* This line should be erased if not required.

(A1) O. Ltd., London — W.14042/M.44. 150,000 Pads. 12/15. Form C.2121.

[initials]

"A" Form. Army Form C. 2121.

MESSAGES AND SIGNALS. No. of Message...........

Prefix........... Code............m. | Words | Charge | This message is on a/c of: ....Service. (Signature of "Franking Officer.") | Recd. at..........m. Date.......... From.......... By..........

Office of Origin and Service Instructions.

Sent At..........m. To.......... By..........

TO APM "Q" 930

Sender's Number	Day of Month	In reply to Number	AAA
* G 641	25		

The joint Divisional prisoners cage has been moved from BILLON FARM and is now situated at F 23 c 9 4

From Adv HEART
Place
Time 10 pm

The above may be forwarded as now corrected.

(Z) [signature] Lt.

Censor. Signature of Addressor or person authorised to telegraph in his name.

* This line should be erased if not required.

(A1) O. Ltd., London— W.14042/M.44. 150,000 Pads. 12/15. Form C.2121.

SECRET. Copy No 23

2nd DIVISION ORDER No. 117.

~~Reference Map 1/~~20,000 and attached sketch. 26th July, 1916.

(1) The 99th Infantry Brigade (less the garrison of MONTAUBAN - 2 coys.) will attack and capture DELVILLE WOOD on the morning of the 27th July.

(2) The attack will be preceded by a bombardment of Heavy Artillery commencing at 6-10.am. Subsequent action of the Artillery and Infantry is shown on the following table :-

Hour.	Artillery Action.	Infantry Action.
6-10.am.	Artillery barrages line marked brown & North of it.	Infantry formed up in and in front of existing trenches.
7-10.am.	Artillery lifts to line marked in red & north of it.	Infantry advances to about line marked in brown and consolidates.
7-40.am.	Artillery lifts to line marked in green & North of it.	Infantry advances to line marked in red.
8-10.am.	Artillery lifts to line marked in blue (final barrage)	Infantry assaults final objective and consolidates.

A line about the line marked in brown when gained will be consolidated as well as the final objective, about 50 yards inside the northern and north eastern edges of the wood.

Divisional artillery will barrage on the same objectives and at the same time as the Heavy Artillery.

(3) A brigade of the 5th Division on our left will attack LONGUEVAL Village and the orchards to the north at the same hours, and the artillery barrages will be the same.

The dividing line between attacks is as shown in green on the sketch.

(4) The 99th Infantry Brigade will form up for the attack in the trenches now held by the Brigade, and also in SOUTH STREET and the new trench running from about S 18 central to near the end of LONGUEVAL ALLEY both of which will be temporarily handed over by G.O.C.5th Infantry Brigade to G.O.C. 99th Infantry Brigade, and re-occupied by 5th Infantry Brigade as soon as vacated. The new trench running N.W. from the Northern end of TRONES WOOD to LONGUEVAL may also be used by the 99th Infantry Brigade.

(5) The 6th Infantry Brigade will be in support to the 99th Infantry Brigade. 2 battalions, 6th Infantry Brigade will be moved up to positions between the trench mentioned last in para 4 and CATERPILLAR WOOD Valley. These two battalions will be at the disposal of G.O.C. 99th Infantry Brigade in the event of his requiring more troops to gain his objective. The remaining two battalions 6th Infantry Brigade will be moved so that they can occupy the positions vacated by the two leading battalions if the former are required by the G.O.C.99th Infantry Brigade and will then be at the disposal of that Commander.

... 2 ...

P.T.O

(6) G.Os. C, 6th and 99th Infantry Brigades will reconnoitre the places of assembly for their brigades and the routes for moving forward. Additional assembly trenches must be dug.

(7) In addition to the assaulting troops, G.O.C., 99th Inf. Brigade will detail parties to deal with dug-outs etc and troops for consolidation. He will also make special arrangements for securing his right flank during the attack and for keeping touch with the 5th Division on his left.

(8) Each man of the assaulting troops will carry at least two Mills grenades and two sandbags and the party detailed for consolidation will be provided with cutting as well as entrenching tools.

(9) The provision of cover for troops detailed to hold the objective after capture is of the utmost importance. Consolidation will be carried out with a view to holding the lines gained mainly with machine and Lewis guns, but they should be constructed so as to allow of lateral movement. At least one communication trench must be dug forward from our present front line.

(10) In the event of the G.O.C, 99th Inf. Brigade not employing the battalions of the 6th Inf, Brigade he will inform Divisional HQ. when these battalions are no longer required in their forward positions: they will then be withdrawn under the orders of the Divisional Commander.

Cancelled

(11) Infantry must take every opportunity of gaining ground under the artillery barrages and of assaulting immediately the barrages lift.

Acknowledge

[signature]

Lieut-Colonel,
General Staff, 2nd Division.

Issued at 7.a.m. to :-

Copy No 1 to 5th Inf. Bde.
2 6th Inf. Bde.
3 99th Inf. Bde
4 10/D.C.L.I.(Pioneers)
5 R.A., 2nd Divn.
6 R.E., "
7 2/Signal Co.R.E.
8 "Q", 2nd Divn.
9. A.D.M.S. 2d Divn.
10 A. D.V.S. "
11 A.P.M. "
12 O.C. Det. Northumberland Hussars.
13 2/Div Gas Officer.
14 XIII Corps "G")
15 XIII Corps "Q")
16 3rd Division.)
17 5th ")
18 30th ") For information.
19 35th ")
20 55th ")
21 1st Cavalry Division.)
22 - 26 G.S. Records)

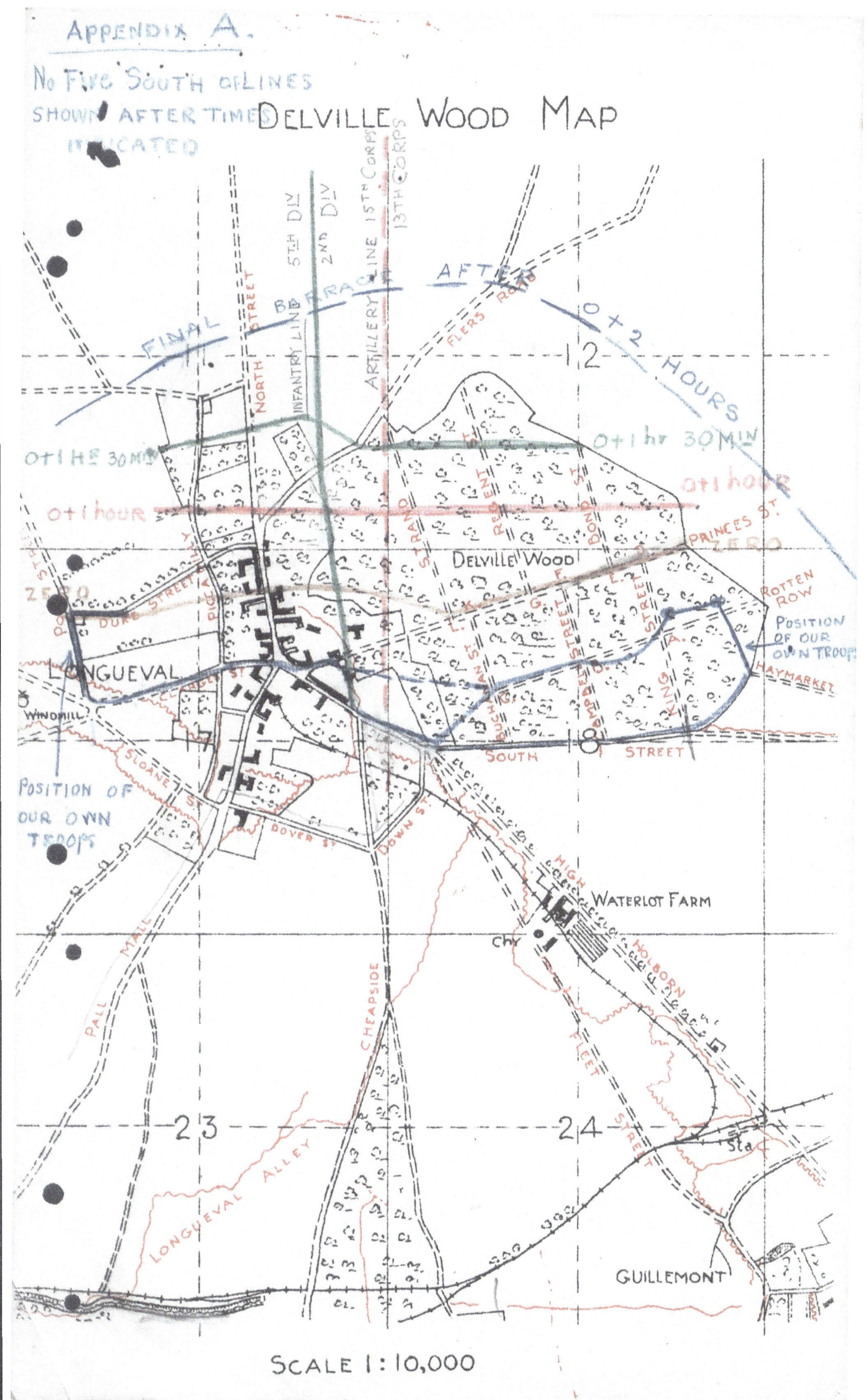

APPENDIX A.
No FIVE SOUTH OF LINES SHOWN AFTER TIMES INDICATED
DELVILLE WOOD MAP
5TH DIV
2ND DIV
INFANTRY LINE
ARTILLERY LINE 15TH CORPS
13TH CORPS
FINAL BARRAGE AFTER 0+2 HOURS
NORTH STREET
FLERS ROAD
0+1 HR 30 MIN
0+1 hr 30 MIN
0+1 hour
0+1 hour
PRINCES ST.
ZERO
ZERO
DELVILLE WOOD
ROTTEN ROW
POSITION OF OUR OWN TROOPS
HAYMARKET
STRAND
REGENT ST
BOND ST
BUCHANAN ST.
CAMPBELL STREET
KING
DUKE STREET
PICCADILLY
LONGUEVAL
WINDMILL
SOUTH
STREET
POSITION OF OUR OWN TROOPS
SLOANE ST
DOVER ST
DOWN ST.
HIGH
WATERLOT FARM
Chy
HOLBORN
PALL MALL
CHEAPSIDE
FLEET STREET
LONGUEVAL ALLEY
11
12
17
18
23
24
Sta
GUILLEMONT
SCALE 1:10,000

Copy No. 24

Amendment to 2nd Division Order No. 117.

26th July, 1916.

Paragraphs 5 and 10 of the above orders are cancelled. The attack will be carried out by the 99th Inf. Brigade only. The 6th Inf. Brigade will remain in its present area, but ready to move at short notice.

The E. Anglian Field Coy. is placed at the disposal of the G.O.C. 99th Inf. Bde. for the operation.

Dgeddes.
Lieut. Colonel,
General Staff, 2nd Division.

Issued to all recipients
of 2nd Div. Order No. 117.

SECRET.

Copy No.....

AMENDMENT No. 2 to 2nd DIVISION ORDER No. 117 dated 26-7-16.

26th July, 1916.

The following Table is substituted for that shown in para. 2, which is cancelled :-

New Para.2. The attack will be preceded by a bombardment of Heavy and Field Artillery commencing at 6-10 a.m. Subsequent action of the Artillery and Infantry is shown on the following Table:-

Hour.	Artillery Action.	Infantry Action.
6-10 a.m.	Artillery barrages line marked brown and North of it.	Infantry formed up in and in front of existing trenches.
7-10 a.m.	Artillery lifts to line marked in red and North of it.	Infantry advances to about line marked in brown and consolidates.
8-10 a.m.	Artillery lifts to line marked in green and North of it.	Infantry advanced to line marked in red.
8-40 a.m.	Artillery lifts to line marked in blue (final barrage).	Infantry assaults final objective and consolidates.

Maps issued with original order must be amended accordingly.

NOTE.

Bombardment by Division on our left begins 1 hour before ours, but their infantry attack takes place at the same time.

ACKNOWLEDGE.

Issued at 11-10 pm

Copies sent to all recipients of 2nd Div. Order No.117.

C. Geddes.
Lieut. Colonel,
General Staff, 2nd Division.

"A" Form. Army Form C. 2121.

MESSAGES AND SIGNALS. No. of Message

Prefix ... Code ... m	Words	Charge	This message is on a/c of:	Recd. at ... m.
Office of Origin and Service Instructions.	Sent		... Service.	Date
	At ... m.			From
	To			
	By		(Signature of "Franking Officer.")	By

TO 2nd Division.

Sender's Number	Day of Month	In reply to Number	AAA
	26		

F.O.O. 52nd Bde reports as follows 18 Pdr Shells which were dropping short at about 8am and 11am into area S.18.b appear to come from direction of western edge of MONTAUBAN aaa Rep

XIII Corps

As this has been frequently reported may the matter be referred to XV Corps. It is suggested that the battery in question may possibly belong to the 33rd Divn.

10/

From 9th D.A.

Place

Time 3.8 pm

X1

The above may be forwarded as now corrected. (Z) G.K. Hayter Lt

Censor. Signature of Addressor or person authorised to telegraph in his name.

* This line should be erased if not required.

T. & W. & J. M. Ltd., London. W 14042/M44. 75,000 12/15. Forms C 2121/10.

Office

matter be referred to XV Corps. It is suggested that the battery in question may possibly belong to the ~~..th~~ 32nd Division.

W. G. Walker

Adv. H.Q. 2nd Divn.
26th July, 1916.

Major-General,
Commanding 2nd Division.

REPORT.

F.OO. 52nd Bde reports as follows :-

18 pdr. shells which were dropping short at about 8.a.m. and 11 am. into area S. 18 b appear to come from direction of western edge of MONTAUBAN AAA

Office

G.A.1001/1/10

XIII Corps.

As this has been frequently reported, may the matter be referred to XV Corps. It is suggested that the battery in question may possibly belong to the ~~30th~~ 33rd Division.

Sg. W.G. Walker

Adv.H.Q. 2nd Divn.
26th July, 1916.

Major-General,
Commanding 2nd Division.

S E C R E T.

2nd Divn. No.

G.S. 935/27

Subject :- COMMUNICATION BETWEEN INFANTRY AND AEROPLANES.

5th Inf. Bde.
6th Inf. Bde.
99th Inf. Bde.
10/D.C.L.I.
RA., 2nd Divn.
R.E., 2nd Divn.
2/Signal Co.
"Q", 2nd Divn.

The aeroplane which works with Infantry is a B.E.2.c., and has the ordinary bullseyes with black stripes (aa) alongside them, and two black streamers (c.c.) on the struts.

9th Squadron, which works with us, also has a black mark on the fusilage (b).

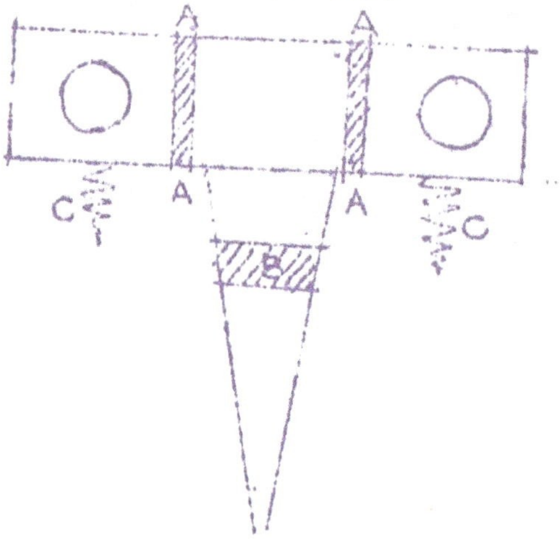

A A C A A C B

The aeroplane carries a Claxon horn to attract the attention of Infantry, and fires a white light meaning " We are ready to observe". As soon as this light is seen, put out ground sheets and "panels" and send Battalion call with panel or lamps.

Machine answers with the same call and Battalion continues with the call till machine sends the same call, Battalion then sends T.

Any other code call can then be sent, such as N N = "Short of ammunition" or any short message. Send slowly - make a long pause between letters.

Flares are sent up from front line only as soon as aeroplane fires a white light.

Calls from aeroplane must be answered. If they are not answered, the aeroplane will probably fly lower, and so run more risk. Six machines have been destroyed in this way since 1st July.

H.Q., 2nd Divn.

26-7-1916.

C.H.Steward Capt: G.S.
for Lieut. Colonel,
General Staff, 2nd Division.

"A" Form.

Army Form C. 2121.

MESSAGES AND SIGNALS.

No. of Message..........

Prefix.......... Code.......... m. Office of Origin and Service Instructions.	Words	Charge	This message is on a/c of: ....Service. (Signature of "Franking Officer.")	Recd. at..........m. Date.......... From.......... By..........
	Sent At..........m. To.......... By..........			

TO { 5th Inf Brigade

*Sender's Number.	Day of Month	In reply to Number	AAA
G 666	26 July		

The Divisional Commander wishes you to ascertain the state of the German Trenches shown in the accompanying air photographs and to take steps to occupy them as a "jumping off" place for a further advance Eastward. AAA Your plan for this operation must include joining up the western end of the trench with "South Street" and the southern end with our present line S. of WATERLOT FARM AAA The operation should be carried out as soon as possible

Operations file

26 7

From 2nd Div

Place

Time 3 pm

The above may be forwarded as now corrected. (Z) [illegible]

Censor. Signature of Addressor or person authorised to telegraph in his name.

* This line should be erased if not required.

(4198) Wt. W14042—M44. 300000 Pads. 12/15. Sir J. C. & S.

"A" Form. Army Form C. 2121

MESSAGES AND SIGNALS. No. of Message

Prefix Code m. Words Charge

Office of Origin and Service Instructions.

Sent At m. To By

This message is on a/c of: Service.

(Signature of "Franking Officer.")

Recd. at m. Date From By

TO TOOLS 865

Sender's Number.	Day of Month	In reply to Number	AAA
* G775	29	G925	

My G.733 reads as follows begins GOC STAR will assume command of left Bde Section of HEART front at 12 noon today aaa Detailed orders will follow aaa acknowledge ends. this is the Bde now on your right

From ADV. HEART

Place

Time 12.25 AM

The above may be forwarded as now corrected. (Z)

Censor. Signature of Addressor or person authorised to telegraph in his name

J. D. Belgrave Major G.S.

* This line should be erased if not required.

(4198) Wt. W14042—M44. 500000 Pads. 12/15. Sir J. C. & S.

"A" Form.
MESSAGES AND SIGNALS.

Army Form C. 2121.

No. of Message

Prefix Code m.	Words	Charge	This message is on a/c of:	Recd. at m.
Office of Origin and Service Instructions.	Sent		Service.	Date
	At m			From
	To			
	By		(Signature of "Franking Officer.")	By

TO STAR (891)

Sender's Number.	Day of Month	In reply to Number	
* G 796	29		AAA

A wounded German officer captured two days ago states that in a dugout situated about S 17 b 7.7 there are some papers of considerable importance AAA I G H Q are asking for these papers and if a search of dugouts in this area could be made if opportunity offers much valuable information might be obtained

From ADV HEART
Place
Time 7.45 pm

The above may be forwarded as now corrected. (Z)

Censor. Signature of Addressor or person authorised to telegraph in his name.

[signature] Major

G.S.

* This line should be erased if not required.

(4198) Wt. W14 42—M44. 300000 Pads. 12/15. Sir J. C. & S.

2nd Divn.No.
G.S. 1001/1/17.

5th Inf. Bde.
6th Inf. Bde.
99th Inf. Bde.
R.A., 2nd Division.

G.O.C., 99th Inf. Bde. will place one Battalion in Divisional Reserve ready to move at an hour's notice from 6 a.m. to-morrow.

H.Q., 2nd Divn. B Belgrave Major for Lieut. Colonel,
29-7-1916. General Staff, 2nd Division.

2nd DIVISION
GENERAL STAFF
No. 2nd Divn. No.
G.S.1001/1/19.
Date

5th Inf. Bde.

I wish to call your attention to the fact that no message was received from the 2/Oxf. & Bucks L.I. for 4 hours after ZERO and none has been received from the 24/Royal Fusiliers as far as I am aware, all day.

Even now I am uncertain whether the trench in S.18.d. is held by us or not.

In view of the fact that I have been receiving constant reports all day by runner from the Artillery O.P. near WATERLOT FARM, I consider that more information and reports should have been forthcoming, and would like you to report what efforts were made to get it them through.

H.Q., 2nd Divn.

30-7-1916.

W. G. Walker
Major-General,
Commanding 2nd Division.

SECRET

2nd DIVISION
GENERAL STAFF
No. 2nd Divn. No.
G.S.1001/1/21.
Date.......

5th Inf. Bde.
6th Inf. Bde.
99th Inf. Bde.
C.R.E., 2nd Divn.
10/D.C.L.I.

The Corps Commander has directed that the following trenches are of immediate importance and must be dug first -

(a). the trenches referred to in G.S.1001/1/20 dated 30-7-1916.

(b). a trench from about S.18.c.7.0. to S.17.d.9.5.

(c). a trench from S.17.d.9.5. to join with the new trench running from the N. end of TRONES WOOD to the S. end of LONGUEVAL.

(d). a communication trench from the S. end of LONGUEVAL to the N. end of BERNAFAY WOOD.

(e). ~~assembly~~ trenches across the trench mentioned in (d). for shelter from shell fire

The C.R.E. will issue instructions to Field Companies R.E. and the 10/D.C.L.I. to ensure that these trenches are proceeded with first.

G.O's C. Brigades will assist with working parties.

H.Q., 2nd Divn.
30-7-1916.

Lieut. Colonel,
General Staff, 2nd Division.

SECRET

Office

2nd Divn. No.
G.S.1061/1/20.

5th Inf. Bde.
6th Inf. Bde.
99th Inf. Bde.
C.R.E., 2nd Divn.
10/D.C.L.I.(Pioneers).

The Divisional Commander wishes efforts to be made to gain ground by digging.

A communication trench, fire stepped to face S. must be dug from the WATERLOT FARM system back to TRONES WOOD and the existing trench deepened.

Trenches must also be dug about 100 yds apart in front of and roughly parallel to the existing trench E. of TRONES.WOOD beginning nearest to the Wood.

1 Section, 226th Fd. Co.R.E. and 1 Company 10/D.C.L.I. will be available for the work under instructions to be issued by the C.R.E. The work will be carried out under the orders of O.C. 226th Fd.Co.R.E. to whom the O.C. Company 10/D.C.L.I. will report.

G.O.C., Inf. Bde. holding right Section will assist with working parties.

H.Q., 2nd Divn.
20-7-1916.

Lieut. Colonel,
General Staff, 2nd Division.

2nd Divn. No.
G.S.1001/1/22.

5th Inf. Bde.
6th Inf. Bde.
99th Inf. Bde.
R.A., 2nd Divn.
R.E., 2nd Divn.
"Q".

DIVISIONAL COMMANDER'S CONFERENCE,
31-7-1916.

(1). Brigadiers report considerable number of dead bodies in LONGUEVAL ALLEY and in the South of DELVILLE WOOD. It was arranged for G.O.C., 5th Inf. Bde. to send 100 men to-night to bury bodies in the first named place and for G.O.C., 6th Inf. Bde. to send a party of 50 men to the last named place.

(2). In future Brigades will render to Divisional Headquarters "G" " TRENCH STRENGTH RETURNS" by first D.R. in the morning.
All that is required is two headings -

(X). Officers and other ranks available for FIGHTING.

(Y). Officers and N.C.O's available in Reserve area to replace casualties.

The above can be sent by telegram under headings X and Y.

(3). Brigadiers report that the white rockets supplied for "S.O.S." are defective and dangerous.

(4). Brigadiers suggest that stretcher bearers going up to forward areas should carry water with them, as water is very scarce in front. 5th Division are being asked for permission to use wells in LONGUEVAL.

H.Q., 2nd Divn.

31-7-1916.

Lieut. Colonel,
General Staff, 2nd Division.

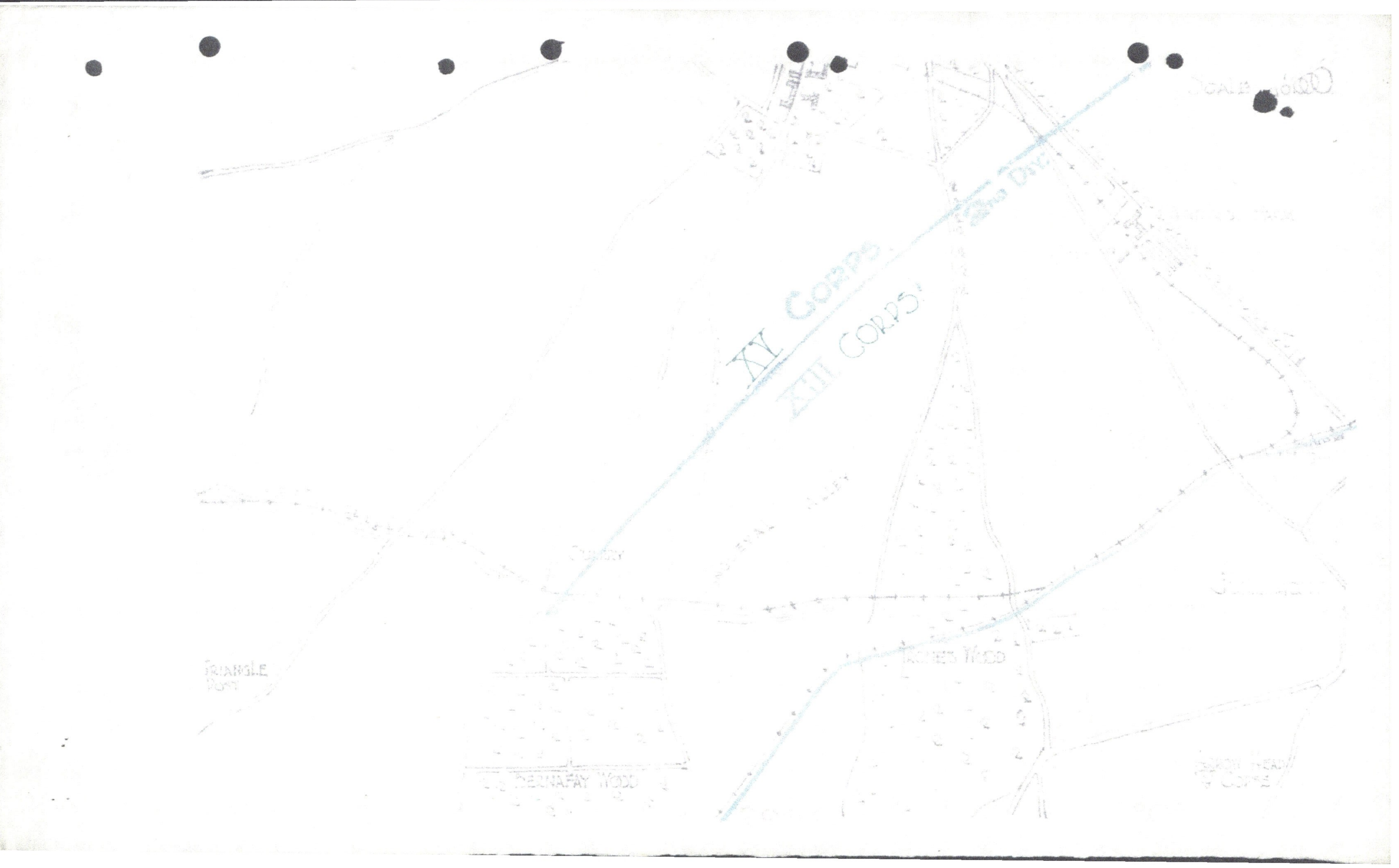
XV CORPS
XIII CORPS
BERNAFAY WOOD
TRIANGLE POINT

5th Inf. Bde.

In your Tactical Progress Report up to 4 p.m. 31st inst., you report as follows :-

> " During the operation in the early morning of 30th, one company of 17/R.Fus. was unable to occupy, as ordered, ANGLE TRENCH, which had not been vacated by the 24/R. Fus. "

Please say at what hour this took place.

C.H. Steward Capt. G.S.
for Lt. Colonel,
General Staff, 2nd Division.

H.Q., 2nd Divn.
31-7-1916.

2

HEADQUARTERS
No. G.S.
222
5th INFANTRY BRIGADE

2nd Division

Reference minute 1, the Company of 17th R. Fus. referred to was ordered in 5th Bde Order No 144 to reach E end of LONGUEVAL ALLEY at 0.8 so as to replace the Company of 24th R. Fusiliers in Angle Trench when it advanced to dig trench for connection of German line with S E corner of Delville Wood. The order for this advance was to emanate from O C 24th R Fusiliers at such time after 0.8 (4.53 AM) as he considered the situation admitted of work being carried out, but the order was not given as O C 24th R. Fus did not consider the conditions admitted of digging. The Company was at once withdrawn on receipt of a message from O C 17th R Fusiliers that accommodation in Angle Trench was not available for the Company

[illegible] Br. General

1/8/16.

Comdg 5th Inf. Bde

GSO II

SECRET. 2nd Divn.No.G.S. 1001/1/51.

NOTES ON EXPERIENCE GAINED DURING THE RECENT OPERATIONS.

(Compiled from a Conference held on 15th August and from reports from Brigadiers).

----

(1). The necessity for following close under our own artillery barrage.

Heavy artillery must not lift too long before the Field Artillery lifts at ZERO, otherwise the enemy will expect an attack - about 2 minutes will probably be sufficient. In this connection it may be possible to "drill" the Germans beforehand, so that when our real attack starts they may have their heads down.

Long halts must be made between artillery lifts in order to allow plenty of time for cleaning up and consolidating ground gained. In villages 8 to 12 hours may be necessary between each lift. The failure of the attack on GUILLEMONT was partly due to the lifts being too quick.

(2). As regards "cleaning up", it is no doubt necessary for a definite "wave" of attack to be told off for this purpose: clearing up parties are not sufficient. Whether this "wave" is the first or one of the succeeding ones depends on circumstances, but as a rule the first "wave" should be told off for this duty and the succeeding "waves" should pass through it to the second, third, etc., objectives.

In "cleaning up" it is not sufficient to bomb dug-out entrances, sentries must be posted to watch the exits to prevent the enemy trying to come up and attack after our troops have passed.

(3). It is most important to have special parties to watch and protect the flanks; this is more particularly the case on the flanks of Battalions and Brigades: flanking parties must be ready to form defensive flanks, in the event of attacks on the flanks of their units failing while theirs have succeeded, and also to prevent the enemy working in on the flanks & rear of our troops, as happened at GUILLEMONT.

(4). As many men as possible must be got over "No Man's Land" as soon as our own artillery has lifted and before the enemy puts down his barrage and gets his machine guns into action. Supporting troops must keep touch with those in front of them so that the latter may be in no doubt that they will be supported. This does not absolve troops in front from using all means in their power to keep connection with their rear and flanks and to communicate with their superiors.

(5). Great care must be exercised in taking over a battle line without giving up ground. The responsibility lies largely with company and platoon commanders. Connection with troops on the flanks while taking over a line and also when flanking troops are carrying out reliefs is of special importance, otherwise touch may be lost and ground which should have been held, given up.

(6). Pigeons have proved most successful; they should be kept at Battalion Head Quarters; larger numbers are required when active operations are in progress and each basket should have its own gas bag.

As regards other means of communication, runners require careful organisation. As a rule they should be worked on the relay system and a man should not have to go more than 400 to 500 yards. Relay posts should be placed in as safe positions as possible, and runner routes should be selected with a view to avoiding the enemy barrage. Runners must know the position of all units in the Brigade.

Telephone wires should always be run out across "No Man's Land"; some of the lines may escape being cut.

(7)........
P.T.O.

(7). The organisation of working parties requires consideration. Troops must be exercised in the drill of forming up, extending and getting to work on their tasks. This must be practised both by day and night and should be carried out from the time when the party reaches the rendezvous. Brigadiers will ask for R.E. assistance while their Brigades are out of the line for the purpose of carrying this out.

(8). As soon as a position has been gained -

(i)(a). Push posts to the front.
(b). Dig as fast and as deep as possible, on a definite plan arranged as far as possible beforehand.
(c). Get Lewis guns into position in front line and support line.
(d). Get some machine guns up into front line, and some just in rear of the flanks of the front line.
(e). Other machine guns should be placed in the support line, the digging of which line should be carried on with the utmost despatch.
(f). Remainder of the Machine Gun Company should be kept in reserve, but, if possible, positions should be prepared for the reserve guns in suitable places.

(ii). Relief of the battalions that formed the front "waves" of attack should be carried out as soon as possible.

(9). To hold the position when it has been gained -

(i). Rely on Machine Guns and Lewis guns for the fire power necessary to beat off a determined attack.
(ii). Only retain a sufficient number of infantry in the forward positions to -
(a). form a chain of posts, especially at night, to prevent penetration of position by small parties of the enemy.
(b). protect machine and Lewis guns from snipers and bombers.
(c). patrol, and clear out, any enemy still lying concealed in the position.
(d). allow of sufficient men for continuous work on the defences.

NOTE. It must be remembered that while machine and Lewis guns can provide all the fire power required to beat off determined attacks, they cannot :-
(a). protect themselves against snipers and bombers.
(b). prevent small parties of the enemy from creeping up and penetrating our lines.
(c). dig trenches.

(10). Up to 25% of an Infantry Brigade was required for carrying parties prior to the attacks on DELVILLE WOOD and on Z...Z trench and GUILLEMONT STATION. This number will probably be considerably reduced if time is given to Brigadiers and Commanding Officers to make their arrangements.

(11). It is not realised how long it takes for orders to reach Company Commanders.

Preliminary orders are sent out from Divisional and Brigade Headquarters, but final arrangements cannot be made until final orders are received from higher commanders.

S.S.119, para.15, says that 6 hours is the maximum that is necessary for orders to pass from Corps to Company H.Q. Under conditions such as prevailed near DELVILLE WOOD and GUILLEMONT this is greatly underestimated. Not only did the actual message take longer than this but even when it was received, arrangements had to be made under conditions which demanded a considerably longer time.

All Commanders must take into consideration the time required for their orders to reach those under their command. It is not sufficient for the orders to reach them; the orders have to be read, understood and acted upon.

(12)......

(12). The hour when an attack should be begun has often been discussed. The early morning undoubtedly assists the assembly of troops and to a certain extent allows of a concealed advance in the semi-darkness.
This hour, however, has drawbacks -

(a). On account of the mist which is usually found in the early morning. In our attacks on Z..Z trench and GUILLEMONT railway station, there is no doubt that some of the assaulting troops lost direction and touch.

(b). Aeroplanes cannot see mirrors and flares for an hour or so after the attack has been launched. In the case of flares, men become absorbed in the fighting, casualties occur and the result is that flares are not lit; this is more particularly the case if the advance is a rapid one.

(c). Our artillery cannot observe so effectively as later in the day.

The afternoon is the best time to attack provided our heavy artillery can counter battery effectively. This appears to be the crux of the whole question and obviously requires most minute and detailed location and registration of the enemy batteries known to be active and also a reserve of guns working with aircraft to deal with guns which open from positions not previously located.

If these measures are adopted (and the French appear to have been successful in doing so), the advantages of a daylight over a dawn attack cannot be overstated.

(13). WOODS. The line should be consolidated about 50 yards from the edge with posts on the edge. If the line is further back it is almost impossible to prevent small parties of the enemy creeping up and occupying the edge of the wood.

H.Q., 2nd Divn.

16-8-1916.

C.W. Geddes.
Lieut. Colonel,
General Staff, 2nd Division.

W 74—664 250,000 3/15 L. S. & Co. Army Form W. 3091.

Cover for Documents.

2nd DIVISION
GENERAL STAFF
No. G.S. 1001/4/
Date

Nature of Enclosures.

OPERATIONS FROM 20th JULY, 1916, to
****

MEMOS, INSTRUCTIONS ETC RECEIVED FROM DIVISION ON RIGHT.

Notes, or Letters written.

S E C R E T.

Reference Trench Map
GUILLEMONT, 1/20,000.

Copy No. ..4.....

55th (WEST LANCASHIRE) DIVISION ORDER No.24.

5th August 1916.

1. The following moves will take place tonight :-

(a). The 165th Infantry Brigade will take over that portion of the front now held by the 164th Infantry Brigade from the junction of the 77th Brigade (French) about A.6.a.4.2 to the road exclusive at S.30.d.5.7.

The Brigadier 165th Infantry Brigade will assume command of the front allotted to him at 6 p.m. at which hour the Battalion of his Brigade, lent to 164th Infantry Brigade and located in DUBLIN and CASEMENT Trenches, will return to his command.

(b). The 165th Infantry Brigade, less three Battalions with the 164th Infantry Brigade, will move into the area now occupied by the 166th Infantry Brigade.

(c). The 166th Infantry Brigade, less two battalions, will move into the CARTET WOOD Area (now occupied by the 165th Infantry Brigade). The remaining two battalions to move into the CITADEL Area.

No movement will take place before 8 p.m., when it will be by platoons at 200 yards interval.

2. The 166th Infantry Brigade will carry on with the completion and construction of the trenches in his area in accordance with a programme that will be handed over to him by the 164th Infantry Brigade.

3. The battalion 165th Infantry Brigade remaining with the 164th Infantry Brigade will return to its Brigade on the night 7th/8th on relief by troops of the 164th Infantry Brigade.

4. Details of moves to be arranged between Brigadiers concerned.

5. Completion of moves to be reported to Division Head-Quarters.

acknowledged

M. Cochrane

Lieut. Colonel.
General Staff, 55th (W.Lanc) Division.

Issued at 4.15 p.m.

Copy No.		Copy No.	
1	XIII Corps "G".	10	1/4 S.Lan.R.
2	" "Q".	11	A.D.M.S.
3	39th (French) Div.	12	A.P.M.
4	2nd Division.	13	Train.
5.	Div.Arty.	14	"Q".
6	Div.Engnrs.	15	G.S.
7	164th Inf. Bde.	16	[illegible]

SECRET.

Copy No. 12......

35th DIVISION ORDER No.44

26.7.1916.

1. On the night of 26/27th July the 105th Infantry Brigade will relieve the 104th Infantry Brigade, taking over the front line trenches from the junction with the French near MALTZ HORN FARM to the junction with the 2nd Division where the railway leaves the eastern edge of TRONES WOOD.
The relief of the front battalion will not commence before 10.30 p.m.

2. On relief 104th Infantry Brigade will bivouac in the Reserve Area near MINDEN POST.

3. The 106th Infantry Brigade will occupy the trenches in GERMANS WOOD area as the 105th Infantry Brigade moves out.

4. Completion of reliefs will be reported to Divisional Headquarters by wire.

5. Details of reliefs will be arranged between Brigades concerned.

E. Makin Major
for Lt-Col. G.S.
35th Division.

Issued at 10 a.m.

Copies to:- A.D.C.(for G.O.C)
G. Branch.
A. Branch.
C.R.E.
C.R.A.
A.D.M.S.
104th Inf. Bde.
105th " "
106th " "
19th North.Fus.(Pioneers)
30th Division.
2nd Division.
153rd Div. (French).
XIII Corps.
35th Div. Signals.
" " Train.
Diary.

Acknowledged [illegible]
[illegible]

W—664 250,000 3/15 L. S. & Co.

Army Form W. 3091.

Cover for Documents.

Nature of Enclosures.

OPERATIONS FROM 20th JULY, 1916, to____________
****

MEMOS., INSTRUCTIONS, ETC., RECEIVED FROM

DIVISION ON THE LEFT.
****

Notes, or Letters written.

SECRET.

5th Division Operation Order No. 109.

29th July, 1916.

Reference - Trench maps 1/10,000.

1. 5th Division will carry out an offensive operation to-morrow 30th instant in conjunction with 51st Division, with a view to establishing a line from DELVILLE WOOD about S.11.d. 80/85 - S.11.d 0/8 - S.11.c. 55/80 - thence N.W. to HIGH WOOD.

2. Preparatory to the above 95th Infantry Brigade will endeavour to establish themselves to-day on the line shown in RED on attached map under the following arrangements :-

(a). From 5, to 5.30 p.m., Heavy Artillery will fire on the line S.11.d. 0/8 - S.11.c. 55/80 thence N.W. towards HIGH WOOD.

(b). From 5 to 5.30 p.m. 5th Divisional Artillery assisted by 33rd Divisional Artillery, will bombard the following points :-

S.11.c 8/8.
S.11.c. 88/20.
S.11.d. 0/8.
S.11.d. 30/57.
N.W. edge of Copse in S.11.d central.

At 5.30 p.m. all above field guns will lift on to an approximate east and west line through S.11.d. 0/8, paying special attention to this point.

Before this lift takes place, the Infantry will endeavour to push forward as close as possible to their objectives, which they will seize immediately the lift occurs.

(c). The Field Artillery mentioned in sub-para. (b) will continue to fire on S.11.d 0/8 and to east and west of it until 8 p.m., at which hour the guns will lift off point S.11.d. 0/8 while keeping up their fire to the flanks and to the north of it.

(d). Infantry patrols will be pushed forward with the object of seizing if possible and consolidating point at S.11.d. 0/8 at 8 p.m.

(e). From 8 p.m. onwards the guns will maintain a barrage on both flanks, and to the north of S.11.d. 0/8.

(f). Every effort will be made to consolidate the several points when gained, and, after dark, to connect them up and securely establish the RED line marked on attached map.

3. 13th Inf. Bde. will relieve the 95th Inf. Bde. to-night under arrangements to be made between Brigadiers concerned.

4. Until further orders the 15th Inf. Bde. will find all carrying parties etc. required by the Brigade in the line.

ACKNOWLEDGE.

done

Lt.Colonel,

Issued at ______ p.m. General Staff, 5th Division.

Copies to C.R.A., C.R.A., 13th, 15th and 95th Bdes., A.D.M.S. and Q.

S E C R E T.

5th Division.
S.485/17. 19

The 5th Division will be relieved by the 17th Division on the night August 1st/2nd.

The 15th Inf. Bde. now in the line, will be relieved by the 52nd Inf. Bde. under the following provisional arrangements :-

The front will be taken over by 3 battalions 2 of which will move up in small parties during daylight to-morrow and will relieve the 2 battalions of 15th Inf. Bde. in support.

The 51st Inf. Bde. will move to the POMMIERS ridge.

The 50th Inf. Bde. will remain in the reserve area probably west of FRICOURT.

The 5th Division after relief will move to an area about RIBEMONT.

Detailed orders for relief will be issued later.

5th Division,
31/7/1916.

Lt.Colonel,
General Staff, 5th Division.

Copies to all concerned.

"C" Form (Duplicate).
MESSAGES AND SIGNALS.

Ar... (In books ...) No. of Mes...

Charges to Pay. £ s. d. | O... Stamp.

Service Instructions.

Handed in at .... Office .... m. Received .... m.

TO 3rd Div

Sender's Number	Day of Month	In reply to Number	AAA
[illegible]	25		

9th Inf Bde will tonight
take over from 76th Inf
Bde of 3rd Div 13th
Corps the [illegible] of
[illegible]
[illegible]
[illegible]
XI [illegible]
[illegible] PALL MALL [illegible]
[illegible] DEVER STREET
[illegible] along eastern side of
CHEAPSIDE [illegible] DOWN
STREET [illegible]
and [illegible] through DELVILLE
WOOD [illegible] SE [illegible] of
CAT ARGYLE [illegible]
[illegible]

FROM
PLACE & TIME [illegible]

Wt.432–M437 500,000 Pads. H W V 5/16 Forms C.2123.

"C" Form (Original).
MESSAGES AND SIGNALS.

Arm… (In books o… No. of Mess…

Prefix......Code......Words......	Received	Sent, or sent out	O… …p.
£ s. d. Charges to collect	From...... By......	At......m. To...... By......	
Service Instructions.			

Handed in at ...... Office ......m. Received ......m.

TO [illegible]

*Sender's Number	Day of Month	In reply to Number	AAA

[illegible] LONGUEVAL [illegible]

FROM
PLACE & TIME [illegible]

* This line should be erased if not required.

Wt. 432—M437 500,000 Pads. H W V 5 16 Forms C. 2123.

W 74—664 250,000 3/15 L. S. & Co.

Army Form W. 3091.

Cover for Documents.

2nd DIVISION
GENERAL STAFF
No. G.S. 1008/5.
Date

Nature of Enclosures.

OPERATIONS FROM 20th JULY , 1916 to ______________

MEMOS, INSTRUCTIONS ETC RECEIVED FROM BRIGADES, R.A. R.E. etc of 2nd DIVISION.

Notes, or Letters written.

Copy No 7

SECRET

Arrangements for Raid by 1st King's on night July 3rd/4th.

1. Objects of Raid are ;-

(a) To inflict as much loss as possible on the enemy.
(b) To destroy suspected mine shaft at S.15.c.4½.4.
(c) To take prisoners (at least 2) and capture Machine Guns
(d) If no prisoners taken, to obtain identification by other means.

2. Troops to be employed :-

5 Officers and 60 men 1st King's, accompanied by demolition party to be detailed by O.C., 182nd Company R.E.
Of these 2 Officers, 48 men 1st King's and party 182nd Coy. R.E. will form assaulting party - 1 Officer and 12 men in close support, who will also find stretcher parties and maintain communication with O.C., Battalion.

3. The itinerary will be as follows:-

(a) The assaulting party followed by the supports will creep out and beyond our own wire, between S.15.c.2.0. and S.21.a.5.8., in sufficient time to be lying down in dead ground about 60 yards from the objective and facing N.N.E. by Zero hour.

(b) At ZERO hour the R.A., Stokes Mortars and Machine Guns will open fire simultaneously.

R.A. Objective - Barrage S.15.d.1.3. and S.21.c.0.9. and German Line S.E. from these points, paying special attention to suspected M.G.Emplacements.
Also at S.15.d.1½.6., S.15.d.8.8., S.15.d.9.8. and S.E. from the latter two points.
These barrages should completely isolate the garrison of the point to be raided from all reinforcements.
Nature of fire - Intense.

Stokes Mortars. - Six Mortars in vicinity of VINCENT STREET to give intense fire at ZERO for one minute and then stop, on objective of raiders.

Machine Guns. - 1 sweeping objective and firing from our Front Line at about S.15.b.2.2. Fire of this gun to cease after 1 minute.
2 other guns placed so as to continuously sweep the ground under Artillery barrage

(c) At 0.1 minutes, Officer i/c Raiding Party will give signal either by "four in hand" method or syren and the assaulting party will at once dash at the position.
Separate parties will already have been detailed for various duties such as to cut wire, if necessary, block communication trenches, bomb dug-outs, seize and carry away Machine Guns if possible, collect and pass out prisoners, search for papers, identifications, etc., Any men not told off for any special jobs will kill Germans for all they are worth.

(d) The time for withdrawal will have to be judged by the Officers on the spot in conjunction with the Officer, 182nd Coy. R.E. but, probably, at the utmost 15 minutes will be spent in the enemy's trenches. The signal for withdrawal will be long blasts on the syren whistles. A code word will also be arranged. Anyone using the word "retire" will be shot at once.
A special party under an Officer will be told off to cover the retirement and remain till they are satisfied that the whole party, including any wounded are well on their way back.
The raiders will return to our trenches by the same way as they went out, taking advantage of the dead ground.

(e).-

(e) If the Officer in charge of Raiders wants any covering fire during the withdrawal, he will flash an electric torch back in direction of our front line. On this signal the six Stokes Mortars (before referred to) will at once open an intense fire over the heads of our men who are withdrawing. This fire will be supplemented by Rifle Grenade fire, which will be arranged by O.C., 1st King's.

4. As soon as the party are all in the O.C. 1st King's will at once inform Brigade Head Quarters – code word "GOFF" which will be passed on to Divisional Artillery, who will stop barrage. Should the telephone wire be out, he will convey the information by firing RED Very Lights, in groups of two, from Battalion Head Quarters. In the event of barrage being again required the code word will be "HUGO" or if telephone wire is out RED Very Lights, fired in groups of three.

A visual signal station for D.D. messages will be established at ALHAMBRA from 11.45 p.m.

5. Dress and Arms for Raiding Party will be as follows:-

Attacking Party – Rifle and Bayonet, 60 rounds Ammunition and 2 Bombs.

Selected Men – Revolvers and Knobkerries and 2 Bombs.

Bombers – Knobkerries and 12 Bombs each.

Every man to carry wirecutters.

Faces blackened and all identification marks and papers removed.

Every Officer and man to be cautioned that, if taken prisoner, he is not to disclose anything, except Number, Rank, Name and Regiment (NOT Battalion).

6. Should the Raiding Party be discovered by the enemy at any time before ZERO hour, the Officer in charge of the party will have a "G" sounded on a bugle, on which Stokes Mortars will take action as already detailed for ZERO. The Artillery being at once informed – Code Word "SAUNDERS". The Raid will then be carried through as described in para. 3

7. O.C., 1st King's will withdraw bombing posts from CENTRAL AVENUE and OLD BOOTS TRENCH at midnight (3rd/4th), they will be re-established as soon as bombardment permits.

They should be warned of the possibility of having to withdraw at anytime after 11.45 p.m., should the Raiding Party be discovered.

8. O.C., 1st King's will send an Officer to notify ZERO hour and explain operations to O.C., Battalion, 51st Division, on our right.

O.C., 17th Middlesex Regt., has already received instructions as to action to be taken by his Battalion.

9. Hd.Qrs. 5th Infantry Brigade, O.C., 228th Coy. R.E., O.C., 182nd Coy. R.E., have been informed of intended enterprise.

10. ZERO hour has already been communicated confidentially to all concerned.

M. Henderson

Major,

3/7/1916. Brigade Major, 6th Infantry Brigade.

Copy No. 1 – 1st King's (to be shown to O.C. 182nd Coy. R.E.
2 – O.C. 6th Bde. T.M. Group (to be shown to O.C. 6th Bde. Machine Gun Company.)
3 – R.A., 2nd Division.
4 – 2nd Division.
5 – Office, 6th Infantry Brigade, to be seen by O.C., 2nd South Staffordshire Regt.

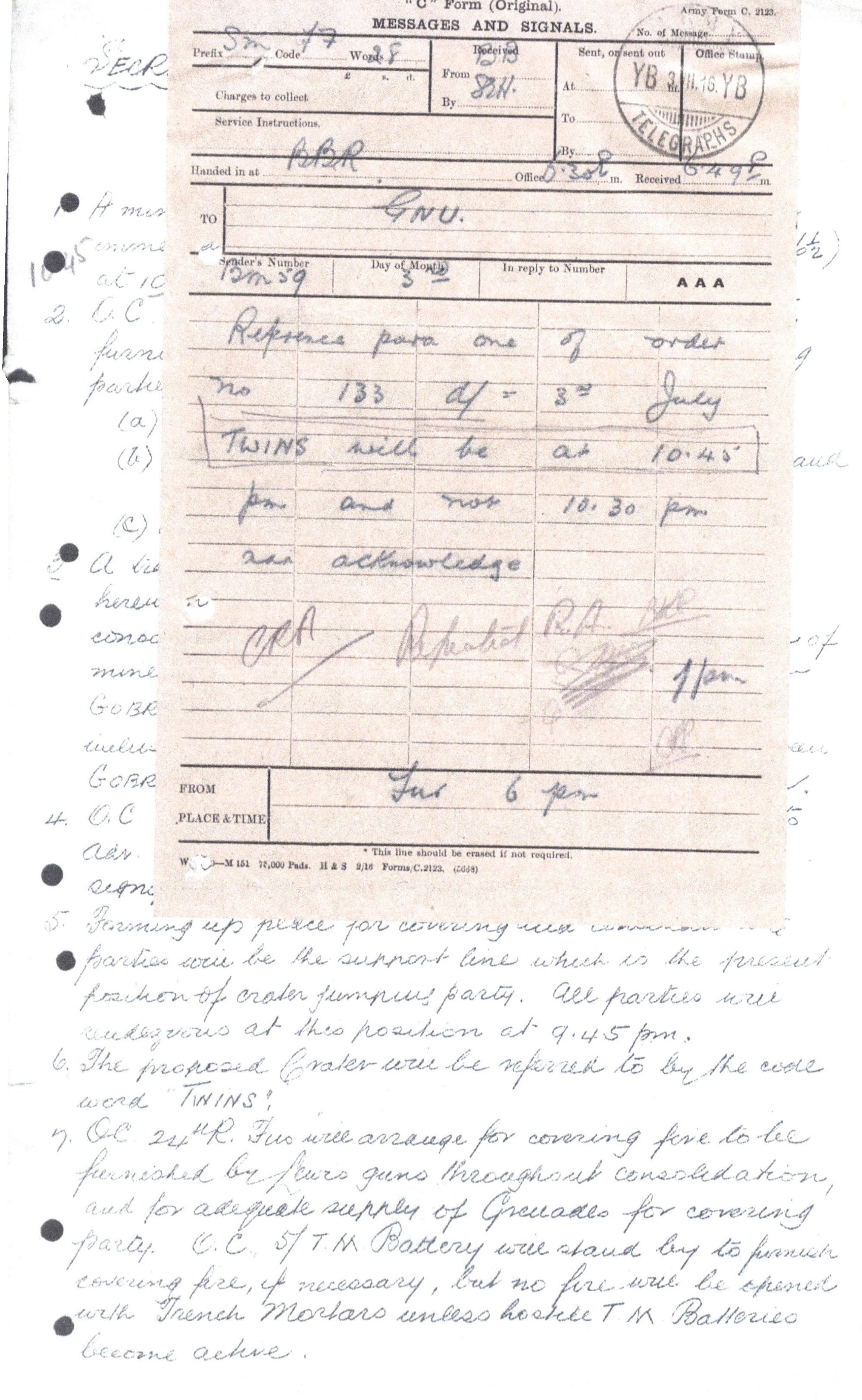

SECR...

"C" Form (Original).

MESSAGES AND SIGNALS.

Army Form C. 2123.

No. of Message ......

Prefix SM Code 47 Words 28	Received BB	Sent, or sent out	Office Stamp
Charges to collect £ s. d.	From 82H	At ......m.	YB 3 VII. 16. YB TELEGRAPHS
Service Instructions.	By	To	
		By	

Handed in at ABR Office 5.30 p m. Received 6.49 p m.

TO GNU.

Sender's Number	Day of Month	In reply to Number	AAA
BM59	3rd		

Reference para one of order no 133 d/- 3rd July TWINS will be at 10.45 pm and not 10.30 pm aaa acknowledge

CRA / Repeated R.A.

1 pm

FROM PLACE & TIME: Fur 6 pm

* This line should be erased if not required.

W...—M 151 75,000 Pads. H & S 2/16 Forms/C.2123. (5068)

1. A mi...
1045 imme...
at 10...
2. O.C. ...
furni...
parti...
(a) ...
(b) ... and
(c) ...
3. A li...
heren...
conso... of
mine...
GOBR...
inclu...
GOBR...
4. O.C. ...
adv...
signi...

5. Forming up place for covering and consolidating parties will be the support line which is the present position of crater jumping party. All parties will rendezvous at this position at 9.45 pm.

6. The proposed Crater will be referred to by the code word "TWINS".

7. O.C. 24th R. Fus will arrange for covering fire to be furnished by Lewis guns throughout consolidation, and for adequate supply of Grenades for covering party. O.C. 5/T.M. Battery will stand by to furnish covering fire, if necessary, but no fire will be opened with Trench Mortars unless hostile T.M. Batteries become active.

SECRET Copy No.

5th Inf Bde Order No 133.

3/7/16.

1. A mine will be blown in CARENCY Section immediately S^o of MOMBER Crater (S.15.a.1½.6½) at ~~10.30~~ 10.45 pm to night.
2. O.C. 24th R. Fus will in conjunction with R.E. furnish the following consolidating and covering parties –
   (a) One Officer and 12 Bombers.
   (b) One Officer 2 N C Os + 30 men with 30 shovels and 10 picks.
   (C) One Officer + 11 other ranks R.E.
3. A tracing showing probable Crater is forwarded herewith to O.C, 24th R.Fus. Crater to be consolidated in the same method as in the case of mine blown on 28/6/16. All troops between GOBRON and Sap leading to LOVE Crater (both inclusive) and as far West as our front line between GOBRON and TANCHOT inclusive to be withdrawn.
4. O.C 24th R. Fus. will send the Code word "BOX" to Adv. Brigade Head Quarters before 10.30 p.m., signifying the danger zone has been cleared.
5. Forming up place for covering and consolidating parties will be the support line which is the present position of crater pumping party. All parties will rendezvous at this position at 9.45 p.m.
6. The proposed Crater will be referred to by the code word "TWINS".
7. OC 24th R. Fus will arrange for covering fire to be furnished by Lewis guns throughout consolidation, and for adequate supply of Grenades for covering party. O.C., 5/T.M Battery will stand by to furnish covering fire, if necessary, but no fire will be opened with Trench Mortars unless hostile T.M. Batteries become active.

8. All ranks will be warned that on no account are they to descend into the Crater. The covering party of Bombers, will, on the explosion of the mine proceed at once to the Crater and work forward round the lips so as to cover the consolidating party effectively. The latter party will follow the Bombers at an interval of 70 yds.

9. O.C. 24th R. Fus will detail a relief of 1 N.C.O and 3 men for each "T" head on W lips of Crater with rations, water, and ample supply of bombs for 24 hours. These men will take over the posts shortly before daylight and may be isolated for the day.

10. Rifles with fixed Bayonets and 1 bandolier will be carried by the consolidating party.

11 O.C. 34th Brigade R.F.A will stand by to barrage enemy's trenches in vicinity of crater from the explosion of the mine. Fire will be called for if required.

12. O.C. 24th R. Fus will detail a carrying party of One Officer and 40 Carriers to report at H.Q. 5th Field Coy R.E at 8.30 pm tonight at CABARET ROUGE. This party will bring up requisite material for consolidation. 5th Field Coy R.E will furnish a guide.

13. O.C. 24th R. Fus will ~~[illegible]~~ synchronise watches with mining Officers concerned.

14. Reports to Adv. Brigade H.Q.

15 Acknowledge.

J D Boyd. Captain
Brigade Major
5th Inf Bde

17th R. Fus.
24th R. Fus.
2nd High. L.I.
2nd Oxf & Bucks L.I
5th Field Coy R.E.
5/T.M. Battery.
5th M.G. Coy.
34th Bde R.F.A
6th Inf Bde.
2nd Division (G)
140th Inf Bde

21/7/16 –

My dear Geddes

I am enclosing 2 copies of an address to my Artillery – Any comments or criticisms will be welcome –

Yours

[illegible]

operations file

BB 227.

P.S. These were written before I had seen or heard of the notes issued by 1st Divn. whose experience seems to agree their soundness.

NOTES FOR FUTURE OPERATIONS.

General Remarks. 1. The fighting in which the Brigade will soon find itself involved has now reached a stage closely assimilating to open warfare - though many of the features pertaining to Trench War, such as bombing and T.M. work, still constantly recur.

Successful results, for the Infantry, will more than ever depend on skilful handling of their commands by Regimental Officers and N.C.Os.

The long period of Trench Warfare to which we have grown accustomed has led us to forget, to a great extent, those principles of mutual support (and above all covering fire) which are so clearly laid down in Ch. VII, para. 105, Field Service Regulations, Part I, which should be re-studied by all.

Covering Fire. 2. (a). It must be impressed on all ranks that they must be prepared to accept the risk of casualties from our own shell fire and to advance as close as possible to their objective under our own artillery barrage.

Casualties will possibly be caused by our own shells but the general result in 9 cases out of 10 will be a successful assault and a great saving of life to our own men.

There comes a moment when the artillery must lift and this is the phsycological moment when success or failure hang in the balance. If the Infantry are close up and can rush in at once before the enemy has time to man his defences and machine guns, all will be well.

This is the secret of the French successes. The reason why so many of our attacks, in the past, have failed, is that the Infantry have been too far from their objective at the moment of the artillery "lift" and in consequence have been caught in the open by concentrated Machine Gun fire before they could get to grips with the enemy.

(b). In addition to covering artillery fire, no forward movement against an unbeaten enemy should be undertaken (unless the nature of the ground absolutely prohibits it) without strong covering rifle, Machine Gun and Lewis Gun fire.

This principle must always be applied down to the smallest units and occasions may often accur when it will be the only form of covering fire.

The STOKES Mortar, whenever it can be employed, is invaluable for covering an Infantry assault and has the additional advantage that it's fire can be kept up after the artillery has been obliged to "lift". Ammuniton supply for the STOKES Mortar is, unfortunately, a very difficult problem in a moving fight.

Lewis Guns, employment of, 3. The adequate supply of ammunition for Lewis Guns is likely to present serious difficulties.

Their particular value probably lies in repelling counter attacks. Lewis Gun fire in an attack, must therefore be carefully regulated and waste of ammunition avoided.

Measures against Counter Attack. 4. All positions captured must be at once put into a state of defence.

Battalion Commanders must always have the pick and shovel supply in mind. Counter attacks are inevitable.

If the Infantry are well protected and Lewis and Machine Guns are well sited, with plenty of ammunition, the more the enemy counter attack the better. Killing Germans is more useful than merely occupying ground.

Officers. 5. The very large number of Officer casualties which occur is apt to seriously prejudice success.

It is without doubt that many of these casualties are avoidable. Battalions should go into action with the smallest necessary number of officers - 3 a company should suffice to start with - the remaining Officers and a proportion of N.C.Os should be held in reserve.

Officers must not take unnecessary risks. It is a very glorious thing to die for one's country but much more useful to live for it and it is the duty of every officer, whilst playing his part to the utmost, to avoid becoming a casualty as long as possible.

The British Soldier thoroughly appreciates the fact that his Officers are prepared to be killed first and it is not, at this stage of the war, desirable for an officer to go out of his way to give further proof of it.

Certain occasions, of course, arise when the officers must sacrifice themselves but, at other times, they should endeavour to control and handle their men as long as possible without doing anything foolhardy.

The men are well aware of their officers' courage and depend on them.

Early casualties in officers means more casualties in other ranks who become as "sheep without a shepherd".

Water Supply.

6. The matter of getting water up to the fighting troops is a very difficult one and will be accentuated by the present hot weather.

O.C. Battalions must improvise every method which occurs to them for taking as much water as possible with the Battalion when it goes up to the firing line.

For instance, certain men in each platoon might be detailed to carry tins or jars of water, or extra water bottles.

Waste of water must be avoided and no unwounded man allowed to drink without permission from an officer or senior N.C.O.

Very Pistols.

7. A reserve of Very Pistols and lights must be kept at Battalion Headquarters.

8. Enough copies of these notes are issued for each Platoon Commander to have one and Commanding Officers must ensure that their contents are made known to all ranks.

A C Daly

21.7.16.

Brigadier General,
Commanding 6th Infantry Brigade.

SECRET.

5TH INFANTRY BRIGADE
ORDER NO.142.

Copy No. 11.

Reference Maps :-
62.D 1/40,000 and
62 N.E. 1/20,000.

2nd Divn GS. 1601/13/72

23rd July 1916.

1. The 5th Infantry Brigade will move to-day to the HAPPY VALLEY (F.26 and 27.) 226th Field Company R.E. and one Bearer Section of 6th Field Ambulance will accompany the 5th Infantry Brigade.

2. Units will proceed independently from their respective Billets at the following times:-

2ND HIGHLAND LT.INFTY and 2ND OXF. & BUCKS LT.INFTY., 10.30 am.
17TH ROYAL FUSILIERS and 24TH ROYAL FUSILIERS, ... 10.45 am.
5TH BRIGADE M.G. COY at 11.15 am.
5TH LIGHT MORTAR BATTERY to follow immediately behind 24TH ROYAL FUSILIERS.
226TH FIELD COY. R.E., at 11.30 am.
BEARER DIVN. 6TH FIELD AMBULANCE at 11.45 am.
5TH BRIGADE HEAD QUARTERS at 12 noon.

Lorries will be provided for packs (2 per Battalion, one for 5th L.M. BATTERY, and one for 5TH BDE.H.Q. The 5th BDE. M.G. COY will arrange to send their Cooks cart on ahead of the detachment if so desired). The above Lorries will not be available until later in the day and parties will remain behind to take charge of packs until loaded on the lorries. Packs will be collected for this purpose at some place in the vicinity of the Head Qrs of the Unit.

3. Route will be as follows :-

Route junction I.35.b.5.0 - Road junction I.36.a.5.8. - VAUX SUR SOMME SAILLY LE SEC, thence to CORBIE-BRAY RD at J.18.c. thence along CORBIE - BRAY RD to Cross Roads at L.13.Central and HAPPY VALLEY.

4. One Mounted Officer per Unit (except 5th L.M.Battery) and Brigade Transport Officer will meet the Staff Captain at Cross Roads L.13 Central at 12 noon. These Officers will be shown the bivouac area for their Unit, water supply etc, and will conduct their Units on arrival at cross roads L.13 Central direct to their respective areas.

5TH L.M. BATTERY will be shown their area on arrival.

5. All Units will move with water carts full.

6. All first line transport will move with their units and will be Brigaded on arrival at HAPPY VALLEY by arrangement of Brigade Transport Officer.

7. Arrival of Battalions etc which is not to be later than 5 pm, in their new areas will be reported at once to Brigade Head Quarters.

8. Brigade Head Quarters will close at CORBIE at 12 noon and open at HAPPY VALLEY at about 4 pm.

9. ACKNOWLEDGE.

J. D. Boyd
Captain.
Brigade Major,
5th Inf. Bde.

Issued at 5.30 am.

Copy No.1 2nd Oxf. & Bucks L.I.
2 2nd Highland L.I.
3 17th Royal Fusiliers.
4 24th Royal Fusiliers.
5 5th Brigade M.G. Coy.
6 5th L.M. Battery.
7 Bde.Transport Officer.
8 " Signal Officer.
9 - 226th Field Coy.R.E.
10 - O.C.,Bearer Sub-Divn 6th Field Amblc
11 - 2nd Divn (G.S.)
12 - 2nd Divn (Q).
13 - Staff Captain.
14 - War Diary.
15 - Office.

****

SECRET. Copy No. 1

99th INF. BDE OPERATION ORDER No. 30.

Ref. Maps:-
1/40,000 and 1/20,000. 23rd July 1916

1. The 99th Inf. Bde will move today to SAND PIT VALLEY, Squares F.13 and 19. It will march via Squares K.9, 10, 11, to N. end of BOIS DE TAILLES, thence by road through L.7, L.1, F.25, ARBRE FILIFORME.

2. 5th Field Company R.E, and Bearer Div. 100th Field Ambulance will remain at MORLANCOURT and will come under the orders of G.O.C. 6th Inf. Bde.

3. E. Anglian Field Company R.E. and Bearer Div. 5th Field Ambulance will join 99th Inf. Bde in SANDPIT VALLEY, and come under the orders of G.O.C. 99th Inf. Bde.

4. The Starting point will be Road Junction E. end of Village K.9.a.

5. The Brigade will pass Starting Point as follows :-

23 R.Fus.	...	10 a.m
1/R.Berks.	...	10.10 am
1/K.R.R.C.	...	10.20 a.m.
99th Coy. M.G.Corps.		10.30 a.m.
99th T.M.Battery.		10.40 a.m.
22 R.Fus.	...	10.50 a.m.

Units will proceed independently by the route ordered.

6. All Units will march with full watercarts.

7. Advance parties for taking over bivouac and guiding Battalions will meet the Staff Captain at Road Junction, Point 107, F.25.b. at 10.15 a.m.

8. ACKNOWLEDGE.

G. Lindsay.
Major.
Brigade Major.
99th Inf.Bde.

Issued at 8.30 am.

Copy No.1.to 2nd Div."G".
2. ,, "Q".
3. 5th Inf.Bde.
4. 6th Inf.Bde.
5. R.A. 2nd.Div.
6. R.E. 2nd Div.
7. Bde Sig.Officer.
8. A.D.M.S. 2nd.Div.
9. 2nd Div'l Train.
10. 5th Field Co.R.E.
11. 100th Field Amb.
12. E.Anglian F'd Coy.

Copy No. 13. 5th Field Amb.
14. 22 R.Fus.
15. 23 R.Fus.
16. 1/R.Berks.
17. 1/K.R.R.C.
18. 99th Coy.M.G.Corps.
19. 99th T.M.Battery.
20. Staff Captain.
21. Bde Transport Officer
22.& 23 War Diary.
24. File.
25, 26, 27, 28, Spares.

Acknowledged
A.B.

2 Divn HQ
GS 1001/15/9

SECRET. A.D.M.S.,2nd Div.No. 4/1140.

SUMMARY OF EVACUATION.

The line about to be taken up by the Division extends roughly from the North of LONGUEVAL to the East of TRONES WOOD T.24.c.5.0.

Field Ambulance Bearers work from Regimental Aid Posts backwards to Bearer Post at North End of BERNAFAY WOOD by hand carriage and wheels. Thence to BRIQUETERIE A.4.b. From this point cars and horse ambulances can be used on the road day and night and proceed via MARICOURT - BILLON FARM (F.30.) - BRONFAY FARM - SAPPER CORNER - MAIN ROAD - DIVES COPSE.

Field Ambulance H.Q. which works line is at SAPPER CORNER (L.15.b.) and acts as a car dump and controls ambulance traffic, enquiring origin of any evacuating cars which pass and automatically sending up another to replace it. Thus the BRIQUETERIE and other places are always supplied with cars. Walking cases are directed on foot or in passing vehicles to BRONFAY FARM (MAIN WALKING DRESSING STATION) (F.29.b.) These are evacuated thence on lorries.
Sick should be sent to BRONFAY FARM.

Medical officers should apply for all medical requirements to Officers in Command Bearer Divisions attached to their Brigade.

H.Q., 2nd Div.,
24.7.16.

[signature] Captain, R.A.M.C.,
for A.D.M.S.,2nd Division.

Copies to :-

O's.C. Nos. 5.6.100 Field Ambulances.
O's.C.Bearer Divisions, Nos. 5.6.100 Fd.Ambs.
Officers in Medical Charge Units.
"G" 2nd Division.
H.Qrs., 5.6.99th Infantry Brigades.

2nd Div No
GS 1001/2/10

SECRET   Copy No 5.....

99th INFANTRY BRIGADE OPERATION NOTES. No 1.

July 24th 1916.

1. CONSOLIDATION OF POSITIONS.

(A). TRENCHES. The immediate digging of very deep and narrow trenches is of the utmost importance.

In order to facilitate and quicken this work the following type of trench will be adopted in the Brigade.

Stages :- (See sketch below).

(i) Dig pits 4 yards long by 2'6" wide. These pits should be made 5 yards apart. Garrison of each pit 4 men.

First stage.

(ii) Dig similar pit 4 yards long, 4 yards in rear of interval.

(iii) Join ends of forward pits to those of rear pits, and generally continue improvement of trench. Thus a trench as per sketch will be made.

Final stage.

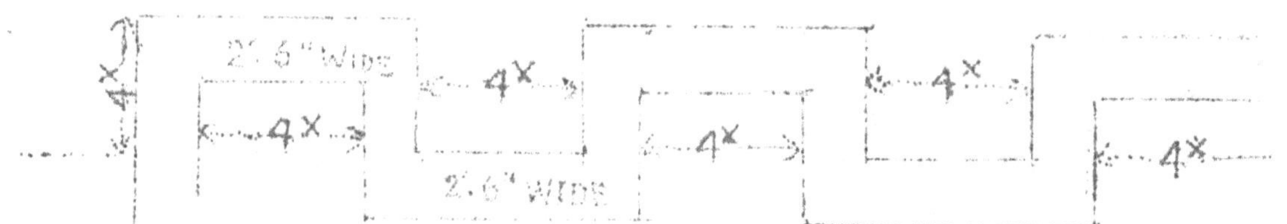

NOTES. (a) Dimensions are given as a rough guide.
(b) Positions for machine guns and Lewis guns should be a primary consideration, and the work of preparing these positions should be begun without a moments delay.

(B). WIRING. This will only be done at night except in exceptionally favourable circumstances.

(C). CROWDING OF FRONT TRENCHES. When a position has been consolidated, and when Machine and Lewis guns are in position, the infantry should be "thinned out" as much as possible.

The idea is to be able to produce sufficient fire power to beat off any counter-attack with the smallest number of men.

Thus a system of defence against counter-attacks which relies principally on Machine guns and Lewis guns, supported by a comparatively small number of Riflemen and Grenadiers

(i) reduces casualties amongst the infantry by the fact that the fewest possible number of men are kept in the front trenches;

(ii) Enables the infantry to be kept in hand, ready for delivering counter-attacks, or a renewal of the offensive.

NOTE :- While it is recognised that the above is a difficult operation, it is one that should be carefully considered by all Comdg. Officers, and acted on whenever possible.

(D). OBSERVATION OF SHELL FIRE. As certain localities are always more heavily shelled than others, the German shell fire should be carefully observed and noted.

This will often enable certain areas to be avoided, or troops moved from them when shelling commences, and thus much unnecessary loss of life avoided.

When a certain area is constantly shelled, it may often be found possible to cover that area by Machine gun fire from flanks, rear or both, and thus avoid the necessity of actually occupying it with troops.

(E). CONSOLIDATING PARTIES. O's C. units must give careful thought to the organisation of these parties. They should not go forward until it is certainthat the objective has been gained, but that they must then be brought forward as rapidly as possible. They must bring with them heavy tools, axes, wire, stakes, sandbags,etc.

(F). ASSISTANCE IN ALL CONSOLIDATION WORK, will be given to battalions by the ~~Xth Xxxxx~~ East Anglian Field Coy. R.E. under arrangements to be made by the O.C. that unit.

2. FIGHTING KIT.

The following will be the fighting kit for infantry of the Bde:-

(a) Rifle, bayonet, scabbard, entrenching tool.
(b) Haversack and mess tin on back.
(c) 170 rounds S.A.A.
(d) 4 sandbags per man.
(e) 2 grenades per man.
NOTE. Definite instructions must be given that no grenades are to be thrown except by the authorised grenadiers.
(f) Steel helmets.
(g) The unexpended portion of the day's ration, iron rations and full water bottle.
(h) A proportion of heavy tools, wire cutters, and gloves to be carried by assaulting waves.
(i) A proportion of Very Lights and Very pistols, and rockets per Company.

3. MOPPING UP PARTIES.

Small parties of riflemen and grenadiers should be told off to follow assaulting waves. These parties are to clear up trenches and dug-outs passed over by the attack. They should be allotted definite tasks.

4. COMMUNICATION WITH REAR.

Careful arrangements must be made by O.s C. units for communi-cation with Rear, sending back of prisoners, working parties and carrying parties whose task is accomplished, etc.

5. ROLE OF MACHINE GUNS.

(a) The O.C. Machine Gun Company will make every effort to
(i) Cover the advance of the infantry.
(ii) Guard its flanks.
(iii) Locate and engage enemy machine guns.

(b) He will also be prepared to push forward a proportion of guns to assist in the consolidation of the position gained.

These guns should not go forward until it is reasonably certain that the infantry has secured the objective. The approximate positions for these guns should be decided before they advance.

(c) Not more than 4 trained gunners per gun should go into action at any one time, the remainder should be held in reserve.

Carrying parties will be provided from the Reserve battalion, and trained gunners must not be used for unskilled work.

(d) Each gun should be accompanied by at least one selected rifleman to protect it against snipers. These will be provided from the reserve battalion.

ROLE OF LEWIS GUNS.

(a) As the successful beating off of a heavy counter-attack will depend ~~xxxxxxx~~ greatly on the work of the Lewis guns, and as the bringing up of magazines may be a matter of great difficulty, it is very necessary to avoid a heavy expenditure of ammunition before the assault has gained its objective.

These guns should not be pushed forward too early, as this will incur serious loss to the gunners. They will go forward earlier than the machine guns, but not before there is a reasonable certainty that the first waves are established in their new position.

(b) Only a proportion of trained Lewis gunners should go into action at any one time, the remainder being kept in reserve.

Carriers, as required, must be detailed from men not trained in the gun, as otherwise trained gunners will be wasted on unskilled work, and this is on no account to be allowed.

7. CARRYING PARTIES FROM ATTACKING BATTALIONS.

O's C. Units must very carefully consider this question, as upon the proper organisation of these parties the ability of a unit to maintain itself in a position gained very greatly depends.

A detailed scheme for carrying parties must be worked out in every unit.

8. CARRYING PARTIES FROM RESERVE BATTALIONS.

The battalion in reserve will have to supply the following parties :-

(a) For Staff Captain.

4 Officers, 8 N.C.O's, 200 privates.

(b) For Machine Gun Company.

(i) 16 selected riflemen for protection against snipers (See para. 5(d)).

(ii) 2 N.C.O's and 64 Privates as carriers.

(c). For Trench Mortar Battery.

4 N.C.O's and 80 men as Carriers.

9. A detailed scheme for Dumps, Rations, Water, Carrying parties, etc. must be drawn up by the Staff Captain.

J C Bott Capt
for Major.
Brigade Major.
99th Inf. Bde.

Copy No.1. to G.O.C.
2. Bde Major.
3. Staff Capt.
4. 2nd Div. "G".
5. 2nd Div. "Q".
6. 22 R. Fus.
7. 23 R. Fus.
8. 1/R. Berks.

Copy No.9. to 1/K.R.R.C.
10. East Anglian F'd Coy R.E.
11. 99th Coy.M.G.Corps.
12. 99th T.M.Battery.
13. 10th D.C.L.I.
14.)
15.) War Diary.
16. File.

SECRET

SECRET. Copy No........4.

2nd DIVISION R.A.M.C. OPERATION ORDER No.47.

(Reference maps : Sheets 1/20,000 & 1/40,000

25th July 1916.

On relief of 3rd Division by the 2nd Division the following movements of Medical Units will take place.

1. On night 24/25th July Bearer Division No. 5 Field Ambulance will accompany 99th Infantry Brigade into the Left Sub-Sector of the line.

2. On 25th July Bearer Division of No 100 Field Ambulance will leave MORLANCOURT at 1.30 p.m., and proceed to its position with the reserve Brigade South of Montauban. They will relieve the Bearer Division of No 7 Field Ambulance. O.C., Bearer Division will detail 1 Officer and 2 N.C.O's to proceed in advance to meet guides at R.E. Dump, CARNOY at 3 p.m. This party after making the necessary investigations will await incoming unit at BRONFAY FARM at 4.30 p.m. and guide them to their destination.

3. On night 25/26 July Bearer Division of No.6 Field Ambulance will proceed with the 5th Infantry Brigade and relieve Bearer Division of No. 8 Field Ambulance, who are evacuating from the Right Sub-Sector of the line. O.C.Bearer Division will detail 1 Officer and 2 N.C.O's. who will proceed in advance to meet guides at R.E.Dump CARNOY A.13.d.3.8. at 8 p.m. This party after making the necessary investigations will await the incoming unit at BRONFAY FARM at 9 p.m. and will guide them to their destination. Bearer Division should leave their present position so as to arrive at BRONFAY FARM at 9 p.m.

4. On 26th July No 5 Field Ambulance will relieve No 142 Field Ambulance at SAPPER CORNER. O.C..No 5 Field Ambulance should send over a small advance party on the preceding day. Details to be arranged between Commanding Officers concerned.

5. Bearer Divisions when proceeding into the line should leave their Horse Ambulances on site occupied by No. 142 Field Ambulance at SAPPER CORNER. They should take their forage carts and water cart to their destination, and return them to Sapper Corner when stores have been unloaded and the water disposed of in petrol tins or otherwise.

6. No.11 San.Sec will move to Citadel,F.21.b. on 25.7.16.

Acknowledge.

[signature] Captain, R.A.M.C.,
for A.D.M.S.,2nd Division.

done! [initials]

Issued at. 12 noon.

Copy No. 1 --- No. 5 Field Ambulance.
2 --- No 6 Field Ambulance.
3 --- No 100 Field Ambulance.
4 --- Bearer Division,No 5 Fd.Amb.
5 --- Bearer Division,No 6 Fd.Amb.
6 --- Bearer Division,No 100 Fd.Amb.
7 --- "G" 2nd Division.)
8 --- "Q" 2nd Division)
9 --- Signals,2nd Division.)For information.
10 --- D.D.M.S., XIII Corps.)
11 --- H.Q.,5th Inf.Bde.)
12 --- H.Q.,6th Inf.Bde.)
13 --- H.Q.,99th Inf.Bde.)
14 --- A.D.M.S.,3rd Division.)
15 --- No 11 Sanitary Section.
16 - 18 --- Office and Records.

[initials]

SECRET

Copy No.....11.....

6TH INFANTRY BRIGADE.

OPERATION ORDER No. 183.

28th July, 1916.

Reference Trench Map MONTAUBAN, 1/20,000, and Map of DEVILLE WOOD.

1. The following reliefs and moves will be carried out tonight, July 28th/29th, under arrangements to be made direct between Officers Commanding Battalions concerned.

(a). 13th Essex Regiment will relieve 22nd Royal Fusiliers and 1st Royal Berkshire Regiment, 2 Companies in OLD BRITISH FRONT LINE, DELVILLE WOOD, 1 Company Support Trench from N of TRONES WOOD to S end of LONGUEVAL VILLAGE, 1 Company and Bn. Headquarters Trenches in S.22.a.b.

(b). 2 Companies 1st King's will be relieved as permanent garrison MONTAUBAN, by the 22nd Royal Fusiliers.

On relief whole of 1st King's will take over accommodation in MONTAUBAN ALLEY now occupied by 1st K.R.R.Corps.

Late Headquarters, 99th Infantry Brigade, are available as Battalion Headquarters.

2. O.C. 6th Light Trench Mortar Battery will reconnoitre possibilities of coming into action in Brigade Area, more particularly with view to helping Brigade on our left in LONGUEVAL.

He will also reconnoitre trench accommodation in S.23.d. with a view to occupation.

3. An Advanced Report Centre is established in QUARRY, S.22.d.9.4. A telephone line connects this point with Brigade Headquarters.

4. Situation of Brigade Headquarters unchanged.

5. Completion of relief to be reported to Brigade Headqrs.

[signature] Captain,
for Brigade Major, 6th Infantry Brigade.

Issued at 4.p.m.

Copy No. 1. 1st King's.
2. 2nd S.Staffs.
3. 13th Essex.
4. 17th Middlesex.
5. 6th Bde. M.G.Coy.
6. 6th L.T.M.Battery.
7. Bde. Grenade.
8. Staff Captain, 6th Bde.
9. 99th Bde.
10. 5th Bde.
11. 2nd Division "G".
12. 100th Fd.Ambulance.

acknowledged
J.B.
28-7.

"A" Form. Army Form C. 2121.

MESSAGES AND SIGNALS.

No. of Message

Prefix ... Code ... m.	Words	Charge	This message is on a/c of:	Recd. at ... m.
Office of Origin and Service Instructions.	Sent		Service.	Date
	At ... m.			From
	To			
	By		(Signature of "Franking Officer.")	By

TO 2nd Dn.

Sender's Number.	Day of Month	In reply to Number	AAA
* BM 95	30th		

attached is a report of patrol which was ordered to proceed to E edge of TRONES WOOD in consequence of an unofficial report having been circulated that the 2nd Division were retiring

G. M. Bullen-Smith
Br. General
Comdg 5th Inf. Bde

From
Place
Time

The above may be forwarded as now corrected. (Z)

Censor. Signature of Addressor or person authorised to telegraph in his name.

* This line should be erased if not required.

(T1809) Wt. 14142—641. 45000 pads. 4/15. Sir J. C. & S.

Secret

2nd Division.

With reference to your General Staff 2nd Divn. No. G.S. 1001/1/19. I submit the following report for the information of the Divn Commander.

The scheme for communication during the operations to-day was fully explained in my orders. I think the O.C. 2/ Oxford and Bucks L.I. erred in not sending several short messages by pigeon post instead of writing a long message to be carried by hand.

In addition to the means of communication described in orders, I received at a late hour (3 a.m.) a wireless set and also an earth induction set, which was specially [illegible] in the other trench [illegible]. The wireless [illegible] working all right, but owing to the crowded trenches he was unable to get the earth induction set to work. As for the wireless

also E end of Longueval Alley
At 5 p.m. the patrol moved to
a point about T.24 c 5.1. No
movement of parties of men or
transport could be discerned
anywhere to N.E. & E.
Considerable quantities of smoke
interfered with observation.
From 5.20 p.m. to 5.40 p.m.
the E. side of Bernafay wood
shelled with H.E. which caused
patrol to make a detour to the South.
The patrol returned in at 5.45 p.m.
The path through TRONES WOOD
rough but clearly marked by
white bands on Trees from point
about T.23.d 66 to T.30.c.27.

Malcolm Mackinnon
2/Lt
O.C. C. Coy.

To Adjutant
94

Ref map Montauban

To Adjt

Report of Reconnaissance patrol carried out by 2/Lt G. Richardson & 1 man

The patrol left E side Bernafay Wood at 4.30 p.m. The officer states that at 4.43 p.m. he reached point S.30 a 3.2. Men in groups of 3 & 5 were visible crossing the sky line running E. to W. of Maltz Horn Farm. 160 men were counted in 10 mins. There was no shelling of this ridge by the enemy from 4.43 p.m. to 5.10 p.m. Hostile artillery were shelling North end of Trones Wood, Waterlot Farm consistently with H.E. Guns were firing from S. SE. Enemy were also shelling Delville Wood with light & Heavy shells

working of the [illegible] to [illegible] day [illegible] by the [illegible] [illegible] for a [illegible].
I am told that the 2nd Oxford and Bucks L.I. were occupying the line by WATERLOT FARM, and the extremely heavy shelling rendered communication of course most difficult. I hope that the officer commanding the battalion concerned, will send forward a detailed statement of the effect on their communication.
As regards the 24th Royal Fusiliers, they [illegible] [illegible], only [illegible] [illegible] [illegible] to the [illegible] [illegible] [illegible] [illegible] [illegible] the officer commanding the battalion should have commenced [illegible] [illegible] [illegible] [illegible] [illegible] [illegible] [illegible] [illegible] [illegible] [illegible] [illegible] [illegible] all day.

I [illegible] appreciate the [illegible] [illegible] in the [illegible] [illegible] [illegible] [illegible] the [illegible] [illegible] [illegible] will take further steps [illegible] [illegible] [illegible] [illegible] [illegible] [illegible] [illegible] [illegible] [illegible] [illegible] that at a [illegible] [illegible] day before [illegible] into the line [illegible] [illegible] [illegible] [illegible] the [illegible]

[illegible]

B.G.

Maj. [illegible]

30.7.16

[illegible] [illegible] [illegible] [illegible] [illegible] [illegible] [illegible] [illegible] [illegible] [illegible] LONGUEVAL ALLEY [illegible] [illegible] [illegible] [illegible] [illegible] [illegible]

[illegible]

B.G.

Seen by G.O.C.

[illegible]

Ref BM543
6 / Bde

21

We sent out patrols last night, but were unable to locate the Batt on our left in the dark. At 3pm we intend to wave a coloured handkerchief from our extreme left, and if necessary send up a Very light. If you could let the 5th Div know about this and get them to do the same, we will probably get connection.

22

By night it is very difficult to find your way about, and by day it is dangerous to leave the trenches, owing to the presence of German snipers.

Situation normal at present

G. Goff Lt Col
1/Kings

1-8-16
10-15 a.m

2

2nd Div.

Will you kindly pass this information to 5th Div. at once.

[illegible]

Capt. [illegible]

1/8/16.

Received 4.35 pm.

[illegible] 1.8. 1.55 pm.

telephoned 5th Div. 4.40 pm.

[illegible]

SECRET
******

Copy No. 12

47th (LONDON) DIVISION OPERATION ORDER No. 81.

2nd July 1916.

1. The following operations will be carried out by 47th Division tomorrow July 3rd and night of July 3rd/4th :-

(a). The Divisional Artillery will carry out "one-round" bombardments. Times and points as follows :-

10-5 a.m.	.	PUITS 8.
10-40 a.m.	.	Dump at H.7. (141st Inf.Bde.Tracing).
11-20 a.m.	.	Trench junction H.5. (- do -).
2-10 p.m.	.	- do - C.5. (- do -).
2-50 p.m.	.	PUITS 6.
3-20 p.m.	.	LIEVIN (M.28).

(b). At 10-15 p.m. and 11 p.m. on July 3rd, and at 5-30 a.m. July 4th, six 18 pdr Batteries and three 4.5" Howr. Batteries of the Divl.Arty. will shoot in conjunction with the IVth Corps H.Arty. on enemy's billets in LIEVIN (M.28).

Cancelled 47 Div G532

(c). The French 120 mm "Courts" will bombard the enemy's trenches in S.3 and S.9 at an hour to be arranged with Br.Gen.Comdg.H.Arty. IVth Corps.

The Artillery of the 2nd and 47th Divisions will shrapnel these trenches when the French guns have ceased firing.

(d). At 3 p.m. 6" Howitzers fire 100 rounds on enemy Machine Gun Emplacements at S.2.b.37.60 and at Southern haunch of salient S.2.b.3.3.

Arrangements for clearing trenches have been made between 140th Inf.Bde. and C.R.A.

2. (a). At 1-45 a.m. on July 4th, the 140th Inf.Bde. will raid the enemy's salient in S.2.b.

(b). The Divisional Artillery will co-operate by forming a barrage in accordance with instructions already issued.

A copy of the orders by 47th Div.Arty. containing programme has been sent to units concerned including IVth Corps H.Arty. and 2nd Div.Arty. Copy No. 6 is forwarded with these orders for information of IVth Corps.

(c). From 1-45 a.m. till 2-15 a.m. a bombardment of the PIMPLE and O.P's North and North-east of the PIMPLE will be carried out by IVth Corps H.Arty. and 2nd Div.Arty. in order to keep down Machine Gun and other fire.

(d). Arrangements for synchronising of watches with Corps H.Arty. and 2nd Div.Arty. is being made by C.R.A. 47th Div.Arty.

3. (a). At 11 a.m. 2nd Division will shoot on The PIMPLE (one round strafe).

(b). At 3 p.m. on July 3rd, IVth Corps H.Arty. will bombard The PIMPLE and the O.P's North and North-east of it.

Arrangements for clearing trenches by 2nd Division have been made between them and IVth Corps H.Arty.

(c).

(c). ~~During the night July 3rd/4th, the IVth Corps H.Arty. will bombard the roads between LIEVIN and LENS.~~ Cancelled

4. Copies of any further orders or instructions issued by units of 47th Division with reference to operations mentioned in paragraphs 1 and 2, will be forwarded to Divl. Hd.Qrs.

5. Acknowledge by wire.

Lt.Colonel,

General Staff,
47th (London) Division.

Issued at 8 p.m.

Copy No. 1. Op.Order File.
2. War Diary.
3. General Staff.
4. 47th Div.Arty.
5. 47th Div.Engrs.
6. 140th Inf.Bde.
7. 141st Inf.Bde.
8. 142nd Inf.Bde.
9. IVth Corps.
10. IVth Corps H.Arty.
11. 1st Division.
12. 2nd Division.
} For information.

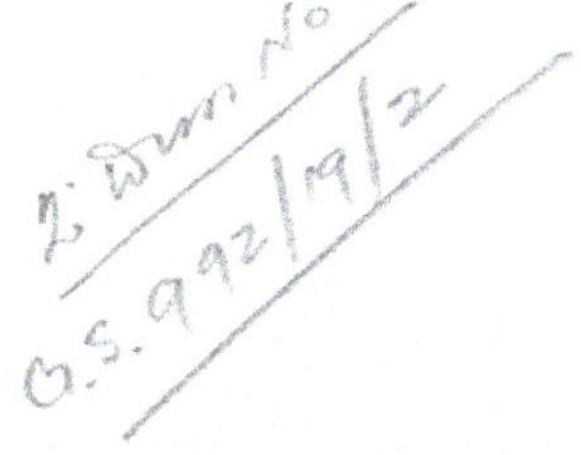

SECRET. Copy No. 16

47th (LONDON) DIVISION OPERATION ORDER No.82.

Ref. Map - 1/40,000, Sheets 36b and 36c.

4th July 1916.

1. The 141st Infantry Brigade will relieve the 140th Infantry Brigade in SOUCHEZ Section on the night of 7th/8th July 1916.

Details of relief to be arranged direct between G.Os.C. Brigades.

2. G.O.C. 141st Infantry Brigade will assume command of the Section on completion of the relief which will be reported to Divisional Headquarters.

Major
for Lt.Colonel,
General Staff,
47th (London) Division.

Issued at 3 p.m.

Copy No.1. Op.Order File
2. War Diary
3. General Staff
4. A.A. & Q.M.G.
5. 47th Div Arty
6. 47th Div Engrs
7. 47th Sigs
8. 140th Inf Bde
9. 141st Inf Bde
10. 142nd Inf Bde
11. 4th R.W.F.
12. 47th Train
13. 47th Med
14. A.P.M.

15. IVth Corps
16. 2nd Division
17. 40th Division
18. R.N.Division.

For information.

acknowledged
5th Bde informed

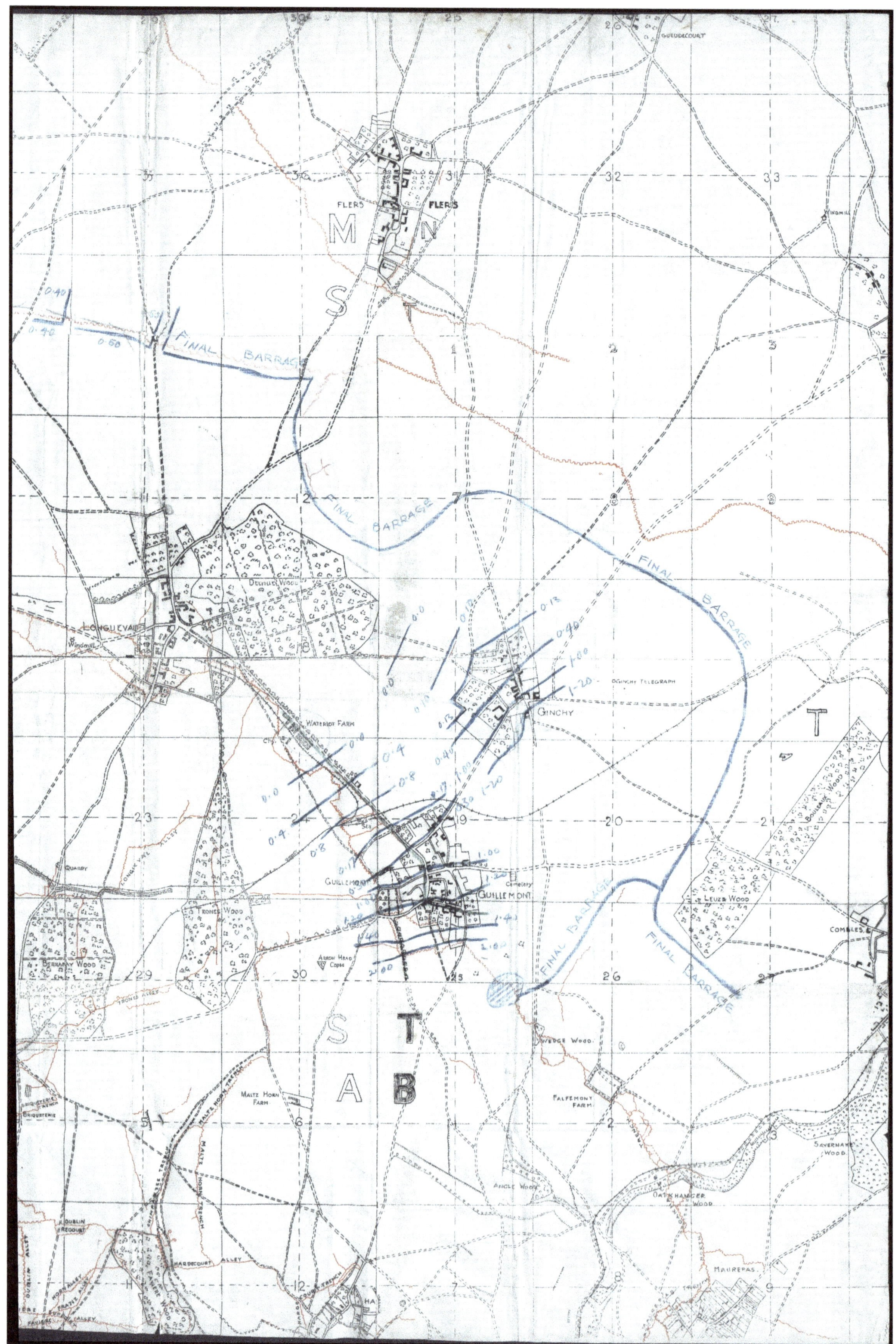

GUEUDECOURT
FLERS
FLERS
M
N
S
T
0.40
0.40
0.50
FINAL BARRAGE
FINAL BARRAGE
FINAL BARRAGE
FINAL BARRAGE
FINAL BARRAGE
FINAL BARRAGE
LONGUEVAL
Windmill
DELVILLE WOOD
WATERLOT FARM
GINCHY
GINCHY TELEGRAPH
0.13
0.40
1.00
1.20
0.4
0.8
GUILLEMONT
GUILLEMONT
Cemetery
1.00
1.20
1.40
2.00
QUARRY
LONGUEVAL ALLEY
TRONES WOOD
BERNAFAY WOOD
ARROW HEAD COPSE
TRONES ALLEY
LEUZE WOOD
BOULEAUX WOOD
COMBLES
T
S
T
A
B
WEDGE WOOD
MALTZ HORN FARM
FALFEMONT FARM
BRIQUETERIE
MALTZ HORN TRENCH
ANGLE WOOD
SAVERNAKE WOOD
OAKHANGER WOOD
HARDECOURT ALLEY
MAUREPAS

Martinpuich
High Wood
Final Barrage
Bazentin-le-Petit
Bazentin-le-Petit Wood
Windmill
Contalmaison Villa
Villa Wood
Middle Wood
Lower Wood
Peake Wood
Bazentin-le-Grand Wood
Bazentin-le-Grand
Longueval
Windmill
Delville
Sabot Copse
Flatiron Copse
Mametz Wood
Wood Support
Quarry
Quarry
Caterpillar Wood
Triangle Post
Trones Wood
Montauban Alley
Bernafay Wood
Montauban
X S
F A
White Trench
Queens Nullah
Maple Trench
Apple Trees
Pommiers Redoubt
Beetle Alley
Montauban Alley
Loop Trench
The Twins
Mill Trench
Chimney Trench
Chimney
Briqueterie
Maltz Horn Farm
Maltz Horn Trench
Dublin Trench
Dublin Alley
Glatz Redoubt
Casement Trench
Dublin Redoubt
Germans Wood
Bedford Trench
Hardecourt Alley
Mametz
Black Hedge
Austrian Support
Austrian Trench
Kasino Point
Bay Point
The Triangle
Breslau Trench
Breslau Point
Brick Point
The Warren
Mine Support
The Castle
Bund Support
Black Alley
Favière
Train Alley
Valley Trench

IVth Corps No. H.R.S. 869.
1st Army G.S. 420/3(a)

2nd DIVISION
GENERAL STAFF
2nd Divn. No.
G.S. 9?2/15/15.
No.
Date.

SECRET

IVth Corps.

Instructions have been received from G.H.Q. to the effect that strict economy in the expenditure of ammunition is now necessary in order to ensure a sufficient supply of ammunition for the main operations: and that ammunition for further wire-cutting on the fronts of the First, Second, and Third Armies cannot be provided.

2. The 2" trench mortar should be the primary weapon to be used for wirecutting purposes and 18 pounder ammunition should only be used for this purpose in exceptional cases in connexion with raids.

3. Further, 18 pounder ammunition should only be used in exceptional cases for the shelling of the enemy's communications and strong points behind his line.

4. At the same time, in order to prevent the enemy from withdrawing troops to reinforce against our main attack, and to wear down his strength, the Commander-in-Chief wishes every effort to be made to continue the carrying out of raids against the enemy trenches on the fronts of the First and Second Armies.

5. It is unlikely that it will be possible to give to Corps any ammunition in addition to that already allotted for the operations now in progress, and the G.O.C. wishes it impressed upon all concerned that, while giving effect to the Commander-in-Chief's wishes as regards raids, every round saved in the carrying out of the Corps programme may help to influence the result of the operations at the decisive point.

3rd July, 1916. (sd) W. de S. Barrow, Major-General, General Staff, First Army.

(2)

C.R.A., 2nd Divn.
5th Inf. Bde.
6th Inf. Bde.
99th Inf. Bde.

For information and guidance.

H.Q., 2nd Divn. Lieut. Colonel,

4-7-1916. General Staff, 2nd Division.

Secret
BM 306.

Report on wire cutting from S30b.89 to S24d.8.5.

1. From S24d.9½.1½ to S30b.9.7½ wire not very visible as it appears to be below the crest of a small ravine, and part of the posts only are visible.

From S24d.9½.1½ to S24d.9½.3 the wire is non existent and constitutes no obstacle — wire near S24d.8.5 has two good avenues cut through it.

Observation was carried out from A.30 [illegible] Central; & on the whole was easy.

3. Ammunition expended — 3300 Shrapnel.

2. Reports timed 5 p.m.

D. M. Graham
Major
BM
3rd Div Art.

29/7/16.

Does not affect us
[illegible]

[illegible]

S E C R E T.

G.2188.

1. With reference to Operation Order No.90, the following modifications in the distribution of the troops are made on account of the greater strength of the Brigades of the 2nd.Division.

(i) 99th.Inf.Bde.
1½ battlns.in front line.
½ " garrison of MONTAUBAN.
2 " in support and reserve, in trenches N.of CATERPILLAR VALLEY.

(ii) 6th.Inf.Bde.
Bde.H.Q.in H.Q.of 76th.Inf.Bde.
3 battlns.in old German trenches now occupied by 76th.Inf.Bde.
1 " in MONTAUBAN ALLEY.

(iii) 106th.Inf.Bde.
Will return to 35th.Division after 2 battlns. of 99th.Inf.Bde.have moved North of CATERPILLAR VALLEY. 106th.Inf.Bde.will communicate with 99th.Inf.Bde.whose H.Q. are at S.27.d.2.8.

(iv) 5th.Inf.Bde.
Will occupy trenches of 8th.Inf.Bde. in front line, TRONES WOOD, BERNAFAY WOOD and LONGUEVAL ALLEY.
The 5th.Inf.Bde.will take over from the 104th. Inf.Bde. the trenches on the E.side of TRONES WOOD North of the Railway.

2. The 6th.Infantry Brigade will arrange for all his units to reconnoitre the approaches to all trenches on the front of the Division, especially LONGUEVAL and DELVILLE WOOD.

H.L. de Poltz

Lieut-Colonel,
General Staff, 3rd.Division.

25th.July 1916.

Copies to:-

8th.Inf.Bde.
99th.Inf.Bde.
76th.Inf.Bde.
106th.Inf.Bde.
2nd.Division.
6th.Inf.Bde.
35th.Division.

SECRET. Copy No: ......

3rd DIVISION OPERATION ORDER No: 90.

24th July, 1916.

Map references Sheets 62.c.N.W. and 62.d.N.E.

1. The operations ordered in operation order No: 89 are cancelled.

2. The 2nd Division will relieve the 3rd Division on July 24th and 25th.

3. (a) On July 24th/25th the 99th Inf Bde will relieve the 9th Inf Bde Headquarters, the front held by the 1st Royal Scots Fusrs., and 4th Royal Fusiliers and all units in support and reserve of the 9th Inf Bde and the 17th Royal Scots, 35th Division, in BERNAFAY WOOD and in the garrison of MONTAUBAN.

The 8th K.O.R.L. will rejoin the 76th Inf Bde as soon as relieved and will move to an area ordered by the 76th Inf Bde. The 17th Royal Scots will join the 106th Inf Bde as directed by the G.O.C. 106th Inf Bde.

The 1st Gordon Highlanders and the front held by them will come under command of the 8th Inf Bde from 10.pm. today.

(b) On July 25th/26th the 5th Inf Bde will relieve the 8th Inf Bde front (including 1st Gordon Highlanders). Arrangements to be made between Brigadiers. 8th Inf Bde to report arrangements to 3rd Div H.Q.

4. Guides at the rate of 1 officer per company and 1 guide per platoon and Vickers detachment will meet relieving units at the R.E. Dump on the CARNOY - MONTAUBAN road near the 8th Inf Bde H.Q. about A.3.c.0.5. at the following times:-

July 24th/25th.

Guides from 1st R.S.F. for 1st R.Berks. at 9.pm.
" " 4th R.Fus. " 1st K.R.R.C. at 10.pm.
" for other units will be at the same place at 9.pm. and will wait for their relieving units.

July 25th/26th

As arranged by Brigadiers 5th and 8th Inf Bdes.

5. Vickers guns will remain in the line together with those relieving them for 24 hours after the infantry have been relieved.

6. Each battalion will leave 1 officer and 1 Senior N.C.O. with the company H.Q. of each company of the relieving unit for 24 hours after the completion of the relief.

7. All trench stores will be handed over and the usual receipts will be sent to 3rd Div H.Q.

All maps, plans and photographs and all information regarding the line and the enemy will be handed over to relieving units.

8. On July 25th the 6th Inf Bde will relieve the 76th Inf Bde in reserve. The relief will be carried out by daylight under arrangements to be made between Brigadiers concerned.

9. Command of Brigade fronts and areas will pass to the relieving Brigadier on completion of the relief of the Sector.

The hour at which command is assumed will be wired to Div.H.Q.

The command of the front and area will pass to the G.O.C. 2nd Div. on completion of the infantry reliefs on the night of July 25th/26th

P.T.O.

Para 10.

10. In the afternoon of July 25th the 6th Inf Bde will relieve the 106th Inf Bde in Divisional reserve in CATERPILLAR VALLEY and MONTAUBAN. The movement will be carried out by small parties under arrangements to be made direct between Brigadiers of 6th and 105th Inf Bdes. The G.O.C. 6th Inf Bde will report to 3rd Div H.Q. when the relief is completed, and his Brigade H.Q. have been established in the QUARRY at S.22c.0.5. After relief the 106th Inf Bde will return to, and will move as directed by the 35th Div.

11. Field Companies R.E. and 20/K.R.R.C.(Pioneers) will be relieved under arrangements to be made between the C.R.E's. of 2nd and 3rd Divisions.

12. Field Ambulances will be relieved under arrangements to be made between the A.D's.M.S. of 2nd and 3rd Divisions.

13. The Divisional Train and all Administrative units of the 3rd Division will move as directed by A.A.& Q.M.G. 3rd Division. Divisional H.Q. will move to the CITADEL.

14. After relief units of the 3rd Division will move to the billets or bivouacs occupied by their relieving units; the exact location of units with map references if possible will be reported to 3rd Division as soon as possible.

Headquarters after relief will be as follows :-

3rd Division H.Q.	CITADEL. F.21.b.central.
8th Inf Bde.	HAPPY VALLEY, L.3.a.
9th Inf Bde.	SAND PITS, E.18.d.
76th Inf Bde.	BOIS des TAILLES (northern part). K.12.a/c.

15. The 3rd Div Artillery will remain in action and will come under command of 2nd Division. The 9th Div Arty will be relieved by 2nd D.A., under arrangements to be made by G.O's.C. R.A.

16. ACKNOWLEDGE.

[illegible]

Lieut-Colonel,
General Staff, 3rd Division.

Issued at 8-50 p.m.

Copies to :-

No: 1 A.D.C. (for G.O.C.)
2 8th Inf Bde.
3 9th Inf Bde.
4 76th Inf Bde.
5 C.R.A.3rd Div.
6 " 9th Div.
7 C.R.E.
8 3rd Div "Q".
9 A.D.M.S.
10 A.P.M.
11 Div Train.
12 5th Div.
13 30th Div.
14 35th Div.
15 XIII Corps "G".
16 " " "Q".
17 3rd Sig Co R.E.
18 20/K.R.R.C.(Pioneers).
19 D.A.D.O.S.
20 A.D.V.S.
21 Camp Commandant.3rd Div.
22 War Diary.
23 2nd Div.
24 File.
25
26

Reference Map 62D. N.E. 1/20,000.

S E C R E T.

Copy No. 2

55TH (WEST LANCASHIRE) DIVISION OPERATION ORDER NO. 20.

25th July, 1916.

164th Inf. Bde.

2/2 W.Lancs.Fd.Coy.R.E. (less Pontoon Section).

1/3 W.Lancs.Fd.Ambnce. (less Tent Division).

1. The units mentioned in the margin will move to-morrow, the 26th July, and relieve the 8th Infantry Brigade group (3rd Division) in the HAPPY VALLEY, i.e:- L.2 and 3.

2. Details of relief will be made between the Infantry Brigade Commanders concerned.

3. Movement to commence at 4 p.m.

Wallace Wright
Lieut. Colonel.

Issued at 11:30 p.m. General Staff, 55th Division.

Copy No. 1 - XIIIth Corps.
2 - 2nd Division.
3 - 3rd Division.
4 - Div. Artillery.
5 - Div. Engineers.
6 - 164th Inf. Bde.
7 - 165th Inf. Bde.
8 - 166th Inf. Bde.
9 - Signals.
10 - A. D. M. S.
11 - A. D. V. S.
12 - Div. Train.
13 - A. P. M.
14 - Div. Supply Col.
15 - A. & Q.
16 - G. S.
17 - File.
18 - War Diary.
19 - G. O. C.

acknowledged 26/7/16

For GSO (1)

Notes at Corps Comdr's Conference
11 AM. 24-7-16.

In case of enemy counter attack.

1 – Successive Lines of defence. See map – & Corps will also send us later, in confirmation.

2 – C.E. will arrange defences of Montauban.

3 – For work, boundary will be as marked on map (A)

4 – Montauban garrison a fixed one, under a separate commander. It was proposed to include the Briqueterie with Montauban, but (& this was later settled) different [illegible] to be separate.

5. Work to be all coordinated. Definite tasks & required – also a time to work to.

Relief of 3rd by 2nd Divn

1. To begin early as possible.

2. Proposed to leave XIII R.S.F. in front line, & to relieve 1/G.H. & R.F. Thus the whole of 9th & 76th Bdes to be relieved by tonight – except for front line Battns. all of these 2 Bdes can be relieved by daylight.

GSO(2) 3. Have warned the 2 Bdes accordingly. GOC 5th Bde has already seen GOC 9th Bde.

4. In relieving, avoid getting in way of troops of 30th Div, & keep to West of Montauban.

~~5. Arrange Kitchen~~

General.

1. Several communications and lines of defence to be organised.

2. RE will construct Div'l HQ forward of main Peronne road, proper, constructed, with light & other conveniences.

8 Bde told

3. 35th Div'l Cmdr said he had no touch with our troops in N. part of Trônes Wood.

8 Bde told

4. 35th Div wants to take over from 8th Bde their portion of Trones Wood N of railway tonight with 1 Battn.

[illegible] 8 Bde told

Details required as to our MGs on 8th Bde front – especially on the Trônes Wood front.

8 Bde told

5 Zero hour for 25th is to be 3.50 AM

9 Bde told

6. Reserves for Longueval defences would be close up – closer than Montauban etc. Consider where to put them.

Div Arty

see OAR GB 220

7. How move guns to West out of Caterpillar Valley. Horse handy. Consider that if we try to get guns out by a narrow bottleneck – it will be risky.

(3)

Relief of Div Arty –

Div Arty

Letting Kirk of relieving personnel only.

Gen. Holdane to let 106th Bde go as soon as possible.

Send in exact position of Bdes to Corps HQ by 3 pm 24/7/16. with the moves for tonight.

Arrange Howick

13 Corps attacks. In case of our plans being upset by a large Boche attack

Up to 2.30 pm we will be on the defensive, with Pinney in Comd

Right Div front

After 2.30 pm we will be on the offensive, with Shea in Comd.

Operation postponed

8 Bde Ops. postponed at least 48 hrs.

Let 8th Bde know this.

Have warned Bdes re reliefs –

Leave in MG's till second night of reliefs –

MONTAUBAN.
PARTS OF SHEETS 57D S.E. 57C S.W. 62D N.E. 62C N.W.
A
Contalmaison
Longueval
Montauban
Mametz
Guillemont
BRITISH FRONT LINE
HIGH HOLBORN
Longueval Alley
REFERENCE
TRENCHES CORRECTED TO 2-6-16.
Scale 1:20,000

TRENCH MAP.

MONTAUBAN.

Scale 1:20,000.

2nd DIVISION
GENERAL STAFF
No. ....
Date ....

Tactical Progress
Reports

1st to 16 July. 1916

S E C R E T.

Intelligence Report - 2nd Division.

From 4.0 p.m. 30th June to 4.0 p.m. 1st July, 1916.

-:-:-:-:-:-:-:-:-:-:-

1. INFORMATION.

1. With reference to the box kites reported in yesterday's Intelligence Report, a string of six went up at 5.25 p.m. from T.12.a, at 7.50 p.m. 2 more ascended, followed by a basket; from this it is presumed that it took 8 kites to lift the basket. A wagon and about 12 men could be seen on the ground from where the kites ascended. They were taken down at about 8.30 p.m.

2. A new line of telegraph posts has been observed along the VIMY - ACHEVILLE Road, these posts carry a cross bar.

3. At 1.30 p.m. our artillery set fire to a house in a row in M.23.c.

4. Shortly after midnight, about six searchlights were seen playing on the sky from the direction of LENS. The enemy were probably searching for our aircraft. Anti-aircraft guns were heard at the same time.

5. At about 8 a.m. this morning, 7 hostile aeroplanes crossed our line from the direction of LENS. At 9.15 a.m. a hostile aeroplane crossed our line flying very low. Rifle fire was directed on it and it went back.

6. One of our patrols reports that the enemy was working in
* barricade front of his * in the trench which is the continuation of INTERNATIONAL AVENUE. This patrol also reports enemy's machine guns at S.15.c.2½.5½, S.15.c.2.6 and a sniper's post at S.15.c.1½.6½.

7. The enemy appear to be digging some new work in M.29.c. About 8 fresh chalk mounds have been observed.

2. HOSTILE MINENWERFER.

Positions estimated as follows :-

Heavy S.15.c.4.4
& S.15.c.5.7

Light. S.19.c.4½.1½.
S.15.a.5.10.
S.15.a.4.6.

3. TRAIN MOVEMENT.

On the BEAUMONT - MERICOURT Line -

6.20 p.m.	one train	moving	towards	MERICOURT.
6.40 p.m.	"	"	"	BEAUMONT.
9.15 a.m.	"	"	"	BEAUMONT.
11.30 a.m.	"	"	"	MERICOURT.

C.H. Stewart Capt. G.S.
for Lieut. Colonel,
General Staff, 2nd Division.

S E C R E T.

Report on Operations and Work done - 2nd Division.

From 4.0 p.m. 30th June to 4.0 p.m. 1st July, 1916.

****

1. OPERATIONS.

BERTHONVAL Section.

Our Lewis guns fired on gaps in the enemy's wire throughout the night.

CARENCY Section.

This morning between 11 a.m. and 1 p.m., the enemy shelled our front and support lines with field guns, 15 cm, howitzers and T.Ms; some damage was done to our trenches. Our Lewis guns dispersed an enemy working party last night in front of the left of this section. Our machine guns fired on gaps in the enemy's wire during the night.

ARTILLERY.

The enemy were active with field guns on our front and support trenches. Yesterday evening, some 15 cm. shells fell in CARENCY. At 11.30 p.m. last night, all our batteries fired for 2 minutes on GIVENCHY. The enemy retaliated by enfilade fire with field guns from the direction of LIEVIN. Our howitzers fired in retaliation for activity of hostile T.Ms.

2. WORK DONE.

BERTHONVAL Section.

Revetting and fire-stepping continued. 30 trench boards laid in CENTRAL AVENUE. Fire trench deepened in 2 places. SNARGATE deepened. One sniping post established.

CARENCY Section.

Bombing posts Nos. 3, 5, 6, 7 and 8 strengthened. Fire steps commenced in ERSATZ AVENUE and in reserve trench between ERSATZ AVENUE and HARTUNG.

H.L. Steward(?) Capt. G.S.
for Lieut. Colonel,
General Staff, 2nd Division.

S E C R E T.

Report on Operations and Work done - 2nd Division.
From 4.0 p.m. 1st to 4.0 p.m. 2nd July, 1916.

1. OPERATIONS.

BERTHONVAL Section.

At 12.30 a.m. our troops carried out a raid and entered the German trench at S.15.c.6.2. A one minute intense bombardment by our Stokes mortars preceded the infantry assault, and our troops entered the German trench with only one casualty. Our men were in the enemy's trench for 15 minutes and it is thought that at least 50 of the enemy were killed, not including any casualties suffered from our bombardment. Our artillery and trench mortars barraged the enemy's trenches round our objective. One prisoner was taken of the 162nd Regt. Our troops suffered some casualties in the withdrawal, but the majority were only slightly wounded.

CARENCY Section.

This morning some shelling of HOLLOWAY with H.E. Our M.Gs. fired at intervals during the night on gaps in the enemy's wire. One enemy sniper was shot. Between 12.45 and 1.25 a.m., front and support lines in this section and ZOUAVE Valley shelled; some damage done to our trenches.

ARTILLERY.

The enemy's barrage was very heavy last night during our raid, but no heavy shells were used. One of our battery positions was shelled with lachrymatory 10.5 cm shell during the morning. Our guns shelled a hostile machine gun emplacement at S.21.b.6.6. Enemy's wire was cut where required.

2. WORK DONE.

BERTHONVAL Section.

On the right, fire trench deepened and parapet and parados repaired. Trenches repaired where blown in by hostile fire. 3 large revetment frames erected in GRANBY Sap.

CARENCY Section.

Trenches repaired where damaged by hostile fire. Fire steps continued in ERSATZ AVENUE . Faulty parapets reconstructed where required along the front line. BANKSIDE deepened.

[signature] for Lieut. Colonel,

General Staff, 2nd Division.

S E C R E T.

Intelligence Report - 2nd Division
From 4.0 p.m. 1st to 4.0 p.m. 2nd July, 1916.

1. HOSTILE MOVEMENT.

1. At 6.40 p.m., two hostile parties of about 20 men each were seen to cross the railway at M.35.a.4.3 marching Northwards.

2. At 6.30 a.m. a party of about 80 men was seen working on trench in T.22.b. Shortly afterwards they moved off towards VIMY.
3. At 9.55 a.m. 18 4-horsed wagons escorted by about a troop of cavalry were seen on the ACHEVILLE - FRESNOY road moving South. At 11.55 a.m. a troop of cavalry was seen moving on the same road towards the South.

4. Chief road traffic seen throughout the day was on the ACHEVILLE - FRESNOY Road.

2. INFORMATION.

1. An enemy aeroplane flew from North to South over our lines at 9 a.m. this morning.

2. The enemy's signal for artillery support at the commencement of our raid last night was 2 twin red lights. The response was practically instantaneous.

3. Enemy's searchlights were again active last night behind the VIMY Ridge.

4. R.A. report a sniper is active opposite INTERNATIONAL TRENCH (S.15.c.4.4½)

3. TRAIN MOVEMENT.

On the BILLY-MONTIGNY - HARNES Line :-

8.45 a.m.	one train	moving	towards	BILLY-MONTIGNY.
9.0 a.m.	"	"	"	- do -
9.20 a.m.	"	"	"	- do -
10.45 a.m.	"	"	"	- do -
12.20 p.m.	"	"	"	- do -

On the HENIN-LIETARD - HARNES Line :-

8.45 a.m.	one train	moving	towards	HENIN-LIETARD.
9.10 a.m.	"	"	"	HARNES.
9.30 a.m.	"	"	"	HARNES.
10.0 a.m.	"	"	"	HARNES.
12.30 p.m.	"	"	"	HENIN-LIETARD.

On the MERICOURT - BEAUMONT Line :-

7.12 a.m.	one train	moving	towards	BEAUMONT.
7.45 a.m.	"	"	"	MERICOURT.
10.40 a.m.	"	"	"	MERICOURT.

9 trains moving South and 5 trains moving North were observed in the distance, but the exact line on which they were moving cannot be definitely stated.

[illegible] Capt. G.S.
for. Lieut. Colonel,
General Staff, 2nd Division.

LATER.

At 6.40 p.m. this evening a large enemys working party was observed working between ACHEVILLE and ROUVROY. They were working on the N.E. side of the road and appeared to be digging a trench. They stretched the whole distance between the two above places.

S E C R E T.

Intelligence Report - 2nd Division.

From 4.0 p.m. 2nd to 4.0 p.m. 3rd July, 1916.

1. INFORMATION.

1. At 8.0 a.m. a hostile aeroplane was observed to rise from the valley East of BOIS-BERNARD.
2. At about 11.10 a.m. the enemy fired 2 Very lights from his front line at S.15.d.4.4. These were shortly followed by 2 more fired from the direction of FRESNOY.
3. Hostile snipers reported very active this afternoon opposite OLD BOOT TRENCH.
4. At 7.25 p.m. yesterday, a large fire was seen behind CITE L'ABATOIRE.

2. HOSTILE MOVEMENT.

At 2.5 p.m. a party of about 20 men was marching towards ACHEVILLE on the ACHEVILLE - VIMY Road.
Traffic observed on roads to-day normal.

3. HOSTILE WORK.

Germans are reported to be doing much work on their lip of the new crater at S.8.b.9.0½.

4. TRAIN MOVEMENT.

The following trains were observed on the BILLY-MONTIGNY - HARNES Line :-

6.0 p.m.	one train moving towards	HARNES.
6.15 p.m.	" " "	HARNES.
1.15 p.m.	" " "	BILLY-MONTIGNY.
3.0 p.m.	" " "	HARNES.
3.5 p.m.	" " "	HARNES.

On the BEAUMONT - MERICOURT Line:-

7.35 p.m.	one train moving towards	MERICOURT.
7.20 a.m.	" " "	BEAUMONT.
8.5 a.m.	" " "	BEAUMONT.
10.10 a.m.	" " "	BEAUMONT.

In the distance the following trains were observed, but the exact line on which they were moving cannot be stated -

4 trains moving South.
2 " " North.
3 " " North west.

[signature] Capt. G.S.
for Lieut. Colonel
General Staff, 2nd Division.

S E C R E T.

Report on Operations and Work done - 2nd Division.

From 4.0 p.m. 2nd to 4.0 p.m. 3rd July, 1916.

****

1. OPERATIONS.

BERTHONVAL Section.

At 4 a.m. the enemy retaliated for our shelling with heavy shrapnel over our front and support trenches. Several small aerial torpedoes were fired during last night and this morning, but they fell behind our front line and did no damage. Our Lewis guns fired on gaps in the enemy's wire during the night.

CARENCY Section.

Slight retaliation for our shelling early this morning. Our machine guns fired on gaps in the enemy's wire during the night. On the whole the enemy were quiet on this front during the day. One of our snipers claims to have hit an enemy sniper this morning.

ARTILLERY.

CARENCY shelled with a 5.9" howitzer at intervals all day. The gun fired from the direction of the ELECTRICITY STATION (M.33) but flashes could not be observed. Some shelling of 130th ALLEY with 77 mm shells. Our artillery fired at the enemy's observation posts and loopholes on the PIMPLE.

2. WORK DONE.

BERTHONVAL Section.

Support trench in front of BROWN'S BURROWS deepened for 30 yards. Front line just North of ERSATZ AVENUE deepened. Traverses in the TRIANGLE revetted.

CARENCY Section.

KINGS TRENCH and LIME STREET deepened and cleaned. 2nd line South of UHLAN Trench cleared where damaged by hostile fire.

W.P. Steward, Capt. G.S.
for Lieut. Colonel,

General Staff, 2nd Division.

S E C R E T.

Report on Operations and Work done - 2nd Division.

From 4.0 p.m. 3rd to 4.0 p.m. 4th July, 1916.

1. OPERATIONS.

BERTHONVAL Section.

At 12.24 a.m. small raiding party entered the German sap at S.15.c.6.2½. The enemy ran away as soon as they saw our men but 2 who failed to escape were killed. The enemy barraged our front line while this operation was taking place.

CARENCY Section.

At 10.45 p.m. we successfully blew two mines immediately South of MOMBER Crater. We had no difficulty in occupying our lips of the craters, and made good progress in the work of consolidation. The enemy put up a barrage on our support trenches and ZOUAVE Valley for about 5 minutes after the mines were exploded. Our artillery replied. Our trench mortars bombarded the enemy's trenches following the explosion of the mines. At 3.0 p.m. the enemy blew a camouflet at S.8.b.9.2. It caused no damage.

ARTILLERY.

This morning the enemy shelled one of our observation stations on the LORETTE SPUR with 77 mm shells. Yesterday evening our artillery fired on a suspected hostile machine gun emplacement and sniper's post at about S.15.d.4.1.

2. WORK DONE.

BERTHONVAL Section.

Front and support lines repaired where damaged by hostile fire. New support trench deepened an average depth of 2 feet for about 30 yards. BROAD STREET deepened. An observation post constructed in CENTRAL AVENUE. Sniper's post commenced in VINCENT STREET.

CARENCY Section.

Consolidation of the new craters formed after the mine explosions last night. COBURG and SOUCHEZ Alleys deepened and cleaned.

C.K. Steward Capt. G.S.
for Lieut. Colonel,
General Staff, 2nd Division.

S E C R E T.

Intelligence Report - 2nd Division.

From 4.0 p.m. 3rd to 4.0 p.m. 4th July, 1916.

1. INFORMATION.

1. At 1.15 p.m. to-day the balloons at MERICOURT and SALLAUMINES were seen to be taken from their sheds. They were soon put back again without ascending.

2. At 1.40 p.m. clouds of smoke were observed to be rising from enemy's lines behind BROADBRIDGE, MILDREN and NEW CUT Craters.

3. The enemy were observed to send up 2 green lights when one of their batteries was firing short. The shelling immediately ceased.

2. HOSTILE WORK.

1. The enemy appear to be doing some new work by MOMBER Crater.

2. It seems probable from reports, that the enemy is attempting to open up the old trench from S.15.c.6.2½ to S.21.b.3.3. He was reported to be working on the Southern end of this trench* and there have been reports that he has been working on the Northern end. It ispossible that he is attempting to advance his front line. It is important that as much information as possible should be obtained regarding this trench.

3. TRAIN MOVEMENT.

Very few trains were observed to-day owing to adverse weather conditions.

[signature] for Lieut. Colonel,

General Staff, 2nd Division.

* early this morning.

S E C R E T.

Report on Operations and Work done - 2nd Division.

From 4.0 p.m. 4th to 4.0 p.m. 5th July, 1916.

-:-:-:-:-:-:-:-:-:-:-:-

1. OPERATIONS.

BERTHONVAL Section.

The enemy threw a few hand grenades at about 11.40 p.m. last night opposite our Southern sub-section for apparently no reason. A quiet day, nothing of interest to report.

CARENCY Section.

The enemy has been very quiet during the last 24 hours. Some heavy trench mortar bombs were fired into HOLLOWAY about midday. Our field guns retaliated.
Hostile snipers have been fairly active. Our snipers claim to have shot 2 of the enemy's snipers.

ARTILLERY.

Last night our artillery fired on GIVENCHY at irregular intervals.
At 3.5 p.m. the enemy fired some 5.9" and 77 mm shells into the ZOUAVE Valley.
On the whole the enemy's artillery has been comparatively inactive.

2. WORK DONE.

BERTHONVAL Section.

OLD BOOT TRENCH and CENTRAL AVENUE cleaned after the rain.
A snipers post has been completed in CENTRAL AVENUE.
Fire steps continued in our second line.

CARENCY Section.

Consolidation of new craters just South of ROMBER Crater continued.
Sap head at KENNEDY Crater strengthened.
BARRABAS trench repaired where damaged by hostile fire.
Support line South of TANCHOT AVENUE strengthened.

[signature] Capt. G.S.
for Lieut. Colonel,

Lieut General Staff, 2nd Division.

S E C R E T.

Intelligence Report - 2nd Division.

From 4.0 p.m. 4th to 4.0 p.m. 5th July, 1916.

-:-:-:-:-:-:-:-:-:-

1. PATROL REPORTS.

At about 1.30 a.m. a party left our trench at about S.8.d.8.5 and reported a large enemy working party just South of IRISH Crater. This party was dispersed by machine gun fire.
At 10.30 p.m. and again at 11.30 p.m. a patrol visited the disused trench which runs South from the enemy's sap at S.15.c.8.3. It was unoccupied. The patrol reports that it is in very bad condition.

2. INFORMATION.

1. A dull clanging sound was heard continuously in the enemy's lines last night, especially between 1 a.m. and 3 a.m.. It resembled hammering of hollow metal and always came from the same place. The direction of the place was difficult to decide but it is thought to have been about S.21.d.5.4, it may have been behind the enemy's front line.

2. A hostile machine gun has been located at about S.15.c.5½.3.

3. HOSTILE WORK.

New work is reported to have been done on the crater at S.15.c.8½.9. This is an old crater behind the German line.

4. TRAIN MOVEMENT.

No hostile train movement observed to-day owing to adverse weather conditions.

[signature] Capt. G.S.
for Lieut. Colonel,

General Staff, 2nd Division.

S E C R E T.

Intelligence Report - 2nd Division.

From 4.0 p.m. 5th to 4.0 p.m. 6th July, 1916.

1. INFORMATION.

1. The enemy is thought to be holding his line weakly from S.15.c.3.6 to S.15.c.10.2. He has shown very little activity on this front and only a few Very lights have been fired.

2. An enemy machine gun is reported to fire from about S.15.c.8.3.

3. Pigeons are reported to have flown over our Northern sub-section towards the direction of LENS.

2. HOSTILE WORK.

1. Fresh sandbags have appeared in the enemy's trench between S.9.c.2.5 to S.9.c.2.3.

2. At S.9.c.2.7 work, which is thought to be a machine gun emplacement, is reported.

3. A loophole plate has been erected by the enemy at S.15.c.5.3½.

3. TRAIN MOVEMENT.

The following trains have been observed :-

On the BILLY-MONTIGNY - HARNES Line.

9.15 a.m.	one train	moving	towards	HARNES.
9.40 a.m.	"	"	"	HARNES.
10.40 a.m.	"	"	"	BILLY-MONTIGNY.
11.5 a.m.	"	"	"	BILLY-MONTIGNY.
11.57 a.m.	"	"	"	HARNES.
12.45 p.m.	"	"	"	BILLY-MONTIGNY.
1.8 p.m.		'		BILLY-MONTIGNY.

On the HENIN-LIETARD - HARNES Line:-

8.25 a.m.	one train	moving	towards	HENIN-LIETARD.
8.40 a.m.	"	"	"	HENIN-LIETARD.
9.35 a.m.	"	"	"	HENIN-LIETARD.
10.15 a.m.	"	"	"	HENIN-LIETARD.
11.2 a.m.	"	"	"	HENIN-LIETARD.
11.25 a.m.	"	"	"	HARNES.
11.45 a.m.	"	"	"	HARNES.
11.53 a.m.	"	"	"	HARNES.
1.48 p.m.	"	"	"	HARNES.
2.45 p.m.	"	"	"	HARNES.

On the MERICOURT - BEAUMONT Line :-

8.5 a.m.	one train	moving	towards	MERICOURT.
10.30 a.m.	"	"	"	MERICOURT.
2.9 p.m.	"	"	"	BEAUMONT.

3 trains were observed in the distance going South but the exact line on which they were moving cannot be stated.

C.H. Stewart. Capt. G.S.
for Lieut. Colonel,
General Staff, 2nd Division.

SECRET.

Report on Operations and Work done - 2nd Division.

From 4.0 p.m. 5th to 4.0 p.m. 6th July, 1916.

1. OPERATIONS.

BERTHONVAL Section.

The enemy shelled this section intermittently during the morning and afternoon with shrapnel.

Some hostile trench mortar activity.

Our Lewis guns fired at intervals throughout the night.

CARENCY Section.

Comparatively quiet during the last 24 hours, except for some hostile trench mortar activity.

Between 12.30 p.m. and 1.30 p.m. hostile trench mortars were active against HOLLOWAY; this was thought to be retaliation for our trench mortar fire.

Gaps in the enemy's wire kept under rifle and machine gun fire during the night.

Our snipers claim one German sniper in this section.

ARTILLERY.

During the morning enemy fired about 30 4.2" shells near the church in ABLAIN ST. NAZAIRE. Intermittent hostile shelling of ZOUAVE Valley.

Our artillery has shelled GIVENCHY and the front north of the PIMPLE.

Enemy's trench shelled when rifle fire was opened on our aeroplanes.

2. WORK DONE.

BERTHONVAL Section.

Trench boards taken up, cleaned and relaid.

New S.A.A. store has been commenced.

MANDORA South widened at intervals along a ridge of 50 yards.

Work continued on the front line between GRANBY and ERSATZ Avenues.

CARENCY Section.

Parados rebuilt in WILSON Trench. Work continued on parados in LIME STREET.

Front line repaired opposite KENNEDY CRATER where damaged by hostile fire.

Work continued on consolidation of lips of the new craters just South of MOMBER Crater.

Some wire put out on the lips of the Northern group of Craters. Our wire is now reported to be very good in front of this part of the line.

[signature] Capt. G.S.
for Lieut. Colonel,
General Staff, 2nd Division.

SECRET.

Report on Operations and Work done - 2nd Division.

From 4.0 p.m. 6th July to 4.0 p.m. 7th July, 1916.

1. OPERATIONS.

BERTHONVAL Section.

On the whole the situation has been quiet during the last 24 hours.

Slight activity on the part of hostile snipers opposite VINCENT STREET.

A few H.E. shells were fired by the enemy which fell in the vicinity of CENTRAL AVENUE.

CARENCY Section.

Comparatively quiet during the last 24 hours except that hostile trench mortars were active principally against the Southern sub-section from 2 p.m. to 4 p.m.

Our trench mortars fired 96 rounds at the enemy's front trench and saps between MOMBER and KENNEDY Craters. Their shooting was reported to be good and effective.

ARTILLERY.

The enemy's artillery has been inactive.

Our artillery fired during the afternoon in retaliation for hostile trench mortar fire.

2. WORK DONE.

BERTHONVAL Section.

Northern sub-section. 50 yards of parapet in front line trench repaired and made bullet-proof. MANDORA South widened 1 ft. for 50 yards, work continuing on fire steps and bays in this trench.

Southern sub-section. TOTTENHAM Trench cleaned and widened.

New snipers post erected in CENTRAL AVENUE and TOTTENHAM Road.

100 yards of SNARGATE drained and cleaned.

CARENCY Section.

Cleaning and drainage of trenches. Trench repaired where damaged by hostile fire. Pumping in progress in PELETIER. Damage repaired in HOLLOWAY due to hostile trench mortar fire.

[signature] Capt. G.S.
for Lieut. Colonel,
General Staff, 2nd Division.

S E C R E T.

Intelligence Report - 2nd Division.
From 4.0 p.m. 6th July to 4.0 p.m. 7th July, 1916.

1. PATROL REPORT.

A patrol last night reconnoitred the ground in front of German trench at about S.15.c.3.5½. The following information was obtained :-

(a) A gap in the enemy's wire was discovered about 3 feet wide. Through this gap the patrol passed but then were confronted by another line of wire about 15 yards from the parapet. This was concertina pattern, very rusty and defied all the attempts which were made to cut it.

(b) When the presence of our patrol was discovered by the enemy, the alarm was given by means of whistles.

(c) A German machine gun was brought up and placed on the parapet. It opened fire as soon as our patrol commenced to retire.

(d) The enemy showed no signs of panic and his trench appeared to be strongly held.

2. INFORMATION.

1. The enemy were distinctly heard working in their trench last night at about S.9.a.1.5.
2. Three compact coils of wire were seen in the German lines at about S.15.c.3.8. These appeared to be ready to put out in the gap which has been cut by our artillery at this point.

3. TRAIN MOVEMENT.

Following trains observed during the day :-

On the BILLY-MONTIGNY - HARNES Line.

10.5 a.m.	one train moving towards	BILLY-MONTIGNY.
1.55 p.m.	" " "	-do-
2.35 p.m.	" " "	-do-
2.46 p.m.	" " "	HARNES.

On the HENIN-LIETARD - HARNES Line.

9.20 a.m.	one train moving towards	HARNES.
10.0 a.m.	" " "	HENIN-LIETARD.
1.45 p.m.	" " "	HARNES.
2.43 p.m.	" " "	HARNES.
3.0 p.m.	" " "	HARNES.

On the BEAUMONT - MERICOURT Line.

10.30 a.m. one train moving towards BEAUMONT.

[signature illegible]
for Lieut. Colonel.
General Staff, 2nd Division.

S E C R E T.

Report on Operations and Work done - 2nd Division.
From 4.0 p.m. 7th July to 4.0 p.m. 8th July, 1916.

****

1. OPERATIONS.

BERTHONVAL Section.

Front and support lines and ZOUAVE Valley barraged for half an hour during our operation in the CARENCY Section. Lewis guns fired in co-operation with this operation.

During the day the enemy has been comparatively quiet.

CARENCY Section.

At 1.5 a.m. our troops attempted to raid the German sap and front line at about S.9.a.1.9.

Our stokes mortars bombarded the line just prior to our infantry assault.

The enemy were very much on the alert and our party was met by a heavy fire; in spite of this our leading party managed to reach the German trench and captured a machine gun but unfortunately the men bringing it back became casualties and the machine gun had to be abandoned. The remaining parties were unable to enter the German trench.

Between 4 and 5 a.m. [illegible] the enemy's trench mortars were active against [illegible] and support line in that vicinity.

Last night our machine guns fired on gaps in the enemy's wire at about S.15.a.6.2. They also fired indirectly on roads in the vicinity of GIVENCHY.

ARTILLERY.

The enemy put up a strong barrage on ZOUAVE Valley during our raid last night. Our artillery fired in retaliation [for hostile T.M. fire] on working party at S.15.a.9.7 and on enemy's trenches to keep down enemy's fire on our aeroplanes.

2. WORK DONE.

BERTHONVAL Section.

TOTTENHAM Road cleaned. Clearing and pumping of CENTRAL AVENUE continued. MANDORA SOUTH widened along whole front. Floor boards taken up, cleaned and relaid.

CARENCY Section.

COBURG trench repaired where blown in by hostile trench mortars. BARRABAS BOYAU cleaned. Parapet of LIME STREET thickened where required. PELLETIER and HOLLOWAY cleared where damaged by hostile fire.

C.K. Steward Capt. G.S.
for Lieut. Colonel,
General Staff, 2nd Division.

S E C R E T.

Report on Operations and Work done - 2nd Division.
From 4.0 p.m. 8th July to 4.0 p.m. 9th July, 1916.

1. OPERATIONS.

BERTHONVAL Section.

Yesterday evening a number of small H.E. shells fell in the vicinity of support line on the Northern flank of this section and also in ZOUAVE Valley.

Hostile machine guns were very active during the night.

At 3.30 a.m. a hostile working party was dispersed by our Lewis gun fire.

CARENCY Section.

Yesterday evening hostile trench mortars were active against COBURG Trench.

Between 11 a.m. and 1 p.m. to-day intermittent fire on our support line and communication trenches by 4.2" Hows. They were thought to be registering.

One of the officers who was stated in the Intelligence Report to be observing artillery fire, was shot by one of our snipers.

Enemy machine guns were active during the night. Our machine guns fired indirectly on BOIS de GIVENCHY during the night.

ARTILLERY.

At 12.40 p.m. to-day slight shelling of our observation posts on the LORETTE SPUR with 77 mm.

Our artillery fired in retaliation for activity of hostile trench mortars.

Working party at S.21.b.5.4 fired on by our field guns.

2. WORK DONE.

BERTHONVAL Section.

Left sub-section. MANDORA South widened for 50 yards, 3 traverses repaired. BROWN'S BURROWS cleaned and debris removed. General cleaning of all trenches.

Right sub-section. 10 yds. of trench rebuilt. 30 yds. of communication trench boarded. Drainage of communication trenches continued. TOTTENHAM Trench cleaned and deepened. A new store for S.A.A. and bombs constructed in ZOUAVE Valley.

CARENCY Section.

COBURG Trench cleaned and sides built up where damaged by hostile trench mortars One sniper's post constructed. Drainage of PELETIER ALLEY and trench of centre picquet in progress. Fire steps in right picquet rebuilt. HOLLOWAY Trench and QUARRY cleaned. Our wire strengthened where required.

[signature] Capt. G.S.
for Lieut. Colonel,
General Staff, 2nd Division.

S E C R E T.

Intelligence Report - 2nd Division.
From 4.0 p.m. 7th July, to 4.0 p.m. 8th July, 1916.

1. PATROL REPORTS.

1. Patrol reports enemy working party last night at S.21.b.2½.1½. This patrol also reports that the enemy appeared to hold their front trench lightly in this portion of the line and flares were sent up from their support line.

2. A patrol reports an enemy's bombing post 50 yards East of INTERNATIONAL Trench. Bombs were exchanged.

2. INFORMATION.

1. Red flares were reported to be, last night, a call used by the enemy for artillery fire. The response was immediate.

2. At 9.30 a.m. this morning columns of smoke were seen rising from behind the PIMPLE.

3. Fresh earth has appeared in the German parapet between KENNEDY and MOMBER Craters.

4. At 12 noon to-day the heads of an enemy working party were seen at S.15.a.9.7. Our artillery was informed and the party was dispersed.

3. TRAIN MOVEMENT.

The following trains observed :-

On the BILLY-MONTIGNY - HARNES Line.

4.5 p.m.	one train	moving	towards	HARNES.
5.35 p.m.	"	"	"	HARNES.
8.55 a.m.	"	"	"	HARNES.
9.55 a.m.	"	"	"	HARNES.
11.50 a.m.	"	"	"	BILLY-MONTIGNY.
12.58 p.m.	"	"	"	BILLY-MONTIGNY.

On the HENIN-LIETARD - HARNES Line.

9.35 a.m.	one train	moving	towards	HARNES.
1.25 p.m.	"	"		HARNES.
2.5 p.m.	"	"	"	HENIN-LIETARD.
2.10 p.m.	"	"	"	HARNES.

On the MERICOURT - BEAUMONT Line.

6.10 p.m.	one train	moving	towards	MERICOURT.
7.20 p.m.	"	"	"	BEAUMONT.

3 trains observed moving South and 2 moving North in the far distance but the exact lines on which they were moving cannot be stated.

[illegible signature] Capt. G.S.
for Lieut. Colonel,
General Staff, 2nd Division.

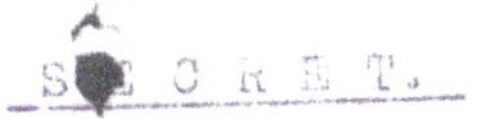
SECRET.

Intelligence Report - 2nd Division,

From 4.0 p.m. 8th July to 4.0 p.m. 9th July, 1916.

1. INFORMATION.

1. At 5.55 p.m. last night a party of about 30 mounted men were seen moving towards ROUVROY on the ROUVROY - ACHEVILLE Road.

2. At 10.10 a.m. a hostile aeroplane was seen to land close to the Northern end of BOIS VILAIN (U.19.b.).

3. During the day, a certain amount of individual movement was seen behind the enemy's lines but no movement of bodies of troops was observed. A few motor lorries were seen moving on the ROUVROY - ACHEVILLE Road.

4. The enemy seem very interested concerning our line just South of IRISH Crater. Numerous periscopes can be seen in his trench about this portion of the line.

5. An officer's patrol reports the enemy's wire to be weak between LOVE Crater and UHLAN Trench.

6. At 6.30 a.m. this morning 2 officers were seen to be observing the effect of their artillery fire opposite our left sub-section of the Northern section. They were wearing gloves and caps with glazed peaks.

2. TRAIN MOVEMENT.

Very little train movement observed during the day.

C.H. Steward Capt. G.S.
for Lieut. Colonel,
General Staff, 2nd Division.

SECRET.

Report on Operations and Work done - 2nd Division.
From 4.0 p.m. 9th July to 4.0 p.m. 10th July, 1916.

1. OPERATIONS.

BERTHONVAL Section.

At about 2 p.m. to-day our reserve lines were shelled with shrapnel.

Enemy's machine guns were active during the night opposite INTERNATIONAL TRENCH.

On the whole a very quiet day in this section.

CARENCY Section.

At 8.34 p.m. yesterday the Germans sprung a mine at S.8.b.9.1½. Our storming party immediately proceeded to the scene of the explosion and met a party of the enemy creeping round the Northern lip of the crater formed. They bombed the enemy who retired. Practically no damage caused to our main line. One of our bombing posts was obliterated. We suffered a few casualties but our position does not appear to have been adversely effected. The enemy barraged our front and support lines for about half an hour after the explosion. Our snipers claim 2 Germans by this new crater to-day. Our artillery retaliated.

2. WORK DONE.

BERTHONVAL Section.

CENTRAL AVENUE and SEAGATE cleaned. Bomb store built in VINCENT STREET. Bombing post completed in VINCENT sap. 40 yards of trench in BROWN'S BURROWS deepened one foot. 12 feet of fire steps constructed. Widening of the new trench between CENTRAL and INTERNATIONAL trenches continued.

CARENCY Section.

Consolidation of new crater blown yesterday evening in progress. WILSON STREET, COBURG and BARNABAS deepened. The opening up of UHLAN ALLEY East of LIME STREET continued. One bomb store rebuilt. General repairs to communication trenches.

[signature] Capt. G.S.
for Lieut. Colonel,
General Staff, 2nd Division.

S E C R E T.

Intelligence Report - 2nd Division.
From 4.0 p.m. 9th July to 4.0 p.m. 10th July, 1916.

1. INFORMATION.

1. At 7.35 p.m. 2 parties of the enemy, each about 20 men strong left AVION by the road running through N.27.c.7.5. They were marching Northwards.

2. At 7.40 p.m. a party of the enemy, about 30 strong, were observed marching towards VIMY on the ACHEVILLE - VIMY Road. These men were wearing helmets.

3. At 7.50 p.m. a hostile machine gun was seen to be mounted on the German parapet at about S.15.a.6½.4½. and opened fire on one of our aeroplanes.

4. It is reported that about 10 Germans have been observed in their line at about S.8.b.9½.1½. They were wearing a head-dress resembling a Highland bonnet with the ribbons pushed well back on the head (more information is required if possible).

2. HOSTILE MOVEMENT.

Movement rather above normal, consisting of small parties, motor and horse transport, observed to-day on the following roads:-

(a) AVION to LENS; chief movement to LENS.
(b) At O.8.c.5.8; chief movement towards HARNES.
(c) LENS to LOISON: chief movement to LOISON.

3. TRAIN MOVEMENT.

Following trains observed:-

On the BILLY-MONTIGNY - HARNES Line.

7.45 a.m.	one train moving towards		BILLY-MONTIGNY
12.35 p.m.	"	"	HARNES.
12.55 p.m.	"	"	HARNES.
1.50 p.m.	"	"	BILLY-MONTIGNY.

On the MERICOURT - BEAUMONT Line.

7.5 p.m.	one train moving towards		BEAUMONT.
7.25 p.m.	" engine	"	BEAUMONT.
7.55 p.m.	" train	"	MERICOURT.

4 trains moving North and 3 moving South were observed in the distance but the exact lines on which they were moving cannot be stated.

[signature] Capt. G.S.
for Lieut. Colonel,
General Staff, 2nd Division.

S E C R E T.

Intelligence Report - 2nd Division.
From 4.0 p.m. 10th July to 4.0 p.m. 11th July, 1918.

1. INFORMATION.

1. The enemy appear to be doing some work in their line at S.15.a.5½.4. They can be seen carrying sandbags along the trench and then appear to go down some steps. Work was observed to be in progress at 4 p.m. yesterday and again this morning. Our artillery was informed in each case and their fire stopped the work.

2. Movement rather above normal of small parties was observed yesterday evening on the roads behind the enemy's lines as follows:-

(a) From 5 p.m. to 5.20 p.m. about 100 men entered AVION from the North in small parties.
(b) About 100 men marching in three parties were observed on the ROUVROY - ACHEVILLE Road moving South.
(c) At about 6 p.m. 50 men were seen entering SALLAUMINES from the West.

To-day the movement behind the enemy's lines has not been above normal, the only movement of any size observed was a party of about 100 men moving towards AVION on the AVION - VIMY Road at 12.20 p.m.

3. The enemy is reported to have considerably strengthened his wire just North of the PIMPLE.

4. This morning Germans were seen walking about behind MOMBER Crater. Our trench mortars were informed.

5. A working party of about 50 strong was seen working this morning at T.22.b. South of MERICOURT.

6. Our patrols report enemy's wire to be strong consisting of 4 bays from about S.21.a.9.8 to S.15.c.7.3. A large hostile working party was reported last night to be working in front of this portion of the line. His work was thought to be wiring.

7. The enemy are reported to be using a mechanical bomb thrower opposite CARENCY Section. More information is required.

2. TRAIN MOVEMENT.

Following trains were observed :-

On the BILLY-MONTIGNY - HARNES Line.

At 11.45 a.m.	one train moving towards	HARNES.
12.3 p.m.	" " "	HARNES.
12.45 p.m.	" " "	BILLY-MONTIGNY.

On the HENIN-LIETARD - HARNES Line.

7.30 p.m.	one train moving towards	HENIN-LIETARD.
8.20 p.m.	" " "	HARNES.
8.25 p.m.	" " "	HENIN-LIETARD.
10.15 a.m.	" " "	HARNES.
12.56 p.m.	" " "	HENIN-LIETARD.

On the MERICOURT - BEAUMONT Line.

6.5 p.m.	one train moving towards	BEAUMONT.
9.38 a.m.	" " "	BEAUMONT.
10.35 a.m.	" " "	MERICOURT.
2.0 p.m.	" " "	MERICOURT.
2.15 p.m.	" " "	MERICOURT.
2.55 p.m.	" " "	BEAUMONT.

5 trains moving North and 4 trains moving South were observed in the distance but the exact lines on which they were moving cannot be stated.

C.H. Stewart Capt. G.S.
for Lieut. Colonel,
General Staff, 2nd Divn.

SECRET.

Report on Operations and Work done - 2nd Division.
From 4 p.m. 10th July to 4.0 p.m. 11th July, 1916.

1. OPERATIONS.

BERTHONVAL Section.

The enemy's machine guns were active during the night opposite this section.

Reserve line in ZOUAVE Valley shelled by heavy minenwerfer from 8 a.m. to 9 a.m. to-day.

CARENCY Section.

The enemy's trench mortars have been active during the last 24 hours, notably :-

(a) Yesterday evening against the WARREN.
(b) Early this morning against both subsections.
(c) 12 noon against out line by Northern group of craters.

Our artillery and trench mortars replied to this activity.

BOMBS were thrown into SOUCHEZ Alley and BOYAU THIRIET apparently by some mechanical thrower.

Enemy's snipers active during the night and early morning.

Our machine guns fired on gaps in the enemy's wire intermittently during the night.

ARTILLERY.

At 1.0 p.m. and 3.0 p.m. to-day the enemy shelled CABARET ROUGE with shrapnel and H.E.

Our artillery fired on working party at S.15.a.5½.4 and on enemy's trenches to keep down rifle and machine gun fire against one of our aeroplanes.

2. WORK DONE.

BERTHONVAL Section.

Front line between CENTRAL AVENUE and OLD BOOTS Trench widened and deepened, also front line North of OLD BOOTS Trench cleaned and repaired.

40 yards of CENTRAL AVENUE cleaned. 2 bomb stores and one ammunition store constructed. New trench to VINCENT Sap lengthened 12 yards. 15 yards of support line deepened and widened. Parapet repaired and entrance rebuilt to GRANBY Sap.

CARENCY Section.

LIME STREET, TRANCHOT, COBURG and BARRABAS Trenches deepened UHLAN Trench opened up and deepened. Work on new battalion H.Q. proceeding. Consolidation of near lip of crater (of 9/7/16 continued. Work continued on BROWN'S BURROWS. ERSATZ AVENUE cleaned.

C. H. Steward Capt. G.S.
for Lieut. Colonel,
General Staff, 2nd Division.

S E C R E T.

Report on Operations and Work done - 2nd Division.
From 4.0 p.m. 11th July to 4.0 p.m. 12th July, 1916.

1. OPERATIONS.

BERTHONVAL Section.

Front line slightly shelled with shrapnel at 10.45 p.m. At 10 p.m. ZOUAVE Valley slightly shelled. Hostile machine guns active throughout the night.

CARENCY Section.

ZOUAVE Valley shelled at intervals during the day with shrapnel and H.E. Hostile trench mortars active in the morning against the vicinity of the WARREN and Northern group of craters. Our artillery retaliated for hostile fire throughout the night. Our snipers claim 4 of the enemy. Hostile snipers very alert on this front.

ARTILLERY.

Intermittent shelling of ZOUAVE Valley during the day. Last night the enemy shelled CABARET ROUGE and 130th ALLEY between 9.30 p.m. and 10.30 p.m. At 3.5 p.m. a 5.9" How. fired 4 rounds into S.20.b. Our artillery fired on 4 enemy working parties. Retaliation for hostile fire. Trenches behind the PIMPLE shelled.

2. WORK DONE.

BERTHONVAL Section.

Front line trenches widened and deepened where required. Fire stepping continued. East end of TOTTENHAM deepened. LADBROOKE GROVE widened, deepened and generally improved. BLUEBELL sap deepened by 1 foot for a length of 15 yards. Fire steps improved and revetment repaired where necessary. 50 yds. of BROWN'S BURROWS fire stepped.

CARENCY Section.

LIME STREET and TRANCHOT trench repaired where damaged by hostile trench mortar fire. More wire put out from LOVE Crater along our front line towards KENNEDY Crater also gaps in front of centre Picquet strengthened. BARRABAS and COBURG deepened also UHLAN Alley. Work on BROWN'S BURROWS continued.

A.P. Steward, Capt. G.S.
for Lieut. Colonel,
General Staff, 2nd Division.

S E C R E T.

Intelligence Report - 2nd Division.
From 4.0 p.m. 11th July to 4.0 p.m. 12th July, 1916.

1. HOSTILE WORK.

1. Hostile working parties were active last night in the enemy's front and support lines in S.21.b. A wiring party was seen at S.15.c.6.2.

2. At 4.0 p.m. yesterday Germans were again seen working in their trench at S.15.a.5½.4. It appears that some work of importance is going on at this place as the enemy working parties are very persistent in spite of our artillery fire.

3. At 4.45 p.m. a working party of about 40 men was seen on the ROUVROY - ACHEVILLE road. They appeared to be carrying out road repairs.

4. At 7.15 a.m. the enemy were seen digging in the trench at S.15.a.6.7½.

2. HOSTILE MOVEMENT.

1. At 8.25 p.m. 11 2-horse wagons were seen moving North from MERICOURT.

2. At 10.45 a.m. a troop of cavalry was seen entering DROCOURT from the East.

3. At 2.15 p.m. a party of about 30 men was seen to enter AVION from the North.

A considerable amount of horse and motor traffic was observed during the day on the ROUVROY - ACHEVILLE road, the chief movement being towards ACHEVILLE

3. HOSTILE MACHINE GUN.

A hostile machine gun reported at S.21.b.2½.6.

4. MISCELLANEOUS.

Enemy's searchlights were reported last night from the direction of LENS.

6. TRAIN MOVEMENT.

The following trains were observed :-

On the BILLY-MONTIGNY - HARNES Line.

9.50 a.m. one train moving towards HARNES.
12.50 p.m. " " " HARNES.

On the HENIN-LIETARD - HARNES Line.

5.35 p.m. one train moving towards HARNES.
5.45 p.m. " " " HENIN-LIETARD.
12.55 p.m. " " " HENIN-LIETARD.

On the BEAUMONT - MERICOURT Line.

8.45 a.m. one train moving towards BEAUMONT.
10.45 a.m. " " " BEAUMONT.
11.0 a.m. " " " MERICOURT.
1.0 p.m. " " " MERICOURT.

5 trains moving North and 4 trains moving South observed in the distance but the exact lines on which they were moving cannot be stated.

[signature] Capt. G.S.
for Lieut. Colonel,
General Staff, 2nd Division.

S E C R E T.

Report on Operations and Work done - 2nd Division.
From 4.0 p.m. 12th July to 4.0 p.m. 13th July, 1916.

1. OPERATIONS.

BERTHONVAL Section.

Enemy's snipers and machine guns active throughout the night.

Enemy fired about 40 small shells between 1 a.m. and 2 a.m., the majority falling on Talus des Zouaves.

CARENCY Section.

At about 12 midnight a German bombing party approached and attempted to bomb one of our posts just North of FOOTBALL Crater. They were driven off by our bombers.

Enemy's trench mortars very active on this front from 11 a.m. to 12.30 p.m. Our artillery and trench mortars replied and silenced them.

Enemy's snipers active during the night.

ARTILLERY.

Enemy shelled CABARET ROUGE intermittently with 77 mm between 9 and 11 p.m. last night. Some shelling of ZOUAVE Valley during the morning.

Our artillery retaliated for hostile fire.

A working party at S.21.b.4.5 was fired on effectively.

Trenches round the PIMPLE shelled.

2. WORK DONE.

BERTHONVAL Section.

2 loophole barricades commenced in OLD BOOTS Trench. One loophole barricade completed in CENTRAL AVENUE. TOTTENHAM Road deepened. New support trench between GOBRON and ERSATZ deepened for 1 ft. over 15 yards. SNARGATE STREET cleaned and trench boards relaid over 24 yards. GRANBY deepened 1½ ft. over 50 yards.

CARENCY Section.

Sap head to KENNEDY Crater prolonged. LIME STREET and TRANCHOT repaired where damaged by hostile trench mortars. Support trench between TRANCHOT and GOBRON strengthened. Fire steps re-made between ERSATZ and HARTUNG. Post and fire steps re-made in HOLLOWAY and THIRIET Alley. Wire balls made and put out North of KENNEDY Crater. 60 yards of wire put out in front of right Picquet and 60 in front of centre Picquet.

H. Pleward Capt. G.S.

for Lieut. Colonel,

General Staff, 2nd Division.

S E C R E T.

Intelligence Report - 2nd Division.
From 4.0 p.m. 12th July to 4.0 p.m. 13th July, 1916.

1. HOSTILE WORK.

1. At 8.55 a.m. a working party of about 60 men was seen at T.22.b.
2. Enemy working parties are again reported to have been active during the night opposite BERTHONVAL Section from about S.15.c.8.2 to S.21.b.1.5. The enemy appears to be doing much work on this portion of his front, both on the front line and on his wire.

2. HOSTILE MOVEMENT.

1. At 9.40 a.m. about 30 men were seen drilling in open order at U.14.a.
2. At 2.45 p.m. about 60 men were seen scattered about a field at N.27.d.; later they fell in and marched away towards Puits 18.
3. Abnormal movement is again reported on the ACHEVILLE - ROUVROY Road chiefly consisting of motor lorries and 2-horse wagons. The movement was not concentrated but chiefly in the direction of ACHEVILLE

3. HOSTILE Machine Gun and Trench Mortars.

A suspected machine gun emplacement just South of IRISH Crater at S.9.c.½.7 has been covered up with some sort of sacking.

Trench mortar positions suspected at S.9.c.2½.5, S.9.c.4½.1½ and S.15.a.5.7.

4. INFORMATION.

1. The mechanical bomb thrower reported in the Intelligence Report of 10th/11th July is now thought to be a revolver gun.
2. The enemy are firing many green lights but their meaning cannot be interpreted. Red lights appear to be a call for artillery fire.

5. TRAIN MOVEMENT. Following trains reported :-

On the HENIN-LIETARD - HARNES Line.

7.25 p.m.	one train	moving	towards	HARNES.
7.30 p.m.	"	"	"	HENIN-LIETARD.
7.50 p.m.	"	"	"	HARNES.
8.50 a.m.	"	"	"	HENIN-LIETARD.
9.30 a.m.	"	"	"	HARNES.
10.20 a.m.	"	"	"	HENIN-LIETARD.
11.10 a.m.	"	"	"	HARNES.
12.50 p.m.	"	"	"	HENIN-LIETARD.
1.55 p.m.	"	"	"	HARNES.
2.5 p.m.	"	"	"	HENIN-LIETARD.
2.13 p.m.	"	"	"	HENIN-LIETARD.
2.40 p.m.	"	"	"	HENIN-LIETARD.

On the MERICOURT - BEAUMONT Line and on the BILLY-MONTIGNY - HARNES Line, practically no movement was observed.

9 trains going South and 3 trains going North were observed in the distance but the exact lines on which they were moving cannot be stated.

W. Steward. Capt. G.S.
for Lieut. Colonel,
General Staff, 2nd Division.

S E C R E T.

Report on Operations and Work done - 2nd Division
From 4.0 p.m. 13th July to 4.0 p.m. 14th July, 1916.

1. OPERATIONS.

BERTHONVAL Section.

Some shelling of our support line during the day. No damage done.

At 2.40 p.m. this morning the enemy fired about 20 shrapnel over ZOUAVE Valley.

CARENCY Section.

Enemy's trench mortars active between 1 and 3 p.m. doing some damage to our front line, our trench mortars replied effectively.

Enemy's snipers reported active opposite GOBRON Trench. 1 German was shot opposite THIRIET Alley at 8.30 a.m. this morning.

ARTILLERY.

Enemy shelled 130th Alley at about 12.45 p.m. to-day. Some shelling of ZOUAVE Valley.

Our artillery fired on hostile working parties and in retaliation for hostile fire.

2. WORK DONE.

BERTHONVAL Section.

8 yards of OLD BOOTS TRENCH revetted. TOTTENHAM Trench deepened, and work on traverses continued. 30 floor boards taken up cleaned and relaid. 20 yds. of parapet thickened in MANDORA South. VINCENT Sap revetted for 15 yds. GRANBY AVENUE deepened and widened over 100 yds.

CARENCY Section.

Cleaning and repairing trenches where damaged by hostile fire. Revetting continued in COBURG ALLEY. BARRABAS deepened Snipers post commenced in GOBRON.

[signature] Capt. G.S.
for Lieut. Colonel,
General Staff, 2nd Division.

S E C R E T.

Intelligence Report - 2nd Division.
From 4.0 p.m. 13th July to 4.0 p.m. 14th July, 1916.

1. HOSTILE MOVEMENT.

1. At 4.0 p.m. yesterday a party of about 30 mounted men was seen going towards ACHEVILLE on the ACHEVILLE - ROUVROY Road.

2. Traffic on the roads behind the German lines opposite our front has been normal to-day. Chief movement has been on the ACHEVILLE - ROUVROY Road.

2. HOSTILE WORK.

1. At 6.30 p.m. last night the enemy were seen working on their sap which leads into KENNEDY Crater and on their front trench just North of the sap.

2. The enemy's wire in front of the BERTHONVAL Section is reported to be strong. This wire has been considerably increased during the last 4 days as will be seen by reports of enemy wiring parties opposite this section.

3. INFORMATION.

1. The enemy appear to have a dump about T.18.c.3.9. Wagons and lorries have been seen to stop there.

2. The enemy have 3 loopholes in position opposite our sap to MOMBER Crater. So far no shots have been fired from them.

3. A hostile machine gun emplacement is suspected at S.9.a.1.1 just East of MILDREN Crater.

4. TRAIN MOVEMENT.

No trains have been observed to-day owing to adverse weather conditions.
In continuation of yesterday's report on hostile trains which were observed after 4 p.m:-

On the HENIN-LIETARD - HARNES Line.

4.20 p.m. one train moving towards				HENIN-LIETARD.
4.45 p.m.	"	"	"	HARNES.
5.30 p.m.	"	"	"	HENIN-LIETARD.
7.5 p.m.	"	"	"	HARNES.
7.30 p.m.	"	"	"	HENIN-LIETARD.
8.5 np.m.	"	"	"	HENIN-LIETARD.

Also after 4 p.m. - 5 trains were seen moving North and 7 moving South in the distance. The exact lines on which they were moving cannot be stated.

[illegible] Capt. G.S.
for Lieut. Colonel,
General Staff, 2nd Division.

S E C R E T.

Report on Operations and Work done - 2nd Division.
From 4.0 p.m. 14th July to 4.0 p.m. 15th July, 1916.
****

1. OPERATIONS.

BERTHONVAL Section.

Enemy's working party fired on last night.

Enemy's artillery active about 2 a.m. with shrapnel and H.E. on support line and ZOUAVE Valley in the Southern sub-section.

Enemy bombed ERSATZ Sap last night. Between 20 and 30 bombs were thrown, all fell short. Our bombers replied.

CARENCY Section.

Hostile trench mortars active between 3.30 p.m. and 4 p.m. opposite Northern sub-section. Our artillery replied and silenced them.

Occasional shelling of communication trench leading from CABARET ROUGE to ZOUAVE Valley.

Hostile trench mortars active against SOUCHEZ LAKE.

Enemy snipers comparatively quiet.

2. WORK DONE.

BERTHONVAL Section.

Front trench revetted, fire steps repaired and parapet heightened. New bomb store made in OLD BOOT STREET. TOTTENHAM Trench deepened and traverse built. New communication trench from front line to SHARGATE deepened. Fire bays in BROWN'S BURROWS revetted.

CARENCY Section.

Progress made for about 40 yards on the joining up of left and centre Picquets; small post established within 40 yards of centre picquet.

Repairs to trenches where damaged by hostile fire. 2 fire steps constructed in BANKSIDE. BRISSON, KENNEDY Sap and GOBRON cleared and deepened. Barricade built up in KENNEDY Sap.

[signature] Capt. G.S.
for Lieut. Colonel,
General Staff, 2nd Division.

S E C R E T.

Intelligence Report - 2nd Division.
From 4.0 p.m. 14th to 4.0 p.m. 15th July, 1916.
****

1. INFORMATION.

1. Yesterday evening enemy's shrapnel was bursting short. Enemy sent up a green light whereupon their range was increased about 200 yards.

2. At 1 a.m. a hostile patrol was seen to leave their line at about S.3.c.½.2. They were fired on and immediately returned to their trench.

3. A hostile sniper was seen on the lip of KENNEDY Crater. He was using a box periscope and exposing a dummy.

2. PATROL REPORT.

One of our patrols crossed FOOTBALL Crater (S.8.b.8.2) and reached enemy's lip. It is reported that the enemy have 2 saps about 20 yards East of their lip about 5 yards apart. These appear to be bombing posts capable of holding about 5 men each. From enemy's lip of the crater their front line is over 60 yds distance; the ground between is grass. Bombs were exchanged with the enemy in his forward post.

3. HOSTILE MACHINE GUN.

Hostile machine gun located at S.9.c.0.0½.

4. HOSTILE WORK.

1. It is reported that the enemy are busily engaged on work on their front line, about 200 yards opposite BLUEBELL Sap; it is thought that their work is construction of a new sap.

2. Enemy heard throughout the night working very hard on their trench South of TWINS Crater (S.15.a.2.7).

W.L. Howard Capt. G.S.
for Lieut. Colonel,
General Staff, 2nd Division.

SECRET.

Report on Operations and Work done - 2nd Division.
From 4.0 p.m. 15th July to 4.0 p.m. 16th July, 1916.

1. OPERATIONS.

BERTHONVAL Section.

Enemy's snipers reported active during the night.

A machine gun fired on CABARET ROAD between 11.30 p.m. and midnight.

At 6.30 a.m. slight shelling of the Southern portion of this section.

CARENCY Section.

Intermittent shelling of 130th ALLEY with H.E. and shrapnel.

Enemy's machine guns active during the night.

Between 3.30 and 4.30 p.m. the enemy fired a few rifle grenades.

Enemy's snipers comparatively quiet during the last 24 hours.

ARTILLERY.

Hostile artillery has shown little activity during the period under review.

Our artillery replied to any hostile shelling and fired on a working party at S.21.b.4.5.

2. HOSTILE WORK.

BERTHONVAL Section.

Fire steps and parados repaired where required and trenches revetted.

CARENCY Section.

Work continued on the joining up of the three picquets at the Northern end of the line. Parapet of centre picquet repaired where damaged by hostile fire. Fire steps built in BANKSIDE. GABRIELLE trench and KENNEDY Sap deepened. Fire stepping continued in front line. KENNEDY Sap, GOBRON and SOUCHEZ LANE revetted. Snipers post commenced in KENNEDY Sap.

C.H. Edward Capt. G.S.
for Lieut. Colonel,
General Staff, 2nd Division.

S E C R E T.

Intelligence Report - 2nd Division.
From 4.0 p.m. 15th July to 4.0 p.m. 16th July, 191[illegible].

INFORMATION.

1. The enemy have erected a loophole plate by FOOTBAL Crater on the South side of his concertina wire.

2. The hostile sniper reported in yesterday's summary as exposing a dummy by KENNEDY Crater, was seen exposing a dummy again to-day but he did not fire.

4. Some of the enemy were seen last night standing on top of their parapet at about S.9.c.3.0. They disappeared when fired on.

4. A small party of the enemy was observed last night working on his wire by MOMBER Crater.

5. A patrol reports that the enemy's wire from S.9.c.2.4 for about 50 yards South is not good.

C.W. Pleward Capt G.S.
for Lieut. Colonel,
General Staff, 2nd Division.

7/12 12 & Bn. 65 Aug 15 E.A.D

1st Shrop Jan – Dec 17 W.O.

2/6 25th CMA Aug 17 Capt. [illegible]

3. 2nd B. M. [illegible] Oct 18 E.A.D

7/12 9 [illegible] Sept 15 Capt [illegible]

2/10 [illegible] Jany & Nov 17 [illegible]

9/4 59 [illegible] Sept. 16 E.A.D

22/9 9 Black Watch Aug Dec 1916 E.A.D

2nd Division
War Diaries
General Staff

July 1916

W 4—664 250,000 3/15 L. S. & Co. Army Form W. 3091.

Cover for Documents.

Nature of Enclosures.

OPERATIONS FROM 20th JULY, 1916, to____________
****

MEMOS., INSTRUCTIONS, ETC., RECEIVED FROM

XIIIth CORPS.
****

Notes, or Letters written.

S E C R E T.
****

XIII Corps.
225/16 (G).

3rd Division.
9th Division.
18th Division.
30th Division.
35th Division.
"Q".
A.P.M.
A.D.A.S.
D.D.M.S.
A.D.O.S.
XV Corps.

Reference map shewing boundaries attached to XIII Corps G.225/15 of to-day's date, the map attached hereto shows that part of the boundary between the XIII Corps and XV Corps from S. of to N. of LONGUEVAL more accurately, after capture of LONGUEVAL VILLAGE & DELVILLE WOOD

[signature]
Major

XIII Corps,
19th July, 1916.

for B.G., G.S.

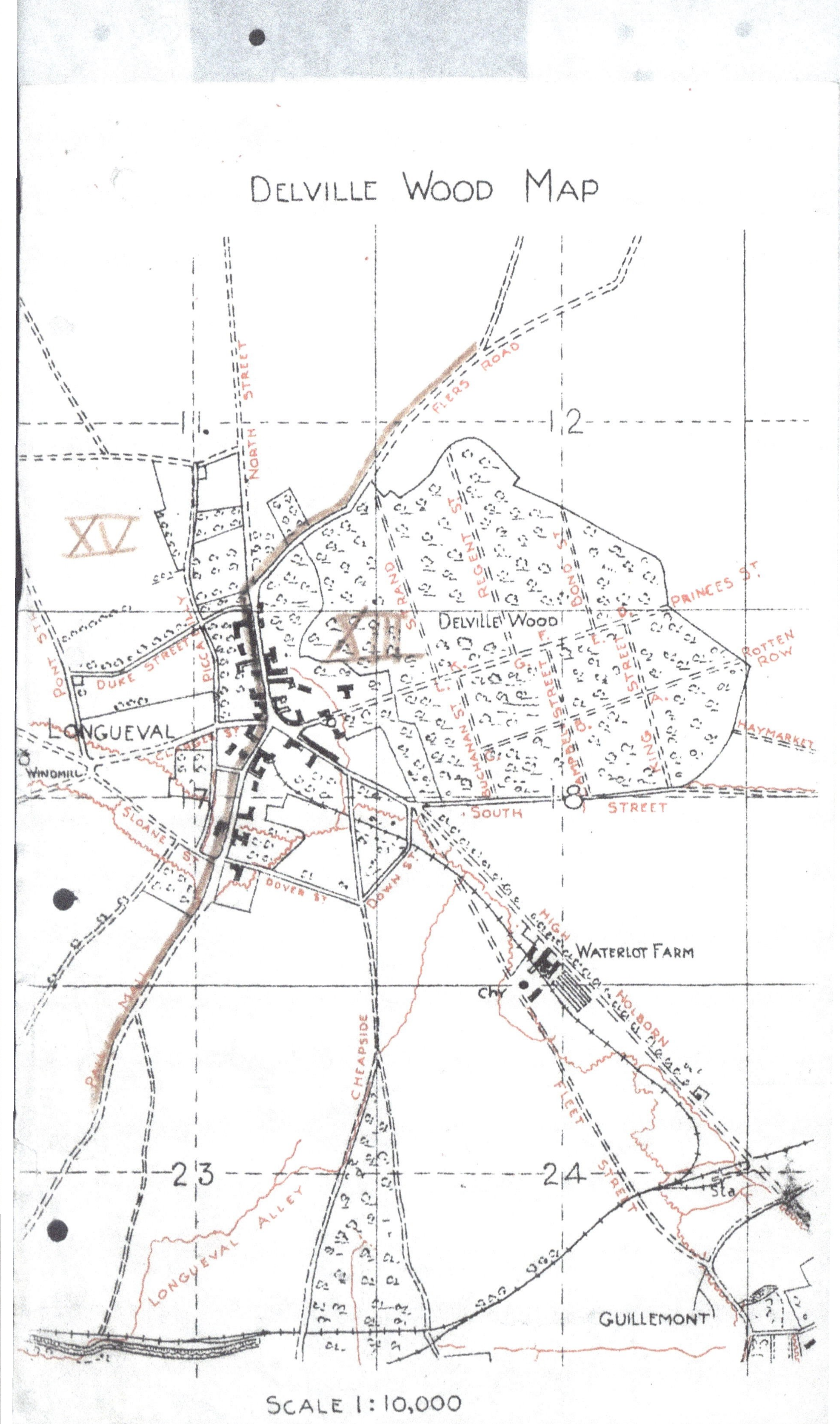
DELVILLE WOOD MAP
NORTH STREET
FLERS ROAD
12
XV
XII
DELVILLE WOOD
PRINCES ST.
ROTTEN ROW
HAYMARKET
DUKE STREET
PONT ST.
PICCADILLY
REGENT ST.
BOND ST.
BUCHANAN ST.
CAMPBELL STREET
KING
LONGUEVAL
WINDMILL
CLARGES ST.
SLOANE ST.
SOUTH STREET
DOVER ST.
DOWN ST.
HIGH HOLBORN
WATERLOT FARM
Chy
CHEAPSIDE
FLEET STREET
23
24
Sta.
LONGUEVAL ALLEY
GUILLEMONT
SCALE 1:10,000

"A" Form.

Army Form C. 2121.

MESSAGES AND SIGNALS.

No. of Message ....

Prefix ...... Code ...... m.	Words	Charge	This message is on a/c of:	Recd. at ......m.
Office of Origin and Service Instructions.	Sent		2 Div No. ...... Service.	Date ......
	At ......m.		[illegible]	From ......
	To			
	By		(Signature of "Franking Officer.")	By ......

TO [illegible]

Sender's Number.	Day of Month.	In reply to Number.	AAA
* A 694	21		

13th Corps and [illegible] Fourth Army state that the establishment of ammunition which it will be possible to maintain in future will be about 850 rounds per 18 pdr. and 650 rounds per gun 4.5 inch total establishment in front of railhead ends addressed RA repeated 2 [illegible]

From 2nd Dn.

Place

Time 1.40 p.m.

The above may be forwarded as now corrected. (Z)

Censor. .... Signature of Addressor or person authorised to telegraph in his name.

[illegible] Robinson Lt Col AA and QMG

* This line should be erased if not required.

225,000 W 14042—M 44. H. W. & V., Ld. 12/15.

"C" Form (Duplicate).
MESSAGES AND SIGNALS.

Army Form C. 2123.
(In books of 60's in duplicate.)

No. of Message

Prefix: Pb Code: 99 Words: 14

NRC

Charges to Pay. £ s. d.

Office Stamp: 21 VII 16 YB

Service Instructions.

Priority

Handed in at NRC Office 9.15 m. Received 1 m.

TO 2nd Divn

Sender's Number	Day of Month	In reply to Number	AAA
865	21st		

It is probable that the general attack will be renewed by fourth army Reserve army and 6th French army on 23rd aaa the task of 13 Corps will be a combined attack on the line FALFEMONT FARM GUILLEMONT by 30th Division and a detachment of 35th Division aaa 3rd Divn will have as objective the clearance of DELVILLE WOOD and LONGUEVAL VILLAGE and connection of GUILLEMONT with Delville Wood aaa meanwhile 2nd Divn will endeavour to gain ground towards GUILLEMONT as far as the Railway

FROM

PLACE & TIME

Wt. 432—M437 500,000 Pads. H W V 5/16 Forms C.2123.

"C" Form (Duplicate).
MESSAGES AND SIGNALS.

Army Form C. 2123.
(In books of 50's in duplicate.)

No. of Message ....

Charges to Pay. £ s. d.

Office Stamp.

Service Instructions.

Handed in at .... Office .... m. Received .... m.

TO 2

Sender's Number	Day of Month	In reply to Number	AAA

aaa 35th Divn the same south of the Railway aaa Consolidation of our own work and prevention of enemy work to continue with all energy aaa added 2nd 3rd 9th 30th 35th Divs 1st Cavalry Division and GOC RA repeated 1st Corps and PC 20 French Corps

FROM 13 Corps
PLACE & TIME 7.30 am

Wt. 432—M437 500,000 Pads. H W V 5/16 Forms C.2123.

S E C R E T.

Copy No.........4

XIII CORPS OPERATION ORDER NO.31.

21st July,1916.

1. (a) The Fourth Army will continue the offensive on the 22nd and 23rd Instant, in conjunction with the French Sixth Army.
The zero hour in each case will be communicated separately.

(b) Tomorrow,22nd instant, the XIII Corps will clear the whole of DELVILLE WOOD.
The XV Corps will capture HIGH WOOD and secure and dig a line from about 300 yards E. of HIGH WOOD to about S.11. central.
The XV Corps will also clear the orchards at North end of LONGUEVAL village.
The III Corps is attacking on left of XV Corps.

(c) On 23rd the XIII Corps will capture the German second line from FALFEMONT FARM (Inclusive) to WATERLOT FARM, including GUILLEMONT.
This attack to be made in conjunction with an attack by the French XX Corps on MAUREPAS.

For (b) above the bombardment on III and XV Corps front will commence at 4 p.m. and be continued at a slow steady rate of fire up to the moment of assault, when the artillery will lift on to objectives to be settled by III and XV Corps.
Bombardment on XIII Corps front to be arranged by XIII Corps.
For (c) above the bombardment will be arranged by XIII Corps in cooperation with French XX Corps.

(d) The 1st and 3rd Cavalry Divisions and 2nd Indian Cavalry Division will remain in present billets and bivouacs.
The 1st Cavalry Division is placed at disposal of XIII Corps for these operations: 2nd Indian Cavalry Division at disposal of XV Corps: 3rd Cavalry Division remains under Army Headquarters.

2. Tomorrow 22nd instant at an hour which will be notified separately the 3rd Division will complete the capture of DELVILLE WOOD and gain touch with the 5th Division of the XV Corps at the N.W.corner of the wood by seizing and forming a strong point in orchard at S.11.d.central from which the FLERS road and NORTH Street can be commanded. The advance on this point to be from the E. or S.E.
The 5th Division working from the W. will establish a strong point about S.11.d.0.3 from which NORTH Street can be commanded.
These operations will be carried out in such a way as to surround any enemy detachments still holding out in the Village of LONGUEVAL: the plan to be arranged between the G.Os.C.3rd and 5th Divisions.
The operation will be preceded by an artillery bombardment to be arranged by G.O.C.3rd Division direct with G.O.C.,R.A.,XIII Corps: no artillery of the XIII Corps will shoot W. of a N. and S.line through S.11.central: XV Corps artillery will not shoot S. of an E. and W.line through S.11.central.
The 3rd Divisional Artillery will be prepared to put on a barrage for the protection of 5th Division on the S.O.S. signal being made by that Division under arrangements to be made between Divisional Commanders concerned.

/The

Acknowledged.
Cd.

The G.O.C.3rd Division will detail a F.O.O. to ~~report at~~ Battalion H.Q. of right battalion of 5th Division prior to the commencement of the operations.

On the 23rd instant at an hour which is being notified separately the 30th Division will attack FALFEMONT FARM and GUILLEMONT simultaneouslywith the French XX Corps, which latter is attacking MAUREPAS.

The boundary between the French and British is a line drawn from MALTZ HORN FARM to point B.2.d.4.8. thence to the railway at B. 3.c.6.6. thence to the railway.

Objective:

The capture of FALFEMONT FARM, including the work S.E. of it, and the enemy's second line defences as far as the railway line, including GUILLEMONT.

The establishment of touch with the French XX Corps on the right and the 3rd Division on the left.

Method of attack.

The attack will be carried out in the form of a right attack starting from MALTZ HORN trench and a left attack starting from between TRONES WOOD and WATERLOT FARM.

Artillery.

The attack will be proceded by an artillery bombardment in accordance with orders to be issued by the G.O.C.,R.A. in consultation with G.O.C.30th Division.

The lifts and barrages of the Corps Artillery are shown on attached map.

The divisional artillery now under G.O.C.35th Division (less such artillery as is detailed by G.O.C.,R.A. for defence of the line) will be at the disposal of G.O.C. 30th Division for the attack.

Preliminary bombardment and wire cutting will be carried out in accordance with orders to be issued by G.O.C., R.A..

The artillery of the French XX Corps are assisting in the preliminary bombardment by fire on FALFEMONT FARM: it will not fire N. of the boundary between Corps after midnight 22/23rd.

4. In conjunction with the attack in para.3 above 3rd Division will capture the German defences as far S. as the railway line and including the trench running from T.19.a.0.3 to S.18.d.3.5.

5. In connection with above attacks Divisional Commanders of 3rd and 30th Divisions will consider the advisability of smoke barrages to cover their left flanks if the wind is favourable.

The attacks will be covered in all cases by advancing Lewis guns into shell holes or other cover prior to the assault: the task of these guns is to keep down fire from the enemy's parapet till the moment of assault.

They should fire in enfilade so far as is possible.

6. On 22nd and 23rd the 1st Cavalry Division will remain in its present billets and bivouacs.

Separate instructions will be issued later.

/7.

7. Corps Headquarters will be at ETINEHEM.

W H Greenly
B.G., G.S..

XIII Corps.

Issued at ......10/15.....p.m.

Copy No. 1 Fourth Army.
2 XV Corps.
3 French XX Corps.
4 2nd Division.
5 3rd Division.
6 30th Division.
7 35th Division.
8 No.9 Squadron, R.F.C.
9)
10) G.O.C., R.A.
11 C.E.
12 A.D.A.S.
13 D.D.M.S.
14 "Q".
15 A.P.M.
16)
17) "G".
18)

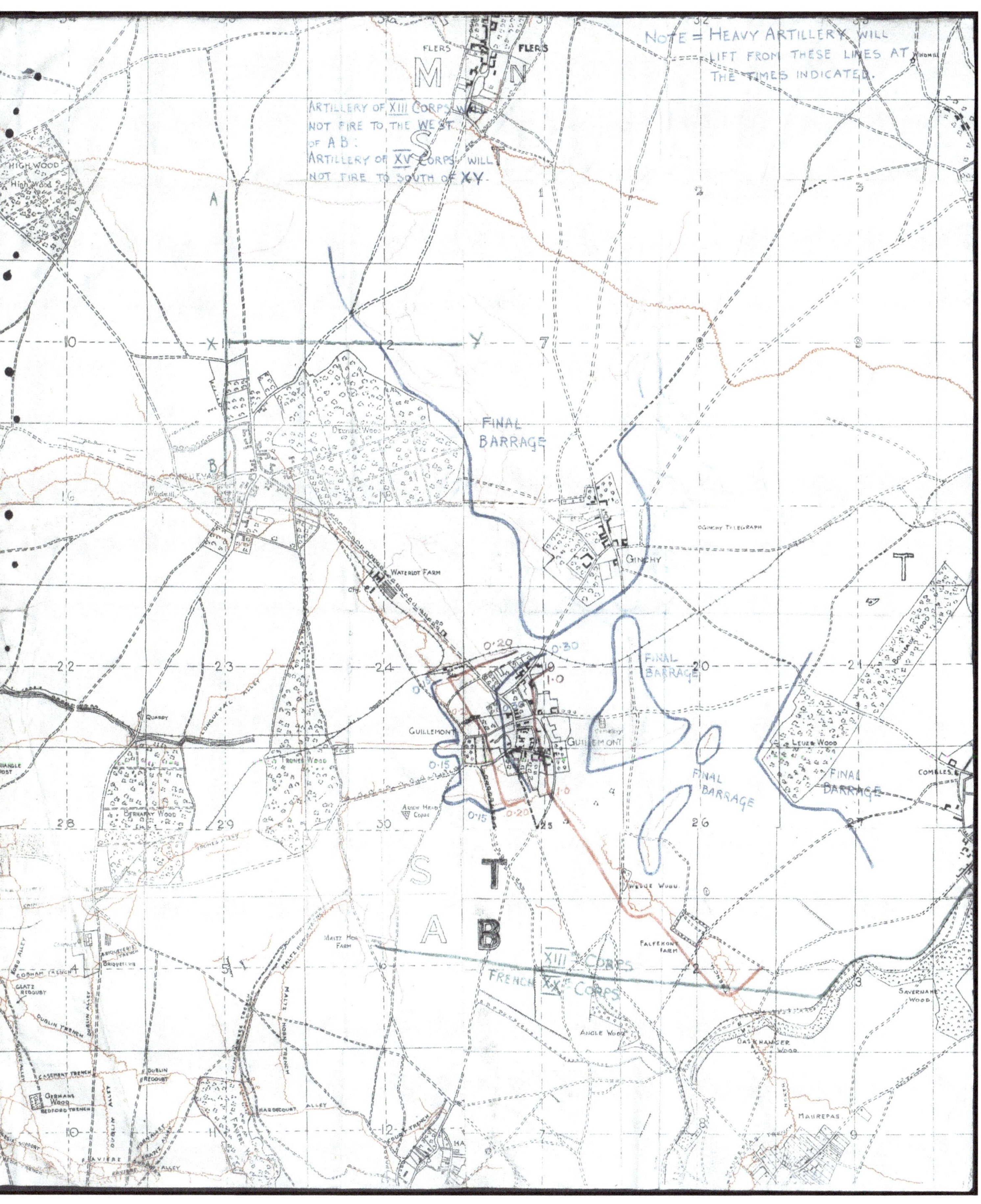

NOTE = HEAVY ARTILLERY WILL LIFT FROM THESE LINES AT THE TIMES INDICATED.
ARTILLERY OF XIII CORPS WILL NOT FIRE TO THE WEST OF AB: ARTILLERY OF XV CORPS WILL NOT FIRE TO SOUTH OF XY.
FLERS
HIGH WOOD
Delville Wood
FINAL BARRAGE
Waterlot Farm
GINCHY
GINCHY TELEGRAPH
0·20
0·30
1·0
0·15
0·20
GUILLEMONT
Guillemont
FINAL BARRAGE
FINAL BARRAGE
Leuze Wood
FINAL BARRAGE
COMBLES
Trones Wood
Bernafay Wood
Quarry
Arrow Head Copse
Wedge Wood
Maltz Horn Farm
Falfemont Farm
XIII CORPS
FRENCH XX CORPS
Angle Wood
Savernake Wood
Oakhanger Wood
Maurepas
Briqueterie
Cobham Trench
Glatz Redoubt
Dublin Trench
Dublin Alley
Casement Trench
Dublin Redoubt
Germans Wood
Bedford Trench
Hardecourt Alley

Accompanies

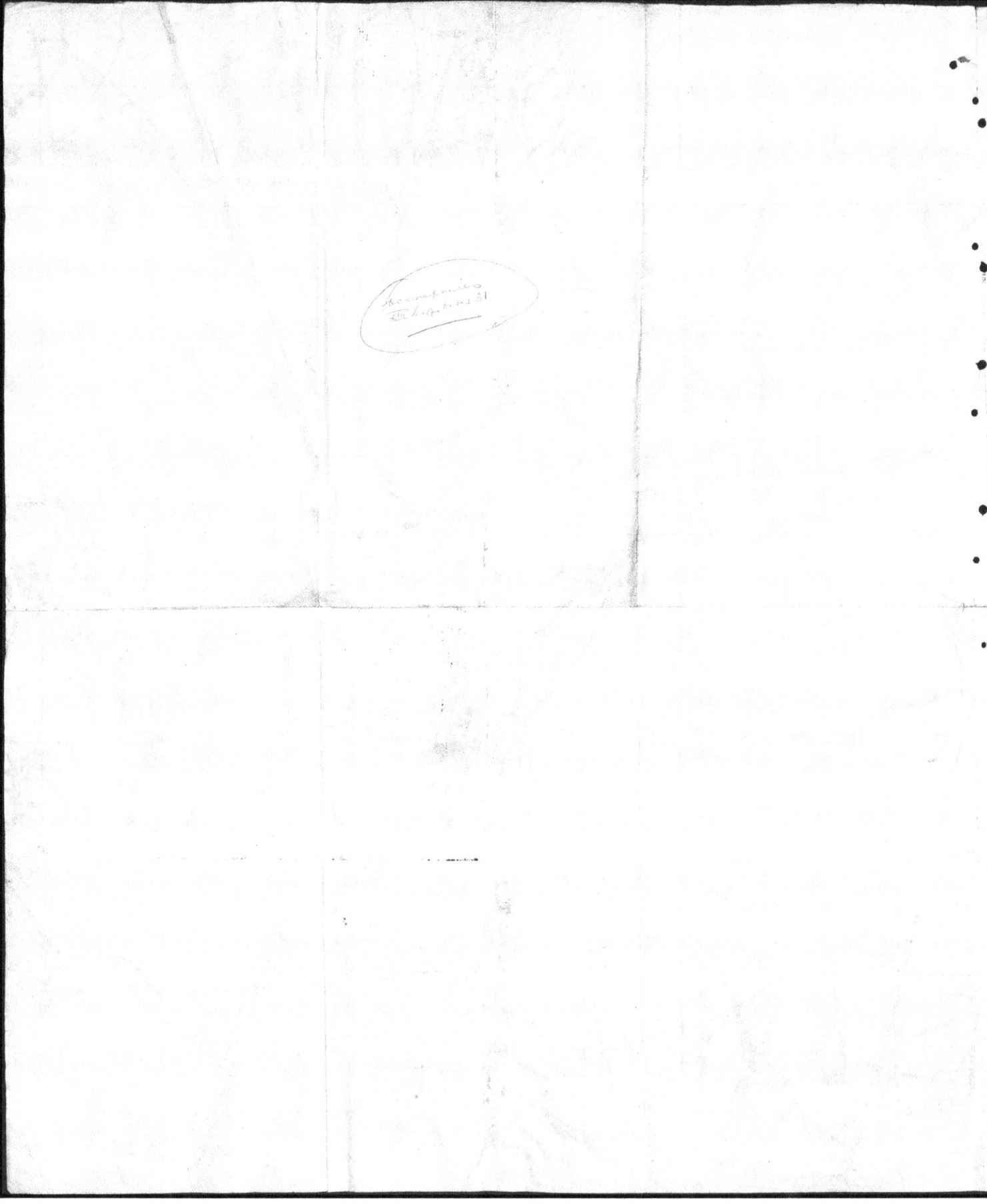

S E C R E T.
****
XIII Corps.
132/81 (G)

2 Divn No
GS 1001/2/3

2nd Division.
~~3rd Division.~~
~~30th Division.~~
~~35th Division.~~
~~G.O.C.R.A.~~
~~No. 9 Squadron R.F.C.~~
~~XV Corps.~~
~~French XX Corps~~.

Reference Operation Order No. 31.

The attack on evening of 22nd by XV Corps will commence at 9.30 p.m.

The attack on 23rd instant by XIII Corps and French XX Corps will commence at 3.40 a.m.

These times are only to be communicated to those whom it immediately concerns. In no case will they be communicated by telephone.

Acknowledge receipt by wire.

Acknowledged

W H Greenly
B.G., G.S.

XIII Corps,
21st July, 1916.

"C" Form (Original). Army Form C. 2123

MESSAGES AND SIGNALS.

No. of Message ....

Prefix .... Code .... Words	Received	Sent, or sent out	Office Stamp.
£ s. d. Charges to collect	From .... By	At .... m. To .... By	
Service Instructions.			

Handed in at NRC Office .... m. Received .... m.

TO 2nd Divn

*Sender's Number	Day of Month	In reply to Number	AAA
904	22		

[illegible] operation [illegible] No 21 para 1(c) 13th Corps [illegible] attack [illegible] 23rd inst aaa [illegible] attack [illegible] will not [illegible] 2nd Division will [illegible] plan accordingly [illegible] proposed [illegible] HQrs [illegible] as [illegible] possible especially [illegible] are [illegible] of [illegible] notice [illegible]

FROM 13th Corps

PLACE & TIME [illegible]

acknowledged [initials illegible]

* This line should be erased if not required.

W 15660—M 151 75,000 Pads. H & S 2/16 Forms/C.2123. (5668)

D.D.M.S. No.
396.

XIII Corps No.
QC1384

2nd Division Q.

For necessary action.

Lieut.-Colonel,
A.Q.M.G., XIII Corps.

22nd July, 1916.

Telephone message from 13 Corps cancelled this order and Tent Division to move to MORLANCOURT.

Headquarters,

XIII Corps.

Will you kindly issue the following orders for the move of the Field Ambulances of the 2nd. Division.

The 3 Bearer Divisions of the Field Ambulances to march with, and be rationed by, their respective Brigades.

The 3 Tent Divisions of the Field Ambulances to proceed forthwith to the Main Dressing Station at J.24.b (ALBERT Combined sheet) and report to O.C. No. 8 Field Ambulance there for duty on arrival.

All motor ambulance wagons of the 2nd. Division to proceed forthwith to the Main Dressing Station.

21st. July 1916.

Colonel,
D.D.M.S. XIII Corps.

"A" Form. Army Form C. 2121.

MESSAGES AND SIGNALS. No. of Message

Prefix Code m. Office of Origin and Service Instructions	Words	Charge	This message is on a/c of: Service. (Signature of "Franking Officer.")	Recd. at m. Date From By
	Sent At m. To By			

TO Operations file B. 23.7.

Sender's Number.	Day of Month	In reply to Number	AAA
*			

2nd DIV bns artillery will move on 23rd inst from their present positions into the reserve areas AAA The move to be so timed that by 7.0 pm on 22nd the inf. bdes. of the division will be (a) one inf. bde BOIS des TAILLES N. of BRAY–CORBIE road R.E. Coys + F.A. of this bde to remain at MORLANCOURT (b) one inf. bde. groups HAPPY VALLEY (c) one inf bde groups SAND PIT Valley Squares F 13 + 19 (d) Pioneer Battn. MORLANCOURT (e) Tent division of

From			
Place			
Time			

The above may be forwarded as now corrected. (Z)

Censor. Signature of Addressor or person authorised to telegraph in his name.

* This line should be erased if not required.

(4198) Wt. W14042—M44. 300000 Pads. 12/15. Sir J. C. & S.

"A" Form. Army Form C. 2121.

MESSAGES AND SIGNALS. No. of Message

Prefix Code m.	Words	Charge	This message is on a/c of:	Recd. at m.
Office of Origin and Service Instructions.	Sent		Service.	Date
	At m.			From
	To			
	By		(Signature of "Franking Officer.")	By

TO

* Sender's Number.	Day of Month	In reply to Number	AAA

F.A at MORLANCOURT AAA
MÉAULTE is placed at the
disposal of 2nd Div for their
rearward echelon AAA The SAND
PIT valley and HAPPY VALLEY
valley will be clear of 6th Div.
troops respectively at 7.30am
& 9.30am. AAA Roads available
(a) Track from MORLANCOURT through
Squares K 9, 10, 11 to BOIS des
TAILLES north (R) road VILLE
MORLANCOURT thence track as in
(a) continuing North of BOIS
des TAILLES north of road
junction K6 d 8.4 thence road to
FILI FORM Tree thence track to
head of SANDPIT valley road

From
Place
Time

The above may be forwarded as now corrected (Z)

Censor. Signature of Addressor or person authorised to telegraph in his name.

* This line should be erased if not required.

(4198) Wt. W14042—M44. 300000 Pads. 12/15. Sir J. C. & S.

"A" Form. Army Form C. 2121.

MESSAGES AND SIGNALS.

No. of Message

Prefix ... Code ... m.	Words	Charge	This message is on a/c of:	Recd. at ... m.
Office of Origin and Service Instructions.	Sent		... Service.	Date
	At ... m.			From
	To			
	By		(Signature of "Franking Officer.")	By

TO

Sender's Number.	Day of Month	In reply to Number	AAA
*			

junction K6d & 4 not to be crossed before 10.0 am. (C) BRAY-CORBIE road and the SOMME valley road to SAILLY-LE-SEC thence to BRAY-CORBIE road AAA BOIS des TAILLES south of BRAY-CORBIE road will be available for temporary halt through the day if required AAA Position of bdes in present area to be reported to H.Q. XIII Corps "Q" by 7.0pm on 23rd AAA Supply and refilling arrangements no change for the present.

From: Troops of 30th Div in Happy Valley
Place: RA
Time: in BOIS des TAILLES RA in Town

The above may be forwarded as now corrected. (Z)

Major [illegible]

Censor. Signature of Addressor or person authorised to telegraph in his name.

* This line should be erased if not required

(4198) Wt. W14042—M44. 300000 Pads. 12/15. Sir J. C. & S.

XIII Corps Q.S. No. 4 QS 143/2

SECRET

MEMO.

The 2nd Division less Artillery will move on 23rd from their present areas into the Reserve Area.

2. The move to be so timed that by 7 p.m. on 23rd the Infantry Brigades of the Division will be -

(a) One Infy. Bde. - BOIS DES TAILLES North (R.E. Coy. and Fd. Ambce. in MORLANCOURT).

(b) One Infy. Bde.Group - HAPPY VALLEY.

(c) One Infy. Bde.Group - SAND PIT VALLEY Sq. F.13.19.

(d) Pioneer Battalion - MORLANCOURT.

(e) Tent Divisions Field Ambulances - MORLANCOURT.

3. MEAULTE is also placed at the disposal of the 2nd Division for their rearward echelons.

4. The SANDPIT VALLEY and the HAPPY VALLEY will be clear of 9th Division troops respectively at 7.30 a.m. and 9.30 a.m.

5. Roads available:-

(a) Track from MORLANCOURT through squares K.9.10.11 to BOIS DES TAILLES North.

(b) Road VILLE - MORLANCOURT thence track as in (a), continuing North of BOIS DES TAILLES North to road junction K.6.d.8.7, thence road to FILIFORM TREE, thence track to head of SANDPIT VALLEY. Road junction K.6.d.8.7 not to be crossed before 10 a.m.

(c) BRAY - CORBIE Road - SOMME VALLEY to SAILLY le SEC, thence to BRAY - CORBIE Road.

6. BOIS DES TAILLES, South of BRAY - CORBIE Road, will be available for temporary halt through the day if required.

7. Position of Brigades in Réserve Area to be reported to Headquarters, XIII Corps 'Q' by 7 p.m. on 23rd instant.

8. No change for the present in Supply refilling arrangements.

2nd Division (Advanced Q.) (Communicated by telephone 10.30 p.m. 22nd; now confirmed).

R.E. Twining

Brigadier General,
D.A.&.Q.M.G. XIII Corps.

22/7/16.

Distribution -

30th Division 'Q'
3rd Division 'Q'
35th Division 'Q'
9th Division 'Q'
'G' XIII Corps.
D.D.M.S. XIII Corps.
A.P.M. XIII Corps.
Camp Commandant XIII Corps.
Camp Commandant, BOIS DES TAILLES North.

Acknowledged

Prefix ...... Code ...... Words ......

£ s. d.

Charges to collect

Service Instructions.

Received From ...... By ......

Sent, or sent out At 7.29 P m. To NRC Collins By ......

TELEGRAPHS

Handed in at NRC Office 6.57 m. Received 7.29 P m.

TO 2nd Divn

*Sender's Number	Day of Month	In reply to Number	AAA
G 914	22nd		

my G 904 the FRENCH attack on MAUREPAS and Operations of 30th Division dependant on it will take place on 24th instant

Operations file

JB 22-7

FROM PLACE & TIME 13th Corps 6.45 Pm

* This line should be erased if not required.

W 15660—M 151 75,000 Pads. H & S 2/16 Forms/C.2123. (5668)

"C" Form (Duplicate).
MESSAGES AND SIGNALS.

Army Form C. 2123.

No. of Message

Charges to Pay. £ s. d.

Office Stamp. 3 VII 15 R

Service Instructions. MCL

Handed in at ... Office 5.45 p.m. Received 4.6 p.m.

TO 2nd Divn

963

Sender's Number	Day of Month	In reply to Number	AAA
G 937	25		

30th Division will be prepared to attack GUILLEMONT only or GUILLEMONT and FALFEMONT FARM together on morning of 26th under French will attack MAUREPAS, when 30th attack FALFEMONT aaa If FALFEMONT not attacked 25th it will be attacked 26th aaa 30th Division working parties will tonight construct such assembly trenches as are necessary for these attacks under arrangements to be made with 3rd and 35th Divisions aaa 30th Division will arrange to patrol tonight and tomorrow night the whole of the enemy defences to

FROM

PLACE & TIME JB. 4.15

W 15660—M 151 75,000 Pads. H & S 5/16 Forms/C.2123. (5666)

Operations file

"C" Form (Original). Army Form C. 2123

MESSAGES AND SIGNALS. No. of Message ......

Prefix ...... Code ...... Words ......

£ s. d.

Charges to collect

Service Instructions

Received From ...... By ......

Sent, or sent out At ...... m. To ...... By ......

Office Stamp. [YS 28 VII 16 ... TELEGRAPHS]

Handed in at ...... Office ...... m. Received ...... m.

TO (2)

*Sender's Number	Day of Month	In reply to Number.	AAA

be attacked in order to
discover where cut and damage
done aaa Tomorrow night the
30th Division will take over
from 3rd and 35th Divisions
such portions of their respective
fronts as are necessary to
form up for the attack
after 3rd and 35th will
remain responsible for defence of
the front now held aaa
Hour of Both attacks will
be notified later aaa 3rd
Division will continue to consolidate
line now held and to
gain ground in DELVILLE WOOD
and towards GUILLEMONT as

FROM

PLACE & TIME

* This line should be erased if not required.

W 12550/4108 75,000 Pads. A. J. W. & Co. 11/15 Forms/C.2123.

"C" Form (Original). Army Form C. 2123.

MESSAGES AND SIGNALS. No. of Message

Prefix Code Words | Received From By | Sent, or sent out At To By | Office Stamp ARMY 13 VII 15 R

£ s. d.

Charges to collect

Service Instructions.

Handed in at Office m. Received m.

TO (3)

*Sender's Number | Day of Month | In reply to Number | AAA

far as the railway aaa
18th will attack the trench
parallel to and NE of
the GUILLEMONT-LONGUEVAL Road when
30th Div attacks GUILLEMONT
aaa Addsd 3rd 30th and
35th Division repts 2nd Divn
GOC RA no 9 Squadron
RBG 15 Corps

FROM 13 Corps

PLACE & TIME 3.35 pm

* This line should be erased if not required.

W 15660—M 151 72,000 Pads. H & S 2/18 Forms/C.2123. (5668)

"C" Form (Duplicate). Army Form C. 2123.

MESSAGES AND SIGNALS. No. of Message

Operations

Service Instructions Priority

Handed in at RG Office 1235a m. Received 12.45a m.

TO 2nd Div

Sender's Number G957 | Day of Month 24th | In reply to Number | AAA

GHQ wire that Germans are believed to be massing large forces on line GINCHY-FLERS possibly with a view to counterattack in direction of MONTAUBAN aaa. Following moves will be carried out immediately aaa Two Battalions 106th Brigade now at CAFTET WOOD will be placed at disposal of GOC 3rd Div. aaa GOC 3rd Division will at once move these two battalions into the valleys in S22B & S23A where they will dig themselves cover immediately aaa Remainder of 106th Brigade to move at once to MONTAUBAN AND come under orders of GOC 3rd Div aaa 90th inf Bde near GLATZ Redoubt will be placed at disposal of GOC 35th Division aaa acknowledge aaa Added 2nd 3rd 30th Div 35th Divs Repeated GOC.RA 15 Corps & 20 French Corps No 9 Squadron RFC. 13 Corps 12.25a

FROM

PLACE & TIME

W 15800—M 151 75,000 Pads [illegible] Forms/C.2123 (5658)

JBB

SECRET

S E C R E T.
****
XIII Corps.
85/2 (G).

2nd Division.

The attached copy of XV Corps Operation Order No. 28 is forwarded for information.

XIII Corps,
24th July, 1916.

B.G., G.S.

SECRET

S E C R E T.

Copy No. 20.

XV CORPS OPERATION ORDER No. 28.

Reference
(a) French maps 1/20,000 Sheets 57d N.E.
& S.W., 62d N.E., 62c N.W.
(b) MARTINPUICH Sheet 1/20,000.

24th July, 1916.

1. (a) A concentration of the enemy is reported on the line FLERS - GINCHY. It is possible that he contemplates an attack against our position near LONGUEVAL.

(b) In the event of a hostile attack, XV Corps is to be prepared to deliver a counter attack, probably against the enemy in LONGUEVAL and DELVILLE WOOD.

2. The intention of the Corps Commander is to strengthen and extend our position and re-adjust our front to enable us to hold a secure position through HIGH WOOD and to assume the offensive against LONGUEVAL, if required.

3. (a) The 51st Division will take over to-night from the 5th Division that portion of its front from the Road Junction at S.10.d.89 (exclusive) to the Southern end of HIGH WOOD.

(b) After relief, the boundary between the 5th and 51st Divisions will be the present boundary as far as S.16.a.29 and thence a line to Road Junction S.10.d.89 and road S.11.d.08 (last named road inclusive to 5th Division).

4. (a) The work ordered in XV Corps G.434 of 24th July will be pressed on.

(b) 5th Division will be responsible for the trench facing LONGUEVAL; and will also undertake any other work required in preparation for an attack on LONGUEVAL and DELVILLE WOOD.

(c) 51st Division will, after relief:-

(i) Continue the duplication of the line in front of the present left of the 5th Division (vide Operation Order No. 27, paragraph 3 (b) (i)).

(ii) be responsible for the trench facing HIGH WOOD.

(iii) complete the trench connecting up with 19th Division and the communication trench from HIGH WOOD to BAZENTIN le GRAND.

5. (a) 51st Division will to-morrow capture and consolidate the Eastern corner of HIGH WOOD.

(b) The arrangements for the bombardment and hour of zero will be notified later.

(Sd.) I.R. Wethered, Major,
for Brigadier General,
General Staff.

Issued at 4.45 p.m.

Copy No. 1 A.D.C. to Corps Commander
2 5th Division
3 do.
4 7th Division
5 do.
6 17th Division.
7 do.
8 33rd Division.
9 do.
10 51st Division
11 do.
12 B.G., R.A.
13 do.
14 do.

Copy No. 15 C.E.
16 Corps Mounted Troops.
17 3rd Squadron R.F.C.
18 Fourth Army) for information.
19 III Corps)
20 XIII Corps)
21 - 24 G.S. and record.

SECRET.

Copy No........1

XIII CORPS OPERATION ORDER NO.32.

24th July,1916.

1. The operations ordered for tomorrow are postponed for at least 48 hours.

2. The 2nd Division will relieve the 3rd Division in the line commencing at once.
G.O.C.2nd Division to report when he has taken over command.
As much as possible of the relief should be effected tonight.
The 106th Infantry Brigade will revert to its own division as soon as it can be spared in the course of the relief: G.O.C.3rd Division to decide when he no longer requires it and report to 35th Division and Corps Headquarters.
The relief of the 3rd Division Artillery by the 2nd Divisional Artillery will be carried out as soon as it can be arranged under orders to be issued by the G.O.C.,R.A..
The 3rd Division, on relief, will move into the Reserve Division area: it will be replaced there brigade by brigade by units of 55th Division which commences detraining tomorrow: on relief by 55th Division units of 3rd Division will move back into the rear portion of the Corps area.

3. The 90th Brigade of 30th Division will remain at the disposal of G.O.C.35th Division until further orders.

4. The 35th Division will arrange to take over from 3rd Division during the early part of tonight the defence of TRONES WOOD N. of the railway line. The left division will be responsible for the defence of LONGUEVAL ALLEY North of TRONES WOOD and of WATERLOT FARM.

5. The strength of the garrisons of the BRIQUETERIE and MONTAUBAN and the names of commanders will be reported to Corps Headquarters at once by Right and Left Divisions respectively: these garrisons will be permanent during the tour of each division in the line, and are to be independent of the remainder of the troops of the division both for attack and defence.

W H Greenly.
B.G.,G.S..

Issued at...4/30...p.m.

Copy No. 1. 2nd Division.
2. 3rd Division.
3. 30th Division.
4. 35th Division.
5. 55th Division.
6.-7. G.O.C.,R.A.
8. XV Corps.

Copy No. 9. "Q".
10. A.D.A.S.
11. War Diary.
12.-14. "G".

acknowledged J.B. 24.7

XIII Corps.
323/8 (G).

2nd Division.
~~3rd Division.~~
~~30th Division.~~
~~35th Division.~~
~~55th Division.~~

Left Division XV Corps reports that their snipers have accounted for 17 Germans during the day, including 1 Officer. It seems probable that under present circumstances enemy is offering great chances to bold use on our part of snipers and Lewis guns from shell holes and other cover. These should be made most of and every effort made to obtain mastery in no man's land and keep enemy from working, and confine him to his trenches.

RECEIVED
JUL. 1916

XIII Corps,
24th July, 1916.

B L Montgomery Major
for B.G., G.S.

XIII Corps. 323/S(G).
G

2nd Division.

Left Division XV Corps reports that their snipers have accounted for 17 Germans during the day, including 1 officer. It seems probable that under present circumstances enemy is offering great chances to bold use on our part of snipers and Lewis guns from shell holes and other cover. These should be made most of and every effort made to obtain mastery in no man's land and keep enemy from working, and confine him to his trenches.

2nd DIVISION
GENERAL STAFF
No. 2 Divn No. 1001/2/3
Date........

XIIIth Corps.
24th July, 1916.

(sd) A.A. Montgomery, Major,
for B.G., G.S.

(G)

5th Inf Bde.
6th Inf. Bde.
99th Inf. Bde.
R.A., 2nd Divn.

For information and guidance.

H.Q., 2nd Divn.
26-7-1916.

B. Belgrave Major
for Lieut. Colonel,
General Staff, 2nd Division.

SECRET.

XIII Corps.
133/84(G).

G.O.C.R.A.
2nd Division.
3rd Division.
30th Division.
35th Division.
55th Division.
XV Corps.

---

1. The boundary between XIII and XV Corps has been modified as shown on attached sketch map by dotted blue line.

1. The 5th Division will take over tonight all ground held by 2nd Division N. and W. of the new boundary.

XIII Corps,
25th July, 1916.

for B.G., G.S..

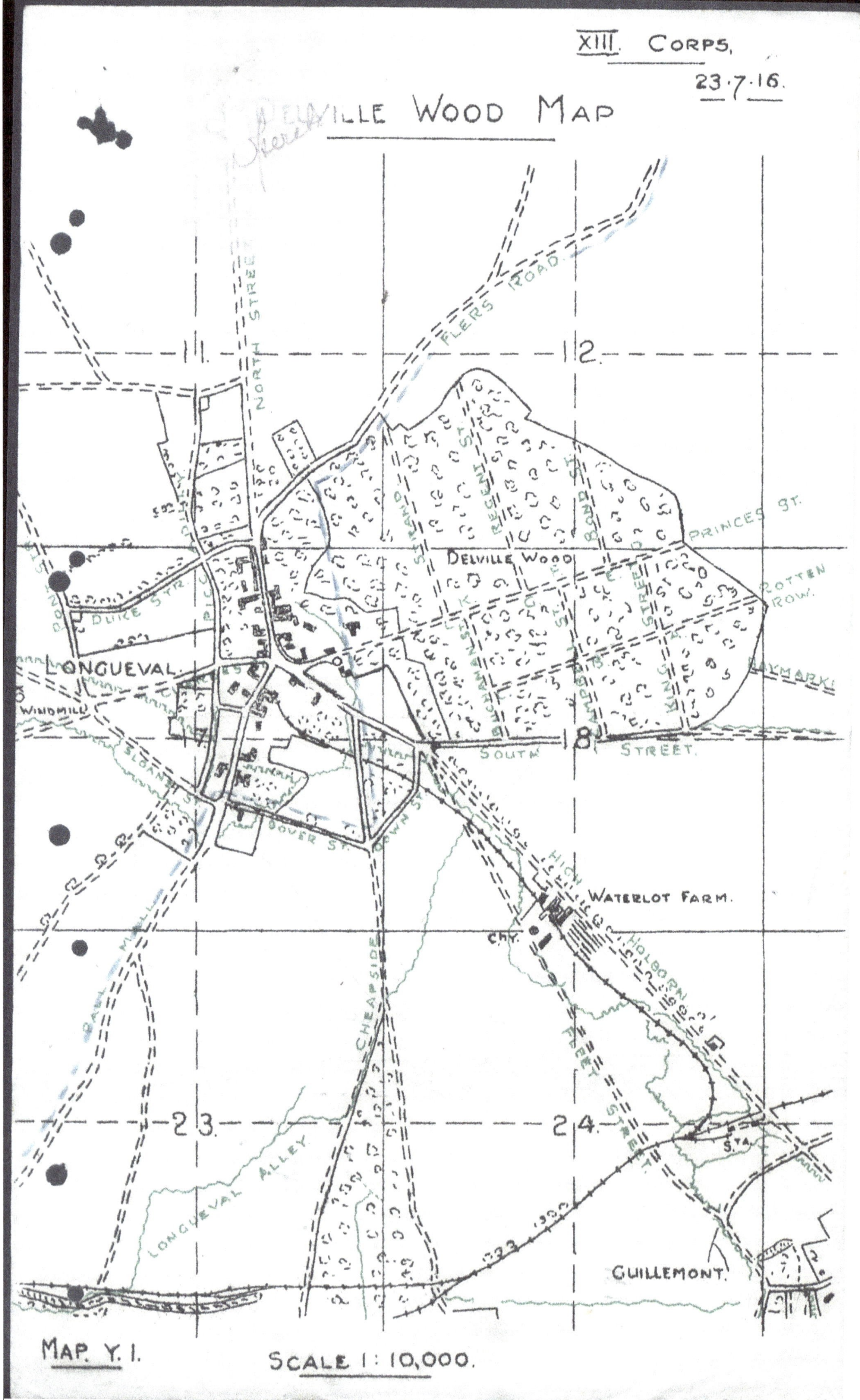

XIII. Corps, 23.7.16.
Delville Wood Map
Flers Road
North Street
12.
11.
Princes St.
Delville Wood
Rotten Row.
Strand
Regent St.
Bond St.
Duke Str.
Longueval.
Windmill
Haymarket
South Street.
Sloane St.
Dover St.
Down St.
Waterlot Farm.
Chy.
Holborn
Cheapside
Fleet Street
23.
24.
Sta.
Longueval Alley
Guillemont.
Map. Y. I.
Scale 1: 10,000.

FURTHER EXAMINATION OF PRISONER OF 3rd Bn., 52nd I.R. 5th Div:

Prisoner says his Battalion arrived in this neighbourhood about 16 days ago, and went into some trenches to the West of LONGUEVAL, relieving a Regiment which he thinks was the 156th or 158th. After 3 or 4 days his Battalionwent into rest for the same period and then returned to the trenches West of LONGUEVAL at night, so he did not see what unit they relieved. After another 3 or 4 days they went to rest, presumably at GUEDECOURT, for 2 days and then came into some shallow and disused trenches near GINCHY.

Whilst there he went back for food to some field cookers, apparently near MORVAL, and saw men wearing the numbers 77 and 99 (77 R.I.R. 2 Guards R.Div: ? and 99 R.I.R., 26 R.D.?)

Prisoner's Battalion was 200 rifle strength on arrival in this neighbourhood and is now 150. He saw no Germans in DELVILLE WOOD to-day when he was captured. The circumstances point to his having deserted.

26-7-16.

CRA

To see & return please.

2nd Lon.

27.7.16.

Major

G.S. XIII Corps

RA

XIII Corps.
320/3(G).

2nd Division.
~~3rd Division.~~
~~30th Division.~~
~~35th Division.~~
~~55th Division.~~

In the event of your division ~~leaving~~ being withdrawn from the Corps a brief account of the fighting in which the division has taken part, stating causes of success or failure and lessons to be deduced therefrom, will be forwarded to this office.

XIII Corps,
29th July, 1916.

Capt
for B.G., G.S..

Fourth Army No.G.S.225.

XIII Corps.

When Divisional Commanders have finished with any reports on operations submitted by their C.R.E's, the C.E., Fourth Army, would like them forwarded to him for his perusal.

H.Q.,Fourth Army,
30th July,1916.

(sd) A.A.Montgomery,
Major-General,
General Staff, FourthArmy.

2.

XIII Corps.
320(G).
/4

2nd Division.
~~3rd Division.~~
~~24th Division.~~
~~30th Division.~~
~~35th Division.~~
~~55th Division.~~

For information and necessary action.

HEADQUARTERS RECEIVED 31 JUL.1916 DIVISION.

XIII Corps,
31st July,1916.

[signature] Capt
for B.G.,G.S..

Fourth Army No. G.S.225.

XIII Corps.

When Divisional Commanders have finished with any reports on operations submitted by their C.R.E's, the C.E., Fourth Army, would like them forwarded to him for his perusal.

H.Q., Fourth Army,
30th July, 1916.

(sd) A.A. MONTGOMERY, Major-General,
General Staff, Fourth Army.

(2)

C.R.E., 2nd Divn.

Please report on any operations in which the Divisional R.E. have taken part, as soon as the Division comes out of the line.

H.Q., 2nd Divn.
31-7-1916.

D. Belgrave Major
for Lieut. Colonel,
General Staff, 2nd Division.

99th Bde 1 V45

I beg to report that on July 27th (in afternoon of) during the attack by my Bn on SELVILLE WOOD a wounded S. African soldier (with a bullet thro his calf & a shrapnel wound in the head) was found about 120 yds beyond the Brown Line. He was in a very weak condition & was in a shell hole screened by a fallen tree

The man was bound up & brought back to Brown line by L/Cpl Stafford & Pte Marshall who reported the case to Capt Taylor.

The man stated that he was Pte NICHOLSON of the 1st S African Regt - was wounded on Tuesday 18th July during the retirement of his Brigade from the wood & had lived on iron rations & ~~ha~~ water found on dead men since.

He stated that during the retirement he saw several of his comrades compelled to surrender & they were shot by the Germans. He also stated that a German officer had

(2)

found him & tormented him by showing him the waterbottle but refusing to let him have a drink.
These facts were not known to me at the time or my battalion would not have taken 2 German officer prisoners!"

H. A. Vernon Lt Col
Cmdg 23rd Bn. R.F.

31/7/16.

2

H.Q. 2nd Division

For information –

R. O. Kellett. B.G.

1/8/16 99.1.K

Retd to Corps

99th Inf. Bde.

I beg to report that on the afternoon of July 27th during the attack by my Bn. on DELVILLE WOOD, a wounded S.African soldier(with a bullet thro' his calf and a shrapnel wound in the head) was found about 120 yards beyond the Brown line. He was in a very weak condition and was in a shell hole screened by a fallen tree.

The man was bound up and brought back to Brown line by L/Cpl. Stafford and Pte. Marshall who reported the case to Capt. Taylor.

The man stated that he was Private NICHOLSON of the 1st S. African Regt., was wounded on Tuesday 18th July during the retirement of his Brigade from the wood and had lived on iron rations and water found on dead men since.

He stated that during the retirement he saw several of his comrades compelled to surrender and they were shot by the Germans. He also stated that a German Officer had found him and tormented him by showing him a waterbottle but refusing to let him have a drink.

These facts were not known to me at the time or my Battalion would not have taken 2 German Officer prisoners !!

31-7-1916.

(sd) H.A. Vernon, Lt. Col.
Commdg. 23/R. Fus.

(2)

XIII Corps.

For information.

(Signed) C Deverell Major-General,

H.Q., 2nd Divn.

2-8-1916.

Commanding 2nd Division.

W 74—664 250,000 3/15 L. S. & Co. Army Form W. 3091.

Cover for Documents.

Nature of Enclosures.

2ND DIVISION
No. G.S. 1001/1/
Date............

OPERATIONS FROM 20th JULY, 1916 to____________
****

MEMOS., INSTRUCTIONS, ETC., ISSUED BY 2nd DIVISION.

Notes, or Letters written.

SECRET

5th Inf. Brigade.

The IVth Corps Heavy Artillery will bombard the PIMPLE and observation posts North and North East of it, commencing at 3 p.m. 3rd July.

It may be necessary for you to clear the " Islands " during the operation, and if so, the code word " HENRY" will be sent to you by wire.

Acknowledge.

H.Q., 2nd Divn. Lieut. Colonel,

2-7-1916. General Staff, 2nd Division.

IVth Corps.

H.R.S. 669.

2/Div No
GS992/16/16

2nd Div.

Herewith certain instructions connected with the installation of gas & smoke.

Please return First Army No G.S. 360/28(a) when done with. Please acknowledge.

H. DePree
B.G. G.S.

2.7.16.

"A" Form.
Army Form C. 2121.

MESSAGES AND SIGNALS.

No. of Message..........

Prefix .... Code .... m. | Words | Charge | This message is on a/c of: | Recd. at ....m.

Office of Origin and Service Instructions.

Sent
At ....m.
To ....
By ....

.... Service.
(Signature of "Franking Officer.")

Date ....
From ....
By ....

TO 4 Corps

Sender's Number.	Day of Month.	In reply to Number.	AAA
* G 268	2		

HRS 669 received from BGGS

From 2nd Div
Place
Time 1035 p

The above may be forwarded as now corrected. (Z)

Censor. Signature of Addressor or person authorised to telegraph in his name.

J Belgrave
Major
GS

* This line should be erased if not required.

28,000. W 14042—M 44. H. W & V., Ld. 12/15.

SECRET

2 Divn No
GS 992/12/12

6th Inf. Bde.
C.R.A., 2nd Divn. (for information).

With reference to paras. 3 and 4 of the attached order, it must be understood that every effort must be made to inform the artillery when raiding party has returned. In any case, artillery support cannot be given after 1-15 a.m. as the artillery of the Division have been allotted another task after that hour.

H.Q., 2nd Divn. Lieut. Colonel,
3-7-1916. General Staff, 2nd Division.

2nd Division

Reference draft of Order 40. . . . :–

I should like the PIMPLE treated thoroughly from the hour of ZERO onwards by:–

(a) Artillery.

(b) As many 2" T.M.'s as can be ~~[illegible]~~ brought to bear on this locality.

With the exception of two slight alterations in map co-ordinates, which are shown in pencil, I have no other observations to make on the draft

J S Boyd Captain
Brigade Major
for
Br. General
Comdg 5th Inf. Bde.

3/7/16.

SECRET

G.S. 992/15/13.

IVth Corps.

I beg to forward herewith an outline plan of an attack which I propose to carry out against the portion of the German line situated between INTERNATIONAL AVENUE and the MOMBER group of craters.

The objective to be taken is the German first line, and its capture will materially improve our position on the VIMY RIDGE, and will, it is hoped, enable us to destroy several enemy mine shafts which are now a source of danger to our present line.

The attack will be delivered about the night 18th/19th July, and will be preceded by a discharge of gas from cylinders.

They will be referred to hereafter as BANANA SKINS in all orders and messages. The success of the operation will depend very largely on the effect produced by the BANANA.

The assaulting troops will be the 5th Inf. Brigade accompanied by a detachment of the 10/D.C.L.I. (Pioneers), probably about 1 company. The 5th Inf. Brigade will take over a section of the present line between INTERNATIONAL AVENUE and UHLAN ALLEY on the night 16th/17th July and the two Infantry Brigades at present holding the BERTHONVAL and CARENCY Sections will contract their fronts on the same night to allow of this being carried out.

In addition to my Divisional Artillery and light mortars, I understand that 3 batteries of 2" trench mortars (12 guns) and 2 batteries of Stokes mortars (16 guns) will be available from sources outside the Division, and I am

basing.....

emplacements and working out a detailed plan on these lines.

The permanent attachment of an officer of the Special Company which will be allotted to this Division for the operation is a matter of early importance.

(Sgd) ... Ballard(?)

H.Q., 2nd Divn. Major-General,

6-7-1916. Commanding 2nd Division.

basing my plans on this accordingly.

I have consulted with Captain GARDEN (O.C. No. 46 Special Battalion) and have arranged for 1020 skins to be provided: this will allow of a front of about 1700 yds, i.e., from CENTRAL AVENUE to COBURG ALLEY, being covered.

Smoke will also be used.

BANANA will be discharged in two instalments lasting about ¾ of an hour each. 15 minutes after the conclusion of the second instalment, the Infantry will assault.

As regards previous Artillery preparation, I am arranging for wire to be cut by 2" trench mortars along the Divisional front for 2 or 3 days before the date fixed for the attack. There will also be periodical bombardments on selected points, but it is obviously undesirable to provoke a German retaliation by trench mortars on account of the danger of damaging the skins.

On account of our front and support lines in the salient between ERSATZ ALLEY and COBURG ALLEY being continually subjected to hostile trench mortar fire, I have arranged for the Skins to be placed in the reserve line for purposes of safety. This will necessitate clearing our saps and first line trenches in the area. This will be done gradually and completed just prior to the bombardment commencing (vide Appendix "A").

An estimate of my requirements for Artillery ammunition is attached (Appendix "B"). I understand that there will be no difficulty in obtaining large quantities of 2" trench mortar and Stokes mortar ammunition.

I should be glad to know at an early date if these proposals are approved: meanwhile I am preparing

emplacements....

APPENDIX "A".

TIME TABLE.
****

ZERO.	0. to 0.10.	Bombardment by Trench mortars and Howitzers.
	0.5.	1st instalment of SKINS begins.
	0.15 to 0.30.	Smoke discharged. 4 candles per 25 yds per minute.
	0.20. (about).	1st instalment of SKINS ends.
	0.30.	2nd instalment of SKINS begins.
	0.30. to 0.40.	Smoke discharged. 3 candles per 25 yds per minute.
	0.45.	2nd instalment of SKINS ends.
	0.45 to 0.57.	Smoke discharged. 4 candles per 25 yds per minute.
	0.60.	Infantry assault.

During the whole period, 18 pdrs. will shrapnel trenches and Howitzers and trench mortars will carry out intermittent bursts of fire.

For estimate of Artillery ammunition vide Appendix "B".

Stokes mortars will bombard enemy's front line for 2 minutes prior to attack and at other periods during the preparatory phase.

APPENDIX "B".

ESTIMATE OF ARTILLERY AMMUNITION.
****

	6" Howr.or French Courts.	4.5" Howr.	18 pdrs.
PRELIMINARY BOMBARDMENTS.......	80	360	-
BARRAGES and SHRAPNEL..........	-	-	2640
BURSTS OF FIRE.................	-	300	-
	80	660	2640

The above figures are approximate only, and do not include barrages and artillery support during consolidation. This may be estimated at -

5000 rounds 18 pdr.)
) per hour.
500 rounds 4.5" Howr.)

A.G.H.Q.

July 7th.1916.

My dear Deedes,

In reply to your letter of the 4th I am afraid we have made no experiments on the effect of White Star Gas on machine guns. I think it would be preferable to aim at their personnel.

White Star Gas, if discharged without nozzles on the parapet pipes, issues very silently, and even without rifle fire I do not think that the discharge would be audible 100 yards away. The discharge without nozzles is also more rapid and therefore heavier concentrations can be obtained. On the other hand a certain amount of gas is deposited as liquid on the ground immediately in front of the parapet, which would cause inconvenience to Infantry raiding parties for probably half to three-quarters of an hour after the discharge ceased.

If nozzles are used there is no deposit on the ground, but the discharge is not so silent. In this case Infantry can follow up a cloud in the open immediately, if there is anything of a wind blowing.

The enemy's trenches should be clear of gas in about five minutes, perhaps it would be safer to say ten minutes, but gas may still be found in their dug-outs for some little while longer, depending on what air currents are caused in the trenches either by the prevailing wind or by movements of men in them.

Many congratulations on becoming G.S.O.1. I see that you have Feilding on your staff. I think he is wasted in Q. I hope that my old Division will make a success of their operation. The discharge should certainly take place at night, in which case I think your raiding parties should have a fairly easy time.

Yours sincerely,

Lieut. Colonel C.P.Deedes, C.M.G.,D.S.O.,
Headquarters, 2nd Division.

SECRET

Office
2: Divn No
GS992/15/7.16

5th Inf. Bde.
6th Inf. Bde.
99th Inf. Bde.
C.R.A., 2nd Divn.

The Divisional Commander wishes G.O's C. Brigades in the line to insist on the utmost vigilance during the next 10 days in order to prevent any possible attempt at raids by the enemy being successful in penetrating our lines. He wishes, therefore, patrolling to be very actively carried out.

H.Q., 2nd Divn.
8-7-1916.

C Deedes
Lieut. Colonel,
General Staff, 2nd Division.

SECRET

2 Divn No
GS 992/15/20

176th Tunnelling Co.R.E.

In the event of operations taking place in the near future, it will be desirable for the numbers of tunnellers employed to be reduced to a minimum.

Will you give this matter your consideration and inform me what dug-out accommodation will, therefore, be vacated temporarily in the ZOUAVE VALLEY.

H.Q., 2nd Divn.
8-7-1916.

Lieut. Colonel,
General Staff, 2nd Division.

SECRET

2 Divn No
GS 992/15/19

C.R.E., 2nd Divn.

About the 16th July, it will be necessary to clear detachments of 10/D.C.L.I.(Pioneers) and Sapping and Dug-out Platoons from all accommodation East of CARENCY. The former will rejoin their Battalion at VILLERS AU BOIS except one company temporarily attached to 5th Inf. Brigade, and the latter will rejoin their units.

(sd) [signature]

H.Q., 2nd Divn.
8-7-1916.

Lieut. Colonel,
General Staff, 2nd Division.

10-7-16

OC 176 Tunnelling Co R.E.

Re

The dugout accommodation in the tunnel gallery as used by our men has been sufficient at various times to hold over 160 men. If necessary the officers dugout would cover another 40 men making a total of 220.

In the support line we have 2 mine galleries with 4 exits that would be sufficient protection for 120 men in each.

These mine galleries are each 180 ft in length and would cover more men if an additional entrance were made [illegible] ample fresh air.

Total accommodation 460 men

[signature]
Capt R.E.

SECRET

5th Inf. Bde.
6th Inf. Bde.
99th Inf. Bde.
C.R.A., 2nd Divn.
C.R.E., 2nd Divn.

Office

2nd Divn No
GS 992/15/14

It is probable that during the next 10 days large carrying parties will be required from all Brigades. It is important, therefore, that all material which can be taken up now should be carried as soon as possible in order that all available labour can be used for carrying up material which can only be taken up at a later date. The demands for carrying parties should reach Divisional Headquarters as soon as requirements are known.

C. Dundas
Lieut. Colonel,
General Staff, 2nd Division.

H.Q., 2nd Divn.
8-7-1916.

2nd Divn. No.
G.S. 992/15/14

7 Dn. Q55481

5th Inf. Bde.
6th Inf. Bde.
99th Inf. Bde.

Smoke candles will probably have to be lighted and used in operations shortly.

G.O's C. Brigades should ensure that they have enough men trained in their use as follows :-

5th Inf. Bde. on a 2 Bn. front.
6th Inf. Bde. on a ½ Bn. front.
99th Inf.Bde. on a 1 Bn. front.

If more men are required to be trained, arrangements will be made for them to be taught at the Divl. Gas School.

Calculations should be made for 2 men at each emplacement 25 yds apart burning 4 candles per ~~minute~~ minute.

H.Q., 2nd Divn.

8-7-1916.

(sd) J.D. BELGRAVE, Major
for Lt. Col.
General Staff, 2nd Division.

(In pads of 50 dupls.) "C" Form (Duplicate). Army Form C. 2123

MESSAGES AND SIGNALS. No. of Message ....

Charges to Pay. £ s. d.

Office Stamp.

Service Instructions.

Handed in at .... Office .... m. Received .... m.

TO Brade

Sender's Number	Day of Month	In reply to Number	AAA
Q 118	8/7		

Refer G S 772/1-7/14 of to day aaa May smoke candles be drawn from your Gas School as required by Battalions

Q.

4.43

Reference attached the scheme is to train men at the Gas School. We cannot have candles burnt all over the place

FROM Brake & QM 8.7

PLACE & TIME

W 15660 M/151. 75,000 Pads. McC. & Co., Ltd., London. 1/16. Forms/C.2123.

Your Q 118 of 8th inst

Reference memo [illegible], dated 7th inst.

No smoke candles are expected to be available for issue before the 14th inst.

[signature]

Lieut.Colonel.

.... Division.

8/7/16.

HD QRS 2ND DIVISION
No. Q5548/1
8 JUL 1916

S E C R E T.

Headquarters,
6th Inf. Bde.
5th Inf. Bde.)
99th Inf. Bde.) For information.
R.A.)
" ")

Your Q118 of 8th inst

Reference memo G.S.992/15/14, dated 6th inst.

No smoke candles are expected to be available for issue before the 14th inst.

[signature]
Lieut. Colonel.
A.A. & Q.M.G. 2nd Division.

8/7/16.

W.

2 Divn No
G.S. 992/15/18

5th Inf. Bde.
6th Inf. Bde.
99th Inf. Bde.
C.R.A. 2nd Divn.
C.R.E. 2nd Divn.
10/D.C.L.I. (Pioneers).
"Q", 2nd Divn.
2/Signal Co.

The attached paper shows the redistribution of the Division when 3 Brigades are in the line.

As far as can be foreseen, the moves will take place on the night 16th/17th July, but an order on the subject will be issued later.

H.Q., 2nd Divn.
8-7-1918.

Lieut. Colonel,
General Staff, 2nd Division.

(i). Left Battalion, Right Brigade.
(ii). Right Battalion, Left Brigade.
(iii). Support Battalion, Left Brigade.

Reserve Battalion -
1 Company - ALHAMBRA.
3 platoons - CABARET ROUGE.
2 Cos. and
1 Platoon - BAJOLLE LINE.

Its Southern boundary will be VINCENT AVENUE inclusive - HORTLEY AVENUE exclusive but giving accommodation in CABARET ROUGE for 2 companies 99th Inf. Bde. - BOYAU 123 exclusive but having all accommodation in the BAJOLLE LINE.

Its Northern Boundary will be BOYAU THIRLEY exclusive - 130 ALLEY common to 5th and 6th Inf. Brigades - 130 ROAD exclusive as far as ARDOUST ROAD - ARDOUST ROAD exclusive.

(c)......

SECRET

REDISTRIBUTION OF FRONTAGE BETWEEN BRIGADES.

(1). On night 16th/17th July the Division will have all three Infantry Brigades in the line, and the frontages allotted to Brigades will be as follows :-

(2).(a). The 99th Inf. Brigade (Advanced Headquarters CABARET ROUGE) will have -

One Battalion in or East of ZOUAVE VALLEY with Head Qrs. at the present Right Battalion Headquarters.

One Battalion distributed between ZOUAVE VALLEY, ALHAMBRA and CABARET ROUGE, with Headquarters at CABARET ROUGE.

Two Battalions in CAMBLAIN L'ABBE.

Its boundaries in forward area will be -

On the South. Southern boundary of Divisional Sector.

On the North. VINCENT AVENUE exclusive - WORTLEY AVENUE inclusive but with accommodation for 2 companies at CABARET ROUGE - BOYAU 123 inclusive but excluding any accommodation in the BAJOLLE LINE.

(b). The 5th Inf. Brigade will have its Advanced Head Qrs. at the present Battalion Headquarters of the support Battalion of the Right Brigade (or at present Adv. H.Q. Left Bde)

Three Battalions in the ZOUAVE VALLEY with Head Qrs. at the present Battalion Head Quarters of -

(i). Left Battalion, Right Brigade.
(ii). Right Battalion, Left Brigade.
(iii). Support Battalion, Left Brigade.

Reserve Battalion -

1 Company	- ALHAMBRA.
3 platoons	- CABARET ROUGE.
2 Cos. and 1 Platoon	- BAJOLLE LINE.

Its Southern boundary will be VINCENT AVENUE inclusive - WORTLEY AVENUE exclusive but giving accommodation in CABARET ROUGE for 2 companies 99th Inf. Bde. - BOYAU 123 exclusive but having all accommodation in the BAJOLLE LINE.

Its Northern Boundary will be BOYAU THIRTY exclusive - 150 ALLEY common to 5th and 6th Inf. Brigades - 150 ROAD exclusive as far as REDOUBT ROAD - REDOUBT ROAD exclusive.

(c)......

(c). The 6th Infy. Brigade (Advanced Headquarters CABARET ROUGE or HOSPITAL ROAD) will have -

One Battalion in ZOUAVE VALLEY - Headquarters, BANKSIDE.

One Battalion distributed between SAVIERE ROAD and -
HOSPITAL ROAD - CARENCY - VILLERS AU BOIS.
Headquarters, CARENCY.

One Battalion, VILLERS AU BOIS.

One Battalion MAISNIL BOUCHE.

<u>Its Southern Boundary</u> will be BOYAU TH IRISH inclusive - 180th ALLEY common to 5th and 6th Inf. Bdes. - 180th ROAD inclusive, as far as REDOUBT road — REDOUBT rd (inclusive).

<u>Its Northern Boundary</u> will be the Northern boundary of the Divisional Sector.

(3). (a). In addition to his own troops, the G.O.C., 5th Inf. Brigade will arrange for accommodation to be available in or East of the ZOUAVE VALLEY for the following :-

2 Batteries Medium Trench Mortars.
2 Batteries Light Trench Mortars.
1 Company 10/D.C.L.I. (Pioneers).
1 Special Company R.E. (about 150 all ranks). 170

(b). In addition to his own troops, G.O.C., 6th Inf. Brigade will arrange for accommodation to be available East of ZOUAVE VALLEY for 1 Battery Medium Trench Mortars.

(4). All detachments of the 10/D.C.L.I. (Pioneers) less 1 Company (vide para. 3(a)) will be withdrawn to VILLERS AU BOIS on the afternoon of the 16th July.

(5). All Sapping and Dug-out Platoons will rejoin their Battalions on the afternoon of the 16th July.

(6). 6th Inf. Brigade will relieve the machine guns of the 5th Inf. Brigade in the MAISTRE, BAJOLLE and BAJOLLE SWITCH Lines on the 15th July under arrangements to be made between Brigadiers concerned.

Secret

992/15/22

5th Inf. Bde.
6th Inf. Bde.
C.R.E., 2nd Divn.
10/D.C.L.I.

The Divisional Commander has decided that one Company 10/D.C.L.I. now employed on the BAJOLLE Line will work in the CARENCY Section under orders to be issued to the Officer Commanding the Company by the G.O.C., Brigade holding the CARENCY Section.

Orders have been issued, through the C.R.E., for the Officer Commanding the Company to report for instructions to G.O.C., 5th Inf. Brigade.to-day.

The Company will continue to live in the BAJOLLE Line until the 18th inst., when it will return to its Battalion, vide my G.S. 992/15/18 of 8th inst.

H.Q., 2nd Divn.

11-7-1916.

[signature]

Lieut. Colonel,

General Staff, 2nd Division.

S E C R E T.
****

Draft burnt.
18D.

ORDERS FOR CARRYING PARTIES.
****

1. Carrying parties will have rifles and bayonets and 1 bandolier of 50 rounds per man. Gas helmets will be worn rolled up on the head as for " GAS ALERT ".
Each man will carry a sandbag to make a pad for his shoulders.

2. Skins will be carried base first.

3. Carrying parties will be divided into detachments, each consisting of 2 officers, 10 N.C.O's and 80 men.

4. Each of these detachments will deal with 20 skins which are carried in 2 wagons.

5. 4 men will be told off to each skin and will march with it, two carrying and two in relief carrying two rifles each. There will be 1 N.C.O. for every two skins, and one officer for every 10 skins.

6. Orders for relief of men carrying will be given by the O.C. Detachment.

7. Each officer will be given a ticket showing the number of the emplacement to which his detachment is to carry the skins. This number will correspond with the number at the emplacement in the line.

8. As each emplacement holds 20 skins, there will be one detachment carrying to each emplacement.

9. One officer will march at the head of each detachment, the other at the rear of it.

10. Detachments carrying skins will move off from the place where they meet the wagons at 10 minutes interval.

11. A Vermorel Sprayer will be found in the second of each pair of wagons. It will be carried by an N.C.O. at the rear of each detachment. These Vermorel Sprayers will be left in the emplacement with the skins.

12. Each detachment will have at least two spare poles and ropes, at least one set, consisting of one pole and two slings, will be found in each wagon with the skins: these will be carried by N.C.O's of the detachments.

13. On arrival at the emplacement, skins and Vermorel Sprayers will be handed over to the men of E. Co. R.E. who will be at the emplacement.

14. All poles will be brought back and handed over as shown in attached table. They will be returned to MONT ST. ELOY by light railway next night when E. Co. R.E. will bring them back from MONT ST. ELOY to CHATEAU DE LA HAIE.

15. Great care will be taken to avoid clanking noises.

H.Q., 2nd Divn.

11-7-1916.

[illegible signature] Lieut. Colonel,
General Staff, 2nd Division.

S E C R E T.
****

INSTRUCTIONS FOR PLACING SKINS IN THE LINE.

1. 10/D.C.L.I. working under the orders of the C.R.E. are responsible for making and numbering the emplacements. They are also responsible that sufficient filled sandbags are at each emplacement to form cover for skins, and firesteps when skins are in.

2. Skins will be carried up to the line in accordance with the attached Table.

3. Brigades are responsible for all the details shown in the attached Table, except the guides found by E. Co. R.E. as shown.

4. Brigades are responsible, as shown in the Table, for the skins from the time they leave CHATEAU DE LA HAIE till they are handed over to E. Co. R.E. at the emplacements.

5. All guides must know the way thoroughly and must "walk the course" beforehand.

6. E. Co. R.E. are responsible for putting the skins into the emplacements and for sandbagging them in.

7. When the skins are in the line, E. Co. R.E. will always have a guard patrolling the line. In case of any leakage, gas helmets will be put on at once and the nearest man of the guard informed.

8. The accompanying sketch shows the routes of carrying parties for each night, and the position of rendezvous, control posts, emplacements, and dumps for poles and slings when carrying has been completed.
   One of these sketches will be given to each O.C., Detachment who will be responsible for it and will hand it in to Brigade Head Quarters on completion of his duty.

9. Wagons will be brought to CHATEAU DE LA HAIE under Divisional arrangements.

H.Q., 2nd Divn. [signature] Lieut. Colonel,

11-7-1916. General Staff, 2nd Division.

Unit. Night 13th/14th July.	No. of skins to put in.	No. of wagons reqd.	Wagons leave CHAU. DE LA HAIE AT -	Guides for wagons: Officers.	Guides for wagons: Men.	Guides for wagons: To be at CHAU. DE LA HAIE AT	Route for wagons via	Place where carrying parties meet wagons.	Carrying Parties: Officers.	Carrying Parties: N.C.O's.	Carrying Parties: Men.	Guides for carrying parties: No.	Guides for carrying parties: Found by.	Route to emplacements and Control Posts each of 1 NCO. at each place mentioned.	Emplacements to be filled	Return route for carrying parties.	Disposal of poles and ropes: Handed over at	Disposal of poles and ropes: Handed over to	Return route for Wagons.	Return of Poles and ropes to MONT ST. ELOY.	REMARKS.
99th Bde.	100	10	9 pm	1	10	8-45 pm	VILLERS AU BOIS- "Overland route" - CABARET ROUGE - ARRAS rd.	BETHUNE - ARRAS rd.at its junc with CENTRAL AVENUE.	10	50	400	1 offr 1 man	99th Bde E.Co RE	Junc.of CENTRAL AV. and ARRAS rd. - Junc.of CENTRAL AV. & OLD BOOTS ST. - Jn.of OLD BOOTS & front line.	17 to 21	TOTTENHAM and WORTLEY AV.	RUGBY DUMP	An NCO 99 Bde	ARRAS - BETHUNE road - "Overland route" (following 5th Bde. wagons).	By rail night 14/15 to ST.ELOY under arrgts made by 99th Bde. thence by E.Co.R.E.	Wagons must not leave VILLERS AU BOIS till after dark.
5th Bde.	80	8	9-15 pm	1	8	8-45 pm	VILLERS AU BOIS- "Overland route" - CABARET ROUGE.	CABARET ROUGE on road outside 99th Bde Hd.Qrs.	8	40	320	1 offr. 1 man	5th Bde E.Co RE	Jn. of ARRAS AV. + ERSATZ AV. - Jn. of ERSATZ AV. with ZOUAVE VALLEY -Jn. of VINCENT ST. with ZOUAVE VALLEY -Jn. of VINCENT ST.with front line.	31 to 34	LADBROKE GROVE & WORTLEY AV.	RUGBY DUMP.	An NCO 99 Bde	"Overland route"	By rail night 14/15 to ST.ELOY under arrgts made by 99th Bde.,thence by E.Co.RE.	Wagons will leave VILLERS AU BOIS to go up,¼ hr.after 99th Bde. wagons.
6th Bde.	100	10	9-30 pm	1	10	8-45 pm	CARENCY - HOSPITAL CORNER - (rd.jn. S.7.d.8.1½) - S.of SOUCHEZ - Xrds.S.14 a.½.6½.	X rds S.14.a. ½.6½. (close to cemetery)	10	50	400	1 offr. 1 man	6th Bde E.Co RE	X rds S.8. c.6½.0. - across ERSATZ ALLEY about S.14 b.4.3. - GRANBY AV. about S.14.d.77. Jn. of GRANBY AV. with front line	43 to 47	INTER-NATIONAL ALLEY - ZOUAVE VALLEY - 130th ALLEY.	CABARET ROUGE dump.	An NCO 6th Bde	CARENCY	By rail night 14/15 under arrgts made by 6th I.Bde.thence by E.Co.RE.	Wagons will not go through CARENCY till after dark. An additional control post of 1 NCO & 2 men will be posted in ZOUAVE VALLEY between ERSATZ AV. & GRANBY AV. to keep the carrying parties of 5th & 6th Bdes. apart.

S E C R E T.
****

INSTRUCTIONS FOR PLACING SKINS IN THE LINE.

1. 10/D.C.L.I. working under the orders of the C.R.E. are responsible for making and numbering the emplacements. They are also responsible that sufficient filled sandbags are at each emplacement to form cover for skins, and firesteps when skins are in.

2. Skins will be carried up to the line in accordance with the attached Table.

3. Brigades are responsible for all the details shown in the attached Table, except the guides found by E. Co. R.E. as shown.

4. Brigades are responsible, as shown in the Table, for the skins from the time they leave CHATEAU DE LA HAIE till they are handed over to E. Co. R.E. at the emplacements.

5. All guides must know the way thoroughly and must "walk the course" beforehand.

6. E. Co. R.E. are responsible for putting the skins into the emplacements and for sandbagging them in.

7. When the skins are in the line, E. Co. R.E. will always have a guard patrolling the line. In case of any leakage, gas helmets will be put on at once and the nearest man of the guard informed.

8. The accompanying sketch shows the routes of carrying parties for each night, and the position of rendezvous, control posts, emplacements, and dumps for poles and slings when carrying has been completed.

One of these sketches will be given to each O.C., Detachment who will be responsible for it and will hand it in to Brigade Head Quarters on completion of his duty.

9. Wagons will be brought to CHATEAU DE LA HAIE under Divisional arrangements.

H.Q., 2nd Divn. [signature], Lieut. Colonel,

11-7-1916. General Staff, 2nd Division.

SECRET

2nd DIVISION
GENERAL STAFF
No. GS992/15/22
Date

5th Inf. Bde.
6th Inf. Bde.
~~XXX~~C.R.E., 2nd Divn.
10/D.C.L.I.

With reference to 2nd Divn. G.S. 992/15/22 dated 11-7-16, the Company 10/D.C.L.I. referred to will continue to work in the CARENCY Section until further orders and will not return to its Battalion on 16th inst.

The whole question of the distribution of the 10/D.C.L.I. will be discussed at to-days conference.

H.Q., 2nd Divn.
~~12~~ 13-7-1916.

Lieut. Colonel,
General Staff, 2nd Division.

SECRET

2nd Divn. G.
G.S.[illegible]/16/28.

5th Inf. Bde.
6th Inf. Bde.
99th Inf. Bde.
C.R.A., 2nd Divn.
C.R.E., 2nd Divn.
[illegible]
"Q", 2nd Divn.
2/Signal Co.

Please consider the following as cancelled :-

2/Div.G.S.[illegible]/17/14 dated [illegible]-7-1916.

2/Div.G.S.[illegible]/17/28 dated 3-7-1916.

H.Q., 2nd Divn.

[illegible]-7-1916.

12

Lt. Colonel,

General Staff, 2nd Divn.

2nd Divn. No.
G.S.992/15/24

IVth Corps.

I had not contemplated any raids as part of the plan of operations after the 11th July (i.e., 18th day of operations), but G.O.C., 99th Inf. Brigade has prepared a plan for a raid opposite ANGEL ALLEY and could carry it out after 5 days notice. The practice trenches are already dug. Other raids might be arranged after about 8 days notice.

As regards a larger operation, I have prepared a scheme for an attack (not a raid) on the portion of the German front line South of the HOMBER group of craters. All details have been worked out and I attach my draft Orders which I was proposing to discuss at a Conference on the 12th. This was unavoidably postponed.

If the Special Company can make arrangements for the skins to be at the CHATEAU DE LA HAIE ready to be loaded on wagons by 7 p.m. on X date, I can hope to have them installed and the assaulting Brigade ready on the X plus 6th, assuming X is not earlier than the 15th. (N.B. Relief takes place on night 13th/14th.).

For this operation I contemplate an expenditure of -

83	rounds	6" Howr. or "French Courts".	
660	,,	4.5" Howr.	
2700	,,	18 pdr., plus	
5000	,,	18 pdr. and)	per hour as a barrage.
500	,,	4.5" Howr.)	

For raids I contemplate expenditure up to

3000 rounds .....

3000 rounds 18 pdr. and 300 rounds 4.5" Howr.	) per raid.

It will be seen from the attached estimate that the carriage of the large amount of T.M. ammunition and other stores is a considerable strain on the troops. The 5th Inf. Brigade, detailed for the attack, will naturally require to be thoroughly trained and rested: the other two Brigades are holding the line and therefore the carriage must be spread over several days. The 5th Inf. Brigade will also be going into the line 2 nights prior to the attack.

Owing to the changes in orders which have been received during the last 2 days, I feel it my duty to point out that some uncertainty has been caused and that this may have re-acted unfavourably on the Regtl. Officers by lessening their confidence in their higher Commanders.

H.Q., 2nd Divn. Major-General,

13-7-1916. Commanding 2nd Division.

SECRET

S E C R E T.
****

NOTES FOR DIVISIONAL CONFERENCE
13-7-1916.

1. Army Commander has decided that our projected operation with skins in the vicinity of the MOMBER group of craters is not to take place. Fire steps must be replaced by Infantry garrisons at once.

He wishes the policy of small raids to be continued and Brigadiers will therefore work out plans and train parties for these. Size of parties are left to Brigadiers and the raids may take the nature of a rush in and rush out, and not necessarily have a fixed time limit. (Vide notes by 47th Divn. which will be issued). Probable diary of events is attached.

2. Owing to the number of crater jumping parties required for the CARENCY Section, and to the more arduous conditions of that Section generally, the BERTHONVAL Section will be increased so as to include the front line system as far as UHLAN ALLEY (common to both Sections), but accommodation in BROWN'S BURROWS, North of ERSATZ, will remain as at present at the disposal of the Brigade holding the CARENCY Section.
This alteration of front will take place on night 13th/14th July when 6th Inf. Brigade relieves 5th Inf.Bde.

3. The general policy as regards defensive work requires bringing up to date.
The division of responsibility between Brigades in the line and the C.R.E. will remain as at present, but see para. 4.

The principal point which has lately been brought to light is the intense mining activity of the enemy about the Northern group of craters.

The lines on which we must work are as follows :-

(a). A continuous front, support, and if possible, reserve line, wired and bullet proof, allowing free movement all along the Divisional front.
At present the situation between COBURG ALLEY and BOYAU THIRIET is not satisfactory in this respect. The "Islands" must be joined up and made into a continuous line as the Germans have done opposite. A support line must also be dug and communications thereto improved.
Between INTERNATIONAL and HARTUNG the support lines require completion, especially on the top of BROWN'S BURROWS.

(b). Dug-out accommodation for all the garrison of the front line system.
This is going on well in most parts, but efforts must be made to provide bomb proof cover all along the line.

(c). Improvement of communication trenches generally - deepening and floor boarding.

(d). Consolidation of KENNEDY CRATER.

(e)........
P.T.O.

(e). Completion of the ALHAMBRA - COLISEUM - ARRAS road Defended Locality.
Plans have been drawn up for this, and the work will be carried out under the C.R.E.

(f). The completion of the trench along the ARRAS - BETHUNE road as far as BOYAU CENTRAL.

(g). Improvement of Overland Route (Q to arrange).

(h). Disposal of "spoil" from mines.

(i). Dump at CABARET ROUGE.

A detailed Programme of Work will be issued.

4. (a). The employment of the 10/D.C.L.I.(Pioneers) requires to be placed on a definite footing.

(b). The Battalion will be administered by its C.O. and will work under instructions conveyed through the C.R.E.

(c). Normally, 2 companies will work in the forward areas under the C.R.E., one in each Brigade Section. The supervision of their technical work will be carried out by the O.C., Field Co. R.E. in the Section in which they are working.
Field Co. Commanders must keep Brigadiers fully informed as to how the Pioneer Company is being employed.

(d). The O.C., 10/D.C.L.I. will arrange for his forward companies being relieved at suitable intervals in consultation with the C.R.E., so as to avoid disturbing continuity of work.

(e). Brigadiers will allot accommodation to the Pioneers Companies working in their Sections and, if necessary, will evacuate an equivalent number of Infantry.

(f). The Pioneer Company in case of attack will come under the orders of the Brigadier and must be allotted a definite duty in the Defence Scheme of the Section.

(g). The remaining 2 Companies will work on back lines and communication trenches under instructions issued through the C.R.E.

5. SNIPING. German snipers are particularly active. Not satisfied that our arrangements for sniping are as good as they might be. Proposed to form a Divisional Sniping Section of about 1 officer and 20 men. The men will be allotted permanent areas and besides sniping will be able to report on alterations in enemy's line, habits, wire and so on. Men work in pairs and always look after the same area. Work in close touch with Brigade Intelligence Officer.
Details will be worked out. Brigadiers to send in names of suitable officers and other ranks.

6. We have 3 Batteries of Medium T.M's and 2 Batteries of Light T.M's of Naval Division. Proposed to carry out a shoot in retaliation for enemy trench mortaring of of CARENCY Section before these are withdrawn. C.R.A. to submit details.

7. PATROLS. Germans are putting low wire in the grass especially in places cut by our guns and T.M's. Patrols must look out for this.

Action against German patrols and working parties.

8. O.C. 2/Signal Co. will explain working of Signal Service in Divisional area, and how it can help operations.

9. Any other G.S. questions which require discussion.

10. Status of Divisional Fund.

11. Other Administrative questions.

SECRET

S E C R E T.

PROBABLE DIARY OF EVENTS.

JULY.

15th. Trench Mortar Shoot by 2nd Division. C.R.A. to arrange details of Medium T.M's. Stokes Mortars to co-operate.

Night 16th/17th. Raid by 47th Division.

Night 18th/19th. Raid by 99th Inf. Brigade.

Night 19th/20th. A Naval Brigade takes over BERTHONVAL Section from 99th Inf. Brigade.

Night 20th/21st. Raid by 47th Division - with BANANA.

About night 22/23rd. Raid by 6th Inf. Brigade.

Night 23rd/24th. 5th Inf. Brigade relieves 6th Inf. Brigade in CARENCY Section.

Night 27th/28th. Naval Brigade relieved in BERTHONVAL Section by 99th Inf. Brigade.

AUGUST.

Night 4th/5th. 6th Inf. Brigade relieves 5th Inf. Brigade in CARENCY Section.

N.B.

Allowance of Artillery ammunition up to and including 20th July for the 2nd Division is -

10,000 rounds 18 pdr.

500 rounds 4.5" Howr.

but this should not be necessarily expended.

SECRET

2nd Divn. No.
G.S. 1001/1/1.

5th Inf. Bde.
6th Inf. Bde.
99th Inf. Bde.
10/D.C.L.I.
R.A., 2nd Divn.
R.E., 2nd Divn.

Reference to Divisional Commander's conversation with you this afternoon - he wishes to call attention to the following points :-

(1). Use of Trench Mortars. 2" trench mortars will be brought up as soon as possible, especially for use against buildings and villages. The same applies to Stokes Mortars.

(2). Infantry must assault on the heels of our barrage.

(3). The necessity of digging in at once on a new position must be impressed on all Commanders. Parties for carrying up heavy tools and sandbags must be told off beforehand.

(4). The supply of food and water are difficulties which must be thought out beforehand.

(5). The enemy has been making extensive use of gas shells. Gas helmets must always be ready for use.

(6). Accuracy in reports is very important. Reports should be verified before being sent on to the Division as accurate, but the Division must be kept informed of the situation as far as it is known. Negative reports are very useful and should be sent in frequently. Brigades will probably be ordered to send reports at stated times.

H.Q., 2nd Divn.

21-7-1916.

[signature]
Lieut. Colonel,
General Staff, 2nd Division.

S E C R E T.
****

Copy No. 23

2nd DIVISION GENERAL STAFF
No. GS 1001/1/2
Date

2nd DIVISION ORDER No. 115.
****

Reference Map 1/40,000
and 1/20,000

APP 43

23rd July, 1916.

(1). The following moves will take place on the 23rd July -

(a). 99th Inf.Bde. to SAND PIT Valley, squares F.13 and 19.

5th Fd.Co.R.E.)
Bearer Div. 100th Fd.Amb.) will remain at MORLANCOURT and will come under orders of G.O.C., 6th Inf. Bde.

99th Inf. Bde. will march to its new area via squares K.9,10,11, to Northern end of BOIS DES TAILLES, thence by road through L.7, L.1, F.25, ARBRE FILIFORME.
99th Inf. Bde. will be clear of MORLANCOURT by 11 a.m. but will not pass road junction K.6.d.8.7. before 10 a.m.

(b). 6th Inf. Bde. will march to an area about the BOIS DES TAILLES, squares K.12 and 18, North of the BRAY - CORBIE road.
6th Inf. Bde. will move via MORLANCOURT, thence by track through squares K.9,10,11, but troops from SAILLY LE SEC can move by road junction J.18.c., thence by main CORBIE - BRAY road; head of column not to reach MORLANCOURT before 11 a.m.; column (including 10/D.C .L.I.) to be clear of SAILLY LE SEC by 10 a.m.

East Anglian Fd.Co.R.E.)
Bearer Div. 5th Fd.Amb.) will march under the orders of G.O.C., 6th Inf. Bde. as far as the N. end of BOIS DES TAILLES, and will proceed thence by the same route as the 99th Inf. Bde. to SAND PIT Valley where they will come under the orders of G.O.C., 99th Inf. Bde.

(c). 5th Inf. Bde.)
226th Fd.Co.R.E.)
Bearer Div. 6th Fd.Amb.) will march to the HAPPY VALLEY, squares F.26 and 27, moving by the SOMME VALLEY road as far as SAILLY LE SEC, thence to BRAY - CORBIE road at J.18.c., thence along the BRAY - CORBIE road. The column will not leave VAUX SUR SOMME before 9-30 a.m.

(d). 10/D.C.L.I. (Pioneers) will move immediately in rear of 6th Inf. Bde. to MORLANCOURT, under orders of G.O.C. 6th Inf. Bde.

(2). (a). Div. Artillery (less Medium Trench Mortar Batteries and S.A.A. Sections and Grenade Wagons D.A.C.) will remain in its present area.

(b). Medium Trench Mortar Batteries, and S.A.A. Sections and Grenade Wagons D.A.C. will move to MORLANCOURT under arrangements to be made by G.O.C., R.A. They will not arrive at MORLANCOURT before 2 p.m. They will march via CORBIE, SOMME VALLEY road as far as SAILLY LE SEC, thence by road junction J.18.c. and road junction K.20.b.

(3)..........

(3). Div. Train will move from its present areas under orders to be issued by the A.A. & Q.M.G.

(4). Advance parties will move to their new areas in sufficient time to ascertain bivouacs, water supply, etc., and to guide the troops to their destinations.

(5). All units will move with watercarts full.

(6). Arrival of troops which is not to be later than 5 p.m., in their new areas will be reported at once to Div. Hd. Qrs.

(7). Advanced Divisional Head Quarters will be at the CITADEL, F.21.b.

(8). Acknowledge.

Lieut. Colonel,

General Staff, 2nd Division.

Issued at 7 a.m.

2 Am to Bdes. RA 10 BC 29 Q

Copy No.1 to 5th Inf. Bde.
2 6th Inf. Bde.
3 99th Inf. Bde.
4 R.A., 2nd Divn.
5 R.E., 2nd Divn.
6 2/Signal Co.
7 10/D,C.L.I.(Pioneers).
8 A.D.M.S., 2nd Divn.
9 A.P.M., 2nd Divn.
10 2/Div. Train.
11 "Q", 2nd Divn.
12 & 13 XIIIth Corps.)
14 3rd Divn.)
15 9th Divn.) For information.
16 18th Divn.)
17 30th Divn.)
18 35th Divn.)
19 1st Cavy.Divn.)
20 - 24 G.S. Records.

2nd DIVISION
GENERAL STAFF
No. G.A. 1001/1/3
Date.

5th Infantry Brigade.
99th Infantry Brigade.

G.O.Cs 5th and 99th Brigades together with such Commanding Officers as can be spared, will carry out a reconnaissance of the line now held by the 3rd Division .

G.O.C. 5th Brigade and party will report at H.Q. 9th Infantry Brigade in MONTAUBAN (S.27 d 2.8) at 5am 24th inst.

G.O.C.99th Brigade and party will report at H.Q. 8th Infantry Brigade at Junction of BRESLAU ALLEY and BACK LANE (A 3 c 0 5) at 5 am 24th inst

Acknowledge

H.Q. 2nd Divn.
23rd July, 1916.

G. Belgrave Major
for Lieut Colonel,
General Staff, 2nd Division

G.O.C. 3rd Division.

With reference to paragraph 10 of your Operation Order of last night, General Daly, Commanding 6th Brigade, is coming to see you this morning. I hope it may not be considered necessary for the Headquarters of 6th Inf. Bde. to be established at the QUARRIES. As my Battalions are up to establishment, you may possibly be able to do with 2 Battalions always instead of the whole Brigade in which case possibly the Headquarters of the Brigade would remain at the present Headquarters of the 76th Brigade.

General Daly will explain full details.

Major-General,

25th July, 1916. Commanding 2nd Division.

C.R.E., 2nd Divn.
5th Inf. Bde.
6th Inf. Bde.
99th Inf. Bde.

The garrison of MONTAUBAN will be employed on work on the defences of the village. The work is being carried out ~~by~~ under the Chief Engineer of the Corps.

H.Q., 2nd Divn. Major for Lt. Colonel,
25-7-1916. General Staff, 2nd Division.

S E C R E T.

2nd DIVISION INSTRUCTIONS No. 139.

25th July, 1916.

The following instructions regarding the policy to be pursued in our new area are forwarded. Work is to commence at once.

1. By Brigades in the line -
Improvement of the front line including wire.
The principal points in this connection are the completion of the Loop in the Northern portion of DELVILLE WOOD by the Brigade holding the left section, and the improvement of the defences of WATERLOT FARM by the Brigade holding the right section.
R.E. and Pioneer assistance will be given (see below)-.

2. The East Anglian Field Co.RE., will construct a strong point in the S.E. corner of the orchard S. of LONGUEVAL under instructions to be given by the C.R.E.

3. The Pioneer Battalion will be employed as follows under the C.R.E:-
1 Company to assist 226th Field Coy. on construction of trench about 70 yards East of TRONES WOOD from the railway to North end of wood. The Right Inf.Bde. will assist with working parties.
This company will then be employed to assist 226th Field Company R.E. on improvement of LONGUEVAL ALLEY as far as BERNAFAY WOOD and construction of trench A from S.23.c.8.4 (junction with 35th Division) to S.23.c. (left of Divisional Area).

1 company to assist E. Anglian Field Coy. in work on new communication trench to run from N. end of BERNAFAY Wood to LONGUEVAL on East side of Divisional boundary.

2 Companies to dig new communication trench under 5th Field Coy. parallel to and on West of BERNAFAY Wood and make shelters.

Field Coy. Commanders will keep Brigadiers informed as to the progress of the work carried out by them and the Pioneer Coys.
In case of attack they will come under the orders of the Brigadier in whose area they are working.

4. 5th Field Coy. R.E. assisted by working parties of the Reserve Brigade will dig a new trench through BERNAFAY Wood from junction of East side of wood with railway to about S.28.a.0.5 and will assist in the construction of cover in CATERPILLAR Wood valley, which will be carried out by the garrison.

5. Garrisons of trenches must start improving cover for themselves at once.

6. New trenches have recently been dug by other units in 2nd Divisional Area and must be occupied as soon as completed.
The principal ones are
(a) From about S.18.b.2.0 to S.18.c.7.5.
(b) From North end of TRONES WOOD towards towards S. end of LONGUEVAL.
(c) Assembly trenches in S.23.c. These are being dug by cavalry working parties.
(d) Trench N.W. and S.W. from WATERLOT FARM.

7......
P.T.O.

7. The dividing lines between Brigades for purposes of command is the GINCHY - LONGUEVAL Road and the trench along it as far West as its junction with the new trench running S.W. towards LONGUEVAL ALLEY thence along this new trench to its junction with old German line about S.1[illegible].c.7.5, thence along LONGUEVAL ALLEY. All the above are inclusive to Right Brigade.

8. Constant activity is necessary and patrols and snipers must be fully employed.
Every effort must be made to gain ground.

Lieut. Colonel,
General Staff, 2nd Division.

Issued to -

5th Inf. Bde.
6th Inf. Bde.
99th Inf. Bde.
10th D.C.L.I.
R.A. 2nd Divn.
R.E. 2nd Divn.
2nd Signal Coy.
"Q" 2nd Divn.

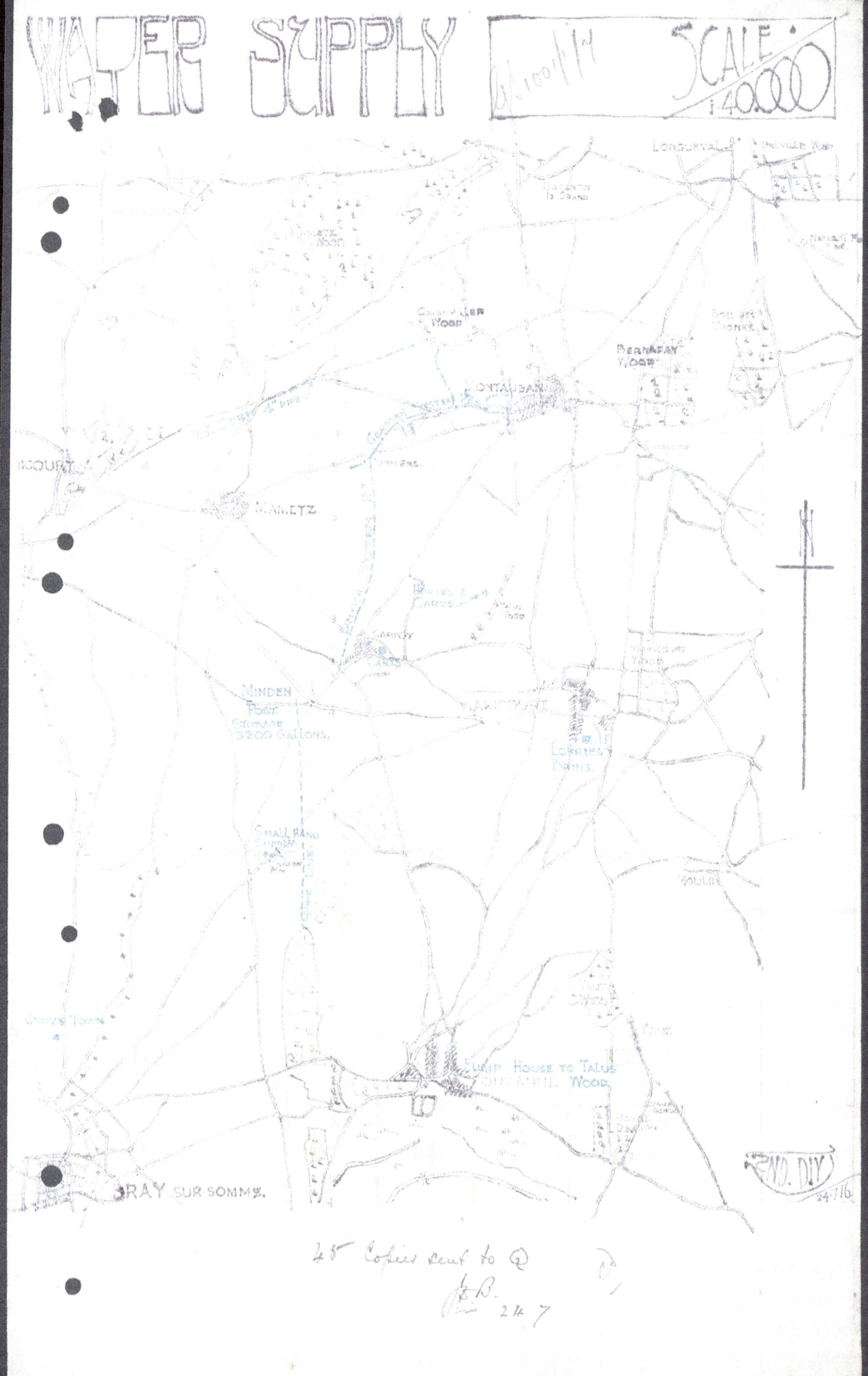
WATER SUPPLY
SCALE 1:40.000
LONGUEVAL
BERNAFAY WOOD
MONTAUBAN
MAMETZ
CARNOY
MINDEN POST STORAGE 3300 GALLONS
SMALL HAND SUPPLY
GROVE TOWN
MOULIN
RAY SUR SOMME
2ND. DIV
24.7.16
48 Copies sent to Q

2nd Division

War Diaries

General Staff

July 1916

DELVILLE WOOD

2nd Division
G.S. 24th Jul 1916

DELVILLE WOOD

LONGUEVAL

SOUTH STREET

GINCHY

WATERLOT FARM

TRONES WOOD

GUILLEMONT

Appendix 47

SECRET.

Copy No.1..

XIII CORPS OPERATION ORDER No. 32.

24th July, 1916.

1. The operations ordered for to-morrow are postponed for at least 48 hours.

2. The 2nd Division will relieve the 3rd Division in the line commencing at once.

G.O.C., 2nd Division to report when he has taken over command.

As much as possible of the relief should be effected to-night.

The 106th Infantry Brigade will revert to its own division as soon as it can be spared in the course of the relief: G.O.C., 3rd Division to decide when he no longer requires it and report to 35th Division and Corps H.Q.

The relief of the 3rd Division Artillery by the 2nd Divisional Artillery will be carried out as soon as it can be arranged under orders to be issued by the G.O.C., R.A.

The 3rd Division, on relief, will move into the Reserve Division area; it will be replaced there brigade by brigade by units of 55th Division which commences detraining to-morrow: on relief by 55th Division units of 3rd Division will move back into the rear portion of the Corps area.

3. The 90th Brigade of 30th Division will remain at the disposal of the G.O.C. 35th Division until further orders.

4. The 35th Division will arrange to take over from 3rd Division during the early part of to-night the defence of TRONES WOOD, N. of the railway.line. The left division will be responsible for the defence of LONGUEVAL ALLEY North of TRONES WOOD and of WATERLOT FARM.

5. The strength of the garrisons of the BRIQUETERIE and MONTAUBAN and the names of commanders will be reported to Corps Headquarters at once by Right and Left Divisions respectively: these garrisons will be permanent during the tour of each division in the line, and are to be independent of the remainder of the troops of the division both for attack and defence.

(sd) W.H. GREENLY

B.G., G.S.

Issued at 4-30 p.m.

SECRET.

Copy No. 21

App 49

2nd DIVISION ORDER No. 116.

Reference Maps, 1/20,000 and 1/40,000.

24th July, 1916.

(1). (a). 99th Inf. Bde. and Bearer Division 5th Fd. Amb. will relieve units of the 3rd Division in the left sub-section of 3rd Div. area on the night 24th/25th July. Detailed arrangements will be made between Brigadiers and A.D'sM.S. concerned.

(b). 99th Inf. Bde. and Bearer Div. 5th Field Ambulance will move from its present area via CAFTET WOOD and MONTAUBAN.

(c). On arrival at MONTAUBAN, 99th Inf. Bde. and Bearer Divn. 5th Field Ambulance will come under the orders of G.O.C. 3rd Division.

(2). (a). 5th Inf. Bde. will relieve units of the 3rd Divn. in the right sub-section of the 3rd Divn. area on the night 25th/26th July. Detailed arrangements will be made between Brigadiers concerned.

(b). 5th Inf. Bde. will move from its present area via X roads F.29.d.2.9. - road junction F.29.b.2.6. - X roads F.18.d.5.3. - CARNOY.

(c). Completion of relief will be reported to Div. Hd. Qrs.

(3). (a). 6th Inf. Bde. will move to-morrow the 25th inst. into the Reserve Brigade area of the 3rd Division and will come under the orders of G.O.C., 3rd Division. Headquarters will be at A.8.b.2.8. Details of relief will be arranged between Brigadiers concerned.

(b). The relief will be carried out in daylight and as early as possible.

(c). Completion of relief will be reported to Div. Hd.Qrs. 3rd and 2nd Divisions.

(4). MONTAUBAN Village will be held by a permanent garrison of two companies under command of Major C.C. HARMAN, 22/R.Fus. who will remain in command during the tour of the Division in the line. The two companies may be changed at the discretion of G.O'sC. Inf. Bdes. in order to provide necessary reliefs, but continuity of work must be ensured. The garrison is on no account to be used for counter-attack.

(5). All first line transport of Inf. Bdes.and R.E. will move on 25th July to HAPPY VALLEY (L.3.).

The tents and shelters of the units of the 3rd Division in HAPPY VALLEY will be taken over as soon as they are vacated by the 3rd Division.

(6). (a). 2nd Div. Artillery will relieve 9th Div. Artillery in the line on nights 26th/27th and 27th/28th under arrangements to be made between C's.R.A. concerned. C.R.A., 2nd Div. will assume command of all Divisional Artillery covering Left Section, XIIIth Corps front at 9 a.m. on 28th.

Completion of reliefs will be reported to Hd.Qrs. 2nd Divn.

(b). Medium trench mortars will be moved into the line as soon as possible under arrangements made by C.R.A.

(7)........
P.T.O.

(7). Field Companies R.E., 2nd Division will relieve Field Companies R.E. 3rd Division under arrangements to be made between C.R.E's concerned. Field Cos. R.E. 2nd Division will move to an area about CARNOY on the 25th July under the orders of the C.R.E.

(8). 10/D.C.L.I.(Pioneers) will relieve 20/K.R.R.C.(Pioneers) in bivouacs at S.13.c. on the afternoon of the 25th. The Battalion will leave MORLANCOURT at 2 p.m. and move via MEAULTE and CARTET WOOD.

(9). Field Ambulances 2nd Division will relieve Field Ambulances 3rd Division under arrangements to be made by A.D'sM.S. concerned.

(10). On completion of Infantry reliefs, G.O.C., 2nd Division will assume command of the Left Section, XIIIth Corps area.

(11). Advanced Head Quarters 2nd Division will close at the CITADEL at 8 p.m. 25th, and will open at COPSE B (A.21.a.) at the same hour.

(12). The following order by G.O.C. 3rd Division will be carried out by 6th Inf. Bde. after the Brigade has taken over the area mentioned in para. 3(a) :-

" In the afternoon of July 25th the 6th Inf. Bde.
" will relieve the 106th Inf. Bde. in Divisional reserve
" in CATERPILLAR VALLEY and MONTAUBAN. The movement will
" be carried out by small parties under arrangements to be
" made direct between Brigadiers of 6th and 106th Inf.Bdes.
" The G.O.C. 6th Inf.Bde. will report to 3rd Div.H.Q. when
" the relief is completed, and his Brigade H.Q. have been
" established in the QUARRY at S.22.c.0.5. After relief
" the 106th Inf. Bde. will return to, and will move as
" directed by the 35th Div. "

Acknowledge.

C. Geddes.
Lieut. Colonel
General Staff, 2nd Division.

Issued at 11-15 p.m.

Copy No.1 to 5th Inf.Bde.
2 6th Inf.Bde.
3 99th Inf.Bde.
4 10/D.C.LI. (Pioneers).
5 R.A., 2nd Divn.
6 R.E., 2nd Divn.
7 2/Signal Co R.E.
8 "Q", 2nd Divn.
9 A.D.M.S., 2nd Divn.
10 A.D.V.S., 2nd Divn.
11 A.P.M., 2nd Divn.
12 OC. Det. Northumberland Hussars.
13 2/Div. Gas Officer.
14 & 15 XIIIth Corps.)
16 3rd Divn.)
17 30th Divn.) For information.
18 35th Divn.)
19 5th Divn.)
20 1st Cav.Divn.)
21 - 25 G.S. Records.

Appendix 50.

S E C R E T.
****

2nd Divn. No.
G.S.1001/2/6.

XIII Corps.
133/84(G).

2nd Divn.

----

1. The boundary between XIII and XV Corps has been modified as shown on attached sketch map by dotted blue line.

2. The 5th Division will take over to-night all ground held by 2nd Division N. and W. of the new boundary.

XIII Corps. (sd) H. Montgomery, Major,

25th July, 1916. for B.G., G.S.

S E C R E T. Appendix 51.

XIII CORPS OPERATION ORDER No. 33.

25th July /16.

1. (a) The XV Corps has been ordered to secure the Eastern corner of HIGH WOOD as early as possible.

(b) The capture of the strong points in the orchards north of LONGUEVAL in S.11.c. and d. the village of LONGUEVAL and DELVILLE WOOD, will form one combined operation to be carried out by the XIII and XV Corps on morning of 27th July.
The whole of the north end of LONGUEVAL Village will be the objective of the XV Corps: DELVILLE WOOD will be the objective of the XIII Corps

(c) The XIII Corps will continue preparations for the attack of the enemy's second line between FALFEMONT FARM and GUILLEMONT, which will not take place before the morning of 28th July.

2. The 2nd Division will attack DELVILLE WOOD on the morning of 27th instant in conjunction with the 5th Division which is attacking LONGUEVAL and the orchards N. of it, including that north of the FLERS ROAD AT S.11.d central.
The details of the plan of attack will be arranged between the 2nd and 5th Divisions.

3. The boundary between the two divisions is shown by the green line on barrage map attached.

The objectives of the 2nd Division are (i) to secure the whole of the wood E. of the boundary line and as far N. as a line shown approximately by the dotted green line, from the E. end of PRINCES STREET to the S.E. corner of the FLERS road orchard at S.11.d.6.5 in touch with the 5th Division which will secure the orchard:
(ii) to consolidate the ground gained and to construct an intermediate line between the present front line and the objective.

4. The attack will take place at an hour, zero, to be notified separately.
The attack will be preceded by an artillery bombardment in accordance with programme issued by G.O.C., R.A. the lifts of the Corps Artillery are shown on attached sketch.
The whole of the available guns of XIII and XV Corps will be employed for this operation.
The boundary line between the artilleries of the two Corps will be a N. and S. line between S.12 and S.11 (shown by dotted red line).

5. Tomorrow morning (26th inst.) the same hour as fixed for the bombardment on 27th inst. an artillery bombardment for one hour by the same guns will be carried out by both Corps.

(Sd) W.H.Greenly.

Issued at 9.15 p.m. B.G., G.S.

SECRET.

2nd Division No. G.S. 1001/2/5.

Appendix 52.

XIII Corps 132/85 (G).

2nd Division.

Special instruction to 2nd Division regarding the bombardment of DELVILLE WOOD on morning of 26th July referred to in para. 6 of XIII Corps Operation Order No. 33.

Special note will be taken and reports forwarded as soon as possible to Corps Headquarters of the distribution and effectiveness of our own artillery fire and the position and intensity of any barrages which the enemy may put up.

Immediately the bombardment lifts at 7.10 a.m. 26th July, patrols will be pushed forward to explore the wood and capture prisoners and endeavour to ascertain the positions of any machine guns or strong points or trenches in the wood which may be manned by the enemy. For this purpose all our own artillery fire will be kept clear of the wood for 1½ hours after the bombardment lifts off the wood.

(Sd) A.A.Montgomery.
Major forB.G., G.S.

XIII Corps.
25th July, 1916.

- 2 -

5th Inf. Bde.
6th Inf. Bde.
99th Inf. Bde.

Forn information.

For information and action (99th Bde. only).

(Sd) J.D.Belgrave.
Major for Lieut. Colonel,
General Staff, 2nd Division.

25/7/16.

S E C R E T. Appendix 53.

2nd DIVISION INSTRUCTIONS No. 139.

****

25th July, 1916.

The following instructions regarding the policy to be pursued in our new area are forwarded. Work is to commence at once.

1. By Brigades in the line -
Improvement of the front line including wire.
The principle points in this connection are the completion of the Loop in the Northern portion of DELVILLE WOOD by the Brigade holding the left section, and the improvement of the defences of WATERLOT FARM by the Brigade holding the right section.
R.E. and Pioneer assistance will be given (see below):-

2. The East Anglian Fd.Co.R.E. will construct a strong point in the S.E. corner of the orchard S. of LONGUEVAL under instructions to be given by the C.R.E.

3. The Pioneer Battalion will be employed as follows under the C.R.E. -
1 company to assist 226th Fd.Co. on construction of trench 70 yards East of TRONES WOOD from the railway to North end of wood. The Right Inf. Bde. will assist with working parties.
This company will then be employed to assist 226th Fd. Co.RE on improvement of LONGUEVAL ALLEY as far as BERNAFAY WOOD and construction of trench A from S.23.c.8.4. (junction with 35th Division) to S.23.c.(left of Divisional Area).
1 company to assist E. Anglian Fd.Co. in work on new communication trench to run from N. end of BERNAFAY WOOD to LONGUEVAL on East side of Divisional boundary.

2 companies to dig new communication trench under 5th Field Coy. parallel to and on West of BERNAFAY WOOD and make shelters.

Field Coy. Commanders will keep Brigadiers informed as to the progress of the work carried out by them and the Pioneer Coys.
In case of attack they will come under the orders of the Brigadier in whose area they are working.

4. 5th Field Coy R.E. assisted by working parties of the Reserve Brigade will dig a new trench through BERNAFAY Wood from junction of East side of wood with railway to about S.28. a.0.5. and will assist in the construction of cover in CATERPILLAR WOOD Valley, which will be carried out by the garrison.

5. Garrisons of trenches must start improving cover for themselves at once.

6. New trenches have recently been dug by other units in 2nd Divisional Area and must be occupied as soon as completed.
The principal ones are :-
(a) From about S.18.b.2.0 to S.18.c.7.5.
(b) From North end of TRONES WOOD towards S. and of LONGUEVAL.
(c) Assembly trenches in S.23.c. These are being dug by cavalry working parties.
(d) Trench N.W. and S.W. from WATERLOT FARM.

7. The dividing lines between Brigades for purposes of command is the GINCHY - LOBGUEVAL Road and the trench along it as far West as its junction with the new trench running S.W. towards LONGUEVAL ALLEY thence along this new trench to its junction with old German line about S.18.c.7.5, thence along LONGUEVAL ALLEY. All the above are inclusive to Right Brigade.

8. Constant activity is necessary and patrols and snipers must be fully employed.

Every effort must be made to gain ground.

(Sd) C. DEEDES. Lieut-Colonel.
General Staff, 2nd Division.

SECRET.

Copy No 24

2nd DIVISION ORDER No. 117.

~~Trones Map~~ 1/20,000 and attached sketch. 26th July, 1916.

(1) The 99th Infantry Brigade (less the garrison of MONTAUBAN - 2 coys.) will attack and capture DELVILLE WOOD on the morning of the 27th July.

(2) The attack will be preceded by a bombardment of Heavy Artillery commencing at 6-10.am. Subsequent action of the Artillery and Infantry is shown on the following table :-

Hour.	Artillery Action.	Infantry Action.
6-10.am.	Artillery barrages line marked brown & North of it.	Infantry formed up in and in front of existing trenches.
7-10.am.	Artillery lifts to line marked in red & north of it.	Infantry advances to about line marked in brown and consolidates.
7-40.am.	Artillery lifts to line marked in green & North of it.	Infantry advances to line marked in red.
8-10.am.	Artillery lifts to line marked in blue(final barrage)	objective and consolidates. Infantry assaults final

A line about the line marked in brown when gained will be consolidated as well as the final objective, about 50 yards inside the northern and north eastern edges of the wood.

Divisional artillery will barrage on the same objectives and at the same time as the Heavy Artillery.

(3) A brigade of the 5th Division on our left will attack LONGUEVAL Village and the orchards to the north at the same hours, and the artillery barrages will be the same.

The dividing line between attacks is as shown in green on the sketch.

(4) The 99th Infantry Brigade will form up for the attack in the trenches now held by the Brigade, and also in SOUTH STREET and the new trench running from about S 18 central to near the bend of LONGUEVAL ALLEY both of which will be temporarily handed over by GOC 5th Infantry Brigade to G.O.C. 99th Infantry Brigade, and re-occupied by 5th Infantry Brigade as soon as vacated. The new trench running N.W. from the Northern end of TRONES WOOD to LONGUEVAL may also be used by the 99th Infantry Brigade.

(5) The 6th Infantry Brigade will be in support to the 99th Infantry Brigade. 2 battalions, 6th Infantry Brigade will be moved up to positions between the trench mentioned last in para 4 and CATERPILLAR WOOD Valley. These two battalions will be at the disposal of G.O.C. 99th Infantry Brigade in the event of his requiring more troops to gain his objective. The remaining two battalions 6th Infantry Brigade will be moved so that they can occupy the positions vacated by the two leading battalions if the former are required by the G.O.C.99th Infantry Brigade and will then be at the disposal of that Commander.

... 2 ...

P.T.O

(6). G.Os. C, 6th and 99th Infantry Brigades will reconnoitre the places of assembly for their brigades and the routes for moving forward. Additional assembly trenches must be dug.

(7) In addition to the assaulting troops, G.O.C., 99th Inf. Brigade will detail parties to deal with dug-outs etc and troops for consolidation. He will also make special arrangements for securing his right flank during the attack and for keeping touch with the 5th Division on his left.

(8) Each man of the assaulting troops will carry at least two Mills grenades and two sandbags and the party detailed for consolidation will be provided with cutting as well as entrenching tools.

(9) The provision of cover for troops detailed to hold the objective after capture is of the utmost importance. Consolidation will be carried out with a view to holding the lines gained mainly with machine and Lewis guns, but they should be constructed so as to allow of lateral movement. At least one communication trench must be dug forward from our present front line.

(10) In the event of the G.O.C, 99th Inf. Brigade not employing the battalions of the 6th Inf, Brigade he will inform Divisional HQ. when these battalions are no longer required in their forward positions: they will then be withdrawn under the orders of the Divisional Commander.

(11) Infantry must take every opportunity of gaining ground under the artillery barrages and of assaulting immediately the barrages lift.

Acknowledge

[signature]
Lieut-Colonel,
General Staff, 2nd Division.

Issued at 7.a.m. to :-

Copy No 1 to 5th Inf. Bde.
2 6th Inf. Bde.
3 99th Inf. Bde
4 10/D.C.L.I.(Pioneers)
5 R.A., 2nd Divn.
6 R.E., "
7 2/Signal Co.R.E.
8 "Q", 2nd Divn.
9. A.D.M.S. 2d Divn.
10 A. D.V.S. "
11 A.P.M. "
12 O.C. Det. Northumberland Hussars.
13 2/Div Gas Officer.
14 XIII Corps "G)
15 XIII Corps "Q")
16 3rd Division.)
17 5th ") For information.
18 30th ")
19 35th ")
20 55th ")
21 1st Cavalry Division.)
22 - 26 G.S. Records)

Copy No. 29

Amendment to 2nd Division Order No. 117.

26th July, 1918.

Paragraphs 5 and 10 of the above orders are cancelled. The attack will be carried out by the 99th Inf. Brigade only. The 6th Inf. Brigade will remain in its present area, but ready to move at short notice.

The E. Anglian Field Coy. is placed at the disposal of the G.O.C. 99th Inf. Bde. for the operation.

[signature]

Lieut. Colonel,
General Staff, 2nd Division.

Issued to all recipients
of 2nd Div. Order No. 117.

Appendix 55.

SECRET.

Copy No. 11.

XIII CORPS ARTILLERY OPERATION ORDER No. 6.

****

26th July, 1916.

1. The 2nd Division (XIII Corps) and the 5th Division (XV Corps) will capture the remainder of LONGUEVAL VILLAGE and DELVILLE WOOD on "Z" day.

2. The dividing line between Corps will be as shewn on the map. The 2nd Division will advance on the right (EAST) of this line and the 5th Division on the left (WEST) of this line.

3. The Artillery of both Corps will prepare and support the attack.

4. The preliminary bombardment will begin at Zero-1 hour at the following rates of fire.

18 pdrs.........2 rounds per gun per minute. (H.E. will be used until final barrage).
4.5" Hows.......1 round per gun per minute.
6" Hows....... - - do - -
8" & 9.2" Hows..1 round per gun per 2 minutes.
12" Hows........ - - do - - 5 "
15" Hows........ - - do - - 10 "

At Zero-7 and 7 minutes before each lift the fire will become intense.

During the preliminary bombardment, the fire of the artillery will be distributed over the whole portion of the Wood NORTH of Zero line and trenches NORTH EAST and EAST of it but mainly concentrated on the SOUTHERN portion.

5. The lifts of the Corps Artillery are shown on the attached map (App. "A").

Divisional Artillery may remain on a little longer if so ordered by the G.O.C. 2nd Division.

6. During the preliminary bombardment the artillery of the French XX Corps and the 35th Divisional Artillery will bombard GUILLEMONT and will lift at Zero on to GINCHY especially the WESTERN and NORTH WESTERN Exits, acting in such a manner as to simulate an attack on GUILLEMONT.

7. From Zero-5 a Section of each Battery of the Counter-battery Group re-inforced by 75 mm and 120 mm batteries firing gas shell will attack selected hostile battery positions and will continue subject to calls from our aeroplanes.

8. After the final lift the Siege Howitzers will maintain a slow rate of fire on the final barrage but will be available for counter battery work if called upon.

9. The date of "Z" day and Zero hour will be communicated later.

10. ACKNOWLEDGE.

(Sd) W.R.Reid. Majro,
Staff Officer to G.O.C., R.A.
XIII Corps.

Issued at 6 a.m.

app 56

Copy No. 26

Amendment to 2nd Division Order No. 117.

26th July, 1918.

Paragraphs 5 and 10 of the above orders are cancelled. The attack will be carried out by the 99th Inf. Brigade only. The 6th Inf. Brigade will remain in its present area, but ready to move at short notice.

The E. Anglian Field Coy. is placed at the disposal of the G.O.C. 99th Inf. Bde. for the operation.

Geddes.

Lieut. Colonel,

General Staff, 2nd Division.

Issued to all recipients
of 2nd Div. Order No. 117.

app 57

S E C R E T.
****

Copy No. 22

AMENDMENT No. 2 to 2nd DIVISION ORDER No. 117 dated 26-7-16.

26th July, 1916.

The following Table is substituted for that shown in para. 2, which is cancelled :-

New Para. 2. The attack will be preceded by a bombardment of Heavy and Field Artillery commencing at 6-10 a.m. Subsequent action of the Artillery and Infantry is shown on the following Table:-

Hour.	Artillery Action.	Infantry Action.
6-10 a.m.	Artillery barrages line marked brown and North of it.	Infantry formed up in and in front of existing trenches.
7-10 a.m.	Artillery lifts to line marked in red and North of it.	Infantry advances to about line marked in brown and consolidates.
8-10 a.m.	Artillery lifts to line marked in green and North of it.	Infantry advanced to line marked in red.
8-40 a.m.	Artillery lifts to line marked in blue (final barrage).	Infantry assaults final objective and consolidates.

Maps issued with original order must be amended accordingly.

N O T E.
****

Bombardment by Division on our left begins 1 hour before ours, but their infantry attack takes place at the same time.

ACKNOWLEDGE.

Issued at 11-10 pm

Copies sent to all recipients of 2nd Div. Order No.117.

[signature]
Lieut. Colonel,
General Staff, 2nd Division.

"A" Form. Army Form C. 2121.

MESSAGES AND SIGNALS. No. of Message

Prefix .... Code .... m.	Words	Charge	This message is on a/c of:	Recd. at .... m.
Office of Origin and Service Instructions.	Sent		.... Service.	Date
	At .... m.			From
	To			
	By		(Signature of "Franking Officer.")	By

TO Adv Head — App. 58

Sender's Number	Day of Month	In reply to Number	AAA
* BMG	27		

Large numbers of gas shells have been fired along road BERNAFAY WOOD – LONGUEVAL ALLEY and MONTAUBAN alley also on MONTAUBAN [illegible] and approaches to front line generally aaa This has greatly hampered communication of all kinds with front and carrying parties [illegible] have been much delayed aaa Report just received ~~that~~ indicates that preparations are now complete in most particulars aaa except that communications except by runner are all broken and it was impossible for men in gas helmets to find and repair broken wire aaa Every effort is ~~[illegible]~~ now being made to repair and it is hoped to have lines working

From

Place

Time

The above may be forwarded as now corrected. (Z)

Censor. Signature of Addressor or person authorised to telegraph in his name.

* This line should be erased if not required.

293146—W. & S. Ltd., London.—W 1789/1402—100,000—7/15. Forms C 2121/10.

"A" Form. Army Form C. 2121.

MESSAGES AND SIGNALS. No. of Message

Prefix ... Code ... m.	Words	Charge	This message is on a/c of:	Recd. at ... m.
Office of Origin and Service Instructions.	Sent		... Service.	Date
	At ... m.			From
	To			
	By		(Signature of "Franking Officer.")	By

TO (2)

Sender's Number	Day of Month	In reply to Number	AAA

in time aaa latest reports indicate that all is otherwise in readiness aaa Except for shells mentioned enemy appears quiet

From OAK

Place

Time 5 am

The above may be forwarded as now corrected. (Z)

Censor. Signature of Addressor or person authorised to telegraph in his name.

* This line should be erased if not required.

395146—W. & S. Ltd., London.—W 1789/1402—100,000—7/15. Forms C 2121/10.

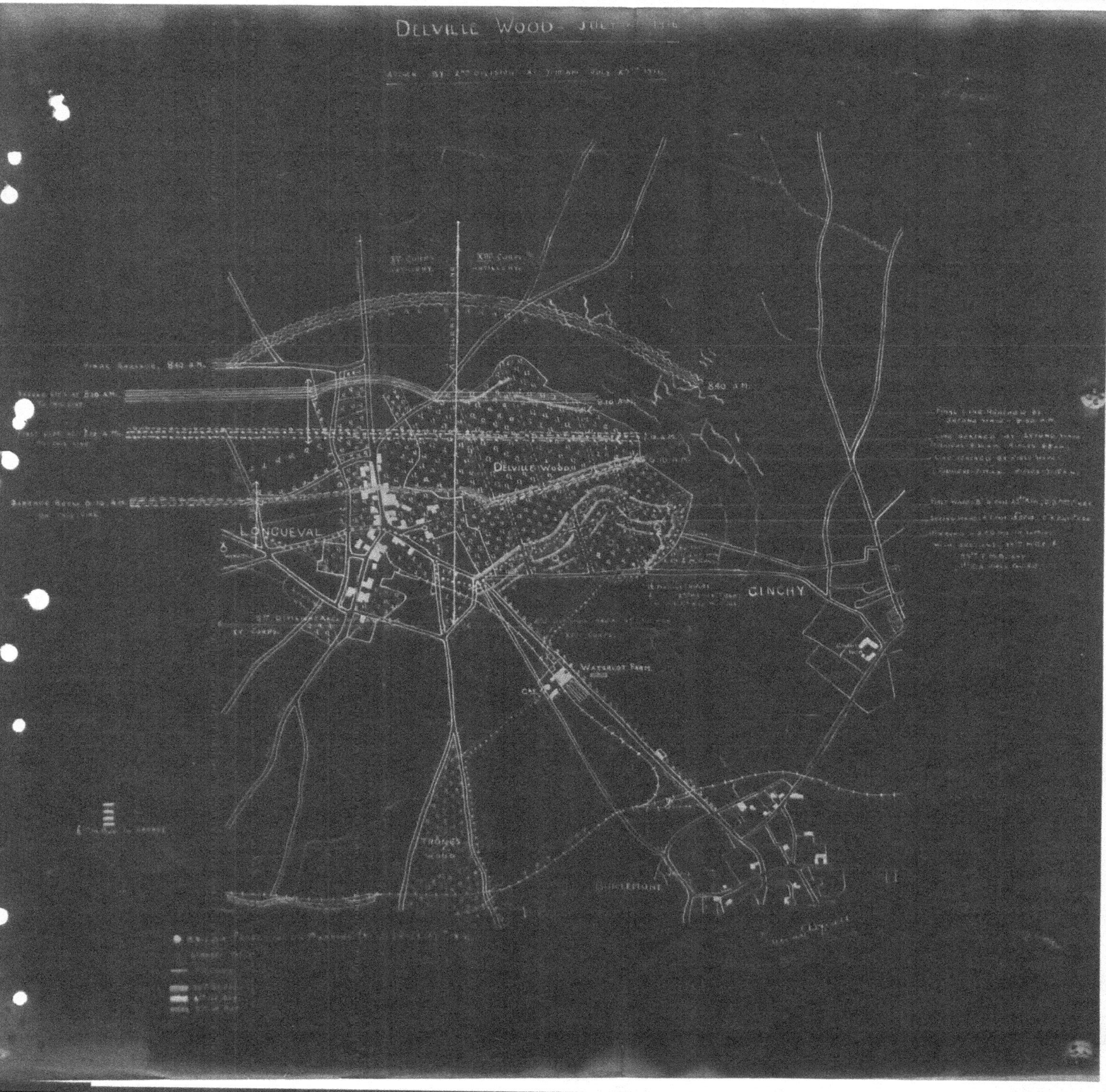
Delville Wood
Longueval
Delville Wood
Ginchy
Waterlot Farm
840 a.m.
Trônes Wood
Guillemont

APPENDIX 59.

G.S. 1001/1/13.

Xlll Corps.

In continuation of my report forwarded last night, the following further information has been received.

Our heavy artillery caused the enemy heavy losses in the wood and had destroyed several machine guns before our infantry advanced, but also caused some loss to our own men during the attack.

Touch was kept with the Norfolks on our left throughout the day.

A very large percentage of our casualties were caused by shell fire after all troops had reached their objective. We had few casualties during the attack. The Germans ran out of the wood and also left the trenches outside the wood and ran over the hill. They were caught by our artillery and suffered very severely.

DELVILLE WOOD is now very thin and men moving in the centre of the wood are exposed to machine gun fire from direction of GUILLEMONT and have suffered some loss from it. A very heavy bombardment is being maintained on DELVILLE WOOD - a good deal of the fire coming from the South East. It is reported that Germans have been coming over in ones and twos and surrendering to the troops near WATERLOT FARM.

There are still a certain number of wounded German prisoners in LONGUEVAL.

Present dispositions are as follows :-

2/S.Staffs. 6th I.Bde. in touch with the 15th Brigade on the N.W. corner of the wood.
2 companies in front line.
1 company in support about Red line on barrage map.
1 company in reserve in that portion of HIGH HOLBURN between South Street and LONGUEVAL ALLEY.

17/Middx. 6th I.Bde. In touch with S.Staffs to left holding Eastern edge of the wood, and still more detachments of other regiments in line with the 17/Mddx.

22/R.Fus. 99th I.Bde. 1 company in trench round S.E. corner of wood.
2 companies in old front line running East and West through the wood.
1 company in trench between N. end of TRONES WOOD and Southern end of LONGUEVAL VILLAGE.

99th Bde.M.G.Co. is being withdrawn and replaced by the 6th Bde. M.G.Co. Latter has now 8 guns in the line.

1/R.Berks. 99th.I.Bde. are collecting in trenches in S.22.a. & b.

23/R.Fus. 99th I.Bde. Collecting in trench running S.W. from the N. end of BERNAFAY WOOD.

1/K.R.R.C. 99th I.Bde. Collecting in MONTAUBAN/VALLEY.

2 companies 1/Kings. 6th I.Bde. garrison of MONTAUBAN VILLAGE.

H.Q. & 2 companies 1/Kings. - BRESLAU Support (A.8.b.)

13/Essex. 6th I.Bde. BACK LANE (A.3.c.)

G.O.C., 6th I.Bde. is making following dispositions -

13/Essex R. 6th Inf. Bde. relieve 22/R.Fusiliers, 99th Inf. Bde. in old British line, DELVILLE WOOD.

2 companies 22/R.Fusiliers, 99th Inf. Bde. will then relieve 2 companies 1/Kings, 6th Inf. Bde. in MONTAUBAN. The whole of the 1/Kings R. will then be in MONTAUBAN ALLEY.

Disposition of 99th Inf. Bde. when above is completed -

99th Bde. will be in area about BUND TRENCH and BRESLAU TRENCH, A.2.c. and /., A.3.c., A.8.a. and b.

Headquarters of Brigades are as follows:-

5th Inf. Bde.........About A.3.c.0.5.
6th Inf. Bde......... " A.8.b.2.8.
99th Inf. Bde......... " A.2.d.5.2.

5th Inf. Bde. 2/High.L.I. holding the front line and 17/R.Fusiliers in support are being relieved to-night by 2/Oxf. & Bucks L.I. and 24/R.Fusiliers respectively.

(Sd) W.G.Walker.

H.Q. 2nd Divn.
28/7/16.

Major-General,
Commanding 2nd Division.

"A" Form.

Army Form C. 2121.

MESSAGES AND SIGNALS.

No. of Message

Prefix Code m. Words Charge

Office of Origin and Service Instructions.

Sent At m. To By

This message is on a/c of: Service.

(Signature of "Franking Officer.")

Recd. at

Date

From

By

TO: FRUIT RA Signals ADMS ADVS STAR RE APM DADOS Train OAK STORM Supply Col Q

Sender's Number.	Day of Month	In reply to Number	AAA
* G745	28		

Following from 4th Army begins aaa Please convey to all ranks HEART my congratulations on the capture of DELVILLE WOOD and my admiration of the splendid work done by the division aaa Ends

835

From: Adv Heart

Place

Time: 4 45 pm

The above may be forwarded as now corrected. (Z)

Censor. Signature of Addressor or person authorised to telegraph in his name. Major

* This line should be erased if not required.

(4198) Wt. W14042—M44 300000 Pads. 12/15. Sir J. C. & S.

S E C R E T.   Appendix 61.

XIII CORPS OPERATION ORDER No. 34.

28th July, 1916.

(Reference GUILLEMONT Trench
map 1/20,000)

1. (a) The XIII Corps has been ordered to capture the enemy's defences between FALFEMONT FARM and GUILLEMONT (both inclusive) in conjunction with an attack by the French XX Corps on MAUREPAS and of other French forces further South.

The XV and III Corps will carry out an artillery bombardment on morning of 30th commencing at 1 hour before zero.

(b) The attack will be made simultaneously by the French and XIII Corps on the 30th instant at an hour to be notified later.

2. The attack of the XIII Corps will be carried out by the 30th Division (strengthened by one Brigade, the 108th, of the 35th Division) and by troops of the 2nd Division.

The boundary between the French XX Corps and the XIII Corps will be a line drawn from MALTZ HORN FARM to point B.2.d.4.8 (point 318 on the French map) thence to the railway at B.3.c.6.6, thence along the railway.

3. Objectives of Divisions:

30th Division.

The capture of the enemy's defences between point B.2.d.4.8, S.E. of FALFEMONT FARM, and GUILLEMONT (inclusive)

The establishment of touch with the French XX Corps on the right and the 2nd Division on the left.

2nd Division.

The capture of the enemy's defences between WATERLOT FARM and GUILLEMONT (exclusive) including the trench which runs parallel to the LONGUEVAL - GUILLEMONT road through T.19.a., S.24.b. and S.18.d.

The establishment of touch with the 30th Division.

The boundary between the two divisions for the attack will be:

the road from WATERLOT FARM CHIMNEY to GUILLEMONT as far as the level crossing at S.24.d.4.9 (road inclusive to 2nd Division) thence a line just S. of trench junction at B.M.138.6 to cross roads at T.19.c.2.8 (exclusive to 2nd Divn.) thence the road (exclusive to 2nd Divn.) to the railway at T.19.a.8.3.

After the capture and consolidation of the objectives given the railway will become the boundary (the station inclusive to 2nd Divn.); time when this boundary will come into force to be arranged between the two divisions.

4. Method of attack.

The 30th and 2nd Divisions will attack simultaneously. The attack of the 30th Division will be carried out in the form of a right attack starting from MALTZ HORN TRENCH, and a left attack starting from between TRONES WOOD and WATERLOT FARM.

The right flank of the right attack will maintain close touch with left flank of French XX Corps, assisting and supporting it in every way possible.

5......

5. Artillery.

The attack will be preceded by an artillery bombardment in accordance with orders to be issued by the G.O.C., R.A. in consultation with G.O.C. 30th and 2nd Divisions.

The lifts and barrages of the Corps Artillery are shown on attached map.

The Divisional Artillery now under G.O.C. 35th Division (less such artillery as is detailed by G.O.C., R.A. for defence of the line) will be at the disposal of G.O.C. 30th Division for the attack.

Preliminary bombardment and wire cutting will be carried out in accordance with orders issued by G.O.C., R.A.

The artillery of the French XX Corps are assisting in the preliminary bombardment by fire on FALFEMONT FARM: it will not fire E. of the boundary between Corps after midnight 29/30th.

6. Defence of the line gained.

Special attention will be paid to the following, and the necessary orders will be issued by Divisions:-

30th Division.

Sweeping with machine gun fire the valleys S.E. and N.W. of the FALFEMONT FARM spur and the slopes facing N.W. between SAVERNAKE WOOD and MAUREPAS.

Bringing enfilade fire of machine guns to bear on the defences along the GINCHY - WEDGE WOOD road, the trench running to GUILLEMONT from LEUZE WOOD through T.20.d. and C. and the trench from T.13.c.8.6 towards GUILLEMONT.

Sweeping with machine gun fire the hollow S. of GINCHY and N. of the railway.

Establishing O.Ps. to observe the front COMBLES - GINCHY TELEGRAPH.

The 30th Division will commence putting into a state of defence a line roughly along the MALTZ HORN FARM - GUILLEMONT road immediately it has been passed by the assaulting troops.

35th Division.

Selecting and at once digging in O.Ps. on the MALTZ HORN FARM plateau.

These O.Ps. are to be established immediately the attacking troops have passed Eastwards of the top: and the provision of cover to be begun at once.

2nd Division.

Will establish strong points at the station and about T.12.a.4.2; also about S.18.d. central.

Will establish O.Ps. immediately to observe the front GINCHY TELEGRAPH - FLERS.

7. The 1st Cavalry Division will remain in billets and bivouacs.

8. Corps Headquarters remain at TEINEHEM.

(Sd) W.H.Greenly.

Issued at 9.0 p.m. B.G., G.S.

SECRET. Copy No......

2nd DIVISION ORDER No. 118.

Reference GUILLEMONT Sheet 29th July, 1916.
1/20,000 corrected to 20-7-16,
and to attached sketch.

(1).(a). XIII Corps has been ordered to capture the enemy's defences between FALFEMONT FARM and GUILLEMONT (both inclusive) in conjunction with attacks by the French to the South.

(b). The attack will be made simultaneously by the French and XIII Corps on the 30th July, at an hour to be notified later.

(2). The attack by the XIII Corps will be carried out by the 30th Division and by the 5th Inf. Brigade of the 2nd Division.

(3). OBJECTIVES OF ATTACK.

The objectives of the 30th Division are :-

The capture of the enemy's defences about GUILLEMONT inclusive, and the establishment of touch with the 2nd Division on their left.

The objective of the 5th Inf. Brigade is the capture of the enemy's defences between WATERLOT FARM and GUILLEMONT (exclusive) including trench which runs parallel to the LONGUEVAL - GUILLEMONT road through T.19.a., S.24.b., and S.18.d.

The establishment of touch with the 30th Division on its right and the joining up of the German trench in S.18.d. with SOUTH STREET (boundary between S.18.b. and d.)

The boundary between 5th Inf. Bde. and the 30th Division for the infantry attack will be the road through WATERLOT FARM chimney to GUILLEMONT as far as level crossing at S.24.d.4.9. (road inclusive to 5th Inf. Bde.) thence a line just South of trench junction at B.M. 138.6. to cross roads at T.19.c.2.8. (exclusive to 2nd Division) thence the road (exclusive to 2nd Division) to the railway T.19.a.8.3.

After the capture and consolidation of the objectives given, the railway will become the boundary (the Station inclusive to 5th Inf. Bde.): time when this boundary will come into force will be notified later.

(4). 30th Division and 5th Inf. Bde. will attack simultaneously, the left attack of the 30th Division starting from between TRONES WOOD and WATERLOT FARM.

(5).........
P.T.O.

(5). The attack will be preceded by an artillery bombardment. The lifts and barrages of the artillery are shown on the attached sketch. Preliminary bombardment and wire cutting will be carried out under orders to be issued by the C.R.A.

Divisional Artillery orders are issued as appendix "A" and will follow shortly.

(6). The infantry of the 30th Division will assault from first objective just after O plus 8 at which hour the barrage will lift to the second line. G.O.C. 5th Inf. Bde. will arrange for his attack so that the infantry reach their objectives at -

(a). GUILLEMONT STATION.
(b). Trench South of it.
(c). The portion of the German trench situated in S.18.d. at the same time as the infantry of the 30th Division reach their first objective.

He will arrange for his attack on the remainder of the trench referred to in para.(3) to be delivered so that his infantry reach it immediately after the barrages lift at O plus 25.

(7). The G.O.C., 5th Inf. Bde. will arrange for machine guns in the S.E. corner of DELVILLE WOOD to sweep the ground between GINCHY VILLAGE and the German trenches during and subsequent to the attack, arranging with G.O.C. 6th Inf. Bde. if he wishes to place any guns in 6th Inf. Bde. line.

(8). After the infantry have reached their final objective the 5th Inf. Bde. will establish strong points at the Railway Station and about T.19.a.4.2. and also about S.18.d.central.

228th Fd Co.R.E. (less 1 Section) will be placed at the disposal of the G.O.C., 5th Inf. Bde. for this purpose.

The C.R.A. will arrange for O.P's to be established immediately, in order to observe the front GINCHY TELEGRAPH - FLERS.

(9). Watches will be synchronised from Divisional Head Quarters at 10 p.m. on the 28th July.

(10). GREEN flares only will be used to indicate the arrival of the infantry on the lines marked O.8 and O.25.

(11). Visual signalling communication will be arranged between a point just N. of WATERLOT FARM and a point in S.22.d. just N.W. of BERNAFAY WOOD, and between the S.W. corner of BERNAFAY WOOD and COPSE B or A.3.c.0.5.

(12). Reports to the CITADEL (F.21.b.).

C. [illegible] Lieut. Colonel,
General Staff, 2nd Division.

Issued at 12 noon.

Copy No.1 to 5th Inf.Bde.
2 6th Inf.Bde.
3 99th Inf.Bde.
4 10/D.C.L.I.(Pioneers).
5 R.A., 2nd Divn.
6 R.E., 2nd Divn.
7 2/Signal Co.
8 "Q", 2nd Divn.
9 A.D.M.S., 2nd Divn.
10 A.D.V.S.
11 A.P.M.

Copy No.12 to O.C.Det North'ld Hrs.
13 2/Div.Gas Offr.
14 XIII Corps "G".
15 XIII Corps "Q".
16 3rd Divn.
17 5th Divn.
18 30th Divn.
19 35th Divn.
20 55th Divn.
21 1st Cav.Divn.
22-26. G.S. Records.

(Copies 14–26) For information.

Delville Wood

PERMANENT OR FINAL BARRAGE HEAVY ART

ARTILLERY

APPENDIX 64.

Copy No 40.

OPERATION ORDER No. 13
by
Brig-General L.W.P. EAST. C.M.G., D.S.O.
Cmdg: Heavy Artillery, XIII Corps.

****

1. The XIII Corps is to attack the German line between WATERLOT CHIMNEY and the work S. of FALFEMONT FARM (inclusive)

2. The 2nd Division is ordered to take the trenches from WATERLOT FARM to GUILLEMONT and also the trench in S.18.d. and T.19.a. The 30th Division assisted by 1 Brigade of 35th Division is to capture GUILLEMONT and the trenches to the South.

3. The XV Corps will protect DELVILLE WOOD and barrage all ground N. of a line running E and W. through T.13 and 14 and this Corps will also assist in Counter Battery work N. of this line. The French are responsible for the destruction of the enemy's defence from WEDGE WOOD inclusive to the S.E.

4. Fire must be kept up continuously on the other portions of the enemy's trenches and defences until Zero (4.45.a.m. the 30th inst). Batteries will lift as shown in accompanying Barrage Map. The 220 mm will fire on GUILLEMONT until 4-15a.m when they will lift on to the trenches in T.20 and 26, one battery paying particular attention to the communication trench from LEUZE WOOD to GUILLEMONT.
The 9.2" and 8" will fire on the trench running S. of GUILLEMONT - a gun on WEDGE WOOD until further orders.
The 6" Hows. will concentrate their fire according to separate programme. There is plenty of 9.2" and 8" ammunition and as heavy a fire as possible is to be kept up on the enemy trenches. If heavy howitzers are taken off for Counter Battery Work, Commanding Officers must try to make up by a more rapid fire on the trenches at other times.

5 F.O.O's must be sent out tomorrw as follows :-

Right Group & C.B. Group	FALFEMONT FARM.
Left Group & Comm Group	GUILLEMONT.

All Groups to assist signals in establishing a station at MALTZ FARM.

6. The Counter Battery Group will tell off Sections or single guns to the most dangerous enemy batteries and will open fire at Zero on these batteries unless called up by aeroplane. After final lift all howitzers will be available for counter battery work with aeroplanes.

7. Details of firing are shewn in the attached Appendix "A"

29th July, 1916. (Sd) F.E. ANDREWS Major, R.A.
Brigade-Major XIII Corps Heavy Artillery.

Appendix "A".

Details of Firing during Night 29/30 and morning of 30th.

6 inch Howitzers.

1. 9 to 10 p.m. Right Group on Trench S.30.b.8.5 to T.25.b.1.5
Left Group on Trench from S.30.b.99.80 to T.25.a.95.45.
Note:- At 9.15 p.m. No. 31 Heavy Battery will fire on trench from T.25.a.15.80, to T.25.a.30.30 for half an hour.

2. 10.30 to 11.30 p.m. Right Group. on S. half of GINCHY - WEDGE WOOD road.
Left Group. on N. half of same.

3. 12.30 to 1.30 a.m. Both Groups on W. edge of GUILLEMONT from Railway line to T.25.c.central.
Right Group S. of point T.25.a.0.9.
Left Group N. of this point.

4. 2.15 to 3.15 a.m. Right Group Road from GUILLEMONT 250 yards E. of ARROW HEAD COPSE down to S.30.d. central.
Left Group Trench in S.18.d. and T.19.a.

5. 4.15 to 4.45 a.m. Right Group MALTZ HORN FARM trench A.6.d.1.6. to S.30.d.4.7. Then on to 0.8 line as ordered in barrage map.

6. 4.40 to 4.53 a.m. Left Group on 0.8 line from 4.40 a.m. to 4.53 a.m. and then as ordered in barrage map.

The Left Group Barrage zones from Area N. of GUILLEMONT and zones A. F. and G. The Right Group barrage zones H. to M. Zones A. B. C. D. and E. are barraged by the heavy Howitzers.

7. Groups will arrange that approximately one third of the 6" Hows. will be on the German Main line trench the whole time from 4.45 a.m. onwards.

8. All guns will be on their 9.15 barrage line at an ordinary rate of fire from 3.30 to 4 a.m. - between 4 a.m. and times ordered in paras. (5) and (6) the guns will play about as they wish in their own line.

9. The 75 mm will fire gas shell into S.E. portion of GUILLEMONT from 4.45 to 4.55 a.m., after which they will fire on LEUZE WOOD.

10. When on final barrage - the Right Group will put 2 6" Hows Btys. on valley in T.26.a. and C. and the Left Group four 6" How. on GINCHY and one 8" Battery on trench at cross roads at T.20.c. The remainder will fire on BOILEAUX and LEUZE WOODS.

11. The 9.2" and 8" will continue on their present barrage until 8 pm, when they will join in the Concentrations as ordered for 6" Hows.

12. The 12" (85th Siege Battery) will fire as follows:-

4.45 a.m. One gun on railway line and walk back; then up N. road until 5.25 when they will lift on to FALFENOY FARM until 5.45 a.m. then on to cemetery.

4.40 to 4.50 a.m. One gun on strong point and dug outs W. edge of GUILLEMONT. Then back and on to WEDGE WOOD

until.

until 5.45 a.m. Then lift on point where trench crosses road at T.30.c.15.00.

13. The 15" (3rd R.M.A.) will fire one round on Quarrt at 4.45 a.m. and two if possible before 4.53. Then on to S.E. corner of GUILLEMONT until 5.15 a.m. Then on to FALFEMONT FARM until 5.40 a.m. The cease fire.

14. Counter Battery Group. When not actively engaged on counter battery work the 60 Pdrs. and 120 mm will search the ground W. of the German main line over which the attack will pass.

Communication Group. The 60 Pdrs. will also sweep this ground at intervals during the night and will also fire as ordered in para. (1).

15. All guns must be as active as possible - a great deal is being asked of us and a very great deal depends on our efforts to-day and to-night and I am sure the officers and men will play up to their utmost.
When not concentra ed howitzers will fire on their own lines as ordered by Group Commanderz

APPENDIX. 65.

REPORT FROM O.C. 52nd L.I. to 5th BRIGADE.

We have made as great effort as possible to attack Station but have not got through. The Stokes Mortars failed to deal with the bombing posts and evidently the bombardment has no effect on the hostile machine guns from straight and almost straight down the main road. I can get no information about position on our right and the present position. Our advance got to within bombing distance of German post after some loss from Machine gun fire which I cannot at present estimate. Our men were bombed from these places and the remainder of them were formed up in a trench. I can get no information, but I know that our leading party got well up to the North face of the Station but they must have been shot. If the 30th Division or other troops succeed in attacking the Station all is clear. The hostile bombing post will have to go and I can meet them by prolonging my present line of consolidation towards the Station. As regards other operation on second objective - attack on right of 24/R.F., of the first wave of three platoons only a few men and no officers have come back. It appears they were enfiladed by machine gun fire from the right. In accordance with the Brig-General's letter I did not send forward second wave because my right would have been in the air.

Recd 2 Div 11.a.m.

"A" Form

MESSAGES AND SIGNALS.

No. of Message

TO 13th Corps
30th Divn

Sender's Number. G 812 | Day of Month 30 | In reply to Number | AAA

Attack on STATION N of GUILLEMONT fa[illegible]d though one attack reached close up to station but men were all killed by machine gun fire aaa Attack on trench in T19a and S24b also failed and few survivors are back on original line aaa Attack on N end of same trench result not known aaa Am trying to arrange another attack on station to [illegible] up with 30th Divn. and for another bombardment of station and trenches on both sides to be carried out aaa Addressed XIII Corps repeated 30th Divn

From 2nd Divn
Place
Time 11.35am

The above may be forwarded as now corrected. (Z)

B. Belgrave
Major

Censor. Signature of Addressor or person authorised to telegraph in his name.

* This line should be erased if not required.

(4.98) Wt. W1.042—M44. 300000 Pads. 12/15. Sir J. C. & S.

"A" Form. Army Form C. 2121.

MESSAGES AND SIGNALS. No. of Message

Prefix Code m. Words Charge

Office of Origin and Service Instructions.

Sent At m. To By

This message is on a/c of: Service. (Signature of "Franking Officer.")

Recd. at m. Date From By

TO Heart

App 67

Sender's Number: BH 65 | Day of Month: 30th | In reply to Number | AAA

Situation as follows at 12 45 pm aaa Coy of 1st AR attacked and reached hostile trench in S18d at 0·8 aaa It is believed that company are still holding on there aaa Grape attacked station but were held up by bombing posts and MG fire at 0·8 aaa A proportion of one wave rushed trenches in vicinity of station and aeroplane reports mirrors flashing at T19a 0 0 aaa At 0·25 three platoons attacked 2nd objective and no information regarding this attack has been obtainable aaa Hostile arty. are maintaining an exceedingly heavy barrage on E end of Longueval Alley and on Bernafay Wood in vicinity of Western edge aaa No digging of trench connecting enemys line with S.E. corner of Delville Wood has yet been possible hitherto

From

Place

Time Fruit 12·50 pm

The above may be forwarded as now corrected. (Z)

Censor. Signature of Addressor or person authorised to telegraph in his name.

* This line should be erased if not required.

93146—W. & S. Ltd., London.—W 1783/1462—100,000—7/15. Forms C 2121/10.

"A" Form. Army Form C. 2121.

MESSAGES AND SIGNALS. No. of Message ....

Prefix .... Code .... m. Office of Origin and Service Instructions.	Words / Charge — Sent: At .... m. To .... By	This message is on a/c of: .... Service. (Signature of "Franking Officer.")	Recd. at .... m. Date .... From .... By ....

TO: 2nd Divn

Sender's Number	Day of Month	In reply to Number	AAA
* G 121	30th		

The 166th Bde of 55th Division will tonight relieve troops of 30th and 35th Divisions in the line on the front now held South of the Guillemont Rly. aaa Touch to be maintained with French on right near Maltz Horn Farm and 2nd Division on left on Eastern edge of TRONES WOOD at railway aaa Relief to be carried out under orders of General Shea aaa G.O.C. 55th Divn will take over command of line when relief complete at an hour to be arranged between the two Divisional Commanders and reported to Corps H.Q. aaa Divisional H.Q. of 30th and 55th to change places aaa 30th Division on relief

From
Place
Time

The above may be forwarded as now corrected. (Z)

Censor. Signature of Addressor or person authorised to telegraph in his name.

* This line should be erased if not required.

93146—W. & S. Ltd., London.—W 1789/1462—100,000—7/15. Forms C 2121/10.

"A" Form. Army Form C. 2121.

MESSAGES AND SIGNALS. No. of Message

Prefix Code m. Words Charge

Office of Origin and Service Instructions.

Sent At m. To By

This message is on a/c of: Service.

(Signature of "Franking Officer.")

Recd. at m. Date From By

TO (2)

Sender's Number | Day of Month | In reply to Number | AAA

will withdraw to Happy Valley one Bde. Citadel two Bdes aaa 35th Division on relief will withdraw to Happy Valley one Bde Sand Pit Valley two Bdes aaa Divisional HQ 35th Divn remain Minden Post aaa 55th Divn. after relief complete will be placed Divnl HQ Billon Farm one Bde in the line one Bde Citadel one Bde Mansel Copse aaa The Bde at Mansel Copse will move after tomorrow to Caftet Wood and Mansel Copse be made available for reserve troops of 2nd Divn Acknowledge aaa Addsd 30th 35th and 55th Divns repeated 2nd Divn GOC RA and Q

From 13th Corps

Place

Time 6.5 pm

The above may be forwarded as now corrected. (Z)

Censor. Signature of Addressor or person authorised to telegraph in his name.

* This line should be erased if not required.

255140—W. & S. Ltd., London.—W 1789/1402—100,000—7/15. Forms C 2121/10.

app 69

S E C R E T.
****

Copy No. 21.....

2nd DIVISION ORDER No.119.

Reference Map, 1/20,000.

31st July, 1916.

(1). On night 1st /2nd August, 99th Inf. Bde. will relieve 6th Inf. Bde. in DELVILLE WOOD Section, under arrangements made by Brigade Commanders concerned.

(2). On relief 6th Inf. Brigade will be in Divisional Reserve, and will occupy the Reserve Brigade area with two Companies as permanent garrison of MONTAUBAN.
1 Bn., 6th Inf. Bde. will be at 1 hour's notice to move.

(3). G.O.C., 99th Inf. Bde. will assume command of the DELVILLE WOOD Section on completion of relief, which will be reported to Div. Hd. Qrs.

[signature]
Lieut. Colonel,
General Staff, 2nd Division.

Issued at 7.30pm

Copy No. 1 to 5th Inf. Bde.
2 6th Inf. Bde.
3 99th Inf. Bde.
4 10/D.C.L.I.(Pioneers).
5 R.A., 2nd Divn.
6 R.E., 2nd Divn.
7 2/Signal Co.
8 "Q", 2nd Divn.
9 A.D.M.S., 2nd Divn.
10 A.D.V.S. ,,
11 A.P.M. ,,
12 O.C., Det. Northumberland Hussars.
13 2nd Divn. Gas Officer.
14 XIII Corps "G".)
15 XIII Corps "Q".) For information.
16 5th Division.)
17 55th Division.)
18-22 G.S. Records.

2nd Division - CASUALTY RETURN FOR WEEK ENDING 29th July, 1916.

UNIT.	KILLED. O.	KILLED. O.R.	WOUNDED. O.	WOUNDED. O.R.	MISSING. O.	MISSING. O.R.	Names of Officers and remarks.*
H.Q., 2nd Division.	-	-	-	-	-	-	* see attached
H.Q., 5th Infy. Bde.	-	-	-	-	-	-	
2/Oxf. & Bucks L.I.	-	7	4	43	-	10	
2/High. L.I.	1	5	3	55	1	8	
17th R. Fusiliers.	1	18	5	108	-	14	
24th R. Fusiliers.	-	49	5	98	-	2	
5th Bde M.G. Coy.	-	3	-	32	-	-	
5th Bde. T.M. Batty.	-	-	-	2 [a]	-	-	[a] 1 of Oxf. & 1 of 24th R.F.
H.Q., 6th Infy. Bde.	-	-	-	-	-	-	
1/Kings Regt.	-	-	1	40	-	-	
2/S. Staff. Regt.	6	42	-	217	-	46	
13th Essex Regt.	-	5	-	4	-	-	
1[illegible]th Middlesex Regt.	1	4	6	5	-	-	
6th Bde. M.G. Coy.	-	3	2	10	1	-	
6th Bde. T.M. Batty.	-	-	-	-	-	-	
H.Q., 99th Inf. Bde.	-	1	1	3	-	-	
1/R. Berks Regt.	1	40	5	170	2	55	
1/K.R.R.C.	4	55	8	182	2	105	
2[illegible] R. Fusiliers.	-	36	4	186	-	19	
23rd R. Fusiliers.	5	55	8	238	-	40	
99th Bde. M.G. Coy.	2	13	5	14	1	2	
99th T.M. Batty.	-	-	-	-	-	-	
10th D.C.L.I.	-	8	3	52	-	6	
H.Q., R.A., 2/Divn.	-	-	-	-	-	-	
34th Bde. R.F.A.	-	-	-	4	-	-	
36th Bde. R.F.A.	-	-	-	~~X~~ 1	-	-	
41st Bde. R.F.A.	1	2	~~X~~	4	-	-	
V.2.T.M.Battery.	-	-	-	3	-	-	
X.2.T.M.Battery.	-	-	1	+	-	-	
Y.2.T.M.Battery.	-	-	-	-	-	-	
Z.2.T.M.Battery.	-	-	-	-	-	-	
H.Q., R.E., 2/Divn.	-	1	-	-	-	-	
5th Field Coy.R.E.	-	-	-	3	-	-	
226th Field Coy.	-	-	-	1	-	-	
E.A.Fd.Coy. R.E.	-	2	-	5	-	-	
2/Signal Coy.R.E.	-	-	-	9	-	1	
R.A.M.C.	-	5	-	43	-	5	
TOTAL.	22	354	61	1532	7	313	

7 /8 /1916.

[signature]
Captain for Major,
D.A.A. & Q.M.G., 2nd Division.

OFFICER CASUALTIES.

To accompany Casualty return for week-ending 29th July, 1916.

Unit	KILLED.	WOUNDED.	MISSING.
2/Oxf. & Bucks. L.I.		2/Lt. J.B.MURRAY, 2/Lt. E.H.VIGARS.(at duty) 2/Lt. P.A.BOBBY. 2/Lt. W.I.B.WARE.	
2/High. L.I.	2/Lt. T.F.PHILLIPS.	2/Lt. W.SHIELDS. T/LT-Col.H.M.CRAIGIE-HALKETT. T/Capt. T.R.GIBBS.	2/Lt. J.F.O'HALLORAN.
17th R. Fusiliers.	2/Lt. R.H.FLETCHER, (14th Bn.)	Lt. E.RICHMOND. Lt. T.ROBINSON.(28th Bn) Capt. L.E.PARSONS. Capt. A.G.KNOCKER. R.ofO. R.Irish.Fus. 2/Lt. S.PENNY, (14th Bn.)	
24th R. Fusiliers.		2/Lt. D.S.O'HAGAN. (30th Bn.) at duty. 2/Lt. H.J.BEACH. Lt. H.COOMBES. 2/Lt. D.H.BIRD. (14th Bn.) 2/Lt. J.H.CHANDLER.	
1/Kings Liverpool R.		2/Lt. H.K.SETH-SMITH. (3rd Bn.)	
2/S.Staffs. R.	2/Lt.(T/Capt.) W.LAKE. Capt. W.E.WANSBROUGH. (3rd Bn.) Lt. J.R.MALPASS. 2/Lt. S.B.THORNTON. 2/Lt. W.L.HOLDCROFT. Lt.(T/Capt.)C.DUTTON.		
13th Middlesex R.	2/Lt. W.HENDRY.	2/Lt. J.F.ENGLEBURTT. Col. H.T.FENWICK.MVO.,DSO., Major F.C.BUCKLEY. Capt. E.I.BELL.(at duty) 2/Lt. G.M.W.ROBERTSON. (27th Bn.) 2/Lt. A.F.ELLIOTT.	
6th Machine Gun Coy.		Lt. M.J.KAVANAGH. (at duty) (of 2/S.Staffs.attached) Capt. B.MILLBURN. (of 1st Hearts. attached)	2/Lt. C.B.CAMPBELL.
H.Qrs. 99th Inf.Bde.		Capt. J.A.BOTT. (17th R.Fus.)	

Killed.	Wounded.	Missing.
1/R.Berks.R.		
2/Lt. R.J.CHILDS.	Lt.(T/Capt) G.S.L. GREGSON-ELLIS.	Lt. J.R.REID.
	2/Lt. F.MOOR.(8th Bn)	2/Lt. H.J.STIDWILL.(3rdBn)
	2/Lt. L.E.PARSONS.	
	2/Lt. C.V.WILSON.	
	2/Lt. J.L.FREEMAN.	
1/K.R.R.C.		
2/Lt.(T/Capt)E.L.HOWELL. (5th Bn.)	2/Lt. H.E.GILL.(3rd Dorst)	Lt.(T/Capt) R.H.SLATER.
2/Lt. A.Y.BAILEY.(5/Bn)	2/Lt, J.W.TAYLOR.	2/Lt. J.W.E.PAUL. (6th Bn)
Lt. C.COLLINS.	2/Lt. J.E.M.SKINNER.	
2/Lt. C.R.S.TURNER. (3rd Dorsets.)	2/Lt. C. WITT.	
	Lt. Hon. F.S.TRENCH. (2nd Bn.)	
	2/Lt. T.I.STEVENSON. (6th Bn.)	
	2/Lt. N.H.NOBLE. (6th Bn)	
	Capt. A.H.BROCKLEHURST.	
22nd Royal Fusiliers.		
	2/Lt. E.W.F.GIBSON.	
	2/Lt. E.WALKER. 29th Bn.	
	2/Lt. W.A.MURRAY.	
	2/Lt. N.WORSHIP. 30th Bn.	
[illegible]rd Royal Fusiliers.		
Capt. C.B.HAYWARD.	Capt.H.A.TAYLOR.	
Lt.(T/Capt)D.C.RANKEN.	2/Lt.S.C.H.WILLIAMS. (15th Bn.)	
2/Lt. R.H.C.BUSHELL. (7th Bn.)	Lieut.J.C.FENTON.	
2/Lt. E.F.H.TAYLOR. (30th Bn.)	2/Lt.A.G.REES.	
2/Lt. E.A.OLIVER.15/Bn.	2/Lt. F.G.BULL.	
	2/Lt.A.S.GARDNER.	
	2/Lt. C.A.MOORE. 30th Bn.	
	2/Lt. F.C.COPPIN.	
99th Machine Gun Coy.		
Capt. C.GRANT.	2/LtA.J.FRENCH.	2/Lt. F.E.GALLICHON.
2/Lt. D.CRAWFORD.	2/Lt. O.F.MORITZ.	
	2/Lt. J.S.FERRIER.	
	2/Lt. K.FLETCHER-BARRETT.	
	2/Lt. S.HEAL. 3/Devon. R.	
10th D.C.L.I.		
	2/Lt. C.HOSKEN.	
	Lt. R.H.DAVENPORT.	
	Lt. C.H.REYNOLDS.	
Royal Artillery.		
Major J.L.MOWBRAY.DSO.	2/Lt. S.H.NOAKS.	
Royal Engineers.		
-	-	-

G.S. 992/15/9
2nd Div.

IVth Corps.

I beg to report on a raid carried out last night by the 13/Essex Regiment, 6th Inf. Brigade, against the German line near VINCENT STREET, S.15.c.5.3. -

The officers and other ranks who took part in the raid were trained for about a week beforehand over dummy trenches in the grounds of the CHATEAU DE LA HAIE, and this training undoubtedly enabled all ranks to be thoroughly aware of the parts they had to play. In addition, many of the raiding party patrolled over the actual ground before the night arrived.

I attach a report from the Officer Commanding 13/Essex Regiment which fully explains the operation.

Great credit is due to Lt. Colonel PAPILLON, and to Captain HAYWARD who commanded the raiding party.

The shooting of the Divisional Artillery was extremely accurate and the wire in front of the point of attack had been very thoroughly cut.

I consider that the following lessons have been learnt from this raid :-

(1). The effect of Stokes mortars.

A one minute bombardment by these weapons was carried out and the enemy were so bewildered and disorganised by the explosions that the raiding party were on top of them before they had time to recover themselves.

(2). The method adopted for starting the raiding party.

A series of strings ran out from the Officer Commanding the party to the 2 officers and 2 N.C.O's in front, and on a pull from the Officer Commanding, the whole party sprang forward. This I consider

superior....

superior to any method of giving the signal to advance either by light or by sound.

(3). Only one casualty occurred in getting into the enemy's trench, but at least two thirds of the total casualties occurred during the return journey, and especially when the men were getting back over their own parapet when they were caught by shrapnel fire directed against our front line trench.

It is for consideration whether it will not be better for the party to lie down in the open after they have left the enemy's trench and then for them to crawl back in their own time as soon as the enemy artillery barrage has died down.

The raid was undoubtedly successful. It has had a great moral effect on the Battalion engaged in it and I think that casualties up to 50 or more were inflicted on the enemy.

H.Q., 2nd Divn. Major-General,

2-7-1916. Commanding 2nd Division.

2nd Division

I forward herewith report of O/C. 1st Essex Regt. on the raid carried out by that Batt. last night.
I think it may be fairly claimed that the raid was a success.
I regret no more prisoners were brought in. I gave instructions that, if possible 2 were to be secured in order that any statements they made might be compared, but the raiding party apparently "saw red" & contented themselves with killing Germans & only Coy Sergt. Major Cattermole remembered to secure a prisoner!
The effect of the 1 minutes intense bombardment by Stokes guns (6 were used for this purpose) was exactly what I had anticipated. The enemy were so bewildered and disorganized by the terrifying explosions that they were thinking only of their own safety and the raiding party was in on top of them before they had time to

2

pull themselves together – there was consequently no difficulty about getting in (thanks to the very thorough manner in which the 9th Battery, under Major Lee Warner D.S.O., had dealt with the enemy's wire) but the difficulties arose in getting back – I understand that at least 2/3rds of the casualties occurred during the return journey & the bulk of these as the men were getting back over our own parapet where they were caught by the shrapnel fire directed against our front line trench – I am thinking of a method to reduce this danger during a future raid.

I thoroughly endorse all that Lt. Colonel Papillon says of Captain Hayward – Captain Hayward was wounded by shrapnel in the arm early in the operations but continued at duty till the raid was over.

Great credit is also due to Lieut. Colonel Papillon himself who took an infinity of trouble to ensure the success of the raid & was in the front line himself

3

all the time –

Other Officers who did excellent work & whilst exposed to great personal danger ~~were~~ are Captain Milburn Comdg 6th Bde M.G. Coy and Captain Parsons Comdg 6/T.M. Group –

I should like to express my appreciation & thanks to the R.A. 2nd Division for the great assistance they afforded us & their excellent shooting –

I think it is reasonable to assume that the fire of our artillery added considerably to the enemy's casualties – ~~The~~ A shoulder strap cut off the jacket of a dead German and 2 books found on the prisoner are being sent with this report –

I very much regret that during the enemy's retaliation a most valuable & experienced Subaltern Officer Lieut. Denison 2/S. Staffordshire R. (which Bn was holding the Northern Sub. Section)

4.

was Killed –

Subject to approval, I propose to organize another raid against the same objective with a view to Killing more Germans and also dealing with the mine shaft reported – This raid would take place either tomorrow or the next night –

A.C. Daly [illegible]
Cmd: 6th Inf. Bde.

2/7/16.

P.S.

The "four in hand" method of starting the raiding party was most successful & did away with the necessity of "Sound" signals – the 2 officers & 2 N.C.O's in front each carried a ball of twine & Captain Hayward held the other end – On a pull from Captain Hayward the whole party sprang silently forward –

6th Infantry Brigade

I beg to report that the raid on the strong point at junction of VINCENT ST. with the German front line, was duly carried out on the night of 1st/2nd July.
The raiding party consisted of —

Capt. Hayward
Lieut Busby
2/Lieut Keeble
100 N.CO.s & men.

Of these 40 N.COs & men formed the covering party, stretcher bearers, signallers and runners, and the remaining 60 N.COs & men formed the storming party with liason party, dug out bombers, identification party, blocking parties and 6 men to search for and bring in suspected machine guns, told off from among them.
The whole party crawled out in the dead ground between the two lines to within about 60 or 70 yards of the objective, and they were in position there by 12.30 a.m.
At Zero hour 12.39 a.m. an intense fire of Artillery, 2" trench mortars and Stokes' guns was opened,

2"

the Artillery and trench mortars forming a box barrage round the objective, and also firing on suspected emplacements, minenwerfer positions and communication trenches in rear. These continued to fire on the same points throughout the raid.

The Stokes' guns fired rapid on the objective for one minute only, and the instant the minute was up a dash was made for the enemy's trenches, and the whole party ~~dashed~~ got in suffering only one casualty on the way.

The strong point was found to be full of Germans, some ten or a dozen of whom had already been killed by the Stokes guns. A fierce fight ensued. A party on the left told off to deal with the Sap in VINCENT STREET found it unoccupied, nor were they any more successful with the supposed Machine gun emplacement to the North of it, which was found to be a mine-shaft. A few Germans were however seen by them, and five were killed.

The left centre party also found a few Germans, of whom one was killed and five took refuge in a dug-out all of these being also killed.

The right centre party found more Germans in their part of the trench. They killed five of them and ran seven to ground in a shallow dug-out, of these latter 6 were killed and one made prisoner.

The bulk of the garrison attempted to withdraw down a communication trench leading Eastward. These were heavily bombed by the right party and twenty were killed and a number more wounded.

The raiding party withdrew after being about a quarter of an hour in the enemy's trenches and came under rather heavy shrapnel fire on the way back.

21

Our Casualties ~~were~~ among the raiding party were —

5 men killed.

2 Officers and 38 men wounded.

2 men missing, believed killed.

The enemy losses must have been considerably over fifty in killed alone, besides any casualties suffered in the bombardment.

The wire was found to be completely cut, and the trenches a good deal damaged by the previous bombardment, and the storming party was over the parapet before the enemy had recovered from the effect of the Stokes guns.

The bulk of our casualties took place during the withdrawal.

I cannot speak too highly of the way in which Capt. Hayward organised and trained the raiding party, and the coolness and courage with which he carried out every detail as planned. Lieut. Busby and 2/Lieut Keeble led their men with great dash and gallantry. The former stayed out till it was light bringing in the dead and wounded, and the latter was the first man into the enemys trench, and shot three Germans before he was himself wounded.

Company Sergt-Major Cattermole also behaved with great gallantry. He killed at least one German during the raid and ~~took~~ another prisoner, and after the withdrawal he exposed himself freely searching for and bringing in wounded. The prisoner taken was unfortunately wounded by shrapnel, though not severely, on the way back.

All ranks behaved with great dash and courage, and I hope to have the honour of bringing some more names to your notice when I have time to make further investigation.

P. R. Papillon Lt Col.
Comdg 13th Essex Regt

5 a.m.
2.7.16

2nd Division

I forward a further report from O/C. 13th Essex Regt relative to last nights raid also a report from Captain Parsons Comdg 6/T.M. Group –

A. C. Daly Br General
Comdg 6th Infantry Bde

2/7/16.

PA with other papers

[illegible] W.G.W.

6th Infantry Brigade

Reference my report on last night's raid I omitted to state that the enemy who withdrew Eastward before our raiding party down the continuation of VINCENT were driven into the barrage of the two Stokes guns which had lifted when the raiding party first attacked. It is therefore reasonable to assume that the enemy suffered further casualties here in addition to the 52 or more killed by the raiding party.

The cooperation of the Stokes guns throughout was most effective and I consider that they contributed materially to the success of the raid.

D. R. Papillon Lt Col.
Comdg 13th Essex Regt.

2.7.16

Raid by 13th Essex Regt. on night of 1/2nd July 1916.
Action of 6th Light Trench Mortar Battery in connection with above.

The objects of the raid being to ascertain nature of important work which enemy were engaged on between S.15.c.4/2.4 and S.15.c.5.2. It was decided to cover that area with intense fire from 5 Mortars (concentrated for the purpose) for the space of one minute while 3 other Stokes Mortars & one 3.7 Trench Howitzer also fired intense for the same time on other selected targets in enemy's front line. It was thus hoped to demoralise the enemy and enable the raiders to enter the trenches without loss. The fire from 2 Mortars was then lifted on to enemy's communication trenches about 100 yards in rear of their front line and a slow fire kept up by these two Mortars and the 3 on the left, thus making an effective barrage & preventing re-inforcements from being rushed up. A signal was arranged with O/C the raiding party for fire to cover the withdrawal, which was given.

Reports from raiders state that numbers of enemy dead were seen in the trenches and it is believed that considering the size of the area covered and the intensity of the fire that large number of the enemy must have been accounted for. A rough sketch of the Mortar positions is attached.

Oswald Parsons Capt.
O/c 6th Light Trench Mortar Battery

2 July 1916

To Brigade Major
6th Infty. Brigade

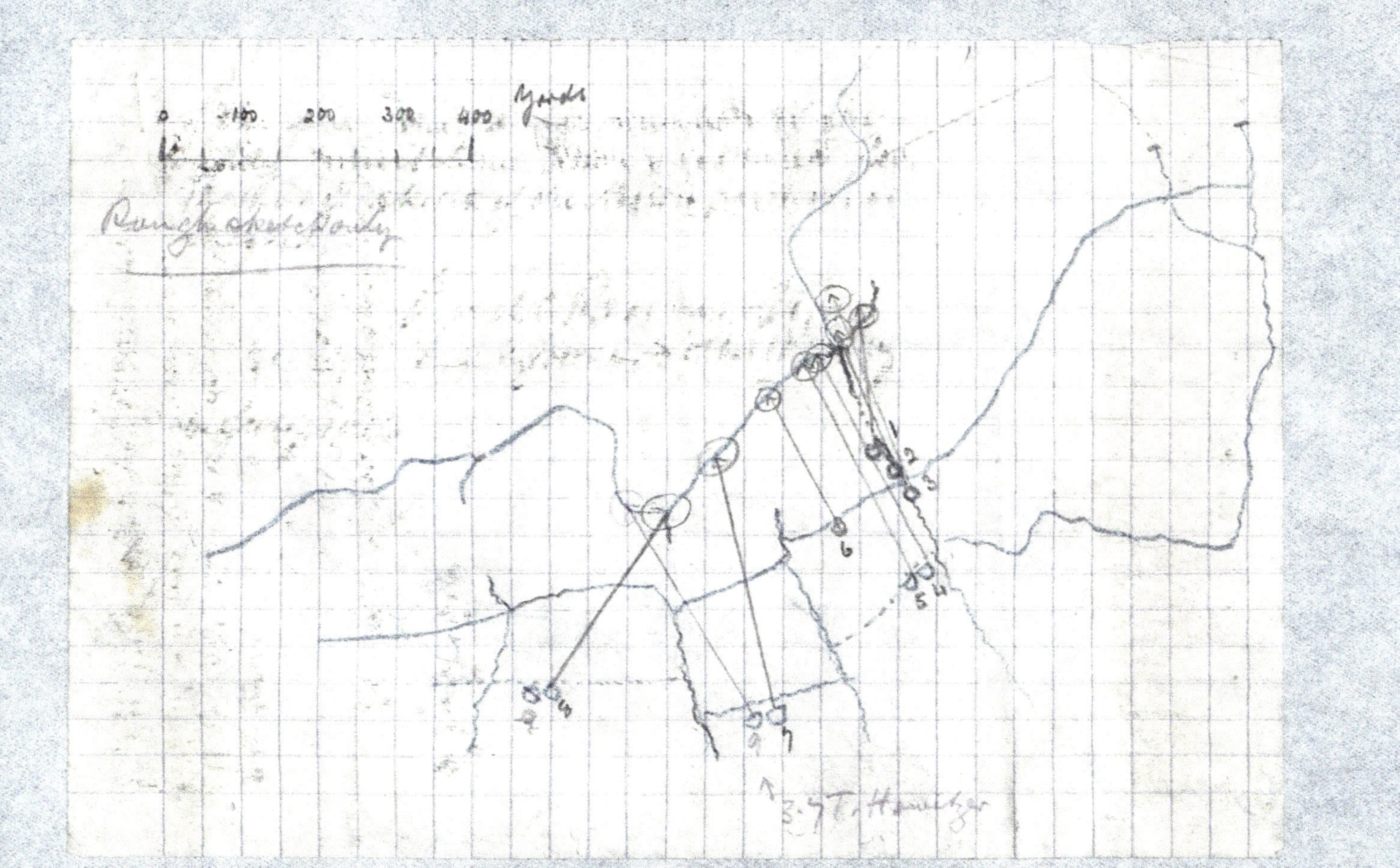

0 100 200 300 400 Yards
Rough sketch only
3·7 T. Howitzer

2nd Division

I omitted, in my report, to attach the "menu" of the supper which was given to the raiding party in the Zouave Valley prior to their enterprise – I forward 2 copies – will you kindly attach one to my report.

A. C. Daly Br General
Comd. 6th Inf Bde

2/7/16.

P.A. with other papers
W. H.J.V.

2nd Divn.

2. Divn No
G.S. 992/14/15

Herewith preliminary report on last night raid —

I have had no opportunity of making detailed enquiries yet owing to Divisional Conference —

I regret better results were not obtained but, of course, things were rather rushed — It was considered however that it was best to make the raid at once as, from information recd. from the prisoner captured the other night which was considered reliable, a relief was in progress last night & it was hoped to catch the enemy in the middle of it — I think, however, that the moral effect was good & the fact was again established that, with wire cut, & a concentrated Stokes gun bombardment our troops can always "get-in" to the enemy's line —

A. Daly Brig-General
Cmd. 6th Infy. Bde.

4/7/16

To
6th Bde ..

Report on raid executed by 1/Kings night 3rd/4th inst

Sir,
I regret to report that the raid executed on the night 3rd/4th did not succeed in its object.
The party started to crawl through the gaps in our wire at 11.40 pm.
15 men got out from VINCENT sap & proceeded north of it – the remaining 45 emerged through 3 gaps in the wire all within 50 yds of the junction of VINCENT street and the front line.
All the parties were clear of our wire by 12 midnight & in ~~all~~ most cases the parties continued too far & arrived to within 20 or 30 yds of the German wire before zero time.
The stokes & artillery opened fire at 12.24 am.
The stokes barrage fell very close to the raiding party wounding 4 men.
At 12.25 am the officer i/c raiding party (Lt Atkinson) blew his siren whistle, which was the prearranged signal.
The right party struck off too far to the right & failed to reach their objective.
The ~~officer~~ ~~of~~ the left party advanced to the north & parallel to VINCENT sap towards the German front line. Two germans were seen in VINCENT sap who were shot by Sergeant Beers. Lt Crosley & some men entered trench north of VINCENT & found it absolutely empty. This officer could not find the mine shaft, but saw a large dug out in that locality. Seeing a light burning in it he & his men dropped 3 or 4 bombs down it.
This party then worked their way to the right & met Lt Atkinson & some men

As the trench seemed completely deserted Lt Atkinson caused the signal to retire to be sounded (a rattle) after the party had been in the trench another 5 ~~ ~~ minutes.
Lights could be seen coming up from the German second line as soon as the bombardment slackened.
Owing to a misunderstanding some men retired too soon. It is thought that a rattle was accidentally sounded by a man who cannot be traced.
The only casualties were 4 men wounded, caused by the Stokes mortar. The German opened no fire of any description on the raiding party, but turned on a barrage onto our front line.
Lt Crowley states that he saw a barricade at the junction of the German front line & Vincent Sap which he & ~~demolished~~ his men pulled down.

[illegible] Kings [illegible]
4th July 1916

Headquarters
2nd Division

G.S. 992/17/17A
2 Div

G.S.
692

1. I forward herewith preliminary reports on raid of night 7/8 July by O.C. 17th Royal Fusiliers, to which I have little to add.

2. I attribute the failure of the raid to the following causes —

(1). The waterlogged condition of the ground owing to the prolonged period of wet weather.

(2). The incomplete cutting of enemy's wire. This was done by the 2nd trench mortars on the day previous to the raid, as the 36th Brigade R.F.A. were unable to do it previously as arranged. A patrol of the 17th Royal Fusiliers reported that it was weakened, and after due consideration it was not thought expedient to do further cutting on the 7th inst.

(3). After the numerous raid operations during the last 10 days, the enemy were very much on the alert.

3. Artillery arrangements were quite satisfactory, and 99th Brigade cooperated as arranged.

4. A further report will be submitted as soon as possible.

G.M. Bullen-Smith
Brig. Genl.
Comdg. 5th Inf. Brigade

8.7.16.

5 Bde 8-7-16 5.a.m

I regret that I am unable at present to send any report of an value as regards last night raid.

Capt Stewart was badly wounded & Lt. Wooton badly schocked & I was not able to question them before they were evacuated. Lt Pollaks is missing. All the men I have questioned give contradictory accounts; they were mostly very shaken & torn by wire & not very coherent.

It appears that owing to the wet state of Very. The wire round the Sap head was strong according to reports & the Germans apparently ready for the raiding party.

Capt Stewart. Lt. Wooton.

C G Higgins Lt Col
W R Fus

the ground & bursts of m.g. fire the whole of the parties were not in their places by zero. The leading parties were formed up however & effected an entry after some difficulty with the wire ~~[illegible]~~ into the water logged trench. I understand Lt Pollak was not seen again after this. I am not clear if an entry into the Sap was effected at all as the accounts all vary. The wire round the Sap head was strong according to reports & the Germans apparently ready for the raiding party.

Capt Stewart. Lt. Noonan.

C G Higgins Lt Col
W R Fusiliers

(3)

A machine gun was seized by 2 of our party & taken out of the trench but could not be got further than the wire both men being hit. According to report.

It appears that the German threw the first bombs.

Our casualties as far as I can ascertain at present were

Lt Pollak & 6 men missing
Capt Stewart. Lt Wootton.

C G Higgins Lt Col
W R Fusiliers

IVth Corps.

With reference to the raid carried out last night by the 5th Inf. Brigade against the German sap and front line about S.9.a.9.9., it appears that owing to the heavy and sodden nature of the ground consequent on the recent rain, more time was taken to reach the German trench than had been experienced in practice.

The leading party got into the German trench and a machine gun was seized, but the two men bringing it back were wounded when returning through the German wire, and it was dropped.

The 3 officers of the party were all casualties and it appears that when they were put out of action, the party was thrown into confusion.

The casualties were :-

1 officer missing.
2 officers wounded.
6 other ranks missing.
12 other ranks wounded.

The artillery and trench mortars co-operated successfully with the Infantry, and a diversion created by Stokes mortars and machine gun fire which was arranged by the G.O.C., 99th Inf. Brigade, was successful in drawing attention and hostile fire away from the point of attack.

I regret the failure of the operation: the party had been well trained and I am satisfied it was gallantly led.

There is no doubt the Germans are very much on the alert along this Divisional front and I do not propose to carry out any more minor raids for the present.

H.Q., 2nd Divn.
8-7-1916.

W. G. Walker. Major-General
Commanding 2nd Division.

To:

2nd Divn HQ
G.S. 992/14/22

G.S. 407.

Headquarters,
2nd Division.

I forward herewith report by O.C., 17th Royal Fusiliers, on the hostile mine which was blown in Northern Sub-section last night.

Consolidation was carried on throughout the night and will be continued to-night.

G. E. Bulkeley-Johnson?
Brigadier General.
Commanding 5th Inf. Bde.

10/7/16.

[illegible]

IV Corps

I forward a report on the consolidation of a new crater formed by the explosion of an enemy mine on the night 9/10 July. The blow came somewhat as a surprise and I consider that the arrangements made by the G.O.C. 5th Brigade in having his consolidating parties formed and ready were good. I also consider that Lt Col? [illegible] Higgens? carried out the work extremely well especially in view of the fact that the stores came just as his battalion was

P.T.O.

Preliminary Report on hostile mine Sprung evening of 1st inst in Carency (2)

At 8.34 pm on 9th inst the German sprung a mine close to Football Crater.

Sgt Harding [illegible] of my left storming party consisting of 19 men calling on the men to turn out & follow up immediately rushed with 2 other men to the place of explosion.

On reaching Football Crater they met a party of the enemy about 7 strong creeping round the northern lip of Football Crater. They bombed them & they retired. Shortly afterwards the remainder of my storming party came up & held the lip. There is no doubt that Sgt Harding by his prompt action saved the near lip from being taken by the enemy.

The effect of the mine was to completely obliterate Sap (10) [illegible] Broadbridge. This point was held by 3 men & they have not been recovered.

The men in Sap 12 were buried but were dug out subsequently.

(2)

The new crater appears to have merely pushed aside our lips of Broadbridge & John Crater a few yards & to have formed a long valley extending from the N. of Football Crater to Mildred Crater.

It does not appear to have affected our position adversely at all. A stretch of our front line from Sap 12 to Sap 9 was blown in & a good part of the support line shaken down.

Consolidation & clearing work was pushed on vigorously by strong parties & the work was well in hand when at about 2. a.m. my covering bombers were withdrawn & the line handed over to the 2/8th & Bucks Lt Infy.

As far as I can tell at present my casualties were:

Killed

5. (3 buried by mine & 2 storming party killed)

Wounded

2 officers

~~...~~ 9 O.R.

C S Higgins Lt Col
1st R. Fusiliers

16-7-16

(1) Report on raid on German Sap at S.9.a.1.9 night of 7/8 July -16

In accordance with 5th Infy Bde order No 135 the raiding party as detailed in my order No 416 left their trenches the night of 7/8 and proceeded by the route reconnoitred to the

To:-
Headquarters
2nd Division

2 Divn No
GS 992/17/21

G
69

I forward herewith a further report by O.C., 17th Royal Fusiliers regarding the raid carried out on night 7/8th July.

J. D. Boyd Captain
for
Brigadier General,
Commanding 5th Inf. Bde.

10/7/16.

Is any of this to be forwarded to Corps?

12.7.

Nothing further
C.D

not collected at this point.

According to my information & observation at 1 minute before zero the first Stokes gun – the signal for assault – fired.

The enemy appeared thoroughly prepared & almost simultaneously

(1)

Report on raid on German Sap at S.9.a.1.9 night of 7/8 July -16

In accordance with 5th Infy Bde order No 135 the raiding party as detailed in my order No 2016 left their trenches the night of 7/8th inst & proceeded by the route reconnoitred to the place of rendez-vous.

Owing to the number of Very lights sent up by the enemy & the more than usual amount of machine gun fire over the route to be crossed the progress of the advance was slower than had been worked out on the basis of reconnaissance reports and the rear of the column had not reached the rendez-vous at zero.

It appears, however, from everything that I can hear as to the subsequent operations, and it is the opinion of the only officer I am able to consult, who took part in the raid, that it was fortunate that greater numbers were not collected at this point.

According to my information & observation at 1 minute before zero the first Stokes gun - the signal for assault - fired.

The enemy appeared thoroughly prepared & almost simultaneously

(2).

a shower of bombs was thrown at the point of rendez-vous, rapid fire was opened by at least 3 machine guns from or in close vicinity to the sap, and trench mortar bombs began to fall on the ground to be crossed by the raiding party.

The first 2 storming parties at once rushed forward to their objectives but the wire was found to be a serious obstacle.

Parties then of course lost their cohesion and it became an affair of individuals seeking to effect entrance through the wire at the point of least resistance.

The wire on the South in front of the so called waterlogged trench appears to have been weakest and the party detailed for this gained their objective. They found the trench empty and made their way towards its junction with the main trench running from the base of the Sap N. Here there was a block and they could make no further progress.

A certain number of men had in the meantime forced their way thro the wire round the Sap & effected an entrance at various points.

(3). Sap area (a) the original objective for this party was found to be full of wire on entering it and no progress could be made here.

Some of the party detailed to establish the N block got in but they have never been seen since and I can get no information as to what progress they made.

A dug-out in the Sap was bombed by one man and he brought out a machine gun. While carrying it over the parapet with the help of another man they were both hit and the gun fell in a shell hole in the wire and could not be recovered.

In the course of the fight all 3 Officers and the N.C.O i/c of the other party had been knocked out and I imagine that the affair must naturally have become very much a matter of individual effort without any control.

Someone, who I cannot find out, nor exactly at what time, gave the signal to withdraw.

The affair then gradually petered out until the enemy started once again throwing a large number of bombs at the men who had remained behind to get in the wounded.

(4). As regards the enemy's wire I would wish to say that I do not consider any blame can be laid on anyone for not having gained fuller information about it.

Owing to the angles made by the wire running round the various arms of the sap & to the fact that the objectives of the attack had to be reached through a narrow gap bounded by the sap & the main trench it was not easy either to cut or to reconnoitre to the same extent as a stretch of wire is in front of a straight trench.

My last patrol stated that the wire extended all along, that no saps could be seen but that the general impression it gave was that it was not strong & would not present a serious obstacle.

From the nature of the ground from our front line to the sap it is extremely hard to bring Lewis gun fire to bear with any accuracy on to the various small arms of the saps; and further on the night of the 7/8 owing to the advanced party going out it was necessarily not possible even to try to do so for some considerable time.

5

There appears nothing more probable, therefore, than that the enemy, being thoroughly on his guard, strengthened his wire with an inner screen of wire.

All men who got thro the wire state that they were confronted with an inner screen of loose wire close to or on the parapet.

Altho the enterprise was not a success, a fact which I regret very deeply, all the Officers of the party and a number of men made very gallant efforts on the ground to try & make it into one, and I would ask permission to send in their names for recognition on a separate list.

I regret extremely that 1 Officer & 7 men are still missing.

These must have been killed or made prisoners in the enemy's trenches.

The ground between our line & the German wire was thoroughly searched the night of the operation & wounded rescued from their wire before light.

Search was again made last night without result.

C. G. Higgins
Lt Col
17th R Fusiliers

9-7-1916

SECRET.

2nd Divn No
G.S. 992/14/16

Copy No 10

5th Infantry Brigade Order No 135.

Reference -
Secret Trench Map 36c S.W.3

6th July 1916.

1 The 17th Royal Fusiliers will carry out a raid on the enemy's trenches East of PELLITIER ALLEY on the night 7th/8th July 1916.

Details will be communicated to all concerned at a conference to be held at Advanced Brigade Head Quarters at 10.30 a.m on the 7th of July

2 Objective -

(a) To destroy enemy's Machine Gun emplacements of which there are at least two and to capture the guns.

(b) To inflict the maximum of loss on the enemy.

(c) To obtain identifications.

3. Strength of raiding party -

3 Officers and about 60 men in all including 4 stretcher bearers, 7 R.E. and 2 miners.

4. Method of carrying out attack -

(a) As soon as it is dark on night 7th/8th July a patrol will move out from central picquet and remain in forming up trench in "no-man's" land to ensure that the raiding party is not surprised when crawling out.

(b) At such time before zero as may be necessary, the raiding party will slip over the parapet and form up facing North in a trench which exists about 30 yds South of Sap at S.9.a.½.9

(c) At Zero hour (to be notified later) the Artillery, Medium Trench Mortars, Light Mortars and machine guns will open fire on objectives as under:-

Artillery - S.3.c.2.2. to S.3.c.1.4 -and- S.9.a.1.6 to S.9.a.½.4 also S.3.c.5½.3 to S.9.a.5.4 } To a depth of 100 yards; including the Pimple

Medium trench mortars -
On the Pimple -

Light Mortars -

On a point at S. 9. a. 1¾. 7 - 50 yards clear of most southerly block held by raiding party. These will fire 1 minute intensive and then reduce to a normal rate of fire.

Machine Guns -

Special instructions have been issued to 5th M. G. Company Commander.

Artillery, Trench Mortars and Machine Gun Detachments - will be prepared to fire at a moments notice from 30 minutes before zero if called upon to do so. Should this be the case and the artillery open fire, trench mortars and machine guns will at once conform.

(d) The bombardment mentioned in (c) will be the signal for the raiding party to attack.
Separate parties have already been detailed for various duties and objectives.

(e) The exact time for withdrawal will be given by the Officers on the spot who will be stationed at the base of the sap, but the duration of the raid will probably not exceed 15 minutes.
The raiders will return to the old trench in "no-mans" land in which they formed up.

(f) At 0.20 hours all Artillery and Trench Mortar fire will automatically slacken and by 0.25 it will stop altogether.

(g) The raiding party will return to our trenches as soon as hostile fire ceases. Right and Left picquets will be warned that some of our own men may lose their way and withdraw to the flanks. A definite rendezvous will be fixed in our own trenches for the raiding party to assemble after withdrawal.

5. Dress and Arms. -

Attacking party - Rifle and bayonet, 60 rounds of ammunition, 2 bombs. Bombers - Knobkerries and 12 bombs each.

5. Dress and Arms (Contd.)

At least 50% will carry wire cutters. Identification party will carry sandbags. Faces and helmets will be blackened and all identification marks, papers etc removed.

All ranks taking part in the raid are to be warned that in the event of capture they are not bound to disclose anything beyond their rank and name, no other information to be given.

All ranks will be warned that the enemy may make use of the word retire.

6. Code words in connection with the raid will be communicated later.

7. Communication will be established by telephone between the centre picquet and Battalion H. Q.
The usual lamp communication will be in use between Battalions and Brigade Head Quarters.
From 10 minutes before zero the 17th Royal Fusiliers will be plugged through to Brigade Head Quarters. The Brigade will not be called up by other Units unless for very urgent reasons.

8. The following are requested to attend at the conference mentioned in para 1.

A Representative of 99th Inf. Bde.
" " " 34th Bde R.F.A.
" " " 36th Bde R.F.A.
O.C., 17th Royal Fusiliers.
" 2nd Highland Lt. Infy.
Captain Stewart, 17th Royal Fusiliers.
O.C., 48th Battery.
Lieut Dyson.
O.C., 5th Brigade M. G. Coy.
" 5/ L. M. Battery.

9 Acknowledge.

[signature]
Captain
Brigade Major
5th Inf. Bde.

Issued at 12.30 pm to:-

Copy No. 1. 17th Royal Fusiliers.
2. 2nd Highland Lt. Infty.
3. 5th Brigade M. G. Coy.
4. 5/ L.M. Battery.
5. 34th Bde R.F.A.
6. 36th Bde R.F.A.
7. 99th Inf. Bde.
8. R.A. H.Qrs.
9. 2nd Division.
10. 141st Inf. Bde.
11. File.

2 Div. No
G.S. 992/17/17

Secret. Copy No. 1.

99th. Inf. Bde. Operation Order No. 54.

Ref. MAP: Secret Trench Map. VIMY. 1/10000. July 7th. 1916.

1. In order to assist the 5th. Inf. Bde. in their tonight's operation, the following programme will be carried out by the 99th. Company, Machine Gun Corps, and the 99th. Trench Mortar Battery.

2. 99th. Company, Machine Gun Corps.
   (a) Between 10 P.M. 7/7/16, and 12-15 a.m. 8/7/16, fire on the Gaps that have been cut in the German wire N. of ANGEL AVENUE, by Y2 Medium Trench Mortar Battery.
   (b) From 12-15 a.m. till 1-30 a.m. 8/7/16, fire normal bursts of fire on German trenches between INTERNATIONAL and ERSATZ, and between a point about 100 yds. S of VINCENT STREET, and RIGHT of Brigade SECTION.

3. 99th. Trench Mortar Battery.
   Fire on German Trenches in the neighbourhood of VINCENT AVENUE, as if a raid was to be carried out there.
   This Fire to Commence at 1 hour 5 mins. a.m. 8/7/16, and last for 1 minute.

4. O.C. 99th. Company M.G. Corps will consult O.C. Y2 T.M.B. as to gaps to be fired on, Vide Para 2 (a) above.

5. 99th. Co., M.G. Corps, and 99th. T.M.B. will Send a representative each to Bde. H. Qrs. to Synchronise watches at 9-30 P.M. 7/7/16.

G. Lindsay, Major
Bde. Major
99th. Inf. Bde.

No. 1 Copy to H. Qrs. 2nd. Div.
" 2 " " H. Qrs. 5th. Inf. Bde.
" 3 " " O.C. 22nd. R. Fus.
" 4 " " O.C. 23rd. R. Fus.
No. 5. (office Copy)

Dictated to:- Representative 99th. Co. M.G. Corps.
" 99th. T.M. Battery.

Issued at:- 4/pm

Acknowledged

2nd Divn. No.
G.S.983/Mining/15.

IVth Corps.

I forward a report on the consolidation of a new crater formed by the explosion of an enemy mine on the night 9th/10th July. The blow came somewhat as a surprise and I consider that the arrangements made by the G.O.C., 5th Inf. Brigade in having his crater jumping parties formed and ready, were good. I also consider that Lieut. Colonel HIGGINS carried out the work extremely well, especially in view of the fact that the blow came just as his Battalion was about to be relieved.

All ranks of the crater jumping party showed resource and dash, especially Sergt. HASTINGS whose name I am forwarding for reward.

H.Q., 2nd Divn.
11-7-1916.

(sd) W.G. WALKER, Major-Genl.
Commanding 2nd Division.

(2)

5th Inf. Bde.

For your information.

H.Q., 2nd Divn.
12-7-1916.

Lieut. Colonel,
General Staff, 2nd Division.

PRELIMINARY REPORT ON HOSTILE MINE
SPRUNG EVENING OF 9th INST IN
CARENCY(2).

At 8-34 p.m. on 9th inst the Germans sprung a mine close to FOOTBALL CRATER.

Sgt. HASTINGS i/c of my left storming party consisting of 19 men calling on the men to turn out and follow up, immediately rushed with 2 other men to the place of explosion.

On reaching FOOTBALL CRATER they met a party of the enemy about 7 strong creeping round the Northern lip of FOOTBALL CRATER. They bombed them and they retired. Shortly afterwards the remainder of my storming party came up and held the lip. There is no doubt that Sgt. HASTINGS, by his prompt action, saved the rear lip from being taken by the enemy.

The effect of the mine was to completely obliterate Sap (10) commanding BROADBRIDGE. This post was held by 3 men and they have not been recovered.

The men in Sap 12 were buried but were dug out subsequently.

The new crater appears to have merely pushed back out lips of BROADBRIDGE and JOHN CRATER a few yards and to have formed a long valley extending from the North of FOOTBALL CRATER to MILDREN CRATER.

It does not appear to have affected our position adversely at all.

A stretch of our front line from SAP 12 to SAP 9 was blown in and a good part of the support line shaken down.

Consolidation and clearing work was pushed on vigourously b y strong parties and the work was well in hand when at about 2 a.m. my covering bombers were withdrawn and the line handed over to the 2/Oxf. & Bucks L.I.

As far as I can tell at present my casualties were :-

KILLED.

5 (3 buried by mines and 2 storming party killed).

WOUNDED.

2 officers, 9 O.R.

10-7-1916. (sd) C.S. HIGGINS, Lt. Col.
17/R. Fus.

(2)

H.Q., 2nd Divn.

I forward herewith report by O.C., 17/R. Fusiliers on the hostile mine which was blown in Northern Sub-Section last night.

Consolidation was carried on throughout the night and will be continued to-night.

10-7-1916. (sd) G. BULLEN SMITH, Br. General,
Commanding 5th Inf. Bde.

S E C R E T.

20 Ann No
G.S.992 | 19 | 3

IVth Corps.
2nd Division.
40th Division.

1. 142nd Infantry Brigade are carrying out two raids on enemy's trenches in M.26.c on night of July 8th/9th.

The second raid will be accompanied by a gas attack.

2. About 11 p.m. one of the two following words will be sent you :-

PUMPKIN - Wind suitable, operations will commence at Zero.

PARSNIP - Operations cancelled.

3. 142nd Infantry Brigade has forwarded to 119th Infantry Brigade a copy of their operation orders. (For information of 40th Division).

4. Acknowledge.

G/1212/86
7th July 1916.

[signature] Lt Col
General Staff,
47th (London) Division.

Headquarters,

2nd Division.

---

2 Divn No
GS 992/14/20

HEADQUARTERS
No G.S.468/3
6th INFANTRY BRIGADE

With reference your No.G.S.992/15/18; as REDOUBT ROAD and 130th ROAD are not passable in daylight may CABARET ROAD be common to both 6th and 5th Brigades, please?

If the Brigade Head Quarters in HOSPITAL ROAD are completed in time I would prefer to occupy them, it is estimated they should be complete in another week at the earliest.

HEADQUARTERS
RECEIVED
10 JUL. 1916
DIVISION.

A. Daly

Brigadier General,

10.7.1916. Commanding, 6th Infantry Brigade.

Discussed at Conference on 12th inst.

[illegible]

I have cancelled these [illegible] orders

P.R.

[illegible]

Secret

2 Divn No GS.992/1/23 — H.Q. 2nd Division

Following Estimate refers to men required to carry up. Bombs, S.A.A, R.E. Material Rations & Water for Operations in connection with BANANA SKINS.

S.A.A.

1. Forward dumps — — 4 × 20 = 80 boxes
2. Intermediate dumps 3 × 30 = 90 "
3. Bde Bomb Stores 2 × 100 = 200

= 340 men making 2 journeys

Bombs

1. 4 × 50 boxes = 200
3 × 100 " = 300
2 × 250 " = 500

= 500 men making 2 journeys

Very Lights

1. 4 × 5 = 20 boxes
2. — — —
3. 2 × 20 = 40 "

= 30 men making 2 journeys

R.E. Material

50 coils French Wire
" " Barbed "
300 Iron Screw posts
15,000 Sandbags

= 275 men making 2 journeys

Rations & Water

1500 rations Meat
" " Biscuits
36 60 gallon Water tanks

= 75 men making 2 journeys

Not required

~~The above makes a~~ A Total of 1250 men
or 312 men working for 4 nights

(1) **Stokes Mortar Ammunition**

4. 200 rounds = 800 rounds per night for 4 days — 100 men making 2 journeys

9.45 pm. adv. Hdqrs.

G. M. Butler? Capt.

Brig Gen
Cmdg 5 Inf Bde

11/7/16

SECRET

No 2

ENLARGED · 4 · TIMES
FROM · AIR · PHOTO · No. 18A 355

REFERENCE
BRITISH TRENCHES
GERMAN Do
DISUSED Do

UHLAN ALLEY

LOVE CRATER

MOMBER CRATER

B. TANCHOT

B. GOBRON

B. HARTUN

ERSATZ AVENUE

A B C D E F G H K L M N O P R S T U V W

APPROX SCALE.

Yds 100 0 100 200 Yds

"A" Form.

Army Form C. 2121.

MESSAGES AND SIGNALS.

No. of Message

Prefix ... Code ... m. Office of Origin and Service Instructions.	Words / Charge / Sent / At ... m. / To / By	This message is on a/c of: ... Service. (Signature of "Franking Officer.")	Recd. at ... m. / Date / From / By
Secret		2 Divn 16 / CS 992/16/7	

TO ~~47th Division~~ 2nd Division ~~Heavy artillery IV Corps~~

Sender's Number.	Day of Month.	In reply to Number.	AAA
*H.R.S. 669/J/1	2nd July		

The 1st Corps propose, if weather conditions admit, to carry out a gas attack at 11.30 pm tonight aaa About 9.30 pm a telephone message will be sent you from this office coded as before aaa This message will be confirmed by wire aaa acknowledge by wire aaa addressed 47th and 2nd Divs and Heavy artillery IV Corps.

From IV Corps

Place

Time 7.0 pm

The above may be forwarded as now corrected. (Z) L A T Bowly Major G.S. IV Corps

Censor. Signature of Addressor or person authorised to telegraph in his name.

* This line should be erased if not required.

925,000 W 14042—M 44 H. W. & V., Ld 12.15

"C" Form (Duplicate). Army Form C. 2123.

MESSAGES AND SIGNALS. No. of Message..................

	Charges to Pay.	Office Stamp.
	£ s. d.	
Service Instructions.		

Handed in at.................................... Office............m. Received............m.

TO	

Sender's Number	Day of Month	In reply to Number	AAA
	2.7.16		

9.35 pm

FROM	4 Corps
PLACE & TIME	9.10 pm

W 15660—M 151 75,000 Pads. H & S 4/16 Forms/C.2123. (5665)

"A" Form. Army Form C. 2121.

MESSAGES AND SIGNALS. No. of Message ....

Prefix .... Code .... m. | Words | Charge | This message is on a/c of: | Recd. at .... m.

Office of Origin and Service Instructions. SECRET

Sent | Service. | Date ....

At .... m. | From ....

To ....

By .... | (Signature of "Franking Officer.") | By ....

TO
2nd-47th Divns. Adv.First Army.
Heavy Artillery. 1st-XVIIth Corps.
G.O.C., R.A. 18 Sqdn R.F.C.

Sender's Number.	Day of Month.	In reply to Number.	
* H.R.S.669/L	3rd July		AAA

Only such operations as Divisional Commanders considerddesirable will be carried out tomorrow fourth AAA
Owing to relief in Ist Corps area IVth Corps Artillery will NOT carry out road shoots AAA
Army and Corps Artillery will carry out billet shoots at 10.45 p.m. Fourth and at 4.0 a.m. and 5.0 a.m. Fifth on M.35.a. only AAA Acknowledge.

Addressed 2nd 47th Divns IVth Corps Heavy Arty G.O.C.R R.A., repeated Ist XVIIth Corps Adv.First Army 18 Sqdn R.F.C.

acknowledged
B.
3.7.

From Fourth Corps.
Place
Time 10.30 pm

The above may be forwarded as now corrected. (Z) L.A.T. Bosty Major B.G.G.S.

Censor. Signature of Addressor or person authorised to telegraph in his name.

* This line should be erased if not required.

225,000. W 14042—M 14. H. W. & V., Ld. 12/15.

2 Divn No
GS 992/16/18

SECRET

1st Army G.S. 420/3(a)

IVth Corps No. H.R.S. 669

IVth Corps.

Instructions have been received from G H.Q. to the effect that strict economy in the expenditure of ammunition is now necessary in order to ensure a sufficient supply of ammunition for the main operations: and that ammunition for further wirecutting on the fronts of the First, Second, and Third Armies cannot be provided.

2. The 2" trench mortar should be the primary weapon to be used for wirecutting purposes and 18-pounder ammunition should only be used for this purpose in exceptional cases in connexion with raids.

3. Further, 18-pounder ammunition should only be used in exceptional cases for the shelling of the enemy's communica:tions and strong points behind his line.

4. At the same time, in order to prevent the enemy from withdrawing troops to reinforce against our main attack, and to wear down his strength, the Commander-in-Chief wishes every effort to be made to continue the carrying out of raids against the enemy trenches on the fronts of the First and Second Armies.

5. It is unlikely that it will be possible to give to Corps any ammunition in addition to that already allotted for the operations now in progress, and the G.O.C. wishes it impressed upon all concerned that, while giving effect to the Commander-in-Chief's wishes as regards raids, every round saved in the carrying out of the Corps programme may help to influence the result of the operations at the decisive point.

3rd July, 1916.

(sd) G.De.S. Barrow. Major General,
General Staff, First Army.

(2)

2nd Division.
~~47th Division.~~
~~G.O.C., R.A.~~

For your information.

L. A. T. B[illegible] Major
for G.S.

4th July, 1916.

Brigadier General,
General Staff, IVth Corps.

RA
Bdes for information & guidance

[illegible]
4.7.

2: Divn NO
GS.992/16/19

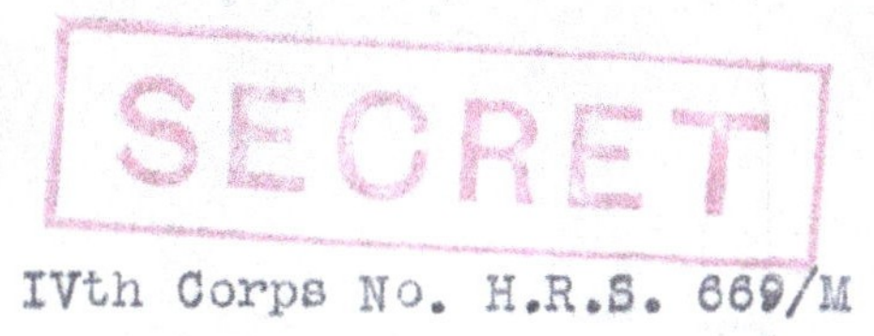

IVth Corps No. H.R.S. 669/M

2nd Division.
~~47th Division.~~
~~B.G., C.H.A., IVth Corps.~~
~~G.O.C., R.A., IVth Corps.~~

---

1. No operations will be carried out in the IVth Corps tomorrow 5th July except for the bombardment of the enemy's billets in M.35.a. at 4.0 a.m. and 5.0 a.m. as ordered in IVth Corps H.R.S. 669/L of yesterday.

2. If weather conditions permit the 1st Corps propose to make a gas and smoke attack tonight July 4th/5th.

3. Please acknowledge by wire.

acknowledged [illegible]

L.A.T. [illegible] Major
for G.S.

4th July, 1916.

Brigadier General,
General Staff, IVth Corps.

"C" Form (Original). Army Form C. 2123.

MESSAGES AND SIGNALS. No. of Message........

Prefix ...... Code* ...... Words 14	Received From CB By Lucock	Sent, or sent out At ....m. To ...... By	Office Stamp.
£ s. d. Charges to collect			
Service Instructions.			

Handed in at ABR Office 2.41p.m. Received 2.51p.m.

TO Gnu

Sender's Number	Day of Month	In reply to Number	AAA
Bm 584	4th		

Your Gs 791/25 has been passed to Fur aaa apparently sent here in error

who made the mistake?

CB.

See attached [illegible]

CHE

FROM PLACE & TIME Fowl 2.30pm

* This line should be erased if not required.

W 15680—M 151 75,000 Pads. H & S 2/16 Forms/C.2123. (5688)

(In pads of 50 dupls.) "C" Form (Duplicate). Army Form C. 2123.

MESSAGES AND SIGNALS. No. of Message ....

	Charges to Pay. £ s. d.	Office Stamp.
Im EKS 18 F? Pm		
Service Instructions.		

Handed in at ...XRO... Office ....m. Received ....m.

TO 2 Div

Sender's Number	Day of Month	In reply to Number	AAA
G997	7.7.16		

Para 1(B) of my HRS/690 of yesterday is cancelled

Acknowledged

[illegible]

FROM

PLACE & TIME 4 Corps 5.50 Pm

W 15650 M/15L 75,000 Pads. McC. & Co., Ltd., London. 1/16. Forms/C.2123.

SECRET

IV Corps No. H.R.S. 669

2 Divn No
GS 992/16/27

HEADQUARTERS 4th CORPS
7 JUL 1916
GENERAL STAFF

2nd Division.
~~G.O.C., R.A.~~
~~D.A. & Q.M.G.~~ } For information

---

1. The present ammunition situation allows of the following allotment of ammunition to your Division which cancels previous orders :-

	18-pdrs.	4.5"
For tonights operation	3,000	300
For your second -,,- including barrage	20,000	2,000
For your daily allowance till noon on July 14th including billet and road shoots in accordance with programme	2,800	350 ~~3,680~~
	25,800	2,650

2. Your defensive dump round the guns should be reduced to 300 rounds 18-pdr per gun, and kept at that figure, and your echelons should be kept full.

H. DePree
Brigadier General,
General Staff, IV Corps.

H.Q., IV Corps,
7th July, 1916.

C.R.A.
To see return please
C. Geddes [illegible]
G.S.
2nd Divn
7.7.16.

G.S. 2nd Div. Seen & returned. [illegible]
8.7.16

"A" Form.

Army Form C. 2121.

MESSAGES AND SIGNALS.

No. of Message

Prefix ... Code ... m. | Words | Charge

Office of Origin and Service Instructions.

SECRET

Sent At ... m. To ... By ...

This message is on a/c of: ... Service. (Signature of "Franking Officer.")

SECRET

Recd. at ... m. Date ... From ... By ...

TO { 2nd Divn
47th Divn
G.O.C.R.A. IV Corps

Sender's Number	Day of Month	In reply to Number	AAA
* H.R.S. 669	12 July		

Corps Commander will hold a conference at Corps H.Q at 9.0 a m tomorrow 13th instant aaa G.Os C 2nd and 47th Divns with their G.S.Os 1st grade and the G.O.C R.A IV Corps will attend aaa Divisional Commanders will be prepared to submit rough projects for big or little raids on their divisional fronts together with approximate dates and estimates of ammunition aaa acknowledge aaa addressed 2nd and 47th Divns and R.A IV Corps

From IV Corps

Place

Time 7.45 p.m

The above may be forwarded as now corrected. (Z) L. A. T. Bowly Major GS

Censor. Signature of Addressor or person authorised to telegraph in his name.

* This line should be erased if not required.

292146—W. & S. Ltd., London.—W 14142/641—60,000—4/15. Forms C 2121/10.

"C" Form (Original).

Army Form C. 2123

MESSAGES AND SIGNALS.

No. of Message ....

Prefix Sm Code 17 Words	Received	Sent, or sent out	Office Stamp.
£ s. d. Charges to collect	From .... By	At .... m. To .... By	YB 8.VII.16 YB
Service Instructions.			

Handed in at .... Office 7.30 m. Received 9.38 a m.

TO G.S. [illegible] Divn

*Sender's Number	Day of Month	In reply to Number	AAA
1005	8.7.16		

One	Sp. Bde Co	will	join	47
Division	and	one	Sp. Bde Co	less
one	section	will	join	2nd
Divn	today	by	bus	from
CEDAR	and	the	former	has.
been	diverted	on	[illegible]	reporting
to	the	CROW	now	there
and	the	latter	on	[illegible]
[illegible]	reporting	at	[illegible]	[illegible]
en	route			

G

~~Q~~

[illegible]

9.40 a

FROM PLACE & TIME: 4 Corps 9.25 am

* This line should be erased if not required.

15660—M 151 75,000 Pads. H & S 2/16 Forms/C.2123. (5668)

SECRET

IVth Corps No. H.R.S. 669/2

2nd Division.
~~47th Division.~~
~~R.N. Division.~~
G.O.C., R.A. IVth Corps.
C.E. "
~~First Army.~~ }
~~Ist Corps.~~ } for information.
~~XVIIth Corps.~~ }
18 Sqdn R.F.C.

2nd Divn No. G.3992/16/29

HEADQUARTERS 4th CORPS 13 JUL 1916 GENERAL STAFF

---

1. The following is the proposed programme of minor operations up to the night of July 20th/21st inclusive:-

July 14th Bombardment of VIMY Station with aeroplane observation, by Corps Artillery.

" 15th Bombardment of LA COULOTTE by Corps Artillery with aeroplane observation.
2nd Division trench mortar bombardment in CARENCY Section.

" 16th Bombardment of SUNKEN ROAD S.16.a.10.3. to S.16.c.0.5.5. with aeroplane observation, by IVth Corps Heavy Artillery.

" Night 16th/17th 47th Division raid in SOUCHEZ Section.

" 17th Bombardment of LA CHAUDIERE by IVth Corps Heavy Artillery with balloon observation.

" 18th Bombardment of LA CHAUDIERE Wood by IVth Corps Heavy Artillery - two bursts of one round each.

" Night 18th/19th 2nd Division raid in BERTHONVAL Section.

" 19th Bombardment of houses at T.2.b.2.0. by IVth Corps Heavy Artillery, with balloon observation.

" 20th Bombardment of FOSSE 7 (T.1.b) by IVth Corps Heavy Artillery, with aeroplane observation.

" Night 20th/21st 47th Division raid with about two companies with the help of gas in the ANGRES Section.

2. The 2nd and 47th Divisions will each prepare one raid for the week following July 20th.

3. Please acknowledge receipt by wire.

W. A. T. Bowly Major G.S.
for Brigadier General,
General Staff, IVth Corps.

13th July, 1916.

Copy to Bde
CRA
Sigs.
CRE.

Acknowledged
B.B.
13.7.

2 Divn No
GS 992/16/28

SECRET

IV Corps No. H.R.S. 609.

~~R.N. Division.~~
~~47th Division.~~
2nd Division.
~~G.O.C., R.A. IV Corps.~~)
~~D.A. & Q.M.G., IV Corps~~)
Advanced First Army.) for information.
~~I Corps.~~)
~~XVII Corps.~~)
~~C.E., IV Corps.~~)

---

1. IV Corps No. H.R.S. 609 of 11th July is amended as follows:-

(a) ON 18th July the 1st Brigade, Royal Naval Division will be relieved in the ANGRES Section by an infantry brigade of the 47th Division and not by the 2nd Brigade Royal Naval Division, and will return to the Reserve Division Area.

(b) On the night 19th/20th July the 2nd Brigade, Royal Naval Division will take over the BERTHONVAL Section from the 2nd Division.

(c) On the night 27th/28th July the 2nd Division will relieve the 2nd Brigade, Royal Naval Division in the BERTHONVAL Section.

2. All details of these reliefs will be arranged between divisions concerned.

3. The 2nd Brigade, Royal Naval Division will come under the orders of the G.O.C., 2nd Division from the commencement of the relief on 19th/20th July and will revert to the command of the Royal Naval Division on completion of its tour of duty in the trenches on 27th/28th July.

4. The dug-out platoons of the battalions of the 2nd Brigade, Royal Naval Division will accompany their battalions into the trenches.

5. The infantry brigade of the 2nd Division relieved from the BERTHONVAL Section will be in Corps Reserve, and its position will be reported to Corps Headquarters.

6. Please acknowledge.

W. A. T. Bro[illegible] Major
for G.S.

H.Q., IV Corps,
13th July, 1916.

Brigadier-General,
General Staff, IV Corps.

Copy to 99th Bdes - CRA cox [illegible]
Detailed orders as to [illegible]
of the 99th Inf Bde will be issued later
[illegible]

acknowledged
[illegible] 13.7.

SECRET

IVth Corps No.H.R.S.809. | 2nd Divn. No. G.S.98/16/28

2nd Division.

1. IVth Corps No.H.R.S. 809 of 11th July is amended as follows :-

(a). On 18th July the 1st Brigade, Royal Naval Division will be relieved in the ANGRES Section by an Infantry Brigade of the 47th Division and not by the 2nd Brigade Royal Naval Division, and will return to the Reserve Division area.

(b). On the night 19th/20th July the 2nd Brigade, Royal Naval Division will take over the BERTHONVAL Section from the 2nd Division.

(c). On the night 27th/28th July the 2nd Division will relieve the 2nd Brigade, Royal Naval Division in the BERTHONVAL Section.

2. All details of these reliefs will be arranged between divisions concerned.

3. The 2nd Brigade, Royal Naval Division will come under the orders of the G.O.C., 2nd Division from the commencement of the relief on 19th/20th July and will revert to the command of the G.O.C., Royal Naval Division on completion of its tour of duty in the trenches on 27th/28th July.

4. The dug-out platoons of the Battalions of the 2nd Brigade, Royal Naval Division will accompany their Battalions into the trenches.

5. The Infantry Brigade of the 2nd Division relieved from the BERTHONVAL Section will be in Corps Reserve, and its position will be reported to Corps Headquarters.

6. Please acknowledge.

H.Q., IVth Corps. (sd) W.A.T. BOWLY, Major G.S.
for Br. General,
13th July, 1916. General Staff, IV Corps.

(2)

5th Inf. Bde. R.A., 2nd Divn.
6th Inf. Bde. R.E., 2nd Divn.
99th Inf. Bde. 2/Signal Co.

For information. Detailed orders as to the relief of the 99th Inf. Brigade will be issued later.

H.Q., 2nd Divn. Lieut. Colonel,

14-7-1916. General Staff, 2nd Division.

SECRET

2 Bm No GS992/18/7

Copy No. 5

OPERATION ORDER FOR 0 + 8. DAY.

BY BRIGADIER GENERAL T. E. MARSHALL,

COMMANDING 4th CORPS HEAVY ARTILLERY.

Headquarters,
1st July 1916.

---

1. 15th H.A.Group and French Artillery will bombard enemy billets as under :-

Time	Target		Ammunition	rounds.
10.0p.m.	Houses - M33b.	- Ammunition allowed	60-pdrs.	8.
			18-pdrs.	16.
			French Long.	8.
			French Court.	4.
10.15p.m.	Houses - N19.	- Ammunition allowed	60-pdrs.	4.
			18-pdrs.	8.
			4.5"Hows.	4
			French Long.	8
10.45p.m.	Houses - M33d.	- Ammunition allowed	60-pdrs.	4.
			18-pdrs.	16
			French Court.	12
5.0a.m. 3/7/16.	Houses - N19.	- Ammunition allowed	60-pdrs.	4.
			18-pdrs.	8
			4.5"Hows.	4
			French Long.	8.

2. 15th H.A.Group will search roads in GIVENCHY, with 18-pdrs.shrapnel, and 60-pdrs., at 3.50 a.m. to 3.55 a.m. 3/7/16 (18-pdrs - 20 rounds, 60-pdrs 6 rounds)

French Artillery will fire at "Zones Regle" at 3.55a.m. 3/7/16

9. S15b9.8.
10. S9d4.3.
11. S9d3.9.
12. S9b9.3.
13. S9b6.7.
14. S9b0.5.

Ammunition allowed - 18 rounds Court.

Cecil Blackburne
Capt.R.A.
Brigade Major,
Heavy Arty. 4th Corps

Copy No. 1 File.
2,3,4.R.A.,IV Corps.
5. 2nd Division.
6. 2nd Div. Arty.
7. 47th Division.
8. 47th Div. Arty.
9. 1st Corps H.A.
10 French Artillery.
11,12,13,14. 15th H.A.Group.

Acknowledged J.B. 1.7.

2nd Divn. No.
G.S. 992/15/7.

C.R.A., 2nd Divn.
C.R.E., 2nd Divn.
5th Inf. Bde.
6th Inf. Bde.
176th Tng. Co. R.E.
182nd ,, ,,

----

(1). At 10-15 p.m. July 2nd and 5 a.m. July 3rd, Army and IVth Corps Artillery will bombard enemy's billets at CITE DE CAUMONT.

(2). At about 4 a.m. July 3rd, IVth Corps Heavy Artillery and 2nd Divisional Artillery will bombard enemy's roads and communication trenches near GIVENCHY.

H.Q., 2nd Divn. (sd) J.D. BELGRAVE, Major for Lt.Col.
1-7-1916. General Staff, 2nd Division.

(2)

IVth Corps.

For information.

H.Q., 2nd Divn. Major-General,
1-7-1916. Commanding 2nd Division.

2 Divn No
GS.992/18/8

SECRET

OPERATION ORDER. Copy No. 5

BY

BRIGADIER-GENERAL. T. E. MARSHALL.

COMMANDING. HEAVY ARTILLERY. IV CORPS.

Headquarters. 2nd JULY '16.

1. 15th H.A.Group will bombard the PIMPLE and Observation posts N., and N.E., of it, commencing at 3.0.pm. This H.Q.,to be notified immediately the bombardment is concluded.

Ammunition allowed :- 120 mm, Court = 350.
4.5" How. = 50.

This bombardment will be repeated from 1.45.am, 4/7/16, to, 2.15.am, 4/7/16.

Ammunition allowed :- 120 mm, Court. = 50.
4.5" How. = 100.

2. 15th H.A.Group will bombard points as under :-

M.G.,at S.2.b.37.60. - 50 rds 6" How.
Trench and wire S.2.b.3½.4. - 50 rds 60-pdr.

To commence at 3.0.pm. This H.Q., to be notified immediately the bombardment is concluded.

[signature]
Captain: R.A.
Brigade-Major.
Heavy Artillery. IV Corps.

Copy No: 1. File.
2.3.4. R.A. IV Corps.
5. 2nd Division.
6. 2nd Divisional Artillery.
7. 47th Division.
8. 47th Divisional Artillery.
9. 1st Corps H.A.
10. French Artillery.
11. 140th Infantry Brigade.
12,13.14.15: 15th H.A.Group.

acknowledged
B.
2.7

004/23 PROGRAMME OF OPERATIONS

Ref Givenchy Trench Maps [illegible]

SECRET

DATE	TIMES	[illegible]	TASK	
28th	9.30 P.M.	18 PRS 12 Rds p gun	**TASK 'A'** 2 minutes intense fire over the following Areas	
		4.5" 6 Rds p gun	4 [illegible] bounding Areas S3D8½3, S4D03, S10B03, S9B13.	All Btys 36th Bde
			" " S9B73, S10B03, S10D06, S9D66.	" " 34th "
			" " S9D66, S10D06, S10B09, S15B69.	" " 41st "
			TASK 'B'	
28th/29th	Odd Intervals Till Dawn	18 PRS 30 Rds a Burst	12 Bursts on Road S9D04 – S9D53	One 18 Pr Bty 36th Bde
			" " S10C2½1 – S10C101.	" " 34th "
		4.5" 20 Rds a Burst	" " about S10a80 & S10C05	4.5" " 36th "
29th	6 A.M.		FEINT BARRAGE on GERMAN FRONT LINE from 50x S. of GRANBY AV. and VINCENT AV.	
	-10 to 00		Ranging	
	00 – 05	2 Rds p gun p min	Barrage on Front Line Trench	2, 18 pr Batteries 41st Bde
	0.5 – 08	4 " "	" " " "	
	0.8 – 011	4 " "	Lift 200x	
	011 – 0.15	6 " "	On Front Line Trench	
	0.15 – 0.17	3 " "	Lift 200x	
	0.17 – 0.20	6 " "	On Front Line Trench	
	00 – 0.17	2	Trench Junctions at S15C2½8, S15C67, S15C7½4, S15C92.	4.5" Bty of 41st Bde
	0.17 – 0.20	4	" " S15a60, S15C99, S15C88, S15D36	34th Bde
29th/30th			TASK 'B' will be repeated except that 4.5" How of 36th Bde will not fire but 4.5" Hows of 34th Bde will fire about S10C05 & S10a80	
30th	11.30 pm		TASK 'A' will be repeated	
30th/1st July	Odd intervals Till Dawn	18 PRS 30 Rds a Burst	12 Bursts of fire on Road S10A1½ to S10A58	2, 18 pdr Btys 41st Bde
		4.5" 20 Rds a Burst	about S10A24 & S10A5½8	4.5" " 41st Bde.

004/29 Continued Secret

Date	Time	Rate of fire etc	Tasks		Allotted.
1st July	11.30 P.M.		TASK A will be repeated.		
2nd July	11 AM	Rds per gun per min	FEINT Barrage between IRISH CRATER & LOVE'S CRATER		
			18 pdrs	4.5" Hows	
	00 to 06	2	Front Trench	Support Trench	2 Btys 18 pdr
	06 " 09	2	Lift 200x	S9C 4½ – S15A5 7	1 " 4.5" How
	09 011	6	Front Trench	Whole Time except 0.13 to 0.18	of 34th Bde.
	0.11 0.13	3	Lift 200x	at ½ rate of fire for 18 pdrs.	
	0.13 0.18		Pause		
	0.18 0.21	6	Front Trench		
	0.18 0.21	4	Support and Communication Trenches to a depth of 400x Back.		3 Btys 18 pdr, 1 " 4.5 How, 36th Bde

2nd Div. No
G.S. 992/16/18

SECRET

IVth Corps No. H.R.S. 669/K.

2nd Division.
~~47th Division.~~
B.G.,C.H.A.,IVth Corps.
G.O.C.,R.A.,IVth Corps.
~~Ist Corps.~~)
~~XVIIth Corps.~~) for information.
~~Adv. First Army.~~)
~~No. 18 Sqdn R.F.C.~~)

With reference to IVth Corps letter No. H.R.S. 669 of 21st June,1916.

1. The following operations will be carried out tomorrow July 3rd, 1916:-

(a) 'One round' bombardments by the Divisional Artillery and Trench Mortars of the 2nd and 47th Divisions at targets and times to be selected by G.O.s C. 2nd and 47th Divisions.

(b) The IVth Corps Heavy Artillery will bombard the PIMPLE and observation posts N and N.E. of it, at a time to be selected by the B.G.,C.H.A.,IVth Corps, in conjunction with G.O.C. 47th Division.

(c) At 10.15 p.m. and 11 p.m. om July 3rd and at 5.30 a.m. on July 4th the Army and IVth Corps Artillery will bombard the enemy's billets in LIEVIN.

(d) The French 120 mm'Courts' will bombard the enemy's trenches in S.3 and S.9. at an hour to be arranged by B.G., C.H.A.,IVth Corps in conjunction with G.O.s C. 2nd and 47th Divisions. The artillery of the 2nd and 47th Divisions will shrapnel these trenches when the French guns have ceased firing.

2. During the night July 3rd/4th :-

(a) The IVth Corps Heavy Artillery will bombard the following roads:-
i. N.19.b.5.8. to M.18.d.0.8. to M.23 Central to M.17.b.8.3.
ii. N.20.a.1.9. to crossroads M. 22.d.5.0. and north to M.22.b.2.2.
iii. N.20.a.1½.0. to N.31.central, to M.35.b.0.4.
iv. N.25.d.4.5. to M.36.b.6.5.

(b) The 47th Division will carry out a raid at a time and place to be selected by the G.O.C. 47th Division.

3. Copies of all orders and instructions with reference to these operations will be forwarded to Corps Headquarters.

4. Please acknowledge by wire.

W. A. T. Bowly Major G.S.
for Brigadier General,
General Staff, IVth Corps.

2nd July, 1916.

SECRET

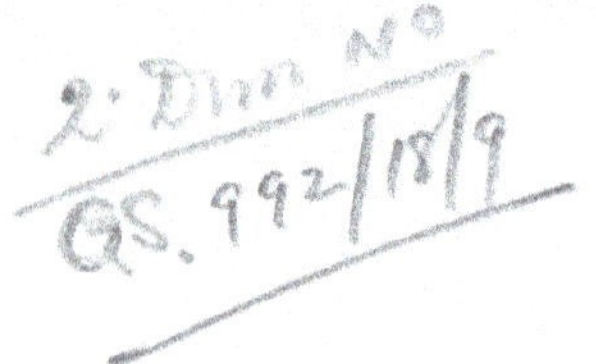

Copy No. 5

OPERATION ORDER for 0 + 11 Day.

BY BRIGADIER-GENERAL. T.E. MARSHALL.,

COMMANDING. HEAVY ARTILLERY. 4th CORPS.

****

Headquarters,
4th JULY.1916.

REFERENCE. Map 1/20000, Sheet 36.c. Edition 7A.

1. The 15th H.A. Group, and French Artillery will bombard the houses in M.35.a., at 10.45.pm, 4/7/16, and again at 4.0.am, and 5.0.am., 5/7/16.

Ammunition allowed :-	Each time.	Total.
18-Pdr.	24	72
4.5"How.	4	12
60-Pdr.	6	18
120mm Long.	6	18.

[signature]

Captain: R.A.
Brigade-Major.
Heavy Artillery. IV Corps.

4/7/16.

Copy No:- 1 File.
2.3.4. R.A. IV Corps.
5. 2nd Division.
6. 2nd Divisional Artillery.
7. 47th Division.
8. 47th Divisional Artillery.
9. 1st Corps H.A.
10. French Artillery.
11.12.13.14. 15th H.A. Group.

acknowledged
JSB

47

IV Corps No. R.A. 681/28/64.

SECRET.

2nd Divisional Artillery.
47th Divisional Artillery.
Heavy Artillery, IV Corps.
IV Corps 'G'.)
2nd Division.) For information.
47th Division.)

The following adjustments of Ammunition Allotment, for Operations in hand, is made :-

From.	To.	Number and Nature.	
Heavy Arty. IV Corps.	2nd D.A.	1,000	A.
"Corps Reserve" held by 2nd D.A.	2nd D.A.	2,500	A.
----do----.	2nd D.A.	2,500	AX.
----do----.	2nd D.A.	400	BX.

This allotment, plus the original allotment, minus ammunition expended since noon 24th ultimo, is to last to noon 14th instant.

If ammunition is required for any special purpose, application must be made to Corps Headquarters for it.

A D Macpherson Capt.
for Brigadier-General,
G.S.O., R.A., IV Corps.

H.Q. IV Corps.
4/7/'16.

SECRET

2 Dvn No
GS992/18/10

Copy No. 5

OPERATION ORDER FOR 0 + 12 DAY.

BY BRIGADIER GENERAL T. E. MARSHALL.,

COMMANDING HEAVY ARTILLERY, IV CORPS.

Headquarters,
5th July 1916.

REFERENCE Map 1/20,000, Sheet 36c. Edition 7a.

1. During the night of 5/6th July, 1916, 15th H.A. Group will fire on roads as follows :-

M18d3.7. - M19b5.8. - M18c1.0.
M18d3.7. - M24a0.0. - N20a2.9.
M36a0.4. - M36b7.4. - M25d5.6.
M36b7.4. - N31b0.2.

Times as follows :-

9.30p.m.	11.55 p.m.
10.5 "	12.20 a.m.
10.30 "	12.35 "
10.50 "	1.0 "
11.20 "	1.10 "
11.25 "	1.45 "

Ammunition allowed 40 rounds - 60-pounder.

[signature]
Capt.R.A.
Brigade Major,
Heavy Arty. IV Corps.

Copy No. 1 File.
2,3, 4, R.A.,IV Corps
5 2nd Division.
6 2nd Div. Arty.
7 47th Division.
8 47th Div. Arty.
9 1st Corps H.A.
10 French Arty.
11,12,13 & 14 15th H.A.Group.

SECRET

IVth Corps No. H.R.S. 669/

2 Divn No
GS992/16/22

HEADQUARTERS 4th CORPS
8 JUL 1916
GENERAL STAFF

2nd Division.
~~47th Division.~~
~~B.G.,C.H.A.,IVth Corps.~~

1. If the wind is favourable the remaining gas cylinders on the 15th and 16th Divisional fronts of the First Corps will be discharged tonight at 11.30 p.m.

2. You will be warned in code as usual.

3. Please acknowledge.

acknowledged

5th July,1916.

J.B. Brady Capt
for Brigadier General,
General Staff, IVth Corps.

SECRET

IVth Corps No. H.R.S. 669/N.

2 Divn No GS 992/16/21

2nd Division.
~~47th Division.~~
~~B.G., C.H.A., IVth Corps.~~
~~G.O.C., R.A., IVth Corps.~~
~~Ist Corps.~~ } for information.
~~Adv. First Army.~~
~~18 Sqdn. R.F.C.~~

During the nights of July 5th/6th and 6th/7th the IVth Corps Heavy Artillery and the Artillery of the 47th Division will bombard the following roads at times to be selected by the B.G., C.H.A., IVth Corps in conjunction with the G.O.C. 47th Divn:-

(i) N.19.b.5.8. to M.18.d.0.8. to M.23.central and M.17.b.6.3. to M.22 central to M.21.d.9.2.

(ii) N.20.a.1.9. to crossroads M.22.d.5.0. and thence North to M.22.b.2.2.

(iii) N.20.a.1½.0. to N.31.central to M.35.b.0.6. to M.33.d.8.3.

(iv) N.25.d.5.7½ to M.36.b.8.5. to M.35.a.6.1.

No fire will be brought to bear on the road N.20.a.0.½. to M.28.d.6.6.

2. The maximum amount of ammunition to be expended will be as under:-

500 rounds of 18-pounder. per night
30 " 4.5" howr. "
40 " 60-pounder. "

3. Please acknowledge by wire.

W. A. T. Bowly Major
for G.S.

5th July, 1916.

Brigadier General,
General Staff, IVth Corps.

SECRET

2 Divn No
GS 992/18/4

Copy No. 5

OPERATION ORDER FOR O + 13 DAY.

BY BRIGADIER GENERAL T. E. MARSHALL.,

COMMANDING HEAVY ARTILLERY, IV CORPS.

Headquarters,
6th July 1916.

REFERENCE Map 1/20,000, Sheet 36c. Edition 7a.

1. Same as for night 5th/6th, both as regards targets, time and ammunition. during night 6th/7th.

2. French Longs, only will fire -

8 rounds rapid at 12.0 noon at N.21.a.6.7.

8 " " " 10.0 p.m. at N.15.d.1.1.

Philip Blackwood
Capt.R.A.
Brigade Major,
Heavy Arty., IV Corps.

Copy No. 1 File.
2,3,4 R.A.,IV Corps.
5 2nd Division.
6 2nd Div.Arty.
7 47th Division.
8 47th Div. Arty.
9 1st Corps H.A.
10 French Arty.
11,12,13,14 15th H.A.Group.

CD

2 Dvn No
GS. 992/16/23

SECRET

IVth Corps No. H.R.S. 669/O.

2nd Division.
~~47th Division.~~
B.G., C.H.A., IVth Corps.
~~G.O.C., R.A., IVth Corps.~~
~~Ist Corps.~~)
~~XVIIth Corps.~~ } for information
~~Adv. First Army.~~ }
~~18 Sqdn R.F.C.~~)

---

1. During the night July 7th/8th

(a) The 2nd Division will carry out a raid on the enemy's trenches about S.9.a.0.8½. at a time to be selected by G.O.C. 2nd Division.

(b) The IVth Corps Heavy Artillery and the Artillery of the 47th Division will bombard the following roads at times to be selected by B.G., C.H.A., IVth Corps in conjunction with G.O.C. 47th Division:-

i. Same roads as during nights 5th/6th and 6th/7th July.

ii. Road N.10.b.9½.1. to M.28.c.1.4. to M.28.b.8.6. to M.28.c.0.4. to M.27.d.5½.9½.

The road ii. will not be shelled until the bombardment of the roads i. is completed.

Cancelled IV Corps 997 BTS T

2. At 12 noon and 10 p.m. July 7th the IVth Corps Heavy Artillery will co-operate with the Ist Corps Heavy Artillery in the bombardment of the enemy's billets N.21.a.6.7. and N.15.d.1.1.

3. Please acknowledge by wire.

W. A. T. Bowly Major
for G.S.
Brigadier General,
General Staff, IVth Corps.

6th July, 1916.

SECRET

2 Divn No
G.S. 992/18/12

Copy No. 5

OPERATION ORDER FOR O + 14 DAY.

BY BRIGADIER GENERAL. T. E. MARSHALL,

COMMANDING HEAVY ARTILLERY, IV CORPS.

Headquarters,
7th July. 1916.

REFERENCE. Map 1/20,000. Sheet 36c. Edition 7a.

1. During the night of 7th/8th July, 1916, 15th H.A. Group will fire on roads as follows :-

(a) Same roads as during nights 5th/6th, and 6th/7th. - Times :- 9.30 p.m.
10.0 p.m.
12.25 a.m.

Ammunition allowed - 15 rounds of 60-pounder.

(b) Roads N.19.b.9½.1. to M.29.c.1.4. to M.28.b.8.6. to M.28.c.0.4. to M.27.d.5½.9½., paying particular attention to portion of road lying in N.19.

Times :- 10.30 p.m.
10.50.p.m.
11.55 p.m.
12.35 am.
1.15 a.m.

Ammunition allowed - 45 rounds of 60-pounder.

P E Bunting
Captain: R.A.
For, Brigade-Major.
Heavy Artillery. IV Corps.

Copy No. 1 File.
2.3.4. R.A. IV Corps.
5. 2nd Division
6. 2nd Divisional A.ty.
7. 47th Division.
8. 47th Division Arty.
9. 1st Corps H.A.
10. French Artillery.
11.12.13.14. 15th H.A. Group.

acknowledged
[illegible] 7.7.

SECRET

H.S. 992/16/24
2 Divn

IV Corps No. H.R.S.669/P.

2nd Division.
~~47th Division.~~
~~B.G., C.H.A.~~
~~G.O.C., R.A.~~
~~I Corps.~~
~~XVII Corps.~~
~~Advanced First Army.~~
~~No. 18 Sqn. R.F.C.~~

1. With reference to proposed programme of operations issued under my H.R.S. 669 of 21st June, the one round bombardments mentioned therein will be carried out at the discretion of the G.Os.C. 2nd and 47th Divisions.

2. The one round bombardment by IV Corps Heavy and Divisional Artillery on the enemy's billets and Headquarters will not take place.

3. The IV Corps H.A. and the 2nd Divisional Artillery will bombard the enemy's roads and communications near XXXXX GIVENCHY if the G.O.C. 2nd Division so desires.

4. The 47th Division will carry out a raid on the night 8th/9th July, the time to be selected by the G.O.C., 47th Divn.

5. Please acknowledge by wire.

J. B. Brady Capt
for/ Brigadier-General,
General Staff, IV Corps.

H.Q., IV Corps.
7th July, 1916.

Acknowledged
J.B.
7.7

2. Dum No
OS 992/118/14

S E C R E T. IV Corps No. R.A. 881/31/64.

2nd Divisional Artillery.
47th Divisional Artillery.
IV Corps 'G'.)
IV Corps 'Q'.)
2nd Division.) For information.
47th Division.)
Heavy Artillery, IV Corps.)

With reference to IV Corps No. H.R.S. 889 of 7/7/'16; the allotment given starts from noon 8th and ends noon 14th. If the 47th D.A. are unable to obtain ammunition from the Park, and it becomes necessary to send ammunition from the 2nd D.A. to 47th D.A. out of the rounds held by 2nd D.A. at present in Corps' Reserve, this Office should be notified.

	A. & AX.	BX.
2nd D.A.	25,800.	2,650.
47th D.A.	14,800.	1,350.
Heavy Arty., IV Corps.	1,349.	233.
Reserve.	6,657.	-.
Total.	48,606.	4,233.

H.Q., IV Corps.
8/7/'16.

[signature] Capt
for Brigadier-General,
G.O.C., R.A., IV Corps.

SECRET

2 Divn No
GS 992/18/13

Copy No. 5

OPERATION ORDER No. 10.

BY BRIGADIER-GENERAL T. E. MARSHALL,

COMMANDING HEAVY ARTILLERY, IV CORPS.

Headquarters,
8th July 1916.

REFERENCE map 1/20,000. Sheet 36c. Edition 7a.

1. From 11.58 p.m. 8-7-16 to 12.30 a.m. 9-7-16, 15th H.A.Group will bombard trenches in M32d, paying special attention to the following points :-

M32d4.4½. - M32d3½.1½. - M32d7½3½. (Trench Mortar)

Ammunition allowed 40 rounds of 4.5" Howitzer.

2. From 12.1 a.m. to 12.25 a.m. 9-7-16, 15th H.A.Group will bombard trenches in M26, paying special attention to the following points :-

M26c8.7. - M26c8½.6. - M26c9.3.

Ammunition allowed 80 rounds of 4.5" Howitzer.

3. From 1.20 a.m. to 1.55 a.m. 9-7-16, 15th H.A.Group will bombard trenches in M26, as in (2), but will, in addition, pay attention to following points :-

M26d7.1½. - M26d6.3. - M26d6.4. - M26d8.5. - M26b7.4½.

Ammunition allowed 80 rounds of 4.5" Howitzer.

4. From 12.1 a.m. to 12.25 a.m. 9-7-16, French Artillery will bombard following points :-

M26d7.1½. - M26d6.3. - M26d6.4. - M26d8.5. - M26b7.4½.

Ammunition allowed 20 rounds of 120 m/m Court.

5. From 11.58 p.m. 8-7-16 to 12.30 a.m. 9-7-16 and again from 1.58 a.m. to 2.35 a.m. 9-7-16, French Artillery and 15th H.A.Group will bombard the "PIMPLE", with a view to prevent observation from that point.

Ammunition allowed 30 rounds of 120 m/m Court.
.. .. 25 .. .. 60-pounder shrapnel.

6. Watches will be synchronised between 9.15 p.m. and 9.30 p.m. 8-7-16.

7. Acknowledge.

Philip Blackburn
Capt.R.A.
Brigade Major,
Heavy Arty.,IV Corps.

Copy No. 1 File.
2,3,4 R.A.,IV Corps.
5 2nd Division.
6 2nd Div. Arty.
7 47th Division.
8 47th Div.Arty.
9 1st Corps H.A.
10 French Arty.
11,12,13,14 15th H.A.Group.

Acknowledged

SECRET

BS992/18/15
2 Div

Copy No. 5

OPERATION ORDER FOR 0 + 16 DAY.

BY BRIGADIER GENERAL. T. E. MARSHALL.

COMMANDING HEAVY ARTILLERY, IV CORPS.

Headquarters.,
9th July 1916.

REFERENCE. Map 1/20,000. Sheet 36c. Edition. 7a.

1. During the night of 9th/10th July, 1916, 15th H.A. Group will fire on roads as follows :-

(a) Same roads as during nights 5th/6th, and 6th/7th.

- Times - 9.30 p.m.
10.0 p.m.
12.25 a.m.

Ammunition allowed :- 9 rounds of 60-Pdr.

(b) Roads N.19.b.9½.1. to M.29.c.1.4. to M.28.b.8.6. to M.28.c.0.4. to M.27.d.5½.9½., paying particular attention to portion of road lying in N.19.

Times :- 10.30 pm.
10.50 pm.
11.55 pm.
12.35 am.
1.15 am.

Ammunition allowed - 31 - rounds of 60-Pounder.

Captain: R.A.
For, Brigade-Major.
Heavy Artillery, IV Corps.

NOTE:- The above is a repetition of OPERATION ORDER for 0 + 14 day for nights 7th/8th, which was cancelled.

Copies to:-

No. 1. File.
2.3.& 4. R.A. IV Corps.
5. 2nd Division.
6 2nd Div Arty.
7. 47th Division.
8. 47th Div Arty.
9. 1st Corps H.A.
11.12.13.14. 15th Group H.A..

2. Divn No.
G.S. 992/1/6/26

SECRET

IVth Corps No. H.R.S. 669/Q

2nd Division.
47th Division.
G.O.C.,R.A.,IVth Corps.
B.G.,C.H.A.,IVth Corps.
Ist Corps.)
XVIIth Corps.) for information.
18 Sqdn. R.F.C.)
Advanced First Army.)

---

1. During tonight July 9th/10th the IVth Corps Heavy Artillery and the artillery of the 47th Division will bombard the following roads at times to be selected by the B.G.,C.H.A., IVth Corps in conjunction with G.O.C. 47th Division:-

(a) Same roads as during nights 5th/6th and 6th/7th July.

(b) Road N.19.b.9½.1. to M.29.c.1.4. to M.28.b.8.6. to M.28.c.0.4. to M.27.d.5½.9½.

Road (b) will not be shelled until the bombardment of roads (a) is completed.

2. Total ammunition allotted:-

600 rounds 18-pounder.
40 " 60-pounder.
30 " 4.5" howr.

3. Please acknowledge by wire.

L. A. T. Bowly Major
for G.S.

9th July,1916.

Brigadier General,
General Staff, IVth Corps.

Acknowledged
H.B.
9/7

S E C R E T. IV Corps No. R.A. 739/4/74.

2nd Divisional Artillery.
47th Divisional Artillery.
Heavy Artillery, IV Corps.
2nd Division.)
47th Division.) For information.
IV Corps 'G'.)
IV Corps 'Q'.)

The instructions as to the proportion of A. to AX. are as follows :-

(1). Allotment for expenditure between 14th and 20th instant - 50% A. to 50% AX.

(2). Proportion to be maintained in Echelons - 75% A. to 25% AX.

(3). Proportion to be maintained in Defensive Dumps - 75% A. to 25% AX.

(4). Proportion of AX to A to be fired between now and the 14th is 64 to 36.

H.Q., IV Corps.
10/7/'16.

Brigadier-General,
G.O.C., R.A., IV Corps.

Copy to :-

M.G., R.A., First Army.

SECRET

2 Div No GS992/16/30

IVth Corps No. H.R.S. 669/2/A

~~B.G., C.H.A., IVth Corps.~~
2nd Division.
~~47th Division.~~
~~R.N. Division.~~
~~G.O.C., R.A., IVth Corps.~~ for information.
~~XVIIth Corps.~~
Adv. ~~First Army.~~
~~18 Sqdn R.F.C.~~

---

1. The IVth Corps Heavy Artillery will bombard VIMY Station tomorrow July 14th at an hour to be selected by B.G., C.H.A., IVth Corps, in consultation with G.O.C. 2nd Division, and notified to Corps Headquarters.

2. Please acknowledge by wire.

13th July, 1916.

W. A. T. Bowly Major G.S.
for Brigadier General,
General Staff, IVth Corps.

By telephone.
tomorrow afternoon
~~after~~ between 2 & 4
exact time will be notified before noon

acknowledged 13/7

S E C R E T. IV Corps No. R.A. 881/31/64.

2 Dvn No GS 992/18/14

IV Corps 'G'.
IV Corps 'Q'.
2nd Divisional Artillery.
47th Divisional Artillery.
2nd Division.
47th Division.
Heavy Artillery, IV Corps.

The attached Table gives Ammunition allotment from noon 13th to noon 20th.

H.Q., IV Corps. A.D. MACPHERSON, Captain, R.A.,
13/7/'16. IV Corps.

(A). The allotment of Ammunition from noon 12th to n[illegible]
follows :-

To.	A. & AX.	B. & BX.	F.	D. & [illegible]
2nd Division.	10,000.	800.	Nil.	Ni[illegible]
47th Division.	20,000.	2,200.	100.	10[illegible]
Heavy Artillery.	1,000. (All AX.).	200.	93.	1,07[illegible]
Corps Reserve.	14,129.	1,521.	Nil.	50[illegible]
Total.	45,129.	4,421.	193.	1,67[illegible]

(B). The above allotment cancels previous allotment[illegible]

(C). For proportion of 'A' to 'AX', see IV Corps No[illegible]

H.Q., IV Corps.
13/7/'16.

Copy to :-
M.G., R.A., First Army.

(A). The allotment of Ammunition from noon 12th to noon 20th for all purposes, including Raids is as follows :-

To.	A. & AX.	B. & BX.	F.	D. & DX.	120 m.m. Court.	120 m.m. Long.
2nd Division.	10,000.	500.	Nil.	Nil.	Nil.	Nil.
47th Division.	20,000.	2,200.	100.	100.	100.	Nil.
Heavy Artillery.	1,000. (All AX.).	200.	95.	1,070.	480.	600.
Corps Reserve.	14,129.	1,521.	Nil.	500.	Nil.	Nil.
Total.	45,129.	4,421.	195.	1,670.	580.	600.

(B). The above allotment cancels previous allotments.

(C). For proportion of 'A' to 'AX', see IV Corps No. R.A. 739/4/74 dated 10/7/'16.

H.Q., IV Corps.
15/7/'16.

[signature] Capt. for Brigadier-General,
G.O.C., R.A., IV Corps.

Copy to :-
M.G., R.A., First Army.

Copy No. 5

OPERATION ORDER No. 12.
by

BRIGADIER GENERAL T. E. MARSHALL, COMMANDING,

HEAVY ARTILLERY, IV CORPS.

Headquarters,
14th July 1916.

REFERENCE Map 1/20,000. Sheet 36c. Edition 7a.

1. French Artillery and 15th H.A.Group will bombard LA COULOTTE, as under :-

7.30 p.m. 15/7/16. - N31c5.1.

7.40 p.m. 15/7/16. - N31c9.½.

Ammunition allowed - 8 rounds 60-pounder.) each
8 " 120 m/m Long.) time.

[signature]

Capt.R.A.
Brigade Major,
Heavy Artillery, IV Corps.

Copies to -
No. 1 File.
2,3,4. R.A.,IV Corps.
5 2nd Division.
6 2nd Div.Arty
7 47th Division.
8 47th Div. Arty.
9 French Artillery.
10,11,12,13,15th H.A.Group.
14 War Diary.

acknowledged
[initials] 14/7

B/

SECRET

IV Corps No. H.R.S. 669/2/B.

2nd Divn No
GS 992/16/31

2nd Division.
~~47th Division.~~
~~R.N.Division.~~
~~G.O.C., R.A., IV Corps.~~
~~B.G., C.H.A., IV Corps.~~

~~I Corps.~~)
~~XVII Corps.~~)
~~Adv: First Army.~~) ~~For information.~~
~~No. 18 Sqdn: R.F.C.~~)

---

1. The IV Corps Heavy Artillery will bombard LA COULOTTE tomorrow July 15th at times to be selected by B.G., C.H.A., IV Corps, in consultation with G.Os.C., 2nd and 47th Divisions.

2. The 2nd Division will carry out a trench mortar bombardment in the CARENCY Section at the discretion of the G.O.C., 2nd Division.

3. Please acknowledge by wire.

W. A. T. Bowly Major
for B.G. G.S.
Brigadier General,
General Staff, IV Corps.

H.Q., IV Corps,
14th July, 1916.

Acknowledged
J.B.
G.S. 14.7

Prefix........ Code............m. | Words | Charge

Office of Origin and Service Instructions.

Sig ex by DR

Sent At ....m. To .... By ....

This message is on a/c of: .... *Service.*

(Signature of "Franking Officer.")

Recd. at ....m. Date .... From .... By ....

TO FIELD ~~[illegible]~~ FISHING

Sender's Number	Day of Month	In reply to Number	AAA
G496	15		

4 Corps H.A will bombard the SUNKEN ROAD S16a 103 to S16c 55 tomorrow July 16th aaa Time depends on weather conditions and will be notified as soon as known aaa Code words for bombardment will be SUNKEN ROAD

From WORK

Place

Time

The above may be forwarded as now corrected. (Z)

Censor

B. Balgrave Major

Signature of Addressor or person authorised to telegraph in his name.

* This line should be erased if not required.

(A1) O. Ltd., London— W.14012/M.44. 150,000 Pads. 12/15. Form C.2121.

Copy No. 5

OPERATION ORDER No. 13.
by
BRIGADIER GENERAL T. E. MARSHALL, COMMANDING.
HEAVY ARTILLERY, IV CORPS.

Headquarters,
15th July 1916.

REFERENCE Map 1/20,000. Sheet 36c. Edition 7a.

1. French Artillery will bombard sunken road in S16a0.8. to S16c5.5. on 16/7/16, with aeroplane observation at time to be arranged by O.C., 18 Squadron R.F.C., when light is suitable.

O.C., 18 Squadron will notify this Office when the shoot will take place, giving as long notice as possible.

Capt.R.A.
Brigade Major,
Heavy Artillery, IV Corps.

Copy No. 1. File.
2,3,4. R.A., IV Corps.
5. 2nd Division.
6. 2nd Div. Arty.
7. 47th Division.
8. 47th Div. Arty.
9. 18 Squadron, R.F.C.
10. French Artillery.
11,12,13,14. 15th H.A.Group.
15. War Diary.

Acknowledged
15.7.

SECRET

IVth Corps No. H.R.S. 669/2/G.

2nd Division.
47th Division.
B.G.,C.H.A.,IVth Corps.
R.N. Division.
G.O.C.,R.A.,IVth Corps.
Ist Corps.
XVIIth Corps.
Adv. First Army.
18 Sqdn R.F.C.

} for information.

---

1. The IVth Corps Heavy Artillery will bombard the SUNKEN ROAD S.16.a.10.3. to S.16.c.5.5. tomorrow July 16th, at times to be selected by the B.G.,C.H.A.,IVth Corps, in consultation with G.O.s C. 2nd and 47th Divisions.

2. Please acknowledge by wire.

Acknowledged

15th July,1916.

for Brigadier General,
General Staff, IVth Corps.

may draw retaliation so Adv. should be warned

15.7

www.ingramcontent.com/pod-product-compliance
Lightning Source LLC
Chambersburg PA
CBHW080822010526
44111CB00015B/2595
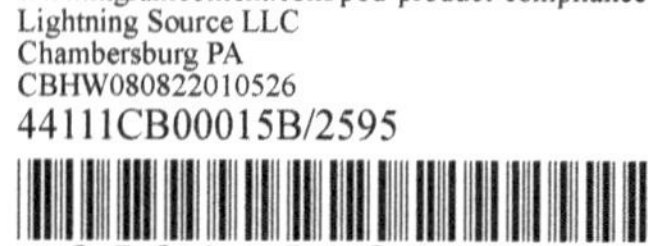